THE
LANGSTON
HUGHES
READER

THE
LANGSTON
HUGHES
READER

George Braziller, Inc.

New York   1958

To My Uncle John

CONTENTS

SHORT STORIES

POEMS

CHILDREN'S POETRY

SONG LYRICS

NOVELS AND HUMOR

PLAYS

AUTOBIOGRAPHY

PAGEANT

ARTICLES AND SPEECHES

SHORT STORIES

The Ways of White Folks

CORA UNASHAMED

Melton was one of those miserable in-between little places, not large enough to be a town, nor small enough to be a village—that is, a village in the rural, charming sense of the word. Melton had no charm about it. It was merely a nondescript collection of houses and buildings in a region of farms—one of those sad American places with sidewalks, but no paved streets; electric lights, but no sewage; a station, but no trains that stopped, save a jerky local, morning and evening. And it was 150 miles from any city at all —even Sioux City.

Cora Jenkins was one of the least of the citizens of Melton. She was what the people referred to when they wanted to be polite, as a Negress, and when they wanted to be rude, as a nigger—sometimes adding the word "wench" for no good reason, for Cora was usually an inoffensive soul, except that she sometimes cussed.

She had been in Melton for forty years. Born there. Would die there probably. She worked for the Studevants, who treated her like a dog. She stood it. Had to stand it; or work for poorer white folks who would treat her worse; or go jobless. Cora was like a tree— once rooted, she stood, in spite of storms and strife, wind, and rocks, in the earth.

She was the Studevants' maid of all work—washing, ironing, cooking, scrubbing, taking care of kids, nursing old folks, making fires, carrying water.

Cora, bake three cakes for Mary's birthday tomorrow night. You Cora, give Rover a bath in that tar soap I bought. Cora, take Ma some jello, and don't let her have even a taste of that raisin pie. She'll keep us up all night if you do. Cora, iron my stockings. Cora, come here . . . Cora, put . . . Cora . . . Cora . . . Cora! Cora!

And Cora would answer, "Yes, m'am."

The Studevants thought they owned her, and they were perfectly right: they did. There was something about the teeth in the trap of economic circumstance that kept her in their power practically all her life—in the Studevant kitchen, cooking; in the Studevant parlor, sweeping; in the Studevant backyard, hanging clothes.

You want to know how that could be? How a trap could close so tightly? Here is the outline:

Cora was the oldest of a family of eight children—the Jenkins niggers. The only Negroes in Melton, thank God! Where they came from originally—that is, the old folks—God knows. The kids were born there. The old folks are still there now: Pa drives a junk wagon. The old woman ails around the house, ails and quarrels. Seven kids are gone. Only Cora remains. Cora simply couldn't go, with nobody else to help take care of Ma. And before that she couldn't go, with nobody to see that her brothers and sisters got through school (she the oldest, and Ma ailing). And before that —well, somebody had to help Ma look after one baby behind another that kept on coming.

As a child Cora had no playtime. She always had a little brother, or a little sister in her arms. Bad, crying, bratty babies, hungry and mean. In the eighth grade she quit school and went to work with the Studevants.

After that, she ate better. Half day's work at first, helping Ma at home the rest of the time. Then full days, bringing home her pay to feed her father's children. The old man was rather a drunkard. What little money he made from closet-cleaning, ash-hauling, and junk-dealing he spent mostly on the stuff that makes you forget you have eight kids.

He passed the evenings telling long, comical lies to the white riff-raff of the town, and drinking licker. When his horse died, Cora's money went for a new one to haul her Pa and his rickety wagon around. When the mortgage money came due, Cora's wages kept the man from taking the roof from over their heads. When Pa got in jail, Cora borrowed ten dollars from Mr. Studevant and got him out.

Cora stinted, and Cora saved, and wore the Studevants' old clothes, and ate the Studevants' left-over food, and brought her pay home. Brothers and sisters grew up. The boys, lonesome, went away, as far as they could from Melton. One by one, the girls left too, mostly in disgrace. "Ruinin' ma name," Pa Jenkins said, "Ruinin' ma good name! They can't go out berryin' but what they come back in disgrace." There was something about the cream-and-tan Jenkins girls that attracted the white farm hands.

Even Cora, the humble, had a lover once. He came to town on a freight train (long ago now), and worked at the livery-stable. (That was before autos got to be so common.) Everybody said he was an I. W. W. Cora didn't care. He was the first man and the last she ever remembered wanting. She had never known a colored lover. There weren't any around. That was not her fault.

This white boy, Joe, he always smelt like the horses. He was some kind of foreigner. Had an accent, and yellow hair, big hands, and grey eyes.

It was summer. A few blocks beyond the Studevants' house, meadows and orchards and sweet fields stretched away to the far horizon. At night, stars in the velvet sky. Moon sometimes. Crickets and katydids and lightning bugs. The scent of grass, Cora waiting. That boy, Joe, a cigarette spark far off, whistling in the dark. Love didn't take long—Cora with the scent of the Studevants' supper about her, and a cheap perfume. Joe, big and strong and careless as the horses he took care of, smelling like the stable.

Ma would quarrel because Cora came home late, or because none of the kids had written for three or four weeks, or because Pa was drunk again. Thus the summer passed, a dream of big hands and grey eyes.

Cora didn't go anywhere to have her child. Nor tried to hide it. When the baby grew big within her, she didn't feel that it was a disgrace. The Studevants told her to go home and stay there. Joe left town. Pa cussed. Ma cried. One April morning the kid was born. She had grey eyes, and Cora called her Josephine, after Joe.

Cora was humble and shameless before the fact of the child. There were no Negroes in Melton to gossip, and she didn't care what the white people said. They were in another world. Of course, she hadn't expected to marry Joe, or keep him. He was of that other world, too. But the child was hers—a living bridge between two worlds. Let people talk.

Cora went back to work at the Studevants'—coming home at night to nurse her kid, and quarrel with Ma. About that time, Mrs. Art Studevant had a child, too, and Cora nursed it. The Studevants' little girl was named Jessie. As the two children began to walk and talk, Cora sometimes brought Josephine to play with Jessie—until the Studevants objected, saying she could get her work done better if she left her child at home.

"Yes, ma'am," said Cora.

But in a little while they didn't need to tell Cora to leave her child at home, for Josephine died of whooping-cough. One rosy afternoon, Cora saw the little body go down into the ground in a white casket that cost four weeks' wages.

Since Ma was ailing, Pa, smelling of licker, stood with her at the grave. The two of them alone. Cora was not humble before the fact of death. As she turned away from the hole, tears came—but at the same time a stream of curses so violent that they made the grave-tenders look up in startled horror.

She cussed out God for taking away the life that she herself had given. She screamed, "My baby! God damn it! My baby! I bear her and you take her away!" She looked at the sky where the sun was setting and yelled in defiance. Pa was amazed and scared. He pulled her up on his rickety wagon and drove off, clattering down the road between green fields and sweet meadows that stretched away to the far horizon. All through the ugly town Cora wept and cursed, using all the bad words she had learned from Pa in his drunkenness.

The next week she went back to the Studevants. She was gentle and humble in the face of life—she loved their baby. In the afternoons on the back porch, she would pick little Jessie up and rock her to sleep, burying her dark face in the milky smell of the white child's hair.

II

The years passed. Pa and Ma Jenkins only dried up a little. Old Man Studevant died. The old lady had two strokes. Mrs. Art Studevant and her husband began to look their age, greying hair and sagging stomachs. The children were grown, or nearly so. Kenneth took over the management of the hardware store that Grandpa had left. Jack went off to college. Mary was a teacher. Only Jessie remained a child—her last year in high-school. Jessie, nineteen now, and rather slow in her studies, graduating at last. In the Fall she would go to Normal.

Cora hated to think about her going away. In her heart she had adopted Jessie. In that big and careless household it was always Cora who stood like a calm and sheltering tree for Jessie to run to in her troubles. As a child, when Mrs. Art spanked her, as soon as she could, the tears still streaming, Jessie would find her way to the kitchen and Cora. At each school term's end, when Jessie had usually failed in some of her subjects (she quite often failed, being a dull child), it was Cora who saw the report-card first with the bad marks on it. Then Cora would devise some way of breaking the news gently to the old folks.

Her mother was always a little ashamed of stupid Jessie, for Mrs. Art was the civic and social leader of Melton, president of the Woman's Club three years straight, and one of the pillars of her church. Mary, the elder, the teacher, would follow with dignity in her footsteps, but Jessie! That child! Spankings in her youth, and scoldings now, did nothing to Jessie's inner being. She remained a plump, dull, freckled girl, placid and strange. Everybody found fault with her but Cora.

In the kitchen Jessie bloomed. She laughed. She talked. She was sometimes even witty. And she learned to cook wonderfully. With Cora, everything seemed so simple—not hard and involved like algebra, or Latin grammar, or the civic problems of Mama's club, or the sermons at church. Nowhere in Melton, nor with anyone, did Jessie feel so comfortable as with Cora in the kitchen. She knew her mother looked down on her as a stupid girl. And with her father there was no bond. He was always too busy buying and selling to bother with the kids. And often he was off in the city. Old doddering Grandma made Jessie sleepy and sick. Cousin Nora (Mother's cousin) was as stiff and prim as a minister's daughter. And Jessie's older brothers and sister went their ways, seeing Jessie hardly at all, except at the big table at mealtimes.

Like all the unpleasant things in the house, Jessie was left to Cora. And Cora was happy. To have a child to raise, a child the same age as her Josephine would have been, gave her a purpose in life, a warmth inside herself. It was Cora who nursed and mothered and petted and loved the dull little Jessie through the years. And now Jessie was a young woman, graduating (late) from high-school.

But something had happened to Jessie. Cora knew it before Mrs. Art did. Jessie was not too stupid to have a boy-friend. She told Cora about it like a mother. She was afraid to tell Mrs. Art. Afraid! Afraid! Afraid!

Cora said, "I'll tell her." So, humble and unashamed about life, one afternoon she marched into Mrs. Art's sun-porch and announced quite simply, "Jessie's going to have a baby."

Cora smiled, but Mrs. Art stiffened like a bolt. Her mouth went dry. She rose like a soldier. Sat down. Rose again. Walked straight toward the door, turned around, and whispered, "What?"

"Yes, ma'am, a baby. She told me. A little child. Its father is Willie Matsoulos, whose folks runs the ice-cream stand on Main. She told me. They want to get married, but Willie ain't here now. He don't know yet about the child."

Cora would have gone on humbly and shamelessly talking about the little unborn had not Mrs. Art fallen into uncontrollable hysterics. Cousin Nora came running from the library, her glasses on a chain. Old Lady Studevant's wheel-chair rolled up, doddering and shaking with excitement. Jessie came, when called, red and

sweating, but had to go out, for when her mother looked up from
the couch and saw her she yelled louder than ever. There was a
rush for camphor bottles and water and ice. Crying and praying
followed all over the house. Scandalization! Oh, my Lord! Jessie
was in trouble.

"She ain't in trouble neither," Cora insisted. "No trouble having
a baby you want. I had one."

"Shut up, Cora!"

"Yes, m'am. . . . But I had one."

"Hush, I tell you."

"Yes, m'am."

III

Then it was that Cora began to be shut out. Jessie was confined
to her room. That afternoon, when Miss Mary came home from
school, the four white women got together behind closed doors in
Mrs. Art's bedroom. For once Cora cooked supper in the kitchen
without being bothered by an interfering voice. Mr. Studevant was
away in Des Moines. Somehow Cora wished he was home. Big and
gruff as he was, he had more sense than the women. He'd probably
make a shot-gun wedding out of it. But left to Mrs. Art, Jessie would
never marry the Greek boy at all. This Cora knew. No man had
been found yet good enough for sister Mary to mate with. Mrs.
Art had ambitions which didn't include the likes of Greek ice-cream
makers' sons.

Jessie was crying when Cora brought her supper up. The black
woman sat down on the bed and lifted the white girl's head in her
dark hands. "Don't you mind, honey," Cora said. "Just sit tight,
and when the boy comes back I'll tell him how things are. If he
loves you he'll want you. And there ain't no reason why you can't
marry, neither—you both white. Even if he is a foreigner, he's a
right nice boy."

"He loves me," Jessie said. "I know he does. He said so."

But before the boy came back (or Mr. Studevant either) Mrs. Art
and Jessie went to Kansas City. "For an Easter shopping trip," the
weekly paper said.

Then Spring came in full bloom, and the fields and orchards at
the edge of Melton stretched green and beautiful to the far horizon.
Cora remembered her own Spring, twenty years ago, and a great
sympathy and pain welled up in her heart for Jessie, who was
the same age that Josephine would have been, had she lived. Sitting
on the kitchen porch shelling peas, Cora thought back over her

own life—years and years of working for the Studevants; years and years of going home to nobody but Ma and Pa; little Josephine dead; only Jessie to keep her heart warm. And she knew that Jessie was the dearest thing she had in the world. All the time the girl was gone now, she worried.

After ten days, Mrs. Art and her daughter came back. But Jessie was thinner and paler than she'd ever been in her life. There was no light in her eyes at all. Mrs. Art looked a little scared as they got off the train.

"She had an awful attack of indigestion in Kansas City," she told the neighbors and club women. "That's why I stayed away so long, waiting for her to be able to travel. Poor Jessie! She looks healthy, but she's never been a strong child. She's one of the worries of my life." Mrs. Art talked a lot, explained a lot, about how Jessie had eaten the wrong things in Kansas City.

At home, Jessie went to bed. She wouldn't eat. When Cora brought her food up, she whispered, "The baby's gone."

Cora's face went dark. She bit her lips to keep from cursing. She put her arms about Jessie's neck. The girl cried. Her food went untouched.

A week passed. They tried to *make* Jessie eat then. But the food wouldn't stay on her stomach. Her eyes grew yellow, her tongue white, her heart acted crazy. They called in old Doctor Brown, but within a month (as quick as that) Jessie died.

She never saw the Greek boy any more. Indeed, his father had lost his license, "due to several complaints by the mothers of children, backed by the Woman's Club," that he was selling tainted ice-cream. Mrs. Art Studevant had started a campaign to rid the town of objectionable tradespeople and questionable characters. Greeks were bound to be one or the other. For a while they even closed up Pa Jenkins' favorite bootlegger. Mrs. Studevant thought this would please Cora, but Cora only said, "Pa's been drinkin' so long he just as well keep on." She refused further to remark on her employer's campaign of purity. In the midst of this clean-up Jessie died.

On the day of the funeral, the house was stacked with flowers. (They held the funeral, not at the church, but at home, on account of old Grandma Studevant's infirmities.) All the family dressed in deep mourning. Mrs. Art was prostrate. As the hour for the services approached, she revived, however, and ate an omelette, "to help me go through the afternoon."

"And Cora," she said, "cook me a little piece of ham with it. I feel so weak."

"Yes, m'am."

The senior class from the high-school came in a body. The Woman's Club came with their badges. The Reverend Doctor McElroy had on his highest collar and longest coat. The choir sat behind the coffin, with a special soloist to sing "He Feedeth His Flocks Like a Shepherd." It was a beautiful Spring afternoon, and a beautiful funeral.

Except that Cora was there. Of course, her presence created no comment (she was the family servant), but it was what she did, and how she did it, that has remained the talk of Melton to this day —for Cora was not humble in the face of death.

When the Reverend Doctor McElroy had finished his eulogy, and the senior class had read their memorials, and the songs had been sung, and they were about to allow the relatives and friends to pass around for one last look at Jessie Studevant, Cora got up from her seat by the dining-room door. She said, "Honey, I want to say something." She spoke as if she were addressing Jessie. She approached the coffin and held out her brown hands over the white girl's body. Her face moved in agitation. People sat stone-still and there was a long pause. Suddenly she screamed. "They killed you! And for nothin'. . . . They killed your child. . . . They took you away from here in the Spring-time of your life, and now you'se gone, gone, gone!"

Folks were paralyzed in their seats.

Cora went on: "They preaches you a pretty semon and they don't say nothin'. They sings you a song, and they don't say nothin'. But Cora's here, honey, and she's gonna tell 'em what they done to you. She's gonna tell 'em why they took you to Kansas City."

A loud scream rent the air. Mrs. Art fell back in her chair, stiff as a board. Cousin Nora and sister Mary sat like stones. The men of the family rushed forward to grab Cora. They stumbled over wreaths and garlands. Before they could reach her, Cora pointed her long fingers at the women in black and said, "They killed you, honey. They killed you and your child. I told 'em you loved it, but they didn't care. They killed it before it was . . ."

A strong hand went around Cora's waist. Another grabbed her arm. The Studevant males half pulled, half pushed her through the aisles of folding chairs, through the crowded dining-room, out into the empty kitchen, through the screen door into the backyard. She struggled against them all the way, accusing their women. At the door she sobbed, great tears coming for the love of Jessie.

She sat down on a wash-bench in the backyard, crying. In the parlor she could hear the choir singing weakly. In a few moments she gathered herself together, and went back into the house. Slowly, she picked up her few belongings from the kitchen and pantry, her aprons and her umbrella, and went off down the alley, home to Ma. Cora never came back to work for the Studevants.

Now she and Ma live from the little garden they raise, and from the junk Pa collects—when they can take by main force a part of his meager earnings before he buys his licker.

Anyhow, on the edge of Melton, the Jenkins niggers, Pa and Ma and Cora, somehow manage to get along.

SLAVE ON THE BLOCK

They were people who went in for Negroes—Michael and Anne—the Carraways. But not in the social-service, philanthropic sort of way, no. They saw no use in helping a race that was already too charming and naive and lovely for words. Leave them unspoiled and just enjoy them, Michael and Anne felt. So they went in for the Art of Negroes—the dancing that had such jungle life about it, the songs that were so simple and fervent, the poetry that was so direct, so real. They never tried to influence that art, they only bought it and raved over it, and copied it. For they were artists, too.

In their collection they owned some Covarrubias originals. Of course Covarrubias wasn't a Negro, but how he caught the darky spirit! They owned all the Robeson records and all the Bessie Smith. And they had a manuscript of Countee Cullen's. They saw all the plays with or about Negroes, read all the books, and adored the Hall Johnson Singers. They had met Doctor DuBois, and longed to meet Carl Van Vechten. Of course they knew Harlem like their own backyard, that is, all the speakeasies and night clubs and dance halls, from the Cotton Club and the ritzy joints where Negroes couldn't go themselves, down to places like the Hot Dime, where white folks couldn't get in—unless they knew the man. (And tipped heavily.)

They were acquainted with lots of Negroes, too—but somehow the Negroes didn't seem to like them very much. Maybe the Carraways gushed over them too soon. Or maybe they looked a little like poor white folks, although they were really quite well off. Or maybe they tried too hard to make friends, dark friends, and the dark friends suspected something. Or perhaps their house in the Village was too far from Harlem, or too hard to find, being back in one of those queer and expensive little side streets that had once been alleys before the art invasion came. Anyway, occasionally, a furtive Negro might accept their invitation for tea, or cocktails; and sometimes a lesser Harlem celebrity or two would decorate their rather slow parties; but one seldom came back for more. As much as they loved Negroes, Negroes didn't seem to love Michael and Anne.

But they were blessed with a wonderful colored cook and maid —until she took sick and died in her room in their basement. And then the most marvellous ebony boy walked into their life, a boy as black as all the Negroes they'd ever known put together.

"He *is* the jungle," said Anne when she saw him.

"He's 'I Couldn't Hear Nobody Pray,'" said Michael.

For Anne thought in terms of pictures: she was a painter. And Michael thought in terms of music: he was a composer for the piano. And they had a most wonderful idea of painting pictures and composing music that went together, and then having a joint "concert-exhibition" as they would call it. Her pictures and his music. The Carraways, a sonata and a picture, a fugue and a picture. It would be lovely, and such a novelty, people would have to like it. And many of their things would be Negro. Anne had painted their maid six times. And Michael had composed several themes based on the spirituals, and on Louis Armstrong's jazz. Now here was this ebony boy. The essence in the flesh.

They had nearly missed the boy. He had come, when they were out, to gather up the things the cook had left, and take them to her sister in Jersey. It seems that he was the late cook's nephew. The new colored maid had let him in and given him the two suitcases of poor dear Emma's belongings, and he was on his way to the Subway. That is, he was in the hall, going out just as the Carraways, Michael and Anne, stepped in. They could hardly see the boy, it being dark in the hall, and he being dark, too.

"Hello," they said. "Is this Emma's nephew?"

"Yes'm," said the maid. "Yes'm."

"Well, come in," said Anne, "and let us see you. We loved your aunt so much. She was the best cook we ever had."

"You don't know where I could get a job, do you?" said the boy. This took Michael and Anne back a bit, but they rallied at once. So charming and naive to ask right away for what he wanted.

Anne burst out, "You know, I think I'd like to paint you."

Michael said, "Oh, I say now, that would be lovely! He's so utterly Negro."

The boy grinned.

Anne said, "Could you come back tomorrow?"

And the boy said, "Yes, indeed. I sure could."

The upshot of it was that they hired him. They hired him to look after the garden, which was just about as big as Michael's grand piano—only a little square behind the house. You know those Village gardens. Anne sometimes painted it. And occasionally they set the table there for four on a spring evening. Nothing grew in the garden really, practically nothing. But the boy said he could plant things. And they had to have some excuse to hire him.

The boy's name was Luther. He had come from the South to his relatives in Jersey, and had had only one job since he got there, shining shoes for a Greek in Elizabeth. But the Greek fired him because the boy wouldn't give half his tips over to the proprietor.

"I never heard of a job where I had to pay the boss, instead of the boss paying me," said Luther. "Not till I got here."

"And then what did you do?" said Anne.

"Nothing. Been looking for a job for the last four months."

"Poor boy," said Michael; "poor, dear boy."

"Yes," said Anne. "You must be hungry." And they called the cook to give him something to eat.

Luther dug around in the garden a little bit that first day, went out and bought some seeds, came back and ate some more. They made a place for him to sleep in the basement by the furnace. And the next day Anne started to paint him, after she'd bought the right colors.

"He'll be good company for Mattie," they said. "She claims she's afraid to stay alone at night when we're out, so she leaves." They suspected, though, that Mattie just liked to get up to Harlem. And they thought right. Mattie was not as settled as she looked. Once out, with the Savoy open until three in the morning, why come home? That was the way Mattie felt.

In fact, what happened was that Mattie showed Luther where the best and cheapest hot spots in Harlem were located. Luther hadn't even set foot in Harlem before, living twenty-eight miles away, as he did, in Jersey, and being a kind of quiet boy. But the second night he was there Mattie said, "Come on, let's go. Working for white folks all day, I'm tired. They needn't think I was made to answer telephones all night." So out they went.

Anne noticed that most mornings Luther would doze almost as soon as she sat him down to pose, so she eventually decided to paint Luther asleep. "The Sleeping Negro," she would call it. Dear, natural childlike people, they would sleep anywhere they wanted to. Anyway, asleep, he kept still and held the pose.

And he *was* an adorable Negro. Not tall, but with a splendid body. And a slow and lively smile that lighted up his black, black face, for his teeth were very white, and his eyes, too. Most effective in oil and canvas. Better even than Emma had been. Anne could stare at him at leisure when he was asleep. One day she decided to paint him nude, or at least half nude. A slave picture, that's what she would do. The market at New Orleans for a background. And call it "The Boy on the Block."

So one morning when Luther settled down in his sleeping pose, Anne said, "No," she had finished that picture. She wanted to paint him now representing to the full the soul and sorrow of his people. She wanted to paint him as a slave about to be sold. And since slaves in warm climates had no clothes, would be please take off his shirt.

Luther smiled a sort of embarrassed smile and took off his shirt.

"Your undershirt, too," said Anne. But it turned out that he had on a union suit, so he had to go out and change altogether. He came back and mounted the box that Anne said would serve just then for a slave block, and she began to sketch. Before luncheon Michael came in, and went into rhapsodies over Luther on the box without a shirt, about to be sold into slavery. He said he must put him into music right now. And he went to the piano and began to play something that sounded like Deep River in the jaws of a dog, but Michael said it was a modern slave plaint, 1850 in terms of 1933. Vieux Carré remembered on 135th Street. Slavery in the Cotton Club.

Anne said, "It's too marvellous!" And they painted and played till dark, with rest periods in between for Luther. Then they all knocked off for dinner. Anne and Michael went out later to one of Lew Leslie's new shows. And Luther and Mattie said, "Thank God!" and got dressed up for Harlem.

Funny, they didn't like the Carraways. They treated them nice and paid them well. "But they're too strange," said Mattie, "they makes me nervous."

"They is mighty funny," Luther agreed.

They didn't understand the vagaries of white folks, neither Luther nor Mattie, and they didn't want to be bothered trying.

"I does my work," said Mattie. "After that I don't want to be painted, or asked to sing songs, nor nothing like that."

The Carraways often asked Luther to sing, and he sang. He

knew a lot of southern worksongs and reels, and spirituals and ballads.

> *"Dear Ma, I'm in hard luck:*
> *Three days since I et,*
> *And the stamp on this letter's*
> *Gwine to put me in debt."*

The Carraways allowed him to neglect the garden altogether. About all Luther did was pose and sing. And he got tired of that.

Indeed, both Luther and Mattie became a bit difficult to handle as time went on. The Carraways blamed it on Mattie. She had got hold of Luther. She was just simply spoiling a nice simple young boy. She was old enough to know better. Mattie was in love with Luther.

As least, he slept with her. The Carraways discovered this one night about one o'clock when they went to wake Luther up (the first time they'd ever done such a thing) and ask him if he wouldn't sing his own marvellous version of John Henry for a man who had just come from Saint Louis and was sailing for Paris tomorrow. But Luther wasn't in his own bed by the furnace. There was a light in Mattie's room, so Michael knocked softly. Mattie said, "Who's that?" And Michael poked his head in, and here were Luther and Mattie in bed together!

Of course, Anne condoned them. "It's so simple and natural for Negroes to make love." But Mattie, after all, was forty if she was a day. And Luther was only a kid. Besides Anne thought that Luther had been ever so much nicer when he first came than he was now. But from so many nights at the Savoy, he had become a marvellous dancer, and he was teaching Anne the Lindy Hop to Cab Calloway's records. Besides, her picture of "The Boy on the Block" wasn't anywhere near done. And he did take pretty good care of the furnace. So they kept him. At least, Anne kept him, although Michael said he was getting a little bored with the same Negro always in the way.

For Luther had grown a bit familiar lately. He smoked up all their cigarettes, drank their wine, told jokes on them to their friends, and sometimes even came upstairs singing and walking about the house when the Carraways had guests in who didn't share their enthusiasm for Negroes, natural or otherwise.

Luther and Mattie together were a pair. They quite frankly lived with one another now. Well, let that go. Anne and Michael prided themselves on being different; artists, you know, and liberal-minded people—maybe a little scatter-brained, but then (secretly, they felt) that came from genius. They were not ordinary people, bothering about the liberties of others. Certainly, the last thing they would do would be to interfere with the delightful simplicity of Negroes.

But Mattie must be giving Luther money and buying him clothes. He was really dressing awfully well. And on her Thursday afternoons off she would come back loaded down with packages. As far as the Carraways could tell, they were all for Luther.

And sometimes there were quarrels drifting up from the basement. And often, all too often, Mattie had moods. Then Luther would have moods. And it was pretty awful having two dark and glowering people around the house. Anne couldn't paint and Michael couldn't play.

One day, when she hadn't seen Luther for three days, Anne called downstairs and asked him if he wouldn't please come up and take off his shirt and get on the box. The picture was almost done. Luther came dragging his feet upstairs and humming:

> *"Before I'd be a slave*
> *I'd be buried in ma grave*
> *And go home to my Jesus*
> *And be free."*

And that afternoon he let the furnace go almost out.

That was the state of things when Michael's mother (whom Anne had never liked) arrived from Kansas City to pay them a visit. At once neither Mattie nor Luther liked her either. She was a mannish old lady, big and tall, and inclined to be bossy. Mattie, however, did spruce up her service, cooked delicious things, and treated Mrs. Carraway with a great deal more respect than she did Anne.

"I never play with servants," Mrs. Carraway had said to Michael, and Mattie must have heard her.

But Luther, he was worse than ever. Not that he did anything wrong, Anne thought, but the way he did things! For instance, he didn't need to sing now all the time, especially since Mrs. Carraway had said she didn't like singing. And certainly not songs like "You Rascal, You."

But all things end! With the Carraways and Luther it happened like this: One forenoon, quite without a shirt (for he expected to pose) Luther came sauntering through the library to change the flowers in the vase. He carried red roses. Mrs. Carraway was reading her morning scripture from the Health and Life.

"Oh, good morning," said Luther. "How long are you gonna stay in this house?"

"I never liked familiar Negroes," said Mrs. Carraway, over her nose glasses.

"Huh!" said Luther. "That's too bad! I never liked poor white folks."

Mrs. Carraway screamed, a short loud, dignified scream. Michael came running in bathrobe and pyjamas. Mrs. Carraway grew tall. There was a scene. Luther talked. Michael talked. Anne appeared.

"Never, never, never," said Mrs. Carraway, "have I suffered such impudence from servants—and a nigger servant—in my own son's house."

"Mother, Mother, Mother," said Michael. "Be calm. I'll discharge him." He turned on the nonchalant Luther. "Go!" he said, pointing toward the door. "Go, go!"

"Michael," Anne cried, "I haven't finished 'The Slave on the Block.'" Her husband looked nonplussed. For a moment he breathed deeply.

"Either he goes or I go," said Mrs. Carraway, firm as a rock.

"He goes," said Michael with strength from his mother.

"Oh!" cried Anne. She looked at Luther. His black arms were full of roses he had brought to put in the vases. He had on no shirt. "Oh!" His body was ebony.

"Don't worry 'bout me!" said Luther. "I'll go."

"Yes, we'll go," boomed Mattie from the doorway, who had come up from below, fat and belligerent. "We've stood enough foolery from you white folks! Yes, we'll go. Come on, Luther."

What could she mean, "stood enough"? What had they done to them, Anne and Michael wondered. They had tried to be kind. "Oh!"

"Sneaking around knocking on our door at night," Mattie went on. "Yes, we'll go. Pay us! Pay us! Pay us!" So she remembered the time they had come for Luther at night. That was it.

"I'll pay you," said Michael. He followed Mattie out.

Anne looked at her black boy.

"Good-bye," Luther said. "You fix the vases."

He handed her his armful of roses, glanced impudently at old Mrs. Carraway and grinned—grinned that wide, beautiful, white-toothed grin that made Anne say when she first saw him, "He looks like the jungle." Grinned, and disappeared in the dark hall, with no shirt on his back.

"Oh," Anne moaned distressfully, "my 'Boy on the Block'!"

"Huh!" snorted Mrs. Carraway.

RED-HEADED BABY

"Dead, dead as hell, these little burgs on the Florida coast. Lot of half-built skeleton houses left over from the boom. Never finished. Never will be finished. Mosquitoes, sand, niggers. Christ, I ought to break away from it. Stuck five years on same boat and still nothin' but a third mate puttin' in at dumps like this on a damned coast-wise tramp. Not even a good time to be had. Norfolk, Savannah, Jacksonville, ain't bad. Ain't bad. But what the hell kind of port's this? What the hell is there to do except get drunk and go out and sleep with niggers? Hell!"

Feet in the sand. Head under palms, magnolias, stars. Lights and the kid-cries of a sleepy town. Mosquitoes to slap at with hairy freckled hands and a dead hot breeze, when there is any breeze.

"What the hell am I walkin' way out here for? She wasn't nothin' to get excited over—last time I saw her. And that must a been a full three years ago. She acted like she was a virgin then. Name was Betsy. Sure ain't a virgin now, I know that. Not after we'd been anchored here damn near a month, the old man mixed up in some kind of law suit over some rich guy's yacht we rammed in a midnight squall off the bar. Damn good thing I wasn't on the bridge then. And this damn yellow gal, said she never had nothing to do with a seaman before. Lyin' I guess. Three years ago. She's probably on the crib-line now. Hell, how far was that house?"

Crossing the railroad track at the edge of town. Green lights. Sand in the road, seeping into oxfords and the cuffs of dungarees. Surf sounds, mosquito sounds, nigger-cries in the night. No street lights out here. There never is where niggers live. Rickety run-down huts, under palm trees. Flowers and vines all over. Always growing, always climbing. Never finished. Never will be finished climbing, growing. Hell of a lot of stars these Florida nights.

"Say, this ought to be the house. No light in it. Well, I remember this half-fallin'-down gate. Still fallin' down. Hell, why don't it go on and fall? Two or three years, and ain't fell yet. Guess *she's* fell a hell of a lot, though. It don't take them yellow janes long to get old and ugly. Said she was seventeen then. A wonder her old woman let me come in the house that night. They acted like it was the first time a white man had ever come in the house. They acted scared. But she was worth the money that time all right. She played like a kid. Said she liked my red hair. Said she'd never had a white man before. . . . Holy Jesus, the yellow wenches I've had, though. . . .

Well, it's the same old gate. Be funny if she had another mule in my stall, now wouldn't it? . . . Say, anybody home there?"

"Yes, suh! Yes, suh! Come right in!"

"Hell, I know they can't recognize my voice. . . . It's the old woman, sure as a yard arm's long. . . . Hello! Where's Betsy?"

"Yes, suh, right here, suh. In de kitchen. Wait till I lights de light. Come in. Come in, young gentleman."

"Hell, I can't see to come in."

Little flare of oil light.

"Howdy! Howdy do, suh! Howdy, if 'tain't Mister Clarence, now, 'pon my word! Howdy, Mister Clarence, howdy! Howdy! After sich a long time."

"You must-a knowed my voice."

"No, suh, ain't recollected, suh. No, suh, but I knowed you was some white man comin' up de walk. Yes, indeedy! Set down, set down. Betsy be here directly. Set *right* down. Lemme call her. She's in de kitchen. . . . You Betsy!"

"Same old woman, wrinkled as hell, and still don't care where the money comes from. Still talkin' loud. . . . She knew it was some white man comin' up the walk, heh? There must be plenty of 'em, then, comin' here now. She knew it was some white man, heh! . . . What yuh sayin', Betsy, old gal? Damn if yuh ain't just as plump as ever. Them same damn moles on your cheek! Com'ere, lemme feel 'em."

Young yellow girl in a white house dress. Oiled hair. Skin like an autumn moon. Gold-ripe young yellow girl with a white house dress to her knees. Soft plump bare legs, color of the moon. Barefooted.

"Say, Betsy, here is Mister Clarence come back."

"Sure is! Claren—Mister Clarence! Ma, give him a drink."

"Keepin' licker in the house, now, heh? Yes? I thought you was church members last time I saw yuh? You always had to send out and get licker then."

"Well, we's expectin' company some of the times these days," smiling teeth like bright-white rays of moon, Betsy, nearly twenty, and still pretty.

"You usin' rouge, too, ain't yuh?"

"Sweet rouge."

"Yal?"

"Yeah, man, sweet and red like your hair."

"Yal?"

No such wise cracking three years ago. Too young and dumb for flirtation then: Betsy. Never like the old woman, talkative, "This here rum come right off de boats from Bermudy. Taste it,

Mister Clarence. Strong enough to knock a mule down. Have a glass."

"Here's to you, Mister Clarence."

"Drinkin' licker, too, heh? Hell of a baby, ain't yuh? Yuh wouldn't even do that last time I saw yuh."

"Sure wouldn't, Mister Clarence, but three years a long time."

"Don't Mister Clarence *me* so much. Yuh know I christened yuh. . . . Auntie, yuh right about this bein' good licker."

"Yes, suh, I knowed you'd like it. It's strong."

"Sit on my lap, kid."

"Sure. . . ."

Soft heavy hips. Hot and browner than the moon—good licker. Drinking it down in little nigger house Florida coast palm fronds scratching roof hum mosquitoes night bugs flies ain't loud enough to keep a man named Clarence girl named Betsy old woman named Auntie from talking and drinking in a little nigger house on Florida coast dead warm night with the licker browner and more fiery than the moon. Yeah, man! A blanket of stars in the Florida sky—outside. In oil-lamp house you don't see no stars. Only a white man with red hair—third mate on a lousy tramp, a nigger girl, and Auntie wrinkled as an alligator bringing the fourth bottle of licker and everybody drinking—when the door . . . slowly . . . opens.

"Say, what the hell? Who's openin' that room door, peepin' in here? It can't be openin' itself?"

The white man stares intently, looking across the table, past the lamp, the licker bottles, the glasses and the old woman, way past the girl. Standing in the door from the kitchen—Look! a damn red-headed baby. Standing not saying a damn word, a damn runt of a red-headed baby.

"What the hell?"

"You Clar—— . . . Mister Clarence, 'cuse me! . . . You hatian, you, get back to you' bed this minute—fo' I tan you in a inch o' yo' life!"

"Ma, let him stay."

Betsy's red-headed child stands in the door looking like one of those goggly-eyed dolls you hit with a ball at the County Fair. The child's face got no change in it. Never changes. Looks like never will change. Just staring—blue-eyed. Hell! God damn! A red-headed blue-eyed yellow-skinned baby!

"You Clarence! . . . 'Cuse me, Mister Clarence. I ain't talkin' to you suh. . . . You, Clarence, go to bed. . . . That chile near 'bout worries de soul-case out o' me. Betsy spiles him, that's why. De

po' little thing can't hear, nohow. Just deaf as a post. And over two
years old and can't even say, 'Da!' No, suh, can't say, 'Da!' "

"Anyhow, Ma, my child ain't blind."

"Might just as well be blind fo' all de good his eyesight do him.
I show him a switch and he don't pay it no mind—'less'n I hit him."

"He's mighty damn white for a nigger child."

"Yes, suh, Mister Clarence. He really ain't got much colored
blood in him, a-tall. Betsy's papa, Mister Clarence, now he were a
white man, too. . . . Here, lemme pour you some licker. Drink,
Mister Clarence, drink."

Damn little red-headed stupid-faced runt of a child, named
Clarence. Bow-legged as hell, too. Three shots for a quarter like a
loaded doll in a County Fair. Anybody take a chance. For Christ's
sake, stop him from walking across the floor! Will yuh?

"Hey! Take your hands off my legs, you lousy little bastard!"

"He can't hear you, Mister Clarence."

"Tell him to stop crawlin' around then under the table before
I knock his block off."

"You varmint. . . ."

"Hey! Take him up from there, will you?"

"Yes, suh, Mister Clarence."

"Hey!"

"You little . . ."

"Hurry! Go on! Get him out then! What's he doin' crawlin'
round dumb as hell lookin' at me up at me. I said, *me*. Get him
the hell out of here! Hey, Betsy, get him out!"

A red-headed baby. Moonlight-gone baby. No kind of yellow-
white bow-legged goggled-eyed County Fair baseball baby. Get him
the hell out of here pulling at my legs looking like me at me like me
at myself like me red-headed as me.

"Christ!"

"Christ!"

Knocking over glasses by the oil lamp on the table where the night
flies flutter Florida where skeleton houses left over from boom
sand in the road and no lights in the nigger section across the rail-
road's knocking over glasses at edge of town where a moon-colored
girl's got a red-headed baby deaf as a post like the dolls you wham
at three shots for a quarter in the County Fair half full of licker
and can't hit nothing.

"Lemme pay for those drinks, will yuh? How much is it?"

"Ain't you gonna stay, Mister Clarence?"

"Lemme pay for my licker, I said."

"Ain't you gonna stay all night?"

"Lemme pay for that licker."

"Why, Mister Clarence? You stayed before."

"How much is the licker?"

"Two dollars, Mister Clarence."

"Here."

"Thank you, Mister Clarence."

"Go'bye!"

"Go'bye."

LITTLE DOG

Miss Briggs had a little apartment all alone in a four story block just where Oakwood Drive curved past the park and the lake. Across the street, beneath her window, kids skated in winter, and in the spring the grass grew green. In summer, lovers walked and necked by the lake in the moonlight. In fall brown and red-gold leaves went skithering into the water when the wind blew.

Miss Briggs came home from work every night at eight, unless she went to the movies or the Women's Civics Club. On Sunday evenings she sometimes went to a lecture on Theosophy. But she was never one to gad about, Miss Briggs. Besides she worked too hard. She was the head bookkeeper for the firm of Wilkins and Bryant, Wood, Coal And Coke. And since 1930, when they had cut down the staff, she had only one assistant. Just two of them now to take care of the books, bills, and everything. But Miss Briggs was very efficient. She had been head bookkeeper for twenty-one years. Wilkins and Bryant didn't know what they would do without her.

Miss Briggs was proud of her record as a bookkeeper. Once the City Hall had tried to get her, but Wilkins and Bryant said, "No, indeed. We can pay as much as the city, if not more. You stay right here with us." Miss Briggs stayed. She was never a person to move about much or change jobs.

As a young girl she had studied very hard in business school. She never had much time to go out. A widowed mother, more or less dependent on her then, later became completely dependent— paralyzed. Her mother had been dead for six years now.

Perhaps it was the old woman's long illness that had got Miss Briggs in the habit of staying home every night in her youth, instead of going out to the theatre or to parties. They had never been able to afford a maid even after Miss Briggs became so well paid—for doctors' bills were such a drain, and in those last months a trained nurse was needed for her mother—God rest her soul.

Now, alone, Miss Briggs usually ate her dinner in the Rose Bud Tea Shoppe. A number of genteel business women ate there, and the colored waiters were so nice. She had been served by Joe or Perry, flat-footed old Negro gentlemen, for three or four years now. They knew her tastes, and would get the cook to make little special dishes for her if she wasn't feeling very well.

After dinner, with a walk of five or six blocks from the Rose Bud, the park would come into view with its trees and lights. The Lyle Apartments loomed up. A pretty place to live, facing the park. Miss Briggs had moved there after her mother died. Trying to keep house alone was just a little too much. And there was no man in view to marry. Most of them would want her only for her money now, at her age, anyway. To move with another woman, Miss Briggs thought, would be a sort of sacrilege so soon after her mother's death. Besides, she really didn't know any other woman who, like herself, was without connections. Almost everybody had somebody, Miss Briggs reflected. Every woman she knew had either a husband, or sisters, or a friend of long standing with whom she resided. But Miss Briggs had nobody at all. Nobody.

Not that she thought about it very much. Miss Briggs was too used to facing the world alone, minding her own business, and going her own way. But one summer, while returning from Michigan where she had taken her two weeks' rest, as she came through Cleveland, on her way from the boat to the station there, she happened to pass a dog shop with a window full of fuzzy little white dogs. Miss Briggs called to the taxi man to stop. She got out and went in. When she came back to the taxi, she carried a little white dog named Flips. At least, the dealer said he had been calling it Flips because its ears were so floppy.

"They just flip and flop," the man said, smiling at the tall middle-aged woman.

"How much is he?" Miss Briggs asked, holding the puppy up.

"I'll let you have him for twenty-five dollars," the man said.

Miss Briggs put the puppy down. She thought that was a pretty steep price. But there was something about Flips that she liked, so she picked him up again and took him with her. After all, she allowed herself very few indulgences. And somehow, this summer, Miss Briggs sort of hated going back to an empty flat—even if it did overlook the park.

Or maybe it was because it overlooked the park that had made it so terrible a place to live lately. Miss Briggs had never felt lonely, not *very* lonely, in the old house after her mother died. Only when she moved to the flat, did her loneliness really come down on her. There were some nights there, especially summer nights, when she thought she couldn't stand it, to sit in her window and see so many people going by, couple by couple, arms locked; or else in groups, laughing and talking. Miss Briggs wondered why she knew no one, male or female, to walk out with, laughing and talking. She knew only the employees where she worked, and with whom she associated but little (for she hated to have people know her business). She knew, of course, the members of the Women's Civics Club, but in a cultural sort of way. The warmth of friendship seldom mellowed her contacts there. Only one or two of the club women had ever called on her. Miss Briggs always believed in keeping her distance, too. Her mother used to say she'd been born poor but proud, and would stay that way.

"Folks have to amount to something before Clara takes up with them," old Mrs. Briggs always said. "Men'll have a hard time getting Clara."

Men did. Now, with no especial attractions to make them keep trying, Miss Briggs, tall and rail-like, found herself left husbandless at an age when youth had gone.

So, in her forty-fifth year, coming back from a summer boarding house in Michigan, Miss Briggs bought herself a little white dog. When she got home, she called on the janitor and asked him to bring her up a small box for Flips. The janitor, a tow-headed young Swede, brought her a grapefruit crate from the A. & P. Miss Briggs put it in the kitchen for Flips.

She told the janitor to bring her, too, three times a week, a dime's worth of dog meat or bones, and leave it on the back porch where she could find it when she came home. On other nights, Flips ate dog biscuits.

Flips and Miss Briggs soon settled on a routine. Each evening when she got home she would feed him. Then she would take him for a walk. This gave Miss Briggs an excuse for getting out, too. In warm weather she would walk around the little lake fronting her apartment with Flips on a string. Sometimes she would even smile at other people walking around the lake with dogs at night. It was nice the way dogs made things friendly. It was nice the way people with dogs smiled at her occasionally because she had a dog, too. But whenever (as seldom happened) someone in the park, dog or no dog, tried to draw her into conversation, Miss Briggs would move on as quickly as she could without being rude. You could never tell just who people were, Miss Briggs thought, or what they might have in their minds. No, you shouldn't think of taking up with strange people in parks. Besides, she was head bookkeeper for Wilkins and Bryant, and in these days of robberies and kidnappings maybe they just wanted to find out when she went for the pay roll, and how much cash the firm kept on hand. Miss Briggs didn't trust people.

Always, by ten o'clock, she was back with Flips in her flat. A cup of hot milk then maybe, with a little in a saucer for Flips, and to bed. In the morning she would let Flips run down the back steps for a few minutes, then she gave him more milk, left a pan of water, and went to work. A regular routine, for Miss Briggs took care of Flips with great seriousness. At night when she got back from the Rose Bud Tea Shoppe, she fed him biscuits; or if it were dog meat night, she looked out on the back porch for the package the janitor was paid to leave. (That is, Miss Briggs allowed the Swede fifty cents a week to buy bones. He could keep the change.)

But one night, the meat was not there. Miss Briggs thought perhaps he had forgotten. Still he had been bringing it regularly for nearly two years. Maybe the warm spring this year made the young janitor listless, Miss Briggs mused. She fed Flips biscuits.

But two days later, another dog meat night, the package was not there either. "This is too much!" thought Miss Briggs. "Come on, Flipsy, let's go downstairs and see. I'm sure I gave him fifty cents this week to buy your bones."

Miss Briggs and the little white beast went downstairs to ask why there was no meat for her dog to eat. When they got to the janitor's quarters in the basement, they heard a mighty lot of happy laughter and kids squalling, and people moving. They didn't sound like Swedes, either. Miss Briggs was a bit timid about knocking, but she finally mustered up courage with Flips there beside her. A sudden silence fell inside.

"You Leroy," a voice said. "Go to de door."

A child's feet came running. The door opened like a flash and a small colored boy stood there grinning.

"Where—where is the janitor?" Miss Briggs said, taken aback.

"You mean my papa?" asked the child, looking at the gaunt white lady. "He's here." And off he went to call his father.

Surrounded by children, a tall broad-shouldered Negro of perhaps forty, gentle of face and a little stooped, came to the door.

"Good evenin'," he said pleasantly.

"Why, are you the janitor?" stammered Miss Briggs. Flips had already begun to jump up on him with friendly mien.

"Yes'm, I'm the new janitor," said the Negro in a softly beautiful voice, kids all around him. "Is there something I can help you to do?"

"Well," said Miss Briggs, "I'd like some bones for my little dog. He's missed his meat two times now. Can you get him some?"

"Yes'm, sure can," said the new janitor, "if all the stores ain't closed." He was so much taller than Miss Briggs that she had to look up at him.

"I'd appreciate it," said Miss Briggs, "please."

As she went back upstairs she heard the new janitor calling in his rich voice, "Lora, you reckon that meat store's still open?" And a woman's voice and a lot of children answered him.

It turned out that the store was closed. So Miss Briggs gave the Negro janitor ten cents and told him to have the meat there the next night when she came home.

"Flips, you shan't starve," she said to the little white dog, "new janitor or no new janitor."

"Wruff!" said Flips.

But the next day when she came home there was no meat on the back porch either. Miss Briggs was puzzled, and a little hurt. Had the Negro forgotten?

Scarcely had she left the kitchen, however, when someone knocked on the back door and there stood the colored man with the meat. He was almost as old as Miss Briggs, she was certain of it, looking at him. Not a young man at all, but he was awfully big and brown and kind looking. So sort of sure about life as he handed her the package.

"I thought some other dog might get it if I left it on the porch," said the colored man. "So I kept it downstairs till you come."

Miss Briggs was touched. "Well, thank you very much," she said.

When the man had gone, she remembered that she had not told him how often to get meat for the dog.

The next night he came again with bones, and every night from then on. Miss Briggs did not stop him, or limit him to three nights a week. Just after eight, whenever she got home, up the back porch steps the Negro would come with the dog meat. Sometimes there would be two or three kids with him. Pretty little brown-black rather dirty kids, Miss Briggs thought, who were shy in front of her, but nice.

Once or twice during the spring, the janitor's wife, instead, brought the dog meat up on Saturday nights. Flips barked rudely at her. Miss Briggs didn't take to the creature, either. She was fat and yellow, and certainly too old to just keep on having children as she evidently did. The janitor himself was so solid and big and strong! Miss Briggs felt better when he brought her the bones for her dog. She didn't like his wife.

That June, on warm nights, as soon as she got home, Miss Briggs would open the back door and let the draft blow through. She could hear the janitor better coming up the rear stairs when he brought the bones. And, of course, she never said more than good-evening to him and thank you. Or here's a dollar for the week. Keep the change.

Flips ate an awful lot of meat that spring. "Your little dog's a regular meat-hound," the janitor said one night as he handed her the bones; and Miss Briggs blushed, for no good reason.

"He does eat a lot," she said. "Goodnight."

As she spread the bones out on paper for the dog, she felt that her hands were trembling. She left Flips eating and went into the parlor, but found that she could not keep her mind on the book she was reading. She kept looking at the big kind face of the janitor in her mind, perturbed that it was a Negro face, and that it stayed with her so.

The next night, she found herself waiting for the dog meat to arrive with more anxiety than Flips himself. When the colored man handed it to her, she quickly closed the door, before her face got red again.

"Funny old white lady," thought the janitor as he went back downstairs to his basement full of kids. "Just crazy about that dog," he added to his wife. "I ought to tell her it ain't good to feed a dog so much meat."

"What do you care, long as she wants to?" asked his wife.

The next day in the office Miss Briggs found herself making errors over the books. That night she hurried home to be sure and be there on time when he brought the dog meat up, in case he came early.

"What's the matter with me," she said sharply to herself, "rushing this way just to feed Flips? Whatever is the matter with me?" But all the way through the warm dusky streets, she seemed to hear the janitor's deep voice saying, "Good evenin'," to her.

Then, when the Negro really knocked on the door with the meat, she was trembling so that she could not go to the kitchen to get it. "Leave it right there by the sink," she managed to call out. "Thank you, Joe."

She heard the man going back downstairs sort of humming to himself, a kid or so following him. Miss Briggs felt as if she were going to faint, but Flips kept jumping up on her, barking for his meat.

"Oh, Flips," she said, "I'm so hungry." She meant to say, *"You're so hungry."* So she repeated it. "You're so hungry! Heh, Flipsy, dog?"

And from the way the little dog barked, he must have been hungry. He loved meat.

The next evening, Miss Briggs was standing in the kitchen when the colored man came with the bones.

"Lay them down," she said, "thank you," trying not to look at him. But as he went downstairs, she watched through the window his beautifully heavy body finding the rhythm of the steps, his big brown neck moving just a little.

"Get down!" she said sharply to Flips barking for his dinner.

To herself she said earnestly, "I've got to move. I can't be worried being so far from a meat shop, or from where I eat my dinner. I think I'll move downtown where the shops are open at night. I can't stand this. Most of my friends live downtown anyway."

But even as she said it, she wondered what friends she meant. She had a little white dog named Flips, that was all. And she was acquainted with other people who worked at Wilkins and Bryant, but she had nothing to do with them. She was the head bookkeeper. She knew a few women in the Civics Club fairly well. And the Negro waiters at the Rose Bud Shoppe.

And this janitor!

Miss Briggs decided that she could not bear to have this janitor come upstairs with a package of bones for Flips again. She was sure he was happy down there with his portly yellow wife and his house full of children. Let him stay in the basement, then, where he belonged. She never wanted to see him again, never.

The next night, Miss Briggs made herself go to a movie before coming home. And when she got home, she fed Flips dog biscuits. That week she began looking for a new apartment, a small one for two, her and the dog. Fortunately there were plenty to be had, what with people turned out for not being able to pay their rent—which would never happen to her, thank God! She had saved her money. When she found an apartment, she deposited the first month's rent at once. On her coming Saturday afternoon off, she planned to move.

Friday night, when the janitor came up with the bones, she decided to be just a little pleasant to him. Probably she would never see him again. Perhaps she would give him a dollar for a tip, then. Something to remember her by.

When he came upstairs, she was aware a long time of his feet approaching. Coming up, up, up, bringing bones for her dog. Flips began to bark. Miss Briggs went to the door. She took the package in one hand. With the other she offered the bill.

"Thank you so much for buying bones for my little dog," she said. "Here, here is a dollar for your trouble. You keep it all."

"Much obliged, m'am," said the astonished janitor. He had never seen Miss Briggs so generous before. "Thank you, m'am! He sure do eat a heap o' bones, your little dog."

"He almost keeps me broke buying bones," Miss Briggs said, holding the door.

"True," said the janitor. "But I reckon you don't have much other expenses on hand, do you? No family and all like me?"

"You're right," answered Miss Briggs. "But a little dog is so much company, too."

"Guess they are, m'am," said the janitor, turning to go. "Well, goodnight, Miss Briggs. I'm much obliged."

"Goodnight, Joe."

As his broad shoulders and tall brown body disappeared down the stairs, Miss Briggs slowly turned her back, shut the door, and put the bones on the floor for Flipsy. Then suddenly she began to cry.

The next day she moved away as she had planned to do. The janitor never saw her any more. For a few days, the walkers in the park beside the lake wondered where a rather gaunt middle-aged woman who used to come out at night with a little white dog had gone. But in a very short while the neighborhood had completely forgotten her.

Laughing to Keep From Crying

WHO'S PASSING FOR WHO?

One of the great difficulties about being a member of a minority
race is that so many kindhearted, well-meaning bores gather around
to help. Usually, to tell the truth, they have nothing to help with,
except their company—which is often appallingly dull.

Some members of the Negro race seem very well able to put up
with it, though, in these uplifting years. Such was Caleb Johnson,
colored social worker, who was always dragging around with him
some nondescript white person or two, inviting them to dinner,
showing them Harlem, ending up at the Savoy—much to the dis-
pleasure of whatever friends of his might be out that evening for
fun, not sociology.

Friends are friends and, unfortunately, overearnest uplifters are
uplifters—no matter what color they may be. If it were the white
race that was ground down intead of Negroes, Caleb Johnson would
be one of the first to offer Nordics the sympathy of his utterly
inane society, under the impression that somehow he would be
doing them a great deal of good.

You see, Caleb, and his white friends, too, were all bores. Or so
we, who lived in Harlem's literary bohemia during the "Negro
Renaissance" thought. We literary ones considered ourselves too
broad-minded to be bothered with questions of color. We liked
people of any race who smoked incessantly, drank liberally, wore
complexion and morality as loose garments, and made fun of anyone
who didn't do likewise. We snubbed and high-hatted any Negro
or white luckless enough not to understand Gertrude Stein, Ulysses,
Man Ray, the theremin, Jean Toomer, or George Antheil. By the
end of the 1920's Caleb was just catching up to Dos Passos. He
thought H. G. Wells good.

We met Caleb one night in Small's. He had three assorted white
folks in tow. We would have passed him by with but a nod had he
not hailed us enthusiastically, risen, and introduced us with great
acclaim to his friends who turned out to be schoolteachers from
Iowa, a woman and two men. They appeared amazed and delighted

30

to meet all at once two Negro writers and a black painter in the flesh. They invited us to have a drink with them. Money being scarce with us, we deigned to sit down at their table.

The white lady said, "I've never met a Negro writer before."

The two men added, "Neither have we."

"Why, we know any number of *white* writers," we three dark bohemians declared with bored nonchalance.

"But Negro writers are much more rare," said the lady.

"There are plenty in Harlem," we said.

"But not in Iowa," said one of the men, shaking his mop of red hair.

"There are no good *white* writers in Iowa either, are there?" we asked superciliously.

"Oh, yes, Ruth Suckow came from there."

Whereupon we proceeded to light in upon Ruth Suckow as old hat and to annihilate her in favor of Kay Boyle. The way we flung names around seemed to impress both Caleb and his white guests. This, of course, delighted us, though we were too young and too proud to admit it.

The drinks came and everything was going well, all of us drinking, and we three showing off in a high-brow manner, when suddenly at the table just behind us a man got up and knocked down a woman. He was a brownskin man. The woman was blonde. As she rose he knocked her down again. Then the red-haired man from Iowa got up and knocked the colored man down.

He said, "Keep your hands off that white woman."

The man got up and said, "She's not a white woman. She's my wife."

One of the waiters added, "She's not white, sir, she's colored."

Whereupon the man from Iowa looked puzzled, dropped his fists, and said, "I'm sorry."

The colored man said, "What are you doing up here in Harlem anyway, interfering with my family affairs?"

The white man said, "I thought she was a white woman."

The woman who had been on the floor rose and said, "Well, I'm not a white woman, I'm colored, and you leave my husband alone."

Then they both lit in on the gentleman from Iowa. It took all of us and several waiters, too, to separate them. When it was over the manager requested us to kindly pay our bill and get out. He said we were disturbing the peace. So we all left. We went to a fish restaurant down the street. Caleb was terribly apologetic to his white friends. We artists were both mad and amused.

"Why did you say you were sorry," said the colored painter to the visitor from Iowa, "after you'd hit that man—and then found out it wasn't a white woman you were defending, but merely a light colored woman who looked white?"

"Well," answered the red-haired Iowan, "I didn't mean to be butting in if they were all the same race."

"Don't you think a woman needs defending from a brute, no matter what race she may be?" asked the painter.

"Yes, but I think it's up to you to defend your own women."

"Oh, so you'd divide up a brawl according to races, no matter who was right?"

"Well, I wouldn't say that."

"You mean you wouldn't defend a colored woman whose husband was knocking her down?" asked the poet.

Before the visitor had time to answer, the painter said, "No! You just got mad because you thought a black man was hitting a *white* woman."

"But she *looked* like a white woman," countered the man.

"Maybe she was just passing for colored," I said.

"Like some Negroes pass for white," Caleb interposed.

"Anyhow, I don't like it," said the colored painter, "the way you stopped defending her when you found out she wasn't white."

"No, we don't like it," we all agreed except Caleb.

Caleb said in extenuation, "But Mr. Stubblefield is new to Harlem."

The red-haired white man said, "Yes, it's my first time here."

"Maybe Mr. Stubblefield ought to stay out of Harlem," we observed.

"I agree," Mr. Stubblefield said. "Good night."

He got up then and there and left the café. He stalked as he walked. His red head disappeared into the night.

"Oh, that's too bad," said the white couple who remained. "Stubby's temper just got the best of him. But explain to us, are many colored folks really as fair as that woman?"

"Sure, lots of them have more white blood than colored, and pass for white."

"Do they?" said the lady and gentleman from Iowa.

"You never read Nella Larsen?" we asked.

"She writes novels," Caleb explained. "She's part white herself."

"Read her," we advised. "Also read the *Autobiography of an Ex-colored Man.*" Not that we had read it ourselves—because we paid but little attention to the older colored writers—but we knew it was about passing for white.

We all ordered fish and settled down comfortably to shocking our white friends with tales about how many Negroes there were passing for white all over America. We were determined to *épater le bourgeois* real good via this white couple we had cornered, when the woman leaned over the table in the midst of our dissertations and said, "Listen, gentlemen, you needn't spread the word, but me and my husband aren't white either. We've just been *passing* for white for the last fifteen years."

"What?"

"We're colored, too, just like you," said the husband. "But it's better passing for white because we make more money."

Well, that took the wind out of us. It took the wind out of Caleb, too. He thought all the time he was showing some fine white folks Harlem—and they were as colored as he was!

Caleb almost never cursed. But this time he said, "I'll be damned!"

Then everybody laughed. And laughed! We almost had hysterics. All at once we dropped our professionally selfconscious "Negro" manners, became natural, ate fish, and talked and kidded freely like colored folks do when there are no white folks around. We really had fun then, joking about that red-haired guy who mistook a fair colored woman for white. After the fish we went to two or three more night spots and drank until five o'clock in the morning.

Finally we put the light-colored people in a taxi heading downtown. They turned to shout a last good-by. The cab was just about to move off, when the woman called to the driver to stop.

She leaned out the window and said with a grin, "Listen, boys! I hate to confuse you again. But, to tell the truth, my husband and I aren't really colored at all. We're white. We just thought we'd kid you by passing for colored a little while—just as you said Negroes sometimes pass for white."

She laughed as they sped off toward Central Park, waving, "Good-by!"

We didn't say a thing. We just stood there on the corner in Harlem dumbfounded—not knowing now *which* way we'd been fooled. Were they really white—passing for colored? Or colored—passing for white?

Whatever race they were, they had had too much fun at our expense—even if they did pay for the drinks.

SOMETHING IN COMMON

Hong Kong. A hot day. A teeming street. A mélange of races. A pub, over the door the Union Jack.

The two men were not together. They came in from the street, complete strangers, through different doors, but they both reached the bar at about the same time. The big British bartender looked at each of them with a wary, scornful eye. He knew that, more than likely, neither had the price of more than a couple of drinks. They were distinctly down at the heel, had been drinking elsewhere, and were not customers of the bar. He served them with a deliberation that was not even condescending—it was menacing.

"A beer," said the old Negro, rattling a handful of Chinese and English coins at the end of a frayed cuff.

"A scotch," said the old white man, reaching for a pretzel with thin fingers.

"That's the tariff," said the bartender, pointing to a sign.

"Too high for this lousy Hong Kong beer," said the old Negro.

The barman did not deign to answer.

"But, reckon it's as good as some we got back home," the elderly colored man went on as he counted out the money.

"I'll bet you wouldn't mind bein' back there, George," spoke up the old white man from the other end of the bar, "in the good old U.S.A."

"Don't *George* me," said the Negro, "'cause I don't know you from Adam."

"Well, don't get sore," said the old white man, coming nearer, sliding his glass along the bar. "I'm from down home, too."

"Well, I ain't from no *down home*," answered the Negro wiping beer foam from his mouth. "I'm from the North."

"Where?"

"North of Mississippi," said the black man. "I mean Missouri."

"I'm from Kentucky," vouched the old white fellow swallowing his whisky. "Gimme another one," to the bartender.

"Half a dollar," said the bartender.

"Mex, you mean?"

"Yeah, mex," growled the bartender picking up the glass.

"All right, I'll pay you," said the white man testily. "Gimme another one."

"They're tough in this here bar," said the old Negro sarcastically. "Looks like they don't know a Kentucky colonel when they see one."

"No manners in these damned foreign joints," said the white man seriously. "How long you been in Hong Kong?"

"Too long," said the old Negro.

"Where'd you come from here?"

"Manila," said the Negro.

"What'd you do there?"

"Now what else do you want to know?" asked the Negro.

"I'm askin' you a civil question," said the old white man.

"Don't ask so many then," said the Negro, "and don't start out by callin' me *George*. My name ain't George."

"What is your name, might I ask?" taking another pretzel.

"Samuel Johnson. And your'n?"

"Colonel McBride."

"Of Kentucky?" grinned the Negro impudently toothless.

"Yes, sir, of Kentucky," said the white man seriously.

"Howdy, Colonel," said the Negro. "Have a pretzel."

"Have a drink, boy," said the white man, beckoning the bartender.

"Don't call me *boy*," said the Negro. "I'm as old as you, if not older."

"Don't care," said the white man, "have a drink."

"Gin," said the Negro.

"Make it two," said the white man. "Gin's somethin' we both got in common."

"I love gin," said the Negro.

"Me, too," said the white man.

"Gin's a sweet drink," mused the Negro, "especially when you're around women."

"Gimme one white woman," said the old white man, "and you can take all these Chinee gals over here."

"Gimme one yellow gal," said the old Negro, "and you can take all your white women anywhere."

"Hong Kong's full of yellow gals," said the white man.

"I mean *high-yellow* gals," said the Negro, "like we have in Missouri."

"Or in Kentucky," said the white man, "where half of 'em has white pappys."

"Here! Don't talk 'bout my women," said the old Negro. "I don't allow no white man to talk 'bout my women."

"Who's talkin' about your women? Have a drink, George."

"I told you, don't *George* me. My name is Samuel Johnson. White man, you ain't in Kentucky now. You in the Far East."

"I know it. If I was in Kentucky, I wouldn't be standin' at this bar with you. Have a drink."

"Gin."

"Make it two."

"Who's payin'?" said the bartender.

"Not me," said the Negro. "Not *me*."

"Don't worry," said the old white man grandly.

"Well, I am worryin'," growled the bartender. "Cough up."

"Here," said the white man, pulling out a few shillings. "Here, even if it is my last penny, here!"

The bartender took it without a word. He picked up the glasses and wiped the bar.

"I can't seem to get ahead in this damn town," said the old white man, "and I been here since Coolidge."

"Neither do I," said the Negro, "and I come before the War."

"Where is your home, George?" asked the white man.

"You must think it's Georgia," said the Negro. "Truth is I ain't got no home—no more home than a dog."

"Neither have I," said the white man, "but sometimes I wish I was back in the States."

"Well, I don't," said the Negro. "A black man ain't got a break in the States."

"What?" said the old white man, drawing up proudly.

"States is no good," said the Negro. "No damned good."

"Shut up," yelled the old white man waving a pretzel.

"What do you mean, shut up?" said the Negro.

"I won't listen to nobody runnin' down the United States," said the white man. "You better stop insultin' America, you big black ingrate."

"You better stop insultin' me, you poor-white trash," bristled the aged Negro. Both of them reeled indignantly.

"Why, you black bastard!" quavered the old white man.

"You white cracker!" trembled the elderly Negro.

These final insults caused the two old men to square off like roosters, rocking a little from age and gin, but glaring fiercely at one another, their gnarled fists doubled up, arms at boxing angles.

"Here! Here!" barked the bartender. "Hey! Stop it now!"

"I'll bat you one," said the white man to the Negro.

"I'll fix you so you can't leave, neither can you stay," said the Negro to the white.

"Yuh will, will yuh?" sneered the bartender to both of them. "I'll see about batting—and fixing, too."

He came around the end of the bar in three long strides. He

grabbed the two old men unceremoniously by the scruff of their necks, cracked their heads together twice, and threw them both calmly into the street. Then he wiped his hands.

The white and yellow world of Hong Kong moved by, rickshaw runners pushed and panted, motor horns blared, pedestrians crowded the narrow sidewalks. The two old men picked themselves up from the dust and dangers of a careless traffic. They looked at one another, dazed for a moment and considerably shaken.

"Well, I'll be damned!" sputtered the old white man. "Are we gonna stand for this—from a Limey bartender?"

"Hell, no," said the old Negro. "Let's go back in there and clean up that joint."

"He's got no rights to put his Cockney hands on Americans," said the old white man.

"Sure ain't," agreed the old Negro.

Arm in arm, they staggered back into the bar, united to protect their honor against the British.

SPANISH BLOOD

In that amazing city of Manhattan where people are forever building things anew, during prohibition times there lived a young Negro called Valerio Gutierrez whose mother was a Harlem laundress, but whose father was a Puerto Rican sailor. Valerio grew up in the streets. He was never much good at school, but he was swell at selling papers, pitching pennies, or shooting pool. In his teens he became one of the smoothest dancers in the Latin-American quarter north of Central Park. Long before the rhumba became popular, he knew how to do it in the real Cuban way that made all the girls afraid to dance with him. Besides, he was very good looking.

At seventeen, an elderly Chilean lady who owned a beauty parlor called La Flor began to buy his neckties. At eighteen, she kept him in pocket money and let him drive her car. At nineteen, younger and prettier women—a certain comely Spanish widow, also one Dr. Barrios' pale wife—began to see that he kept well dressed.

"You'll never amount to nothin'," Hattie, his brown-skinned mother said. "Why don't you get a job and work? It's that foreign blood in you, that's what it is. Just like your father."

"*Que va?*" Valerio replied, grinning.

"Don't you speak Spanish to me," his mama said. "You know I don't understand it."

"O.K., mama," Valerio said, "*Yo voy a trabajar.*"

"You better *trabajar*," his mama answered. "And I mean work, too! I'm tired o' comin' home every night from that Chinee laundry and findin' you gone to the dogs. I'm gonna move out o' this here Spanish neighborhood anyhow, way up into Harlem where some real *colored* people is, I mean American Negroes. There ain't nobody settin' a decent example for you down here 'mongst all these Cubans and Puerto Ricans and things. I don't care if your father was one of 'em, I never did like 'em real well."

"Aw, ma, why didn't you ever learn Spanish and stop talking like a spook?"

"Don't you spook me, you young hound, you! I won't stand it. Just because you're straight-haired and yellow and got that foreign blood in you, don't you spook me. I'm your mother and I won't stand for it. You hear me?"

"Yes, m'am. But you know what I mean. I mean stop talking like most colored folks—just because you're not white you don't have to get back in a corner and stay there. Can't we live nowhere else but way up in Harlem, for instance? Down here in 106th Street, white and colored families live in the same house—Spanish-speaking families, some white and some black. What do you want to move further up in Harlem for, where everybody's all black? Lots of my friends down here are Spanish and Italian, and we get along swell."

"That's just what I'm talkin' about," said his mother. "That's just why I'm gonna move. I can't keep track of you, runnin' around with a fast foreign crowd, all mixed up with every what-cha-ma-call-it, lettin' all shades o' women give you money. Besides, no matter where you move, or what language you speak, you're still colored less'n your skin is white."

"Well, I won't be," said Valerio, "I'm American, Latin-American."

"Huh!" said his mama. "It's just by luck that you even got good hair."

"What's that got to do with being American?"

"A mighty lot," said his mama, "in America."

They moved. They moved up to 143rd Street, in the very middle of "American" Harlem. There Hattie Gutierrez was happier —for in her youth her name had been Jones, not Gutierrez, just plain colored Jones. She had come from Virginia, not Latin America. She had met the Puerto Rican seaman in Norfolk, had lived with him there and in New York for some ten or twelve years and borne him a son, meanwhile working hard to keep him and their house in style. Then one winter he just disappeared, probably missed his boat in some far-off port town, settled down with another woman, and went on dancing rhumbas and drinking rum without worry.

Valerio, whom Gutierrez left behind, was a handsome child, not quite as light as his father, but with olive-yellow skin and Spanish-black hair, more foreign than Negro. As he grew up, he became steadily taller and better looking. Most of his friends were Spanish-speaking, so he possessed their language as well as English. He was smart and amusing out of school. But he wouldn't work. That was what worried his mother, he just wouldn't work. The long hours and low wages most colored fellows received during depression times never appealed to him. He could live without struggling, so he did.

He liked to dance and play billiards. He hung out near the Cuban theater at 110th Street, around the pool halls and gambling places, in the taxi dance emporiums. He was all for getting the good things out of life. His mother's moving up to black 143rd Street didn't improve conditions any. Indeed, it just started the ball rolling faster, for here Valerio became what is known in Harlem as a big-timer, a young sport, a hep cat. In other words, a man-about-town.

His sleek-haired yellow star rose in a chocolate sky. He was seen at all the formal invitational affairs given by the exclusive clubs of Harlem's younger set, although he belonged to no clubs. He was seen at midnight shows stretching into the dawn. He was even asked to Florita Sutton's famous Thursday midnight-at-homes where visiting dukes, English authors, colored tap dancers, and dinner-coated downtowners vied for elbow room in her small Sugar Hill apartment. Hattie, Valerio's mama, still kept her job ironing in the Chinese laundry—but nobody bothered about his mama.

Valerio was a nice enough boy, though, about sharing his income with her, about pawning a ring or something someone would give him to help her out on the rent or the insurance policies. And maybe, once or twice a week, mama might see her son coming in as she went out in the morning or leaving as she came in at night, for Valerio often slept all day. And she would mutter, "The Lord knows, cause I don't, what will become of you, boy! You're just like your father!"

Then, strangely enough, one day Valerio got a job. A good job, too—at least, it paid him well. A friend of his ran an after-hours night club on upper St. Nicholas Avenue. Gangsters owned the place, but they let a Negro run it. They had a red-hot jazz band, a high-yellow revue, and bootleg liquor. When the Cuban music began to hit Harlem, they hired Valerio to introduce the rhumba. That was something he was really cut out to do, the rhumba. That wasn't work. Not at all, *hombre!* But it was a job, and his mama was glad.

Attired in a yellow silk shirt, white satin trousers, and a bright red sash, Valerio danced nightly to the throbbing drums and seed-filled rattles of the tropics—accompanied by the orchestra's usual instruments of joy. Valerio danced with a little brown Cuban girl in a red dress, Concha, whose hair was a mat of darkness and whose hips were nobody's business.

Their dance became the talk of the town—at least, of that part of the town composed of night-lifers—for Valerio danced the rhumba as his father had taught him to dance it in Norfolk when he was ten years old, innocently—unexpurgated, happy, funny, but beautiful, too—like a gay, sweet longing for something that might be had, some time, maybe, some place or other.

Anyhow, business boomed. Ringside tables filled with people who came expressly to see Valerio dance.

"He's marvelous," gasped ladies who ate at the Ritz any time they wanted to.

"That boy can dance," said portly gentlemen with offices full of lawyers to keep track of their income tax. "He can dance!" And they wished they could, too.

"Hot stuff," said young rum-runners, smoking reefers and drinking gin—for these were prohibition days.

"A natural-born eastman," cried a tan-skin lady with a diamond wrist-watch. "He can have anything I got."

That was the trouble! Too many people felt that Valerio could have anything they had, so he lived on the fat of the land without making half an effort. He began to be invited to fashionable cocktail parties downtown. He often went out to dinner in the East 50's with white folks. But his mama still kept her job in the Chinese laundry.

Perhaps it was a good thing she did in view of what finally happened, for to Valerio the world was nothing but a swagger world tingling with lights, music, drinks, money, and people who had everything—or thought they had. Each night, at the club, the orchestra beat out its astounding songs, shook its rattles, fingered its drums. Valerio put on his satin trousers with the fiery red sash to dance with the little Cuban girl who always had a look of pleased surprise on her face, as though amazed to find dancing so good.

Somehow she and Valerio made their rhumba, for all their hip-shaking, clean as a summer sun.

Offers began to come in from other night clubs, and from small producers as well. "Wait for something big, kid," said the man who ran the cabaret. "Wait till the Winter Garden calls you."

Valerio waited. Meanwhile, a dark young rounder named Sonny, who wrote number bets for a living, had an idea for making money off of Valerio. They would open an apartment together where people could come after the night clubs closed—come and drink and dance—and love a little if they wanted to. The money would be made from the sale of drinks—charging very high prices to keep the riffraff out. With Valerio as host, a lot of good spenders would surely call. They could get rich.

"O.K. by me," said Valerio.

"I'll run the place," said Sonny, "and all you gotta do is just be there and dance a little, maybe—you know—and make people feel at home."

"O.K.," said Valerio.

"And we'll split the profit two ways—me and you."

"O.K."

So they got a big Seventh Avenue apartment, furnished it with deep, soft sofas and lots of little tables and a huge icebox and opened up. They paid off the police every week. They had good whisky. They sent out cards to a hundred downtown people who didn't care about money. They informed the best patrons of the cabaret where Valerio danced—the white folks who thrilled at becoming real Harlem initiates going home with Valerio.

From the opening night on, Valerio's flat filled with white people from midnight till the sun came up. Mostly a sporty crowd, young blades accompanied by ladies of the chorus, race-track gentlemen, white cabaret entertainers out for amusement after their own places closed, musical-comedy stars in search of new dance steps —and perhaps three or four brown-skin ladies-of-the-evening and a couple of chocolate gigolos, to add color.

There was a piano player. Valerio danced. There was impromptu entertaining by the guests. Often famous radio stars would get up and croon. Expensive night-club names might rise to do a number —or several numbers if they were tight enough. And sometimes it would be hard to stop them when they really got going.

Occasionally guests would get very drunk and stay all night, sleeping well into the day. Sometimes one might sleep with Valerio.

Shortly all Harlem began to talk about the big red roadster

Valerio drove up and down Seventh Avenue. It was all nickel-plated—and a little blonde revue star known on two continents had given it to him, so folks said. Valerio was on his way to becoming a gigolo de luxe.

"That boy sure don't draw no color lines," Harlem commented. "No, sir!

"And why should he?" Harlem then asked itself rhetorically. "Colored folks ain't got no money—and money's what he's after, ain't it?"

But Harlem was wrong. Valerio seldom gave a thought to money—he was having too good a time. That's why it was well his mama kept her job in the Chinese laundry, for one day Sonny received a warning, "Close up that flat of yours, and close it damn quick!"

Gangsters!

"What the hell?" Sonny answered the racketeers. "We're payin' off, ain't we—you and the police, both? So what's wrong?"

"Close up, or we'll break you up," the warning came back. "We don't like the way you're running things, black boy. And tell Valerio to send that white chick's car back to her—and quick!"

"Aw, nuts!" said Sonny. "We're paying the police! You guys lay off."

But Sonny wasn't wise. He knew very well how little the police count when gangsters give orders, yet he kept right on. The profits had gone to his head. He didn't even tell Valerio they had been warned, for Sonny, who was trying to make enough money to start a number bank of his own, was afraid the boy might quit. Sonny should have known better.

One Sunday night about 3:30 A.M., the piano was going like mad. Fourteen couples packed the front room, dancing close and warm. There were at least a dozen folks whose names you'd know if you saw them in any paper, famous from Hollywood to Westport.

They were feeling good.

Sonny was busy at the door, and a brown bar-boy was collecting highball glasses, as Valerio came in from the club where he still worked. He went in the bedroom to change his dancing shoes for it was snowing and his feet were cold.

O, rock me, pretty mama, till the cows come home . . .

sang a sleek-haired Harlemite at the piano.

Rock me, rock me, baby, from night to morn . . .

when, just then, a crash like the wreck of the Hesperus resounded through the hall and shook the whole house as five Italian gentlemen in evening clothes who looked exactly like gangsters walked in. They had broken down the door.

Without a word they began to smash up the place with long axes each of them carried. Women began to scream, men to shout, and the piano vibrated, not from jazz-playing fingers, but from axes breaking its hidden heart.

"Lemme out," the piano player yelled. "Lemme out!" But there was panic at the door.

"I can't leave without my wrap," a woman cried. "Where is my wrap? Sonny, my ermine coat!"

"Don't move," one of the gangsters said to Sonny.

A big white fist flattened his brown nose.

"I ought to kill you," said a second gangster. "You was warned. Take this!"

Sonny spit out two teeth.

Crash went the axes on furniture and bar. Splintered glass flew, wood cracked. Guests fled, hatless and coatless. About that time the police arrived.

Strangely enough, the police, instead of helping protect the place from the gangsters, began themselves to break, not only the furniture; but also the *heads* of every Negro in sight. They started with Sonny. They laid the barman and the waiter low. They grabbed Valerio as he emerged from the bedroom. They beat his face to a pulp. They whacked the piano player twice across the buttocks. They had a grand time with their night sticks. Then they arrested all the colored felows (and no whites) as the gangsters took their axes and left. That was the end of Valerio's apartment.

In jail Valerio learned that the woman who gave him the red roadster was being kept by a gangster who controlled prohibition's whole champagne racket and owned dozens of rum-running boats.

"No wonder!" said Sonny, through his bandages. "He got them guys to break up our place! He probably told the police to beat hell out of us, too!"

"Wonder how he knew she gave me that car?" asked Valerio innocently.

"White folks know everything," said Sonny.

"Aw, stop talking like a spook," said Valerio.

When he got out of jail, Valerio's face had a long night-stick scar across it that would never disappear. He still felt weak and sick and hungry. The gangsters had forbidden any of the night clubs to employ him again, so he went back home to mama.

"Umm-huh!" she told him. "Good thing I kept my job in that Chinee laundry. It's a good thing . . . Sit down and eat, son . . . What you gonna do now?"

"Start practicing dancing again. I got an offer to go to Brazil— a big club in Rio."

"Who's gonna pay your fare way down yonder to Brazil?"

"Concha," Valerio answered—the name of his Cuban rhumba partner whose hair was a mat of darkness. "Concha."

"A woman!" cried his mother. "I might a-knowed it! We're weak that way. My God, I don't know, boy! I don't know!"

"You don't know what?" asked Valerio, grinning.

"How women can help it," said his mama. "The Lord knows you're *just* like your father—and I took care o' him for ten years. I reckon it's that Spanish blood."

"*Que va!*" said Valerio.

ON THE WAY HOME

Carl was not what you would call a drinking man. Not that he had any moral scruples about drinking, for he prided himself on being broad-minded. But he had always been told that his father (whom he couldn't remember) was a drunkard. So in the back of his head, he didn't really feel it right to get drunk. Except for perhaps a glass of wine on holidays, or a bottle of beer if he was out with a party and didn't want to be conspicuous, he was a teetotaler.

Carl had promised his mother not to drink *at all*. He was an only child, fond of his mother. But she had raised him with almost too much kindness. To adjust himself to people who were less kind had been hard. But since there were no good jobs in Sommerville, he came away to Chicago to work. Every month, for a Sunday, he went back home, taking the four o'clock bus Saturday afternoon, which put him off in front of his boyhood door in time for supper —with country butter, fresh milk, and home-made bread.

After supper he would go uptown with his mother in the cool of evening, if it was summer, to do her Saturday-night shopping. Or if it was winter, they might go over to a neighbor's house and pop corn or drink cider. Or friends might come to their home and sit around the parlor talking and playing old records on an old victrola—Sousa's marches, Nora Bayes, Bert Williams, Caruso—

records that most other people had long ago thrown away or forgotten. It was fun, old-fashioned, and very different from the rum parties most of his office friends indulged in in Chicago.

Carl had definitely promised his mother and himself not to drink. But this particular afternoon, he stood in front of a long counter in a liquor store on Clark Street and heard himself say, strangely enough, "A bottle of wine."

"What kind of wine?" the clerk asked brusquely.

"That kind," Carl answered, pointing to a row of tall yellow bottles on the middle shelf. It just happened that his finger stopped at the yellow bottles. He did not know the names or brands of wines.

"That's sweet wine," the clerk said.

"That's all right," Carl affirmed, for he wanted to get the wine quickly and go.

The clerk wrapped the bottle, made change, and turned to another customer. Carl took the bottle and went out. He walked slowly, yet he could hardly wait to get to his room. He had never been so anxious to drink before. He might have stopped at a bar, since he passed many, but he was not used to drinking at bars. So he went to his room.

It was quiet in the big, dark, old rooming house. There was no one in the hall as he went up the wide, creaking staircase. All the roomers were at work. It was Tuesday. He would have been at work, too, had he not received at the office about noon a wire that his mother was suddenly very ill, and he had better come home. He knew there was no bus until four o'clock. It was one now. He would get ready to go soon. But he needed a drink. Did not men sometimes drink to steady their nerves? In novels they took a swig of brandy—but brandy made Carl sick. Wine would be better— milder.

In his room he tore open the package and uncorked the bottle even before he hung his hat in the closet. He took his toothbrush out of a glass on his dresser and poured the glass a third full of the amber-yellow wine. He tried to keep himself from wondering if his mother was going to die.

"Please, no!" he prayed. He drank the wine.

He sat down on the bed to get his breath back. That climb up the steps had never taken his breath before, but now his heart was beating fast, and sweat had come out on his brow, so he took off his coat, tie, shirt, and got ready to wash his face.

He had better pack his bag first. Then, he suddenly thought, he had no present for his mother—but he caught himself in the middle of the thought. This was not Saturday, not one of his monthly Saturdays when he went home. This was Tuesday and there was this telegram from the Rossiters in his pocket that had suddenly broken the whole rhythm of his life:

YOUR MOTHER GRAVELY ILL STOP COME HOME AT ONCE.

John and Nellie Rossiter had been neighbors since childhood. They would not frighten him needlessly. His mother must be very ill indeed, so he need not think of taking her a present. He went to the closet door to pull out the suitcase, but his hands did not move. The wine, amber-yellow in its tall bottle, stood on the dresser beside him. Warm, sweet, forbidden.

There was no one in the room. Nobody in the whole house perhaps except the landlady. Nobody really in all Chicago to talk to in his trouble. With a mother to take care of on a small salary, room rent, a class at business college, books to buy, there's not much time left to make friends or take girls out. In a big city it's hard for a strange young man to know people.

Carl poured the glass full of wine again—drank it. Then he opened the top drawer, took out his toilet articles and put them on the bed. From the second drawer he took a couple of shirts. Maybe three would be better, or four. This was not a week end. Perhaps he had better take some extra clothing—in case his mother was ill long, and he had to stay a week or more. Perhaps he'd better take his dark suit in case she . . .

It hit him in the stomach like a fist. A pang of fear spread over his whole body. He sat down trembling on the bed.

"Buck up, old man!" The sound of his own voice comforted him. He smiled weakly at his face in the mirror.

"Be a man!"

He filled the glass full this time and drank it without stopping. He had never drunk so much wine before and this was warm, sweet, and palatable. He stood, threw his shoulders back, and felt suddenly tall as though his head were touching the ceiling. Then, for no reason at all, he looked at himself in the mirror and began to sing. He made up a song out of nowhere that repeated itself over and over:

> *In the spring the roses*
> *In the spring begin to sing*
> *Roses in the spring*
> *Begin to sing . . .*

He took off his clothes, put on his bathrobe, carefully drained the bottle, then went down the hall to the bathroom, still singing. He ran a tub full of water, climbed in, and sat down. The water in the tub was warm like the wine. He felt good remembering a dark grassy slope in a corner of his mother's yard where he played with a little girl when he was very young at home. His mother came out, separated them, and sent the little girl away because she wasn't of a decent family. But now his mother would never dismiss another little girl be—

Carl sat up quickly in the tub, splashed water over his back and over his head. Drunk? What's the matter? What's the matter with you? Thinking of your mother that way and maybe she's dy— Say! Listen, don't you know you have to catch a four o'clock bus? And here he was getting drunk before he even started on the way home. He trembled. His heart beat fast, so fast that he lay down in the tub to catch his breath, all but his head covered with the warm water.

To lie quiet that way was fine. Still and quiet. Tuesday. Everybody working at the office. And here he was, Carl Anderson, lying quiet in a deep tub of warm water. Maybe someday in a few years with a little money saved up, and no expenses at home, and a car to take girls out in the spring,

> *When the roses sing*
> *In the spring . . .*

He had a good voice and the song that he had made up himself about roses sounded good with wine on his breath as he sang, so he stood up in the tub, grabbed a towel, and began to sing quite lustily. Suddenly there was a knock at the door.

"What's going on in there?"

It was the landlady's voice in the hall outside. She must have heard him singing downstairs.

"Nothing, Mrs. Dyer! Nothing! I just feel like singing."

"Mr. Anderson? Is that you? What're you doing in the house this time of day?"

"I'm on the way home to see my mother. She . . ."

"You sound happier than a lark about it. I couldn't imagine . . ."

He heard the landlady's feet shuffling off down the stairs, back to her ironing.

"She's . . ." His head began to go round and round. "My mother's . . ." His eyes suddenly burned. To step out of the tub, he held tightly to the sides. Drunk, that's what he was! Drunk!

He lurched down the hall, fell across the bed in his room, and buried his head in the pillows. He stretched his arms above his head to the rods of the bedstand. He felt ashamed. With his head in the pillows all was dark. His mother dying? No! No! But he was drunk.

In the dark he seemed to feel his mother's hand on his head when he was a little boy, and her voice saying, "Be sweet, Carl. Be a good boy. Keep clean. Mother loves you. She'll look our for you. Be sweet—and remember what you're taught at home."

Then the roses in the song he had made up and the wine he had drunk began to go around and around in his head and he felt as if he had betrayed his mother and home singing about roses and spring and dreaming of cars and pretty girls with that yellow telegram in his coat pocket on the back of the chair beside the bed that suddenly seemed to go around and around.

But when he closed his eyes, it stopped. He held his breath. He buried his head deeper in the pillows. He lay very still. It was dark and warm. And quiet, and darker than ever. A long time passed, a very long time, dark, and quiet, and peaceful, and still.

"Mr. Anderson! Hey, Mr. Anderson!"

In the darkness far off, somebody called, then nearer—but still very far away—then knocking on a distant door.

"Mr. Anderson!"

The voice was quite near now, sharper. The door opened, light streamed in. A hand shook his shoulder. He opened his eyes. Mrs. Dyer stood there, looking down at him in indignant amazement.

"Mr. Anderson, are you drunk?"

"No, Mrs. Dyer," he said in a daze, blinking at the landlady standing above him. The electric light bulb she had switched on hurt his eyes.

"Mr. Anderson, they's a long-distance call for you on the phone down in the hall. Get up. Tie up that bathrobe. Hurry on down there and get it, will you? I've been yelling for you for five minutes."

"What time is it?" Carl sat bolt upright. The landlady stopped in the door.

"It's after dinner time," she said. "Must be six-thirty, seven o'clock."

"Seven o'clock?" Carl gasped. "I've missed my bus!"

"What bus?"

"The four o'clock bus."

"I guess you have," said the landlady. "Alcohol and timetables don't mix, young man. That must be your mother on the phone now." Disgusted, she went downstairs, leaving his door open.

The phone! Carl felt sick and unsteady on his legs. He pulled his bathrobe together and stumbled down the stairs. The phone! A kind of weakness rushed through his veins. The telephone! He had promised his mother not to drink. She said his father . . . He couldn't remember his father. He died long ago. Now his mother was . . . Anyhow, he should have been home by seven o'clock, at her bedside, holding her hand. He could have been home an hour ago. Now, maybe she . . .

He picked up the receiver. His voice was hoarse, frightened. "Hello. Yes, this is Carl . . . Yes, Mrs. Rossiter . . ."

"Carl, honey, we kept looking for you on that six o'clock bus. My husband went out on the road a piece to meet you in his car. We thought it might be quicker. Carl, honey . . ."

"Yes, Mrs. Rossiter . . ."

"Your mother . . ."

"Yes, Mrs. Rossiter . . ."

"Your mother just passed away. I thought maybe you ought to know in case you hadn't already started. I thought maybe . . ."

For a moment he couldn't hear what she said. Then he knew that she was asking him a question—that she was repeating it.

"I could have Jerry drive to Chicago and get you tonight. Would you like to have me do that, since there's no bus now until morning?"

"I wish you would, Mrs. Rossiter. But then, no—listen! Never mind! There's two or three things I ought to do before I come home. I ought to go to the bank. I must. But I'll catch that first bus home in the morning. First thing in the morning, Mrs. Rossiter, I'll be home."

"We're your neighbors and your friends. You know *this* is your home, too, so come right here."

"Yes, Mrs. Rossiter, I know. I will. I'll be home."

He ran back upstairs and jumped into his clothes, feeling that he had to get out. Had to get out! His body burned. His throat was dry. He picked up the wine bottle and looked at the label. Good wine! Warm and easy to the throat! Hurry before perhaps the landlady came. Hurry! She wouldn't understand this haste.

Did she die alone?

Quickly he put on his coat and plunged down the steps. Outside it was dark. The street lights seemed dimmer than usual.

Did she die alone?

At the corner, there was a bar, palely lighted. He had never stopped there before, but this time he went in. He could drink all he wanted to now.

Alone, at home, alone! Did she die alone?

The bar was big and dismal, like a barn. A juke box played a raucous hit song. A woman stood near the machine singing to herself.

Carl went up to the bar.

"What'll it be?" The bartender passed his towel over the counter in front of him.

"A drink," Carl said.

"Whisky?"

"Yes."

"Can you make it two?" asked the woman in a warm low voice.

"Sure," Carl said. "Make it two."

"What's the matter? You're shivering!" she exclaimed.

"Cold," Carl said.

"You've been drinking?" the woman said. "But it don't smell like whisky."

"Wasn't," Carl said. "Was wine."

"Oh! I guess you can mix up your drinks, heh? O.K. Try it. But if that wine along with this whisky knocks you out," she purred, "I'll have to take you home to my house, little boy."

"Home?" Carl asked.

"Yes," the woman said, "home with me. You and me—home."

She put her arm around his shoulders.

"Home?" Carl said.

"Home, sure, baby! Home to my house."

"Home?" Carl was about to repeat when suddenly a volley of uncontrolled sobs shook his body, choking the word, "Home." He leaned forward with his head in his arms and wept like a kid.

"Home. . . . . home . . . home . . ."

The bartender and the woman looked at him in amazement. The juke box stopped.

The woman said gently, "You're drunk, fellow. Come on, buck up! I'll take you home. It don't have to be to my house either— if you don't want to go. Where do you live? I'll see that you get home."

TAIN'T SO

Miss Lucy Cannon was a right nice old white woman, so Uncle Joe always stated, except that she really did *not* like colored folks, not even after she come out West to California. She could never get over certain little Southern ways she had, and long as she knowed my Uncle Joe, who hauled her ashes for her, she never would call him *Mister*—nor any other colored man *Mister* neither for that matter, not even the minister of the Baptist Church who was a graduate of San Jose State College. Miss Lucy Cannon just wouldn't call colored folks *Mister* nor *Missus*, no matter who they was, neither in Alabama nor in California.

She was always ailing around, too, sick with first one thing and then another. Delicate, and ever so often she would have a fainting spell, like all good Southern white ladies. Looks like the older she got, the more she would be sick and couldn't hardly get around— that is, until she went to a healer and got cured.

And that is one of the funniest stories Uncle Joe ever told me, how old Miss Cannon got cured of her heart and hip in just one cure at the healer's.

Seems like for three years or more she could scarcely walk—even with a cane—had a terrible bad pain in her right leg from her knee up. And on her left side, her heart was always just about to give out. She was in bad shape, that old Southern lady, to be as spry as she was, always giving teas and dinners and working her colored help to death.

Well, Uncle Joe says, one New Year's Day in Pasadena a friend of hers, a Northern lady who was kinda old and retired also and had come out to California to spend her last days, too, and get rid of some parts of her big bank full of money—this old lady told Miss Cannon, "Darling, you just seem to suffer so all the time, and you say you've tried all the doctors, and all kinds of baths and medicines. Why don't you try my way of overcoming? Why don't you try faith?"

"Faith, honey?" says old Miss Lucy Cannon, sipping her jasmine tea.

"Yes, my dear," says the Northern white lady. "Faith! I have one of the best faith-healers in the world."

"Who is he?" asked Miss Lucy Cannon.

"She's a woman, dear," said old Miss Northern white lady. "And she heals by power. She lives in Hollywood."

"Give me her address," said Miss Lucy, "and I'll go to see her. How much do her treatments cost?"

Miss Lucy warn't so rich as some folks thought she was.

"Only Ten Dollars, dearest," said the other lady. "Ten Dollars a treatment. Go, and you'll come away cured."

"I have never believed in such things," said Miss Lucy, "nor disbelieved, either. But I will go and see." And before she could learn any more about the healer, some other friends came in and interrupted the conversation.

A few days later, however, Miss Lucy took herself all the way from Pasadena to Hollywood, put up for the week end with a friend of hers, and thought she would go to see the healer, which she did, come Monday morning early.

Using her customary cane and hobbling on her left leg, feeling a bit bad around the heart, and suffering terribly in her mind, she managed to walk slowly but with dignity a half-dozen blocks through the sunshine to the rather humble street in which was located the office and home of the healer.

In spite of the bright morning air and the good breakfast she had had, Miss Lucy (according to herself) felt pretty bad, racked with pains and crippled to the use of a cane.

When she got to the house she was seeking, a large frame dwelling, newly painted, she saw a sign thereon:

MISS PAULINE JONES

"So that's her name," thought Miss Lucy. "Pauline Jones, Miss Jones."

Ring And Enter said a little card above the bell. So Miss Lucy entered. But the first thing that set her back a bit was that nobody received her, so she just sat down to await Miss Jones, the healer who had, she heard, an enormous following in Hollywood. In fact, that's why she had come early, so she wouldn't have to wait long. Now, it was only nine o'clock. The office was open—but empty. So Miss Lucy simply waited. Ten minutes passed. Fifteen. Twenty. Finally she became all nervous and fluttery. Heart and limb! Pain, pain, pain! Not even a magazine to read.

"Oh, me!" she said impatiently, "What is this? Why, I never!"

There was a sign on the wall that read:

BELIEVE

"I will wait just ten minutes more," said Miss Lucy, glancing at her watch of platinum and pearls.

But before the ten minutes were up, another woman entered

the front door and sat down. To Miss Lucy's horror, she was a colored woman! In fact, a big black colored woman!

Said Miss Lucy to herself, "I'll never in the world get used to the North. Now here's a great—my friend says great faith-healer, treating darkies! Why, down in Alabama, a Negro patient wouldn't dare come in here and sit down with white people like this!"

But, womanlike, (and having still five minutes to wait) Miss Lucy couldn't keep her mouth shut that long. She just had to talk, albeit to a Negro, so she began on her favorite subject—herself.

"I certainly feel bad this morning," she said to the colored woman, condescending to open the conversation.

"Tain't so," answered the Negro woman placidly—which sort of took Miss Lucy back a bit. She lifted her chin.

"Indeed, it is so," said she indignantly. "My heart is just about to give out. My breath is short."

"Tain't so a-tall," said the Negro calmly.

"Why!" gasped Miss Lucy, "such impudence! I tell you *it is so!* I could hardly get down here this morning."

"Tain't so," said the Negro calmly.

"Besides my heart," went on Miss Lucy, "my right hip pains me so I can hardly sit here."

"I say, tain't so."

"I tell you it *is* so," screamed Miss Lucy. "Where is the healer? I won't sit here and suffer this—this impudence. I can't! It'll kill me! It's outrageous."

"Tain't so," said the large black woman serenely, whereupon Miss Lucy rose. Her pale face flushed a violent red.

"Where is the healer?" she cried, looking around the room.

"Right here," said the colored woman.

"What?" cried Miss Lucy. "You're the—why—you?"

"I'm Miss Jones."

"Why, I never heard the like," gasped Miss Lucy. "A *colored* woman as famous as you? Why, you must be lying!"

"Tain't so," said the woman calmly.

"Well, I shan't stay another minute," cried Miss Lucy.

"Ten Dollars, then," said the colored woman. "You've had your treatment, anyhow."

"Ten Dollars! That's entirely too much!"

"Tain't so."

Angrily Miss Lucy opened her pocketbook, threw a Ten Dollar bill on the table, took a deep breath, and bounced out. She went three blocks up Sunset Boulevard walking like the wind, conversing with herself.

" 'Tain't so,' " she muttered. " 'Tain't so!' I tell her I'm sick and she says, 'Tain't so!' "

On she went at a rapid gait, stepping like a young girl—so mad she had forgotten all about her infirmities, even her heart—when suddenly she cried, "Lord, have mercy, my cane! For the first time in three years, I'm *without* a cane!"

Then she realized that her breath was giving her no trouble at all. Neither was her leg. Her temper mellowed. The sunshine was sweet and warm. She felt good.

"Colored folks do have some funny kind of supernatural conjuring powers, I reckon," she said smiling to herself. Immediately her face went grim again. "But the impudence of 'em! Soon's they get up North—calling herself *Miss* Pauline Jones. The idea! Putting on airs and charging me Ten Dollars for a handful of *Tain't so's!*"

In her mind she clearly heard, "Tain't so!"

ONE FRIDAY MORNING

The thrilling news did not come directly to Nancy Lee, but it came in little indirections that finally added themselves up to one tremendous fact: she had won the prize! But being a calm and quiet young lady, she did not say anything, although the whole high school buzzed with rumors, guesses, reportedly authentic announcements on the part of students who had no right to be making announcements at all—since no student really knew yet who had won this year's art scholarship.

But Nancy Lee's drawing was so good, her lines so sure, her colors so bright and harmonious, that certainly no other student in the senior art class at George Washington High was thought to have very much of a chance. Yet you never could tell. Last year nobody had expected Joe Williams to win the Artist Club scholarship with that funny modernistic water color he had done of the high-level bridge. In fact, it was hard to make out there was a bridge until you had looked at the picture a long time. Still, Joe Williams got the prize, was feted by the community's leading painters, club women, and society folks at a big banquet at the Park-Rose Hotel, and was now an award student at the Art School—the city's only art school.

Nancy Lee Johnson was a colored girl, a few years out of the South. But seldom did her high-school classmates think of her as colored. She was smart, pretty and brown, and fitted in well with the life of the school. She stood high in scholarship, played a swell game of basketball, had taken part in the senior musical in a soft, velvety voice, and had never seemed to intrude or stand out except in pleasant ways, so it was seldom even mentioned—her color.

Nancy Lee sometimes forgot she was colored herself. She liked her classmates and her school. Particularly she liked her art teacher, Miss Dietrich, the tall red-haired woman who taught her law and order in doing things; and the beauty of working step by step until a job is done; a picture finished; a design created; or a block print carved out of nothing but an idea and a smooth square of linoleum, inked, proofs made, and finally put down on paper—clean, sharp, beautiful, individual, unlike any other in the world, thus making the paper have a meaning nobody else could give it except Nancy Lee. That was the wonderful thing about true creation. You made something nobody else on earth could make—but you.

Miss Dietrich was the kind of teacher who brought out the best in her students—but their own best, not anybody else's copied best. For anybody else's best, great though it might be, even Michelangelo's, wasn't enough to please Miss Dietrich dealing with the creative impulses of young men and women living in an American city in the Middle West, and being American.

Nancy Lee was proud of being American, A Negro American with blood out of Africa a long time ago, too many generations back to count. But her parents had taught her the beauties of Africa, its strength, its song, its mighty rivers, its early smelting of iron, its building of the pyramids, and its ancient and important civilizations. And Miss Dietrich had discovered for her the sharp and humorous lines of African sculpture, Benin, Congo, Makonde. Nancy Lee's father was a mail carrier, her mother a social worker in a city settlement house. Both parents had been to Negro colleges in the South. And her mother had gotten a further degree in social work from a Northern university. Her parents were, like most Americans, simple ordinary people who had worked hard and steadily for their education. Now they were trying to make it easier for Nancy Lee to achieve learning than it had been for them. They would be very happy when they heard of the award to their daughter—yet Nancy did not tell them. To surprise them would be better. Besides, there had been a promise.

Casually, one day, Miss Dietrich asked Nancy Lee what color frame she thought would be best on her picture. That had been the first inkling.

"Blue," Nancy Lee said. Although the picture had been entered in the Artist Club contest a month ago, Nancy Lee did not hesitate in her choice of a color for the possible frame since she could still

see her picture clearly in her mind's eye—for that picture waiting
for the blue frame had come out of her soul, her own life, and had
bloomed into miraculous being with Miss Dietrich's help. It was, she
knew, the best water color she had painted in her four years as a
high-school art student, and she was glad she had made something
Miss Dietrich liked well enough to permit her to enter in the con-
test before she graduated.

It was not a modernistic picture in the sense that you had to
look at it a long time to understand what it meant. It was just a
simple scene in the city park on a spring day with the trees still
leaflessly lacy against the sky, the new grass fresh and green, a flag
on a tall pole in the center, children playing, and an old Negro
woman sitting on a bench with her head turned. A lot for one pic-
ture, to be sure, but it was not there in heavy and final detail like
a calendar. Its charm was that everything was light and airy, happy
like spring, with a lot of blue sky, paper-white clouds, and air show-
ing through. You could tell that the old Negro woman was looking
at the flag, and that the flag was proud in the spring breeze, and
that the breeze helped to make the children's dresses billow as they
played.

Miss Dietrich had taught Nancy Lee how to paint spring, people,
and a breeze on what was only a plain white piece of paper from
the supply closet. But Miss Dietrich had not said make it like any
other spring-people-breeze ever seen before. She let it remain Nancy
Lee's own. That is how the old Negro woman happened to be
there looking at the flag—for in her mind the flag, the spring, and
the woman formed a kind of triangle holding a dream Nancy Lee
wanted to express. White stars on a blue field, spring, children,
ever-growing life, and an old woman. Would the judges at the Artist
Club like it?

One wet, rainy April afternoon Miss O'Shay, the girls' vice-
principal, sent for Nancy Lee to stop by her office as school closed.
Pupils without umbrellas or raincoats were clustered in doorways
hoping to make it home between showers. Outside the skies were
gray. Nancy Lee's thoughts were suddenly gray, too.

She did not think she had done anything wrong, yet that tight
little knot came in her throat just the same as she approached Miss
O'Shay's door. Perhaps she had banged her locker too often and
too hard. Perhaps the note in French she had written to Sallie
halfway across the study hall just for fun had never gotten to Sallie
but into Miss O'Shay's hands instead. Or maybe she was failing in
some subject and wouldn't be allowed to graduate. Chemistry! A
pang went through the pit of her stomach.

She knocked on Miss O'Shay's door. That familiarly solid and competent voice said, "Come in."

Miss O'Shay had a way of making you feel welcome, even if you came to be expelled.

"Sit down, Nancy Lee Johnson," said Miss O'Shay. "I have something to tell you." Nancy Lee sat down. "But I must ask you to promise not to tell anyone yet."

"I won't, Miss O'Shay," Nancy Lee said, wondering what on earth the principal had to say to her.

"You are about to graduate," Miss O'Shay said. "And we shall miss you. You have been an excellent student, Nancy, and you will not be without honors on the senior list, as I am sure you know."

At that point there was a light knock on the door. Miss O'Shay called out, "Come in," and Miss Dietrich entered. "May I be a part of this, too?" she asked, tall and smiling.

"Of course," Miss O'Shay said. "I was just telling Nancy Lee what we thought of her. But I hadn't gotten around to giving her the news. Perhaps, Miss Dietrich, you'd like to tell her yourself."

Miss Dietrich was always direct. "Nancy Lee," she said, "your picture has won the Artist Club scholarship."

The slender brown girl's eyes widened, her heart jumped, then her throat tightened again. She tried to smile, but instead tears came to her eyes.

"Dear Nancy Lee," Miss O'Shay said, "we are so happy for you." The elderly white woman took her hand and shook it warmly while Miss Dietrich beamed with pride.

Nancy Lee must have danced all the way home. She never remembered quite how she got there through the rain. She hoped she had been dignified. But certainly she hadn't stopped to tell anybody her secret on the way. Raindrops, smiles, and tears mingled on her brown cheeks. She hoped her mother hadn't yet gotten home and that the house was empty. She wanted to have time to calm down and look natural before she had to see anyone. She didn't want to be bursting with excitement—having a secret to contain.

Miss O'Shay's calling her to the office had been in the nature of a preparation and a warning. The kind, elderly vice-principal said she did not believe in catching young ladies unawares, even with honors, so she wished her to know about the coming award. In making acceptance speeches she wanted her to be calm, prepared, not nervous, overcome, and frightened. So Nancy Lee was asked to think what she would say when the scholarship was conferred upon her a few days hence, both at the Friday morning high-school assembly hour when the announcement would be made, and at the evening banquet of the Artist Club. Nancy Lee promised the vice-principal to think calmly about what she would say.

Miss Dietrich had then asked for some facts about her parents, her background, and her life, since such material would probably be desired for the papers. Nancy Lee had told her how, six years before, they had come up from the Deep South, her father having been successful in achieving a transfer from the one post office to another, a thing he had long sought in order to give Nancy Lee a chance to go to school in the North. Now, they lived in a modest Negro neighborhood, went to see the best plays when they came to town, and had been saving to send Nancy Lee to art school, in case she were permitted to enter. But the scholarship would help a great deal, for they were not rich people.

"Now Mother can have a new coat next winter," Nancy Lee thought, "because my tuition will all be covered for the first year. And once in art school, there are other scholarships I can win."

Dreams began to dance through her head, plans and ambitions, beauties she would create for herself, her parents, and the Negro people—for Nancy Lee possessed a deep and reverent race pride. She could see the old woman in her picture (really her grand-mother in the South) lifting her head to the bright stars on the flag in the distance. A Negro in America! Often hurt, discriminated against, sometimes lynched—but always there were the stars on the blue body of the flag. Was there any other flag in the world that had so many stars? Nancy Lee thought deeply but she could remember none in all the encyclopedias or geographies she had ever looked into.

"Hitch your wagon to a star," Nancy Lee thought, dancing home in the rain. "Who were our flag-makers?"

Friday morning came, the morning when the world would know—her high-school world, the newspaper world, her mother and dad. Dad could not be there at the assembly to hear the announcement, nor see her prize picture displayed on the stage, nor listen to Nancy Lee's little speech of acceptance, but Mother would be able to come, although Mother was much puzzled as to why Nancy Lee was so insistent she be at school on that particular Friday morning.

When something is happening, something new and fine, some-thing that will change your very life, it is hard to go to sleep at night for thinking about it, and hard to keep your heart from pounding, or a strange little knot of joy from gathering in your throat. Nancy Lee had taken her bath, brushed her hair until it glowed, and had gone to bed thinking about the next day, the big day when, before three thousand students, she would be the one student honored, her painting the one painting to be acclaimed as the best of the year from all the art classes of the city. Her short speech of gratitude was ready. She went over it in her mind, not word for word (because she didn't want it to sound as if she had learned it by heart) but she let the thoughts flow simply and sincerely through her consciousness many times.

When the president of the Artist Club presented her with the medal and scroll of the scholarship award, she would say:

"Judges and members of the Artist Club. I want to thank you for this award that means so much to me personally and through me to my people, the colored people of this city who, sometimes, are discouraged and bewildered, thinking that color and poverty are against them. I accept this award with gratitude and pride, not for myself alone, but for my race that believes in American opportunity and American fairness—and the bright stars in our flag. I thank Miss Dietrich and the teachers who made it possible for me to have the knowledge and training that lie behind this honor you have conferred upon my painting. When I came here from the South a few years ago, I was not sure how you would receive me. You received me well. You have given me a chance and helped me along the road I wanted to follow. I suppose the judges know that every week here at assembly the students of this school pledge allegiance to the flag. I shall try to be worthy of that pledge, and of the help and friendship and understanding of my fellow citizens of whatever race or creed, and of our American dream of 'Liberty and justice for all!' "

That would be her response before the students in the morning. How proud and happy the Negro pupils would be, perhaps almost as proud as they were of the one colored star on the football team. Her mother would probably cry with happiness. Thus Nancy Lee went to sleep dreaming of a wonderful tomorrow.

The bright sunlight of an April morning woke her. There was breakfast with her parents—their half-amused and puzzled faces across the table, wondering what could be this secret that made her eyes so bright. The swift walk to school; the clock in the tower almost nine; hundreds of pupils streaming into the long, rambling old building that was the city's largest high school; the sudden quiet of the homeroom after the bell rang; then the teacher opening her record book to call the roll. But just before she began, she looked across the room until her eyes located Nancy Lee.

"Nancy," she said, "Miss O'Shay would like to see you in her office, please."

Nancy Lee rose and went out while the names were being called

and the word *present* added its period to each name. Perhaps, Nancy
Lee thought, the reporters from the papers had already come.
Maybe they wanted to take her picture before assembly, which
wasn't until ten o'clock. (Last year they had had the photograph of
the winner of the award in the morning papers as soon as the
announcement had been made.)

Nancy Lee knocked at Miss O'Shay's door.

"Come in."

The vice-principal stood at her desk. There was no one else in
the room. It was very quiet.

"Sit down, Nancy Lee," she said. Miss O'Shay did not smile. There
was a long pause. The seconds went by slowly. "I do not know how
to tell you what I have to say," the elderly woman began, her eyes
on the papers on her desk. "I am indignant and ashamed for myself
and for this city." Then she lifted her eyes and looked at Nancy
Lee in the neat blue dress sitting there before her. "You are not
to receive the scholarship this morning."

Outside in the hall the electric bells announcing the first period
rang, loud and interminably long. Miss O'Shay remained silent. To
the brown girl there in the chair, the room grew suddenly smaller,
smaller, smaller, and there was no air. She could not speak.

Miss O'Shay said, "When the committee learned that you were
colored, they changed their plans."

Still Nancy Lee said nothing, for there was no air to give breath
to her lungs.

"Here is the letter from the committee, Nancy Lee." Miss O'Shay
picked it up and read the final paragraph to her.

" 'It seems to us wiser to arbitrarily rotate the award among the
various high schools of the city from now on. And especially in this
case since the student chosen happens to be colored, a circumstance
which unfortunately, had we known, might have prevented this
embarrassment. But there have never been any Negro students in
the local art school, and the presence of one there might create
difficulties for all concerned. We have high regard for the quality of
Nancy Lee Johnson's talent, but we do not feel it would be fair
to honor it with the Artist Club award.' " Miss O'Shay paused.
She put the letter down.

"Nancy Lee, I am very sorry to have to give you this message."

"But my speech," Nancy Lee said, "was about. . . ." The words
stuck in her throat. ". . . about America. . . ."

Miss O'Shay had risen, she turned her back and stood looking out
the window at the spring tulips in the school yard.

"I thought, since the award would be made at assembly right after our oath of allegiance," the words tumbled almost hysterically from Nancy Lee's throat now, "I would put part of the flag salute in my speech. You know, Miss O'Shay, that part about 'liberty and justice for all.' "

"I know," said Miss O'Shay slowly facing the room again. "But America is only what we who believe in it, make it. I am Irish. You may not know, Nancy Lee, but years ago we were called the dirty Irish, and mobs rioted against us in the big cities, and we were invited to go back where we came from. But we didn't go. And we didn't give up, because we believed in the American dream, and in our power to make that dream come true. Difficulties, yes. Mountains to climb, yes. Discouragements to face, yes. Democracy to make, yes. That is it, Nancy Lee! We still have in this world of ours democracy to *make*. You and I, Nancy Lee. But the premise and the base are here, the lines of the Declaration of Independence and the words of Lincoln are here, and the stars in our flag. Those who deny you this scholarship do not know the meaning of those stars, but it's up to us to make them know. As a teacher in the public schools of this city, I myself will go before the school board and ask them to remove from our system the offer of any prizes or awards denied to any student because of race or color."

Suddenly Miss O'Shay stopped speaking. Her clear, clear blue eyes looked into those of the girl before her. The woman's eyes were full of strength and courage. "Lift up your head, Nancy Lee, and smile at me."

Miss O'Shay stood against the open window with the green lawn and the tulips beyond, the sunlight tangled in her gray hair, her voice an electric flow of strength to the hurt spirit of Nancy Lee. The Abolitionists who believed in freedom when there was slavery must have been like that. The first white teachers who went into the Deep South to teach the freed slaves must have been like that. All those who stand against ignorance, narrowness, hate, and mud on stars must be like that.

Nancy Lee lifted her head and smiled. The bell for assembly rang. She went through the long hall filled with students toward the auditorium.

"There will be other awards," Nancy Lee thought. "There're schools in other cities. This won't keep me down. But when I'm a woman, I'll fight to see that these things don't happen to other girls as this has happened to me. And men and women like Miss O'Shay will help me."

She took her seat among the seniors. The doors of the auditorium closed. As the principal came onto the platform, the students rose and turned their eyes to the flag on the stage.

One hand went to the heart, the other outstretched toward the flag. Three thousand voices spoke. Among them was the voice of a dark girl whose cheeks were suddenly wet with tears, ". . . one nation indivisible, with liberty and justice for all."

"That is the land we must make," she thought.

TRAGEDY AT THE BATHS

"That it should happen in my Baths!" was all she could say. "That it should happen in my Baths!" And try as they would, nobody could console her. Señora Rueda was quite hysterical. Being a big strong woman, her screams alarmed the neighborhood.

She and her now-deceased husband had owned the Baths for years—the Esmeralda Baths—among the cleanest and most respectable in Mexico City, family baths where only decent people came for their weekly tub or shower or *baño de vapor*. Indeed, her establishment, with its tiled courtyard and splashing fountain, was a monument to the neighborhood, a middle-class section of flats and shops near the Loreto. Now this had happened!

Why! Señora Rueda had known the young man for years—that is, he had been a customer of the Esmeralda Baths since his youth, coming there for his weekly shower and swim in the little tiled tank. Sometimes, when he was flush, he took a private tub, and a good steaming out—which cost a *peso*. Juan Maldonado was the young man's name. He was a tall nice-looking boy.

That Sunday morning when he presented himself at the wicket and asked for a private tub for two—himself and his wife—Señora Rueda was not especially surprised. Even by reading the papers, one can't keep up with all the marriages that take place—and young men will eventually get married.

As she handed Juan his change she looked up to see beside him a vibrant black-haired girl with the soft Indian-brown complexion of a Mexican *mestiza*. Señora Rueda smiled. A nice couple, she thought as the attendant showed them to their room and their tub. Two beautiful youths, she thought, and sighed.

Some bathhouses, she knew, did not allow the sexes to mingle within their walls, but Señora Rueda did not mind when they were legally married. Being respectable neighborhood baths, nothing but decent people were her patrons, anyway. She had no reason to suspect young Maldonado.

But an hour later there was another tale to tell! Not even smelling salts then could calm poor Señora Rueda. Oh, why did it have to happen in her Baths? *Por dios,* why?

This is the story as it came to me. It may not be wholly true for, in the patios and courtyards of Loreto, romantic and colorful additions have probably been added by those who know Juan and his family. The Mexicans love sad, romantic tales with many embroidered touches of sentimental heartbreak and ironic frustration. But, although versions of what led up to that strange Sunday morning in the Esmeralda Baths may vary in the telling, what actually happened therein—everybody knows. And it was awful!

In the first place, they were not married, Juan and that woman!

He met her in a very strange way, anyhow. The mounted police were charging a demonstration against the government. The Zocalo was filled with people trampling the grass and the flowers. Juan crossed the square on the way to the shop where he worked, giving the demonstrators a wide berth—as his particular politics were not involved that day. But just as he got midway across the Zocalo, the police began to charge on horses and the crowd began to run, so Juan was forced to run, too.

Everyone was trying to reach the shelter of the *portales* opposite the Palace, or the gates of the Cathedral, or the safety of a side street. Juan was heading toward Avenida Madero, the clatter of the horses' hoofs behind him when, just in front of him, a woman stumbled and fell.

Juan stopped running and picked her up, lifted her in his arms and went on. Once out of the square, in the quiet of a side street, he put her down on her feet and offered her his handkerchief to wipe the dust and tears from her face. Then he saw that she was young and very beautiful with the soft Indian-brown complexion of a Mexican mestiza.

"Ay, Señor," she said to the tall young man in front of her, "how can I ever thank you?"

But just at that moment a man approached, hatless and wild-eyed. He, too, had been caught in the spinning crowd, had seen his wife fall, but could not get to her—and then she had disappeared! For a while, the husband was frantic, but finally he caught sight of her around the corner faced by a tall young man who was offering her his handkerchief and gazing deep into her lovely eyes.

"You don't need to thank me," the young man was saying, "just let me look at you," as the girl caught sight of her approaching husband.

"Sunday at the Maximo," she whispered. "I want to thank you alone."

"At your service," said the young man, as the panting husband arrived.

Now, the husband was also a fairly young man, but neither as tall nor as handsome as Maldonado. He was much too short and frail to be married to so charming a woman. He kept an *escritorio,* a writing room, in the Portal of Santo Domingo on the little square, where letters were written for peasants who had no education, and where people could get legal documents copied on the typewriter, or have their names penned with decorative flourishes on a hundred calling cards.

The husband, too, there in the side street that day, thanked young Maldonado for having rescued his wife from the feet of the crowd and the hoofs of the police horses. Then they all shook hands and went their way, the tall young man going south, the pretty girl and her prosaic husband north.

But the following Sunday Maldonado waited at the entrance of the Cinema Maximo, where a Bogart film was being shown, and about five o'clock, sure enough, she appeared, alone. She was even prettier than the day he had picked her up in the Zocalo, and very shy, as if ashamed of what she was doing.

They took seats way up in the balcony, where lovers sit and hold hands in the dark. And soon they were holding hands, too.

"There was something about the strength of your arms the other day," she said, "even before I looked into your eyes, that made me want to stay with you forever."

"Stop!" yelled a cop, firing across the screen.

"And there was something in the feel of your body lying in my arms that made me never want to put you down," said Juan.

"My name is Consuelo Aguilar," the girl said softly. "You have met my husband."

"Tell me about him," said Juan.

"He is crazy about me," Consuelo answered, "and terribly jealous! He wants to be a writer, but all he writes is letters for peasants."

"And if he knew you were here—?"

"But he won't know. He stays home on Sundays and writes poems! When I tell him they're no good, he says I don't love him and threatens to commit suicide. He is very emotional, my little husband."

"And where does he think you are now?"

"At my aunt's."

It was really love, and at first sight, so they say in the patios of Loreto. But they also say that Juan was a little dumb, and a little inexperienced in the ways of women.

They kept on meeting in *cines* and dance halls, and things began to be more and more dangerous for both of them, for husbands very often kill lovers in Mexico—and go free. It is the thing to do! But what this husband did was even worse! At least, Señora Rueda thought so.

But what his wife did was terrible, too. In Catholic lands where divorces are practically impossible, and where women are never supposed to leave their husbands, anyhow—this wife planned to run away with Maldonado! But, being young and foolish (or so they say in Loreto), for some strange reason or other, on the Sunday of their elopement, they planned to take a bath first. And that is how the couple happened to be in Señora Rueda's quiet Esmeralda Baths.

There the husband came and caught them! Or, rather, he deliberately followed them there. The miracle was that he did not kill them both! Instead, he bought a season's ticket for a whole year of baths (probably not realizing what he was doing) then went into the corridor outside the room where Juan and Consuelo were bathing—and shot *himself!*

Then it was that the uproar began, and such an uproar! People commenced to emerge from their tubs, clad and unclad, to run and scream. Doors began to open, and steam escaped into the courtyard. In the excitement, someone turned off the water main and the fountain stopped running. Naturally, Consuelo and Maldonado came out to see what was going on—and stumbled over the bleeding body of Señor Aguilar at their feet.

"Oh, my God!" Consuelo cried. "He said he would kill himself if I ran away with you."

"How did he ever know you were coming away with *me?*" asked the young man in astonishment.

"I told him," said Consuelo. Her eyes were hard. "I wanted to see if he really would commit suicide. He threatened to so often. But now, darling," she turned softly toward Juan, "with him gone, we can get married."

"But suppose he had killed *us!*" said Maldonado, trembling in the doorway with only a towel about his body.

"That little coward," sneered Consuelo, "wasn't man enough!"

"But he did kill himself," said Maldonado slowly, turning back into the room away from the body on the floor and the crowd that had gathered.

"Kiss me," purred Consuelo, lifting her pretty face toward Juan's, as she closed their door.

"Get away from me!" cried Juan, suddenly sickened with horror. Flinging open the door, he gave her a terrific push into the hall.

Consuelo fell prone over the body of her husband and, beginning to realize that she was, after all, a widow, and that there were six good typewriters to be inherited from the escritorio, she commenced to sob in approved fashion on the floor, embracing the corpse of her late spouse, hysterically—as a good wife should.

When the police got through asking questions of them both, and of Señora Rueda, Juan went home alone and left Consuelo still crying at the Baths. It took him a long time to get over the fact that she had told her husband—and the sound of that single pistol shot echoed in his head for months.

But the saddest thing of all, so they say in Loreto, was that when the details of their tragic triangle appeared in the papers, Juan's employer read them with such scandalized interest that he promptly dismissed him from his work. Consuelo lost only a husband she didn't want. But young Maldonado lost his *job*.

As for Señora Rueda, she swore never to rent another tub to a couple.

BIG MEETING

The early stars had begun to twinkle in the August night as Bud and I neared the woods. A great many Negroes, old and young, were plodding down the dirt road on foot on their way to the Big Meeting. Long before we came near the lantern-lighted tent we could hear early arrivals singing, clapping their hands lustily and throwing out each word distinct like a drumbeat. Songs like "When the Saints Go Marching Home" and "That Old-time Religion" filled the air.

In the road that ran past the woods, a number of automobiles and buggies belonging to white people had stopped near the tent so that their occupants might listen to the singing. The whites stared curiously through the hickory trees at the rocking figures in the tent. The canvas, except behind the pulpit, was rolled up on account of the heat, and the meeting could easily be seen from the road, so there beneath a tree Bud and I stopped, too. In our teens, we were young and wild and didn't believe much in revivals, so we stayed outside in the road where we could smoke and laugh like the white folks. But both Bud's mother and mine were under the tent singing, actively a part of the services. Had they known we were near, they would certainly have come out and dragged us in.

From frequent attendance since childhood at these Big Meetings held each summer in the South, we knew the services were divided into three parts. The testimonials and the song-service came first. This began as soon as two or three people were gathered together, continuing until the minister himself arrived. Then the sermon followed, with its accompanying songs and shouts from the audi ence. Then the climax came with the calling of the lost souls to the mourners' bench, and the prayers for sinners and backsliders. This was where Bud and I would leave. We were having too good a time being sinners, and we didn't want to be saved—not yet, anyway.

When we arrived, old Aunt Ibey Davis was just starting a familiar song:

> *Where shall I be when that first trumpet sound?*
> *Lawdy, where shall I be when it sound so loud?*

The rapidly increasing number of worshipers took up the tune in full volume sending a great flood of melody billowing beneath the canvas roof. With heads back, feet and hands patting time, they repeated the chorus again and again. And each party of new arrivals swung into rhythm as they walked up the aisle by the light of the dim oil lanterns hanging from the tent poles.

Standing there at the edge of the road beneath a big tree, Bud and I watched the people as they came—keeping our eyes open for the girls. Scores of Negroes from the town and nearby villages and farms came drawn by the music and the preaching. Some were old and gray-headed; some in the prime of life; some mere boys and girls; and many little barefooted children. It was the twelfth night of the Big Meeting. They came from miles around to bathe their souls in a sea of song, to shout and cry and moan before the flow of Reverend Braswell's eloquence, and to pray for all the sinners in the county who had not yet seen the light. Although it was a colored folks' meeting, whites liked to come and sit outside in the road in their cars and listen. Sometimes there would be as many as ten or twelve parties of whites parked there in the dark, smoking and listening, and enjoying themselves, like Bud and I, in a not very serious way.

Even while old Aunt Ibey Davis was singing, a big red buick drove up and parked right behind Bud and me beneath the tree. It was full of white people, and we recognized the driver as Mr. Parkes, the man who owned the drugstore in town where colored people couldn't buy a glass of soda at the fountain.

> *It will sound so loud it will wake up the dead!*
> *Lawdy, where shall I be when it sound?*

"You'll hear some good singing out here," Mr. Parkes said to a woman in the car with him.

"I always did love to hear darkies singing," she answered from the back seat.

Bud nudged me in the ribs at the word *darkie*.

"I hear 'em," I said, sitting down on one of the gnarled roots of the tree and pulling out a cigarette.

The song ended as an old black woman inside the tent got up to speak. "I rise to testify dis evenin' fo' Jesus!" she said. "Ma Saviour an' ma Redeemer an' de chamber wherein I resusticates ma soul. Pray fo' me, brothers and sisters. Let yo' mercies bless me in all I do an' yo' prayers go with me on each travelin' voyage through dis land."

"Amen! Hallelujah!" cried my mother.

Just in front of us, near the side of the tent, a woman's clear soprano voice began to sing:

> *I am a po' pilgrim of sorrow*
> *Out in this wide world alone . . .*

Soon others joined with her and the whole tent was singing:

> *Sometimes I am tossed and driven,*
> *Sometimes I don't know where to go . . .*

"Real pretty, ain't it?" said the white woman in the car behind us.

> *But I've heard of a city called heaven*
> *And I've started to make it my home.*

When the woman finished her song she rose and told how her husband left her with six children, her mother died in a poorhouse, and the world had always been against her—but still she was going on!

"My, she's had a hard time," giggled the woman in the car.

"Sure has," laughed Mr. Parkes, "to hear her tell it."

And the way they talked made gooseflesh come out on my skin.

"Trials and tribulations surround me—but I'm goin' on," the the woman in the tent cried. Shouts and exclamations of approval broke out all over the congregation.

"Praise God!"

"Bless His Holy Name!"

"That's right, sister!"

"Devils beset me—but I'm goin' on!" said the woman. "I ain't got no friends—but I'm goin' on!"

"Jesus yo' friend, sister! Jesus yo' friend!" came the answer.

"God bless Jesus! I'm goin' on!"

"Dat's right!" cried Sister Mabry, Bud's mother, bouncing in her seat and flinging her arms outward. "Take all this world, but gimme Jesus!"

"Look at mama," Bud said half amused, sitting there beside me smoking. "She's getting happy."

"Whoo-ooo-o-o! Great Gawd-a-Mighty!" yelled old man Walls near the pulpit. "I can't hold it dis evenin'! Dis mawnin', dis evenin', dis mawnin', Lawd!"

"Pray for me—cause I'm goin' on!" said the woman. In the midst of the demonstration she had created she sat down exhausted, her armpits wet with sweat and her face covered with tears.

"Did you her her, Jehover?" someone asked.

"Yes! He heard her! Halleloo!" came the answer.

"Dis mawnin', dis evenin', dis mawnin', Lawd!"

Brother Nace Eubanks began to line a song:

> *Must Jesus bear his cross alone*
> *An' all de world go free?*

Slowly they sang it line by line. Then the old man rose and told of a vision that had come to him long ago on that day when he had been changed from a sinner to a just man.

"I was layin' in ma bed," he said, "at de midnight hour twenty-two years past at 714 Pine Street in dis here city when a snow-white sheep come in ma room an' stood behind de wash bowl. Dis here sheep, hit spoke to me wid tongues o' fiah an' hit said, 'Nace, git up! Git up, an' come wid me!' Yes, suh! He had a light round 'bout his head like a moon, an' wings like a dove, an' he walked on hoofs o' gold an' dis sheep hit said, 'I once were lost, but now I'm saved, an' you kin be like me!' Yes, suh! An' ever since dat night, brothers an' sisters, I's been a chile o' de Lamb! Pray fo' me!"

"Help him, Jesus!" Sister Mabry shouted.

"Amen!" chanted Deacon Laws. "Amen! Amen!"

> *Glory! Hallelujah!*
> *Let de halleluian roll!*
> *I'll sing ma Saviour's praises far an' wide!*

It was my mother's favorite song, and she sang it like a paean of triumph, rising from her seat.

"Look at ma," I said to Bud, knowing that she was about to start her nightly shouting.

"Yah," Bud said. "I hope she don't see me while she's standing up there, or she'll come out here and make us go up to the mourners' bench."

"We'll leave before that," I said.

> *I've opened up to heaven*
> *All de windows of ma soul,*
> *An' I'm livin' on de halleluian side!*

Rocking proudly to and fro as the second chorus boomed and swelled beneath the canvas, mama began to clap her hands, her lips silent now in this sea of song she had started, her head thrown back in joy—for my mother was a great shouter. Stepping gracefully to the beat of the music, she moved out toward the center aisle into a cleared space. Then she began to spring on her toes with little short rhythmical hops. All the way up the long aisle to the pulpit gently she leaped to the clap-clap of hands, the pat of feet, and the steady booming song of her fellow worshipers. Then mama began to revolve in a dignified circle, slowly, as a great happiness swept her gleaming black features, and her lips curved into a smile.

> *I've opened up to heaven*
> *All de windows of my soul . . .*

Mama was dancing before the Lord with her eyes closed, her mouth smiling, and her head held high.

> *I'm livin' on de halleluian side!*

As she danced she threw her hands upward away from her breasts as though casting off all the cares of the world.

Just then the white woman in Mr. Parkes' car behind us laughed, "My Lord, John, it's better than a show!"

Something about the way she laughed made my blood boil. That was *my mother* dancing and shouting. Maybe it was better than a show, but nobody had any business laughing at her, least of all white people.

I looked at Bud, but he didn't say anything. Maybe he was thinking how often we, too, made fun of the shouters, laughing at our parents as though they were crazy—but deep down inside us we understood why they came to Big Meeting. Working all day all their lives for white folks, they *had* to believe there was a "Halleluian Side."

I looked at mama standing there singing, and I thought about how many years she had prayed and shouted and praised the Lord at church meetings and revivals, then came home for a few hours' sleep before getting up at dawn to go cook and scrub and clean for others. And I didn't want any white folks, especially whites who wouldn't let a Negro drink a glass of soda in their drugstore or give one a job, sitting in a car laughing at mama.

"Gimme a cigarette, Bud. If these dopes behind us say any more, I'm gonna get up and tell 'em something they won't like."

"To hell with 'em," Bud answered.

I leaned back against the gnarled roots of the tree by the road and inhaled deeply. The white people were silent again in their car, listening to the singing. In the dark I couldn't see their faces to tell if they were still amused or not. But that was mostly what they wanted out of Negroes—work and fun—without paying for it, I thought, work and fun.

To a great hand-clapping, body-rocking, foot-patting rhythm, mama was repeating the chorus over and over. Sisters leaped and shouted and perspiring brothers walked the aisles bowing left and right, beating time, shaking hands, laughing aloud for joy, and singing steadily when, at the back of the tent, the Reverend Duke Braswell arrived.

A tall, powerful, jet-black man, he moved with long steps through the center of the tent, his iron-gray hair uncovered, his green-black coat jim-swinging to his knees, his fierce eyes looking straight toward the altar. Under his arm he carried a Bible.

Once on the platform, he stood silently wiping his brow with a large white handkerchief while the singing swirled around him. Then he sang, too, his voice roaring like a cyclone, his white teeth shining. Finally he held up his palms for silence and the song gradually lowered to a hum, hum, hum, hands and feet patting, bodies still moving. At last, above the broken cries of the shouters and the undertones of song, the minister was able to make himself heard.

"Brother Garner, offer up a prayer."

Reverend Braswell sank on his knees and every back bowed. Brother Garner, with his head in his hands, lifted his voice against a background of moans:

"Oh, Lawd, we comes befo' you dis evenin' wid fear an' tremblin' —unworthy as we is to enter yo' house an' speak yo' name. We comes befo' you, Lawd, cause we knows you is mighty an' powerful in all de lands, an' great above de stars, an' bright above de moon. Oh, Lawd, you is bigger den de world. You holds de sun in yo' right hand an' de mornin' star in yo' left, an' we po' sinners ain't nothin', not even so much as a grain o' sand beneath yo' feet. Yet we calls on you dis evenin' to hear us, Lawd, to send down yo' sweet Son Jesus to walk wid us in our sorrows to comfort us on our weary road cause sometimes we don't know which-a-way to turn! We pray you dis evenin', Lawd, to look down at our wanderin' chilluns what's gone from home. Look down in St. Louis, Lawd, an' look in Memphis, an' look down in Chicago if they's usin' Thy name in vain dis evenin', if they's gamblin' tonight, Lawd, if they's doin' any ways wrong—reach down an' pull 'em up, Lawd, an' say, 'Come wid me, cause I am de Vine an' de Husbandman an' de gate dat leads to Glory!' "

Remembering sons in faraway cities, "Help him, Jesus!" mothers cried.

"Whilst you's lookin' down on us dis evenin', keep a mighty eye on de sick an' de 'flicked. Ease Sister Hightower, Lawd, layin' in her bed at de pint o' death. An' bless Bro' Carpenter what's come out to meetin' here dis evenin' in spite o' his broken arm from fallin' off de roof. An' Lawd, aid de pastor dis evenin' to fill dis tent wid yo' Spirit, an' to make de sinners tremble an' backsliders shout, an' dem dat is widout de church to come to de moaners' bench an' find rest in Jesus! We ask Thee all dese favors dis evenin'. Also to guide us an' bless us wid Thy bread an' give us Thy wine to drink fo' Christ de Holy Saviour's sake, our Shelter an' our Rock. Amen!"

There's not a friend like de lowly Jesus . . .

Some sister began, high and clear after the passion of the prayer,

No, not one! . . . No, not one!

Then the preacher took his text from the open Bible. "Ye now therefore have sorrow: but I will see you again, and your hearts shall rejoice, and your joy no man taketh from you."

He slammed shut the Holy Book and walked to the edge of the platform. "That's what Jesus said befo' he went to the cross, children—'I will see you again, and yo' hearts shall rejoice!' "

"Yes, sir!" said the brothers and sisters. " 'Deed he did!"

Then the minister began to tell the familiar story of the death of Christ. Standing in the dim light of the smoking oil lanterns, he sketched the life of the man who had had power over multitudes.

"Power," the minister said. "Power! Without money and without titles, without position, he had power! And that power went out to the poor and afflicted. For Jesus said, 'The first shall be last, and the last shall be first.' "

"He sho did!" cried Bud's mother.

"Hallelujah!" mama agreed loudly. "Glory be to God!"

"Then the big people of the land heard about Jesus," the preacher went on, "the chief priests and the scribes, the politicians, the bootleggers, and the bankers—and they begun to conspire against Jesus because *He had power*! This Jesus with His twelve disciples preachin' in Galilee. Then came that eve of the Passover, when he set down with His friends to eat and drink of the vine and the settin' sun fell behind the hills of Jerusalem. And Jesus knew that ere the cock crew Judas would betray Him, and Peter would say, 'I know Him not,' and all alone by Hisself He would go to His death. Yes, sir, He knew! So He got up from the table and went into the garden to pray. In this hour of trouble, Jesus went to pray!"

Away at the back of the tent some old sister began to sing:

> *Oh, watch with me one hour*
> *While I go yonder and pray . . .*

And the crowd took up the song, swelled it, made its melody fill the hot tent while the minister stopped talking to wipe his face with his white handkerchief.

Then to the humming undertone of the song, he continued, "They called it Gethsemane—that garden where Jesus fell down on His face in the grass and cried to the Father, 'Let this bitter hour pass from me! Oh, God, let this hour pass.' Because He was still a young man who did not want to die, He rose up and went back into the house—but His friends was all asleep. While Jesus prayed, His friends done gone to sleep! But, 'Sleep on,' he said, 'for the hour is at hand.' Jesus said, 'Sleep on.' "

"Sleep on, sleep on," chanted the crowd, repeating the words of the minister.

"He was not angry with them. But as Jesus looked out of the house, He saw that garden alive with men carryin' lanterns and swords and staves, and the mob was everywhere. So He went to the door. Then Judas come out from among the crowd, the traitor Judas, and kissed Him on the cheek—Oh, bitter friendship! And the soldiers with handcuffs fell upon the Lord and took Him prisoner.

"The disciples was awake by now, Oh, yes! But they fled away because they was afraid. And the mob carried Jesus off.

"Peter followed Him from afar, followed Jesus in chains till they come to the palace of the high priest. There Peter went in, timid and afraid, to see the trial. He set in the back of the hall. Peter listened to the lies they told about Christ—and didn't dispute 'em. He watched the high priest spit in Christ's face—and made no move. He saw 'em smite Him with the palms of they hands—and Peter uttered not a word for his poor mistreated Jesus."

"Not a word! . . . Not a word! . . . Not a word!"

"And when the servants of the high priest asked Peter, 'Does you know this man?' he said, 'I do not!'

"And when they asked him a second time, he said, 'No!'

"And yet a third time, 'Do you know Jesus?'

"And Peter answered with an oath, 'I told you, No!'

"Then the cock crew."

"De cock crew!" cried Aunt Ibey Davis. "De cock crew! Oh, ma Lawd! De cock crew!"

"The next day the chief priests taken counsel against Jesus to put Him to death. They brought Him before Pilate, and Pilate said, 'What evil hath he done?'

"But the people cried, 'Crucify Him!' because they didn't care. So Pilate called for water and washed his hands.

"The soldiers made sport of Jesus where He stood in the Council Hall. They stripped Him naked, and put a crown of thorns on His head, a red robe about His body, and a reed from the river in His hands.

"They said, 'Ha! Ha! So you're the King! Ha! Ha!' And they bowed down in mockery before Him, makin' fun of Jesus.

"Some of the guards threw wine in His face. Some of the guards was drunk and called Him out o' His name—and nobody said, 'Stop! That's Jesus!'"

The Reverend Duke Braswell's face darkened with horror as he pictured the death of Christ. "Oh, yes! Peter denied Him because he was afraid. Judas betrayed Him for thirty pieces of silver. Pilate said, 'I wash my hands—take Him and kill Him.'

"And His friends fled away! . . . Have mercy on Jesus! . . . His friends done fled away!"

"His friends!"

"His friends done fled away!"

The preacher chanted, half moaning his sentences, not speaking them. His breath came in quick, short gasps with an indrawn,

"Umn!" between each rapid phrase. Perspiration poured down his face as he strode across the platform wrapped in this drama that he saw in the very air before his eyes. Peering over the heads of his audience out into the darkness, he began the ascent to Golgotha, describing the taunting crowd at Christ's heels and the heavy cross on His shoulders.

"Then a black man named Simon, blacker than me, come and took the cross and bore it for Him. Umn!

"Then Jesus were standin' alone on a high hill, in the broilin' sun, while they put the crosses in the ground. No water to cool His throat! No tree to shade His achin' head! Nobody to say a friendly word to Jesus! Umn!

"Alone, in that crowd on the hill of Golgotha, with two thieves bound and dyin', and the murmur of the mob all around. Umn!

"But Jesus never said a word! Umn!

"They laid they hands on Him, and they tore the clothes from His body—and then, and then," loud as a thunderclap, the minister's voice broke through the little tent, "they raised Him to the cross!"

A great wail went up from the crowd. Bud and I sat entranced in spite of ourselves, forgetting to smoke. Aunt Ibey Davis wept. Sister Mabry moaned. In their car behind us the white people were silent as the minister went on:

They brought four long iron nails
And put one in the palm of His left hand.
The hammer said . . . Bam!
They put one in the palm of His right hand.
The hammer said . . . Bam!
They put one through His left foot . . . Bam!
And one through His right foot . . . Bam!

"Don't drive it!" a woman screamed. "Don't drive them nails! For Christ's sake! Oh! Don't drive 'em!"

And they left my Jesus on the cross!
Nails in His hands! Nails in His feet!
Sword in His side! Thorns circlin' His head!
Mob cussin' and hootin' my Jesus! Umn!
The spit of the mob in His face! Umn!
His body hangin' on the cross! Umn!
Gimme piece of His garment for a souvenir! Umn!
Castin' lots for His garments! Umn!
Blood from His wounded side! Umn!
Streamin' down His naked legs! Umn!

Droppin' in the dust—umn—
That's what they did to my Jesus!
They stoned Him first, they stoned Him!
Called Him everything but a child of God.
Then they lynched Him on the cross.

In song I heard my mother's voice cry:

Were you there when they crucified my Lord?
Were you there when they nailed Him to the tree?

The Reverend Duke Braswell stretched wide his arms against the white canvas of the tent. In the yellow light his body made a cross-like shadow on the canvas.

Oh, it makes me to tremble, tremble!
Were you there when they crucified my Lord?

"Let's go," said the white woman in the car behind us. "This is too much for me!" They started the motor and drove noisily away in a swirl of dust.

"Don't go," I cried from where I was sitting at the root of the tree. "Don't go," I shouted, jumping up. "They're about to call for sinners to come to the mourners' bench. Don't go!" But their car was already out of earshot.

I didn't realize I was crying until I tasted my tears in my mouth.

Other Stories

THANK YOU, M'AM

She was a large woman with a large purse that had everything in it but hammer and nails. It had a long strap and she carried it slung across her shoulder. It was about eleven o'clock at night, and she was walking alone, when a boy ran up behind her and tried to snatch her purse. The strap broke with the single tug the boy gave it from behind. But the boy's weight, and the weight of the purse combined caused him to lose his balance so, instead of taking off full blast as he had hoped, the boy fell on his back on the sidewalk, and his legs flew up. The large woman simply turned around and kicked him right square in his blue jeaned sitter. Then she reached down, picked the boy up by his shirt front, and shook him until his teeth rattled.

After that the woman said, "Pick up my pocketbook, boy, and give it here."

She still held him. But she bent down enough to permit him to stoop and pick up her purse. Then she said, "Now ain't you ashamed of yourself?"

Firmly gripped by his shirt front, the boy said, "Yes'm."

The woman said, "What did you want to do it for?"

The boy said, "I didn't aim to."

She said, "You a lie!"

By that time two or three people passed, stopped, turned to look, and some stood watching.

"If I turn you loose, will you run?" asked the woman.

"Yes'm," said the boy.

"Then I won't turn you loose," said the woman. She did not release him.

"I'm very sorry, lady, I'm sorry," whispered the boy.

"Um-hum! And your face is dirty. I got a great mind to wash your face for you. Ain't you got nobody home to tell you to wash your face?"

"No'm," said the boy.

"Then it will get washed this evening," said the large woman start-ing up the street, dragging the frightened boy behind her.

He looked as if he were fourteen or fifteen, frail and willow-wild, in tennis shoes and blue jeans.

The woman said, "You ought to be my son. I would teach you right from wrong. Least I can do right now is to wash your face. Are you hungry?"

"No'm," said the being-dragged boy. "I just want you to turn me loose."

"Was I bothering *you* when I turned that corner?" asked the woman.

"No'm."

"But you put yourself in contact with *me*," said the woman. "If you think that that contact is not going to last awhile, you got another thought coming. When I get through with you, sir, you are going to remember Mrs. Luella Bates Washington Jones."

Sweat popped out on the boy's face and he began to struggle. Mrs. Jones stopped, jerked him around in front of her, put a half-nelson about his neck, and continued to drag him up the street. When she got to her door, she dragged the boy inside, down a hall, and into a large kitchenette-furnished room at the rear of the house. She switched on the light and left the door open. The boy could hear other roomers laughing and talking in the large house. Some of their doors were open, too, so he knew he and the woman were not alone. The woman still had him by the neck in the middle of her room.

She said, "What is your name?"

"Roger," answered the boy.

"Then, Roger, you go to that sink and wash your face," said the woman, whereupon she turned him loose—at last. Roger looked at the door—looked at the woman—looked at the door—*and went to the sink.*

"Let the water run until it gets warm," she said. "Here's a clean towel."

"You gonna take me to jail?" asked the boy, bending over the sink.

"Not with that face, I would not take you nowhere," said the woman. "Here I am trying to get home to cook me a bite to eat and you snatch my pocketbook! Maybe you ain't been to your supper either, late as it be. Have you?"

"There's nobody home at my house," said the boy.

"Then we'll eat," said the woman. "I believe you're hungry—or been hungry—to try to snatch my pocketbook."

"I wanted a pair of blue suede shoes," said the boy.

"Well, you didn't have to snatch *my* pockebook to get some suede shoes," said Mrs. Luella Bates Washington Jones. "You could of asked me."

"M'am?"

The water dripping from his face, the boy looked at her. There was a long pause. A very long pause. After he had dried his face and not knowing what else to do dried it again, the boy turned around, wondering what next. The door was open. He could make a dash for it down the hall. He could run, run, run, run, *run!*

The woman was sitting on the day-bed. After awhile she said, "I were young once and I wanted things I could not get."

There was another long pause. The boy's mouth opened. Then he frowned, but not knowing he frowned.

The woman said, "Um-hum! You thought I was going to say *but,* didn't you? You thought I was going to say, *but I didn't snatch people's pocketbooks.* Well, I wasn't going to say that." Pause. Silence. "I have done things, too, which I would not tell you, son —neither tell God, if he didn't already know. So you set down while I fix us something to eat. You might run that comb through your hair so you will look presentable."

In another corner of the room behind a screen was a gas plate and an icebox. Mrs. Jones got up and went behind the screen. The woman did not watch the boy to see if he was going to run now, nor did she watch her purse which she left behind her on the day-bed. But the boy took care to sit on the far side of the room where he thought she could easily see him out of the corner of her eye, if she wanted to. He did not trust the woman *not* to trust him. And he did not want to be mistrusted now.

"Do you need somebody to go to the store," asked the boy, "maybe to get some milk or something?"

"Don't believe I do," said the woman, "unless you just want sweet milk yourself. I was going to make cocoa out of this canned milk I got here."

"That will be fine," said the boy.

She heated some lima beans and ham she had in the icebox, made the cocoa, and set the table. The woman did not ask the boy anything about where he lived, or his folks, or anything else that would embarrass him. Instead, as they ate, she told him about her job in a hotel beauty-shop that stayed open late, what the work was like, and how all kinds of women came in and out, blondes, red-heads, and Spanish. Then she cut him a half of her ten-cent cake.

"Eat some more, son," she said.

When they were finished eating she got up and said, "Now, here, take this ten dollars and buy yourself some blue suede shoes. And next time, do not make the mistake of latching onto *my* pocketbook *nor nobody else's*—because shoes come by devilish like that will burn your feet. I got to get my rest now. But I wish you would behave yourself, son, from here on in."

She led him down the hall to the front door and opened it. "Goodnight! Behave yourself, boy!" she said, looking out into the street.

The boy wanted to say something else other than, "Thank you, m'am," to Mrs. Luella Bates Washington Jones, but he couldn't do so as he turned at the barren stoop and looked back at the large woman in the door. He barely managed to say, "Thank you," before she shut the door. And he never saw her again.

PATRON OF THE ARTS

Although it was just four o'clock of an autumn afternoon, the lights were on in the corners of Darby's little fifth floor studio apartment, those soft rose-colored lights that make even an ugly woman look charming—particularly if she is as smartly groomed as many New York women of color are. Through the windows with their *tete de negre* drapes, one saw a wind-blown, autumn-leafed view of aristocratic Sugar Hill, and southward the less well-kept regions of Harlem through which, in spite of poverty, fame had stalked to carry off a Josephine Baker or an Eartha Kitt.

Darby looked out, puffing impatiently on a cigarette and waiting for the lady to arrive. She was thirty-five and, according to the poets, there is no woman so charming as the woman of thirty-five. Darby had read this somewhere. He was twenty-one, fresh out of college: Today he had everything in readiness, the little anchovies, the ice in the bowl, the Barcardi and the limes. He knew what she liked, this green-eyed brownskin Mrs. Oldham who had been one of his first friends in New York. Back home in Oklahoma over his drawing board in art class in high school, Darby had dreamed of women like Cornelia Oldham. There were none in the West.

Now that he knew her—and had known her—there was a little girl at the Art Students League downtown he liked much better— a struggling young artist like himself in a strange city. He wished he could marry her.

Standing in reverie, Darby heard the elevator door close. He straightened his tie—despite the fact that he might shortly take it off. You see, he was only twenty-one, and he wanted to look his best at first.

The bell rang. He went to his door and there was Cornelia. Taller than Darby, sleek in black and white, green-eyed and wise and old. He took her in his arms, but the very first words she said caused him to jump halfway across the room.

"Darling," she whispered, panting, looking at him with her great green eyes like a cat's, "I have told. . . . my husband. . . . all."

Something stopped beating in Darby's breast. It was his heart. "What?" he cried.

"Yes, dear, I have told him I love you!"

Darby stood behind the sofa. He stared at her with wide young eyes. He knew she had a husband, to be sure, a large dark man. But that personage had always seemed quite remote, far-away at home in St. Albans, or working at his Seventh Avenue office. This was Darby's first experience with a married woman. And he never dreamed that they told their husbands all.

"What—what," stuttered the young man as soon as he could talk, "what—did—your husband say?"

"He rose," Cornelia panted, "and stalked out of the room."

Her green eyes in her cafe-au-lait face were full of tragedy. At once Darby had visions of an irate spouse still stalking—right on up to his apartment with a pistol in his hand.

"Lord!" Darby cried, "Cornelia, why did you do that?"

"I love you," she said, "that's why."

"But—but maybe he'll come here and shoot up the place!"

"Let him," she cried. "First we'll mix a cocktail." She took off her wraps and sat down. The youth stood behind the sofa shaking his head.

"I—I will not fix a cocktail," he said. She leaned her head back for a kiss. "Suppose he were tailing you! Why, he'd find us in a— a compromising position!" Darby retreated toward the wall.

"Darling!" Cornelia cried, rising to come swiftly toward him, her green eyes gleaming, her dark hair done by Frankie, "Don't worry. . . ."

Just then there was a ring at the door. Darby stood as if petrified while Cornelia returned to the sofa. Finally he managed to move his legs, close his mouth, and turn the door knob.

The janitor stood in the hall.

"I'll take them socks, Mr. Middlefield, you said you wanted ma wife to mend."

"Could you come back later, *please?*" said Darby.

"Yes, suh," said the man.

"Let's get out of here," Darby said as he closed the door. "Your husband might come at any moment now, Cornelia."

"He's still in his office, darling."

"I don't care," said Darby, "let's go."

Thinking how his mother back home in Tulsa would feel if she read in the papers that he was killed over a *married* woman, he opened the closet and took out his coat.

"If you leave me," Cornelia said, "I will shoot myself."

"There's nothing here for you to shoot yourself with," said Darby, putting on his coat.

"Then I'll grind up glass and eat it."

"Don't be a fool!" cried Darby.

"I am," said Cornelia, "about you!"

"I want *you* to go home," Darby begged desperately.

"I won't," answered Cornelia.

"Then I'm going out to a phone and call your husband and explain everything to him. After all, you're just my patron, Mrs. Oldham. You paid me well to paint your portrait."

"Is that all I am to you?" cried Cornelia. She poured herself a huge drink, not bothering to mix it.

"That's all I'll ever admit," said the young man. "I'm going to explain fully to your husband *now*—our relationship. After that, please take your portrait home. It's finished." He pointed toward the easel where rested the oil painting he had made of her.

"You coward!" said Mrs. Oldham, "afraid of my husband! Why, you and I could go to Paris and be free."

"I don't want to go to Paris," said Darby, "I'm going to a phone."

He left Cornelia in front of the cocktail shaker as he rushed out. From the pay station in the drug store at the corner, Darby finally got Dr. Oldham on the phone.

"I am Darby Middlefield," said the young man nervously.

"Who?" said Mr. Oldham.

"Middlefield, the artist."

"The artist?"

"I'm calling you about your wife."

"My wife? Why about *my* wife?"

"Because I want to make it plain to you, Dr. Oldham, we're nothing to each other."

"What? But why?"

Darby repeated what he had just said.

"My dear boy," said Dr. Oldham, "my wife and I have lived apart for years. Our divorce is pending."

"But—but—"

"Whoever you are," said Dr. Oldham, "from the sound of your voice, you must be very young. You need not worry about me."

"But I thought she had told you all?" said Darby plaintively.

"She probably did," explained Dr. Oldham. "But I am so bored at Cornelia's frequent affairs with young men immature enough to be her sons, that I usually walk out of the room when she begins her confidences. I've heard them for years so I am no longer amused, damn it!"

"You mean you don't care?"

"I certainly don't," said Dr. Oldham. "Cornelia's a woman of forty-seven who can take care of herself."

"Forty-seven?" said Darby. "She told me she was thirty-five!"

"I can smell your youth!" said Dr. Oldham. He hung up the phone.

"Thirty-five! *Forty-seven!*" Darby murmured to himself as he left the booth. "Thirty-five! That lying chick!"

When he got back to his apartment Cornelia had gone. Without partaking of any ground glass, she had drunk *half* of his bottle of Bacardi instead.

Lying on the tray beside the bottle was a little note:

> *Dearest Darby:*
>   *Please keep the picture you painted*
>   *of me to take with you when you go*
>   *back to Oklahoma. Perhaps, when you*
>   *are older, you might like to remember*
>   *how your patron looked. Don't forget.*
>   *Love,*
>   *Cornelia*

POEMS

The Weary Blues

THE WEARY BLUES

Droning a drowsy syncopated tune,
Rocking back and forth to a mellow croon,
  I heard a Negro play.
Down on Lenox Avenue the other night
By the pale dull pallor of an old gas light
  He did a lazy sway . . .
  He did a lazy sway . . .
To the tune o' those Weary Blues.
With his ebony hands on each ivory key
He made that poor piano moan with melody.
  O Blues!
Swaying to and fro on his rickety stool
He played that sad raggy tune like a musical fool.
  Sweet Blues!
Coming from a black man's soul.
  O Blues!
In a deep song voice with a melancholy tone
I heard that Negro sing, that old piano moan—
  "Ain't got nobody in all this world,
  Ain't got nobody but ma salf.
  I's gwine to quit ma frownin'
  And put ma troubles on the shelf."
Thump, thump, thump, went his foot on the floor.
He played a few chords then he sang some more—
  "I got the Weary Blues
  And I can't be satisfied.
  Got the Weary Blues
  And can't be satisfied—
  I ain't happy no mo'
  And I wish that I had died."
And far into the night he crooned that tune.
The stars went out and so did the moon.

The singer stopped playing and went to bed
While the Weary Blues echoed through his head.
He slept like a rock or a man that's dead.

THE NEGRO SPEAKS OF RIVERS

I've known rivers:
I've known rivers ancient as the world and older than the flow of
    human blood in human veins.

My soul has grown deep like the rivers.

I bathed in the Euphrates when dawns were young.
I build my hut near the Congo and it lulled me to sleep.
I looked upon the Nile and raised the pyramids above it.
I heard the singing of the Mississippi when Abe Lincoln went down
      to New Orleans, and I've seen its muddy bosom turn all
    golden in the sunset.
I've known rivers:
Ancient, dusky rivers.

My soul has grown deep like the rivers.

Montage of a Dream Deferred

NOTE: In terms of current Afro-American popular music and the sources from which it has progressed—jazz, ragtime, swing, blues, boogie-woogie, and be-bop—this poem on contemporary Harlem, like be-bop, is marked by conflicting changes, sudden nuances, sharp and impudent interjections, broken rhythms, and passages some-times in the manner of the jam session, sometimes the popular song, punctuated by the riffs, runs, breaks, and disc-tortions of the music of a community in transition.

L. H.

BOOGIE SEGUE TO BOP

DREAM BOOGIE

Good morning daddy!
Ain't you heard
The boogie-woogie rumble
Of a dream deferred?

Listen closely:
You'll hear their feet
Beating out and beating out a—

    You think
    It's a happy beat?

Listen to it closely:
Ain't you heard
something underneath
like a—

    What did I say?

Sure,
I'm happy!
Take it away!

89

Hey, pop!
Re-bop!
Mop

Y-e-a-h!

PARADE

Seven ladies
and seventeen gentlemen
at the Elks Club Lounge
planning planning a parade;
Grand Marshal in his white suit
will lead it.
Cadillacs with dignitaries
will precede it.
And behind will come
with band and drum
on foot . . . on foot . . .
on foot . . .

Motorcycle cops
white,
will speed it
out of sight
if they can:
Solid black,
can't be right.

Marching . . . marching . . .
marching . . .
noon till night . . .
    I never knew
    that many Negroes
    were on earth,
    did you?
    I never knew!
    PARADE!
A chance to let
    PARADE!
the whole world see
    PARADE!
old black me!

CHILDREN'S RHYMES

When I was a chile we used to play,
"One—two—buckle my shoe!"
and things like that. But now, Lord,
listen at them little varmints!

> By what sends
> the white kids
> I ain't sent:
> I know I can't
> be President.

There is two thousand children
in this block, I do believe!

> What don't bug
> them white kids
> sure bugs me:
> We knows everybody
> ain't free!

Some of these young ones is cert'ly bad—
One batted a hard ball right through my window
and my gold fish et the glass.

> What's written down
> for white folks
>
> ain't for us a-tall:
> "Liberty and Justice—
> Huh—For All."
>
> Oop-pop-a-da!
> Skee! Daddle-de-do!
> Be-bop!
>
> Salt'peanuts!

De-dop!

SISTER

That little Negro's married and got a kid
Why does he keep on foolin' around Marie?
Marie's my sister—not married to me—

But why does he keep on foolin' around Marie?
Why don't she get a boy-friend
I can understand—some decent man?

> Did it ever occur to you, son
> the reason Marie runs around with trash
> is she wants some cash?

Don't decent folks have dough?

> Unfortunately usually no!

Well, anyway, it don't have to be a married man.

> Did it ever occur to you, boy
> that a woman does the best she can?

> ## Comment on Stoop

So does a man.

PREFERENCE

I likes a woman
six or eight and ten years older'n myself.
I don't fool with these young girls.
Young girls'l say,
    Daddy, I want so-and-so.
    I needs this, that, and the other.
But a old woman'll say,
    Honey, what does YOU need?
    I just drawed my money tonight
    and it's all your'n.
That's why I likes a older woman
who can appreciate me:
When she conversations you
it ain't forever, Gimme!

NECESSITY

Work
I don't have to work.
I don't have to do nothing
but eat, drink, stay black, and die.

This little old furnished room's
so small I can't whip a cat
without getting fur in my mouth
and my landlady's so old
her features is all run together
and God knows she sure can overcharge—
Which is why I reckon I does
have to work after all.

QUESTION

Said the lady, Can you do
what my other man can't do—
That is
love me, daddy—
and feed me, too?

FIGURINE

De-dop!

BUDDY

That kid's my buddy,
still and yet
I don't see him much.
He works downtown for Twelve a week.
Has to give his mother Ten—
she says he can have
the other Two
to pay his carfare, buy a suit,
coat, shoes,
anything he wants out of it.

JUKE BOX LOVE SONG

I could take the Harlem night
and wrap around you
Take the neon lights and make a crown,
Take the Lenox Avenue busses,

Taxis, subways,
And for your love song tone their rumble down.
Take Harlem's heartbeat,
Make a drumbeat,
Put it on a record, let it whirl,
And while we listen to it play,
Dance with you till day—
Dance with you, my sweet brown Harlem girl.

ULTIMATUM

Baby, how come you can't see me
when I'm paying your bills
each and every week?

If you got somebody else,
tell me—
else I'll cut you off
without your rent.
I mean
without a cent.

WARNING

Daddy,
don't let your dog
curb you!

CROON

I don't give a damn
For Alabam'
Even if it is my home.

NEW YORKERS

I was born here,
That's no lie, he said,
right here beneath God's sky.

I wasn't born here, she said,
I come—and why?
Where I come from
folks work hard
all their lives
until they die
and never own no parts
of earth nor sky.
So I come up here.
Now what've I got?
　　　You!
She lifted up her lips
in the dark:
The same old spark!

WONDER

Early blue evening.
Lights ain't come on yet.
　　　Looky yonder!
They come on now!

EASY BOOGIE

Down in the bass
That steady beat
Walking walking walking
Like marching feet.

Down in the bass
That easy roll,
Rolling like I like it
In my soul.

　　　Riffs, smears, breaks.

Hey, Lawdy, Mama!
Do you hear what I said?
Easy like I rock it
In my bed!

DIG AND BE DUG

MOVIES

The Roosevelt, Renaissance, Gem, Alhambra:
Harlem laughing in all the wrong places
        at the crocodile tears
        of crocodile art
        that you know
        in your heart
        is crocodile:

        (Hollywood
        laughs at me,
        black—
        so I laugh
        back.)

TELL ME

        Why should it be my loneliness,
        Why should it be my song,
        Why should it be my dream
                deferred
                overlong?

NOT A MOVIE

Well, they rocked him with road-apples
because he tried to vote
and whipped his head with clubs
and he crawled on his knees to his house
and he got the midnight train
and he crossed that Dixie line
now he's livin'
on a 133rd.

He didn't stop in Washington
and he didn't stop in Baltimore

neither in Newark on the say.
Six knot was on his head
but, thank God, he wasn't dead,
And there ain't no Ku Klux
on a 133rd.

NEON SIGNS

WONDER BAR
• • •

WISHING WELL
• • •

MONTEREY
• • •

MINTON'S
(altar of Thelonious)
• • •

MANDALAY
• • •

Spots where the booted
and unbooted play

LENOX
• • •

CASBAH
• • •

POOR JOHN'S
• • •

Mirror-go-round
where a broken glass
in the early bright
smears re-bop
sound

NUMBERS

If I ever hit for a dollar
gonna salt every dime away
in the Post Office for a rainy day.

I ain't gonna
play back a cent.

(Of course, I might
combinate a little
with my rent.)

WHAT? SO SOON!

I believe my old lady's
pregnant again!

Fate must have
some kind of trickeration
to populate the
cullud nation!

COMMENT AGAINST LAMP POST

You call it fate?

FIGURETTE

De-daddle-dy!
De-dop!

MOTTO

I play it cool
and dig all jive
That's the reason
I stay alive.
My motto,
As I live and learn,
        is:
Dig and Be Dug
In Return.

DEAD IN THERE

Sometimes
A night funeral

Going by
Carries home
A re-bop daddy.

Hearse and flowers
Guarantee
He'll never hype
Another paddy.

It's hard to believe,
But dead in there,
He'll never lay a
Hype nowhere!

He's my ace-boy,
Gone away.
Wake up and live!
He used to say.

Squares
Who couldn't dig him,
Plant him now—
Out where it makes
No diff' no how.

SITUATION

When I rolled three 7's
in a row
I was scared to walk out
with the dough.

DANCER

Two or three things in the past
failed him
that had not failed people
of lesser genius.

In the first place
he didn't have much sense.
He was no good at making love
and no good at making money.

So he tapped,
    trucked,
    boogied,
    sanded,
    kittered,
until he made folks say,
    Looky yonder
    at that boy!
    Hey!

But being no good at lovin'—
the girls left him.
(When you're no good for dough they go.)
With no sense, just wonderful feet,
What could possibly be all-reet?
Did he get anywhere? No!

Even a great dancer
can't C.P.T.
a show.

ADVICE

Folks, I'm telling you,
birthing is hard
and dying is mean—
so get yourself
a little loving
in between.

GREEN MEMORY

A wonderful time—the War:
when money rolled in
and blood rolled out.

But blood
was far away
from here—

Money was near.

WINE-O

Setting in the wine-house
Soaking up a wine-souse
Waiting for tomorrow to come—
Then
Setting in the wine-house
Soaking up a new souse.
Tomorrow. . . .
Oh, hum!

RELIEF

My heart is aching
for them Poles and Greeks
on relief way across the sea
because I was on relief
once in 1933.

I know what relief can be—
it took me two years to get on W.P.A.
If the war hadn't come along
I wouldn't be out of the barrel yet.
Now, I'm almost back in the barrel again.

To tell the truth,
if these white folks want to go ahead
and fight another war,
or even two,
the one to stop 'em won't be me.

Would you?

BALLAD OF THE LANDLORD

Landlord, landlord,
My roof has sprung a leak.
Don't you 'member I told you about it
Way last week?

Landlord, landlord,
These steps is broken down.

When you come up yourself
It's a wonder you don't fall down.

Ten bucks you say I owe you?
Ten bucks you say is due?
Well, that's ten bucks more'n I'll pay you
Till you fix this house up new.

What? You gonna get eviction orders?
You gonna cut off my heat?
You gonna take my furniture and
Throw it in the street?

Um-huh! You talking high and mighty.
Talk on—till you get through.
You ain't gonna be able to say a word
If I land my fist on you.

Police! Police!
Come and get this man!
He's trying to ruin the government
And overturn the land!

Copper's whistle!
Patrol bell!
Arrest.

Precinct Station.
Iron cell.
Headlines in press:

MAN THREATENS LANDLORD

• • •

TENANT HELD NO BAIL

• • •

JUDGE GIVES NEGRO 90 DAYS IN COUNTY JAIL

CORNER MEETING

Ladder, flag, and amplifier:
what the soap box
used to be.

The speaker catches fire
looking at their faces.

His words
jump down to stand
in listeners' places.

PROJECTION

On the day when the Savoy
leaps clean over to Seventh Avenue
and starts jitterbugging
with the Renaissance,
on that day when Abyssinia Baptist Church
throws her enormous arms around
St. James Presbyterian
and 409 Edgecombe
stoops to kiss 12 West 133rd,
on that day—
Do, Jesus!
Manhattan Island will whirl
like a Dizzy Gillespie transcription
played by Inez and Timme.
On that day, Lord,
Willie Bryant and Marian Anderson
will sing a duet,
Paul Robeson
will team up with Jackie Mabley,
and Father Divine will say in truth,
    Peace!
    It's truly
    wonderful!

EARLY BRIGHT

FLATTED FIFTHS

Little cullud boys with beards
re-bop be-bop mop and stop.

Little cullud boys with fears,
frantic, kick their CC years

into flatted fifths and flatter beers
that at a sudden change become
sparkling Oriental wines
rich and strange
silken bathrobes with gold twines
and Heilbroner, Crawford,
Nat-undreamed-of Lewis combines
in silver thread and diamond notes
on trade-marks inside
Howard coats.

Little culled boys in berets
          oop pop-a-da
horse a fantasy of days
          ool ya koo
and dig all plays.

TOMORROW

Tomorrow may be
a thousand years off:

Two dimes and a nickle only

says this particular
cigarette machine.

Others take a quarter straight.

Some dawns
wait.

MELLOW

Into the laps
of black celebrities
white girls fall
like pale plums from a tree
beyond a high tension wall
wired for killing
which makes it
more thrilling.

LIVE AND LET LIVE

Maybe it ain't right—
but the people of the night
will give even
a snake
a break.

GAUGE

Hemp . . . .
A stick . . . .
A roach . . . .
Straw . . . .

BAR

That whiskey will cook the egg.

Say not so!
Maybe the egg
will cook the whiskey.

You ought to know!

CAFE: 3 A.M.

Detectives from the vice squad
with weary sadistic eyes
spotting fairies.

Degenerates,
some folks say.

But God, Nature,
or somebody
made them that way.

Police lady or Lesbian
over there?

Where?

DRUNKARD

Voice grows thicker
as song grows stronger
as time grows longer until day
trying to forget to remember
the taste of day.

STREET SONG

Jack, if you got to be a rounder
Be a rounder right—
Just don't let mama catch you
Makin' rounds at night.

125TH STREET

Face like a chocolate bar
full of nuts and sweet.
Face like a jack-o'-lantern,
candle inside.
Face like slice of melon,
grin that wide.

DIVE

Lenox Avenue
by daylight
runs to dive in the Park
but faster . . .
faster . . .
after dark.

WARNING: AUGMENTED

Don't let your dog curb you!
Curb your doggie
Like you ought to do,
But don't let that dog curb you!

You may play folks cheap,
Act rough and tough,
But a dog can tell
When you're full of stuff.
Them little old mutts
Look all scriggly and bad,
But they got more sense
Than some people ever had.
Cur dog, fice dog, keary blue—
Just don't let your dog curb you!

UP BEAT

In the gutter
boys who try
might meet girls
on the fly
as out of the gutter
girls who will
may meet boys
copping a thrill
while from the gutter
both can rise:
But it requires
plenty eyes.

JAM SESSION

Letting midnight
out on bail
    pop-a-da
having been
detained in jail
    oop-pop-a-da
for sprinkling salt
on a dreamer's tail
    pop-a-da
While Be-Bop boys
    Implore Mecca
    to achieve
    six discs

with Decca,
Little cullud boys
    with fears,
        frantic,
nudge their draftee years.

        Pop-a-da!

VICE VERSA TO BACH

THEME FOR ENGLISH B

The instructor said,

        Go home and write
        a page tonight.
        And let that page come out of you—
        Then, it will be true.

I wonder if it's that simple?

I am twenty-two, colored, born in Winston-Salem.
I went to school there, then Durham, then here
to this college on the hill above Harlem.
I am the only colored student in my class.
The steps from the hill lead down into Harlem,
through a park, then I cross St. Nicholas,
Eighth Avenue, Seventh, and I come to the Y,
the Harlem Branch Y, where I take the elevator
up to my room, sit down, and write this page:

It's not easy to know what is true for you or me
at twenty-two, my age. But I guess I'm what
I feel and see and hear. Harlem, I hear you:
hear you, hear me—we two—you, me talk on this page.
(I hear New York, too.) Me—who?

Well, I like to eat, sleep, drink, and be in love.
I like to work, read, learn, and understand life.
I like a pipe for a Christmas present,
or records—Bessie, bop, or Bach.

I guess being colored doesn't make me not like
the same things other folks like who are other races.
So will my page be colored that I write?
Being me, it will not be white.
But it will be
a part of you, instructor.
You are white—
yet a part of me, as I am a part of you.
That's American.
Sometimes perhaps you don't want to be a part of me.
Nor do I often want to be a part of you.
But we are, that's true!
As I learn from you,
I guess you learn from me—
although you're older—and white—
and somewhat more free.

This is my page for English B.

COLLEGE FORMAL: RENAISSANCE CASINO

Golden girl
in a golden gown
in a melody night
in Harlem town
lad tall and brown
tall and wise
college boy smart
eyes in eyes
the music wraps
them both around
in mellow magic
of dancing sound
till they're the heart
of the whole big town
gold and brown

LOW TO HIGH

How can you forget me?
But you do!

You said you was gonna take me
Up with you—
Now you've got your Cadillac,
you done forgot that you are black.
How can you forget me
When I'm you?

But you do.

How can you forget me,
fellow, say?
How can you low-rate me
this way?
You treat me like you damn well please,
Ignore me—though I pay your fees.
How can you forget me?

But you do.

BOOGIE: 1 A. M.

Good evening, daddy!
I know you've heard
The boogie-woogie rumble
Of a dream deferred
Trilling the treble
And twining the bass
Into midnight ruffles
Of cat-gut lace.

HIGH TO LOW

God knows
We have our troubles, too—
One trouble is you:
you talk too loud,
cuss too loud,
look too bad,
don't get anywhere,
and sometimes it seems
you don't even care.
The way you send your kids to school

stockings down,
(not Ethical Culture)
the way you shout out loud in church,
(not St. Philips)
and the way you lounge on doorsteps
just as if you were down South,
(not at 409)
the way you clown—
the way, in other words,
you let me down—
me, trying to uphold the race
and you—
well, you can see,
we have our problems,
too, with you.

LADY'S BOOGIE

See that lady
Dressed so fine?
She ain't got boogie-woogie
On her mind—

But if she was to listen
I bet she'd hear,
Way up in the treble
The tingle of a tear.

Be-bach!

DEFERRED

This year, maybe, do you think I can graduate?
I'm already two years late.
Dropped out six months when I was seven,
a year when I was eleven,
then got put back when we come North.
To get through high school at twenty's kind of late—
But maybe this year I can graduate.

Maybe now I can have that white enamel stove
I dreamed about when we first fell in love

eighteen years ago.
But you know,
rooming and everything
then kids,
cold-water flat and all that.
But now my daughter's married
And my boy's most grown—
quit school to work—
and where we're moving
there ain't no stove—
Maybe I can buy that white enamel stove!

Me, I always did want to study French.
It don't make sense—
I'll never go to France,
but night schools teach French.
Now at last I've got a job
where I get off at five,
in time to wash and dress,
so, s'il-vous plait, I'll study French!
Someday,
I'm gonna buy two new suits
at once!

All I want is
one more bottle of gin.

All I want is to see
my furniture paid for.

All I want is a wife who will
work with me and not against me. Say,
baby, could you see your way clear?

Heaven, heaven, is my home!
This world I'll leave behind.
When I set my feet in glory
I'll have a throne for mine!

I want to pass the civil service.

I want a television set.

You know, as old as I am,
I ain't never
owned a decent radio yet?

I'd like to take up Bach.

Montage
of a dream
deferred.

Buddy, have you heard?

REQUEST

Gimme $25.00
and the change.
I'm going
where the morning
and the evening
won't bother me.

SHAME ON YOU

If you're great enough
and clever enough
the government might honor you.
But the people will forget—
Except on holidays.

A movie house in Harlem named after Lincoln,
Nothing at all named after John Brown.

Black people don't remember
any better than white.

If you're not alive and kicking,
shame on you!

WORLD WAR II

What a grand time was the war!
Oh, my, my!
What a grand time was the war!
My, my, my!

In wartime we had fun,
Sorry that old war is done!

What a grand time was the war,
     My, my!

Echo:

          Did
          Somebody
          Die?

DREAM DEFERRED

MYSTERY

When a chile gets to be thirteen
and ain't seen Christ yet,
she needs to set on de moaner's bench
night and day.

Jesus, lover of my soul!

Hail, Mary, mother of God!

Let me to thy bosom fly!

Amen! Hallelujah!

Swing low, sweet chariot,
Coming for to carry me home.

Sunday morning where the rhythm flows,
how old nobody knows—
yet old as mystery,
older than creed,
basic and wondering
and lost as my need.

          Eli, eli!
          Te deum!
          Mahomet!
          Christ!

Father Bishop, Effendi, Mother Horne,
Father Divine, a Rabbi black
as black was born,
a jack-leg preacher, a Ph.D.

The mystery
and the darkness
and the song
and me.

SLIVER OF SERMON

When pimps out of loneliness cry:
   Great God!
Whores in final weariness say:
   Great God!
Mothers who've lost their last sons weep:
   Great God!
   Oh, God!
   My God!

   Great
   God!

TESTIMONIAL

If I just had a piano
if I just had a organ,
if I just had a drum,
how I could praise my Lord!

But I don't need no piano,
   neither organ
   nor drum
for to praise my Lord!

PASSING

On sunny summer Sunday afternoons in Harlem
when the air is one interminable ball game
and grandma cannot get her gospel hymns
from the Saints of God in Christ
on account of the Dodgers on the radio,
on sunny Sunday afternoons
when the kids look all new
and far too clean to stay that way,

and Harlem has its
washed-and-ironed-and-cleaned-best out,
the ones who've crossed the line
to live downtown
miss you,
Harlem of the bitter dream,
since their dream has
come true.

NIGHTMARE BOOGIE

I had a dream
and I could see
a million faces
black as me!
A nightmare dream:
Quicker than light
All them faces
Turned dead white!
Boogie-woogie,
Rolling bass,
Whirling treble
of cat-gut lace.

SUNDAY BY THE COMBINATION

I feel like dancin', baby,
till the sun goes down.

But I wonder where
the sunrise
Monday morning's gonna be?

I feel like dancin'!
Baby, dance with me!

CASUALTY

He was a soldier in the army,
But he doesn't walk like one.

He walks like his soldiering
Days are done.

Son! . . . Son!

NIGHT FUNERAL IN HARLEM

Night funeral
in Harlem:

Where did they get
Them two fine cars?

Insurance man, he did not pay—
His insurance lapsed the other day—
Yet they got a satin box
For his head to lay.

Night funeral
in Harlem:

Who was it sent
That wreath of flowers?

Them flowers came
from that poor boy's friends—
They'll want flowers, too,
When they meet their ends.

Night funeral
in Harlem:

Who preached that
Black boy to his grave?

Old preacher-man
Preached that boy away—
Charged Five Dollars
His girl friend had to pay.

Night funeral
in Harlem:

When it was all over
And the lid shut on his head
and the organ had done played
and the last prayers been said

and six pallbearers
Carried him out for dead
And off down Lenox Avenue
That long black hearse sped,
     The street light
     At his corner
     Shined just like a tear—
That boy that they was mournin'
Was so dear, so dear
To them folks that brought the flowers,
To that girl who paid the preacher-man—
It was all their tears that made
That poor boy's
Funeral grand.

Night funeral
in Harlem.

BLUES AT DAWN

I don't dare start thinking in the morning
I don't dare start thinking in the morning.
     If I thought thoughts in bed,
     Them thoughts would bust my head—
So I don't dare start thinking in the morning.

I don't dare remember in the morning.
Don't dare remember in the morning.
     If I recall the day before,
     I wouldn't get up no more—
So I don't dare remember in the morning.

DIME

     Chile, these steps is hard to climb.
          Grandma, lend me a dime.
     Montage of a dream deferred:
          Grandma acts like
          She ain't heard.
     Chile, Granny ain't got no dime.
          I might've knowed
          It all the time.

ARGUMENT

White is right,
Yellow mellow,
Black, get back!

> Do you believe that, Jack?

Sure do!

> Then you're a dope
> for which there ain't no hope.
> Black is fine!
> And, God knows,
> It's mine!

NEIGHBOR

Down home
he sets on a stoop
and watches the sun go by.
In Harlem
when his work is done
he sets in a bar with a beer.
He looks taller than he is
and younger than he ain't.
He looks darker than he is, too.
And he's smarter than he looks.

> He ain't smart.
> That cat's a fool.

Naw, he ain't neither.
> He's a good man,
> except that he talks too much.
> In fact, he's a great cat.
> But when he drinks,
> he drinks fast.

> Sometimes
> he don't drink.

True
he just
lets his glass
set there.

EVENING SONG

A woman standing in the doorway
Trying to make her where-with-all:
Come here, baby, darlin'!
Don't you hear me call?

If I was anybody's sister,
I'd tell her, Gimme a place to sleep.
But I ain't nobody's sister,
I'm just a poor lost sheep.

Mary, Mary, Mary,
Had a little lamb.
Well, I hope that lamb of Mary's
Don't turn out like I am.

CHORD

Shadow faces
In the shadow night
Before the early dawn
Bops bright.

FACT

There's been an eagle on a nickle,
An eagle on a quarter, too.
But there ain't no eagle
On a dime.

JOE LOUIS

They worshipped Joe.
A school teacher

whose hair was gray
said:

> Joe has sense enough to know
> He is a god.
> So many gods don't know.

"They say" . . . "They say" . . . "They say" . . .
But the gossips had no
"They say"
to latch onto
for Joe.

SUBWAY RUSH HOUR

> Mingled
> breath and smell
> so close
> mingled
> black and white
> so near
> no room for fear.

BROTHERS

> We're related—you and I,
> You from the West Indies,
> I from Kentucky.

> Kinsmen—you and I,
> You from Africa,
> I from the U. S. A.

> Brothers—you and I—

LIKEWISE

The Jews:
> Groceries
> Suits
> Fruit

Watches
Diamond rings
THE DAILY NEWS
Jews sell me things.
Yom Kippur, no!
Shops all over Harlem
close up tight that night.

Some folks blame high prices on the Jews.
(Some folks blame too much on Jews.)
But in Harlem they don't answer back,
Just maybe shrug their shoulders,
"What's the use?"

What's the use
In Harlem?
What's the use?
What's the Harlem
use in Harlem
what's the lick?

Hey!
Baba-re-bop!
Mop.
On a be-bop kick!

Sometimes I think
Jews must have heard
the music of a
dream deferred.

SLIVER

Cheap little rhymes
A cheap little tune
Are sometimes as dangerous
As a sliver of the moon.

A cheap little tune
to cheap little rhymes
Can cut a man's
Throat sometimes.

HOPE

He rose up on his dying bed
and asked for fish.
His wife looked it up in her dream book
and played it.

DREAM BOOGIE: VARIATION

Tinkling trebel,
Rolling bass,
High noon teeth
In a midnight face,
Great long fingers
On great big hands,
Screaming pedals
Where his twelve-shoe lands,
Looks like his eyes
Are teasing pain,
a Few minutes late
For the Freedom Train.

LENOX AVENUE MURAL

HARLEM

What happens to a dream deferred?

Does it dry up
like a raisin in the sun?
Or fester like a sore—
And then run?
Does it stink like rotten meat?
Or crust and sugar over—
like a syrupy sweet?

Maybe it just sags
like a heavy load.

Or does it explode?

GOOD MORNING

Good morning, daddy!
I was born here, he said,
watched Harlem grow
until colored folks spread
from river to river
across the middle of Manhattan
out of Penn Station
dark tenth of a nation,
planes from Puerto Rico,
and holds of boats, chico,
up from Cuba Haiti Jamaica,
in busses marked New York
from Georgia Florida Louisiana
to Harlem Brooklyn the Bronx
but most of all to Harlem
dusky sash across Manhattan
I've seen them come dark
    wondering
    wide-eyed
    dreaming
out of Penn Station—
but the trains are late.
The gates open—
but there're bars
at each gate.

    What happens
    to a dream deferred?

Daddy, ain't you heard?

SAME IN BLUES

I said to my baby,
Baby, take it slow.
I can't, she said, I can't!
I got to go!

    There's a certain
    amount of traveling
    in a dream deferred.

Lulu said to Leonard,
I want a diamond ring.
Leonard said to Lulu,
You won't get a goddamn thing!

> A certain
> amount of nothing
> in a dream deferred.

Daddy, daddy, daddy,
All I want is you.
You can have me, baby—
but my lovin' days is through.

> A certain
> amount of impotence
> in a dream deferred.

Three parties
On my party line—
But that third party,
Lord, ain't mine!

> There's liable
> to be confusion
> in a dream deferred.

From river to river
Uptown and down,
There's liable to be confusion
when a dream gets kicked around.

> You talk like
> they don't kick
> dreams around
> Downtown.

I expect they do—
But I'm talking about
Harlem to you!

LETTER

Dear Mama,
    Time I pay rent and get my food

and laundry I don't have much left
but here is five dollars for you
to show you I still appreciates you.
My girl-friend send her love and say
she hopes to lay eyes on you sometime in life.
Mama, it has been raining cats and dogs up
here. Well, that is all so I will close.

    Your son baby
      Respectable as ever,
        Joe

ISLAND

Between two rivers,
North of the park,
like darker rivers
The streets are dark.

Black and white,
Gold and brown—
Chocolate-custard
Pie of a town.

Dream within a dream
Our dream deferred.

Good morning, daddy!

Ain't you heard?

Other Poems

BALLAD OF MARY'S SON

It was in the Spring.
The Passover had come.
There was fasting in the streets and joy.
But an awful thing
Happened in the Spring—
Men who knew not what they did
Killed Mary's Boy.

He was Mary's Son,
And the Son of God was He—
Sent to bring the whole world joy.
There were some who could not hear,
And some were filled with fear—
So they built a Cross
For Mary's Boy.

To His Twelve Disciples
He gave them of His bread.
He gave them to drink of His wine.
*This is my body
And this is my blood,* He said.
*My Cross for you
Will be a sign.*

He went into the garden
And He knelt there to pray.
He said, *Oh, Lord, Thy will be done!*
The soldiers came
And took my Lord away.
They made a Cross
For Mary's Son.

*This is my body
And this is my blood!*

127

His body and His blood divine!
He died on the Cross
That my soul should not be lost.

His body and His blood
Redeem mine.

ACCEPTANCE

God, in His infinite wisdom
Did not make me very wise—
So when my actions are stupid
They hardly take God by surprise.

PASTORAL

Between the little clouds of heaven
They thought they saw
The Saviour peeping through.
For little tears of heaven
They mistook the gentle dew,
And believed the tiny flowers
That grew upon the plain
To be souvenirs of Jesus,
The Child, come back again.

DEAR LOVELY DEATH

Dear lovely death
That taketh all things under wing—
Never to kill—
Only to change
Into some other thing
This suffering flesh,
To make it either more or less,
But not again the same.
Dear lovely Death,
Change is thy other name.

POET TO BIGOT

I have done so little
For you,
And you have done so little
For me,
That we have good reason
Never to agree.

I, however,
Have such meagre
Power,
Clutching at a
Moment,
While you control
An hour.

But your hour is
A stone.

My moment is
A flower.

TESTAMENT

What shall I leave my son
When I am dead and gone?
    Room in hell to join me
    When he passes on.
What shall I leave my daughter,
The apple of my eye?
    A thousand pounds of salt
    For tears if she should cry.
What shall I leave my wife
Who nagged me to my death?
    I'll leave her more to nag about
    Than she's got breath.

CONSERVATORY STUDENT STRUGGLES WITH HIGHER INSTRUMENTATION

The saxophone
Has a vulgar tone.
I wish it would
Let me alone.

The saxophone
Is ordinary.
More than that,
It's mercenary!

The saxophone's
An instrument
By which I wish
I'd never been
Sent!

ELDERLY POLITICIANS

The old, the cautious, the over-wise—
Wisdom reduced to the personal equation:
Life is a system of half-truths and lies,
Opportunistic, convenient evasion.
Elderly,
Famous,
Very well paid,
They clutch at the egg
Their master's
Goose laid:
$$$$$
$$$$
$$$
$$
$

FREEDOM'S PLOW

When a man starts out with nothing,
When a man starts out with his hands
Empty, but clean,
When a man starts out to build a world,
He starts first with himself
And the faith that is in his heart—
The strength there,
The will there to build.

First in the heart is the dream—
Then the mind starts seeking a way.
His eyes look out on the world,
On the great wooded world,
On the rich soil of the world,
On the rivers of the world.

The eyes see there materials for building,
See the difficulties, too, and the obstacles.
The mind seeks a way to overcome these obstacles.
The hand seeks tools to cut the wood,
To till the soil, and harness the power of the waters.
Then the hand seeks other hands to help,
A community of hands to help—
Thus the dream becomes not one man's dream alone,
But a community dream.
Not my dream alone, but *our* dream.
Not my world alone,
But *your world and my world,*
Belonging to all the hands who build.

A long time ago, but not too long ago,
Ships came from across the sea
Bringing Pilgrims and prayer-makers,
Adventurers and booty seekers,
Free men and indentured servants,
Slave men and slave masters, all new—
To a new world, America!

With billowing sails the galleons came
Bringing men and dreams, women and dreams.

In little bands together,
Heart reaching out to heart,
Hand reaching out to hand,
They began to build our land.
Some were free hands
Seeking a greater freedom,
Some were indentured hands
Hoping to find their freedom,
Some were slave hands
Guarding in their hearts the seed of freedom.
But the word was there always:
    FREEDOM.

Down into the earth went the plow
In the free hands and the slave hands,
In indentured hands and adventurous hands,
Turning the rich soil went the plow in many hands
That planted and harvested the food that fed
And the cotton that clothed America.
Clang against the trees went the ax in many hands
That hewed and shaped the rooftops of America.
Splash into the rivers and the seas went the boat-hulls
That moved and transported America.
Crack went the whips that drove the horses
Across the plains of America.
Free hands and slave hands,
Indentured hands, adventurous hands,
White hands and black hands
Held the plow handles,
Ax handles, hammer handles,
Launched the boats and whipped the horses
That fed and housed and moved America.
Thus together through labor,
All these hands made America.

Labor! Out of labor came the villages
And the towns that grew to cities.
Labor! Out of labor came the rowboats
And the sailboats and the steamboats,
Came the wagons and the coaches,
Covered wagons, stage coaches,
Out of labor came the factories,
Came the foundries, came the railroads.

Came the marts and markets, shops and stores,
Came the mighty products moulded, manufactured,
Sold in shops, piled in warehouses,
Shipped the wide world over:
Out of labor—white hands and black hands—
Came the dream, the strength, the will,
And the way to build America.
Now it is Me here, and You there.
Now it's Manhattan, Chicago,
Seattle, New Orleans,
Boston and El Paso—
Now it is the U. S. A.

A long time ago, but not too long ago, a man said:
    ALL MEN ARE CREATED EQUAL . . .
    ENDOWED BY THEIR CREATOR
    WITH CERTAIN UNALIENABLE RIGHTS . . .
    AMONG THESE LIFE, LIBERTY
    AND THE PURSUIT OF HAPPINESS.
His name was Jefferson. There were slaves then,
But in their hearts the slaves believed him, too,
And silently took for granted
That what he said was also meant for them.
It was a long time ago,
But not so long ago at that, Lincoln said:
    NO MAN IS GOOD ENOUGH
    TO GOVERN ANOTHER MAN
    WITHOUT THAT OTHER'S CONSENT.
There were slaves then, too,
But in their hearts the slaves knew
What he said must be meant for every human being—
Else it had no meaning for anyone.
Then a man said:
    BETTER TO DIE FREE
    THAN TO LIVE SLAVES.
He was a colored man who had been a slave
But had run away to freedom.
And the slaves knew
What Frederick Douglass said was true.

With John Brown at Harper's Ferry, Negroes died.
John Brown was hung.
Before the Civil War, days were dark,

And nobody knew for sure
When freedom would triumph.
"Or if it would," thought some.
But others knew it had to triumph.
In those dark days of slavery,
Guarding in their hearts the seed of freedom,
The slaves made up a song:
   Keep Your Hand On The Plow! Hold On!
That song meant just what it said: *Hold On!*
Freedom will come!
   Keep Your Hand On The Plow! Hold On!
Out of war it came, bloody and terrible!
But it came!
Some there were, as always,
Who doubted that the war would end right,
That the slaves would be free,
Or that the union would stand,
But now we know how it all came out.
Out of the darkest days for a people and a nation,
We know now how it came out.
There was light when the battle clouds rolled away.
There was a great wooded land,
And men united as a nation.

America is a dream.
The poet says it was promises.
The people say it *is* promises—that will come true.
The people do not always say things out loud,
Nor write them down on paper.
The people often hold
Great thoughts in their deepest hearts
And sometimes only blunderingly express them,
Haltingly and stumblingly say them,
And faultily put them into practice.
The people do not always understand each other.
But there is, somewhere there,
Always the *trying* to understand,
And the *trying* to say,
"You are a man. Together we are building our land."

America!
Land created in common,
Dream nourished in common,

Keep your hand on the plow! Hold on!
If the house is not yet finished,
Don't be discouraged, builder!
If the fight is not yet won,
Don't be weary, soldier!
The plan and the pattern is here,
Woven from the beginning
Into the warp and woof of America:
    ALL MEN ARE CREATED EQUAL.
    NO MAN IS GOOD ENOUGH
    TO GOVERN ANOTHER MAN
    WITHOUT THAT OTHER'S CONSENT.
    BETTER DIE FREE,
    THAN TO LIVE SLAVES.
Who said those things? Americans!
Who owns those words? America!
Who is America? You, me!
We are America!
To the enemy who would conquer us from without,
We say, NO!
To the enemy who would divide
And conquer us from within,
We say, NO!
    FREEDOM!
      BROTHERHOOD!
        DEMOCRACY!
To all the enemies of these great words:
We say, NO!

A long time ago,
An enslaved people heading toward freedom
Made up a song:
    Keep Your Hand On The Plow! Hold On!
The plow plowed a new furrow
Across the field of history.
Into that furrow the freedom seed was dropped.
From that seed a tree grew, is growing, will ever grow.
That tree is for everybody,
For all America, for all the world.
May its branches spread and its shelter grow
Until all races and all peoples know its shade.
    KEEP YOUR HAND ON THE PLOW! HOLD ON!

Translations

EPIGRAM

by *Armand Lanusse*
(Louisiana Creole, U. S. A.)

"Do you not wish to renounce the Devil?"
Asked a good priest of a woman of evil
Who had so many sins that every year
They cost her endless remorse and fear.
"I wish to renounce him forever," she said,
"But that I may lose every urge to be bad,
Before pure grace takes me in hand,
Shouldn't I show my daughter how to get a man?"

VERSE WRITTEN IN THE ALBUM OF MADEMOISELLE

by *Pierre Dalcour*
(Louisiana Creole, U. S. A.)

The evening star that in the vaulted skies
Sweetly sparkles, gently flashes,
To me is less lovely than a glance of your eyes
        Beneath their brown lashes.

FLUTE PLAYERS

by Jean Joseph Rabéarivelo
(Madagascar)

Your flute,
  you carved from the shin bone of a strong bull,
  and you polished it on barren hills beaten by sun.
His flute,
  he carved from a reed trembling in the breeze
  and cut its little holes beside a flowing brook
  drunk on dreams of moonlight.
Together
  you made music in the late afternoon
  as if to hold back the round boat
  sinking on the shores of the sky,
  as if to save it from its fate:
  but are your plaintive incantations
  heard by the gods of the wind,
  and of the earth, and of the forest,
  and of the sand?
Your flute
  throws out a beat like the march of an angry bull
  toward the desert
  but who comes back running,
  burned by thirst and hunger
  and defeated by weariness
  at the foot of a shadeless tree
  with neither leaves nor fruit.
His flute
  is like a reed that bends
  beneath the weight of a bird in flight—
  but not a bird captured by a child
  whose feathers are stroked,
  but a bird lost from other birds
  who looks at his own shadow for company
  in the flowing water.
Your flute
  and his—
  regret their beginnings
  in the sorrows of your songs.

GUINEA

by *Jacques Roumain*
(*Haiti*)

It's the long road to Guinea
Death takes you down
Here are the boughs, the trees, the forest
Listen to the sound of the wind in its long hair
    of eternal night

It's the long road to Guinea
Where your fathers await you without impatience
Along the way, they talk
They wait
This is the hour when the streams rattle
    like beads of bone

It's the long road to Guinea
No bright welcome will be made for you
In the dark land of dark men:
Under a smoky sky pierced by the cry of birds
Around the eye of the river
    the eyelashes of the trees open on decaying light

There, there awaits you beside the water a quiet village,
And the hut of your fathers, and the hard ancestral stone
    where your head will rest at last.

SHE LEFT HERSELF ONE EVENING

by *Léon Damas*
(*French Guiana*)

SHE LEFT HERSELF ONE EVENING
to prowl around
my misery
like a mad dog
like a naked dog

like a doggish dog
quite mad
quite naked
quite doggishly
dog

thus simply
the drama began

I

by 'Francisca'
(Mexico)

I want to play
boys and girls
I want to play
come here
we're going to jump
run and climb
over walls
and sing
do a lot of
things
make a lot of noise

Start the rocks
flying
hear them bounce
kick
hard
on the sidewalks

Destroy
all the flowers
break the pots
Frighten the
hens
so that they will sing
with us

Let the dogs
howl

let them bark
let the birds
sing
let the cats
jump
and let them all
laugh at us

Let's play
boys and girls until
our hot souls
are tired
and when we
can't lift
our arms any longer
and our legs
are worn out
we'll yell
at the moon:
> Look moon
this is playing!

OPINIONS OF THE NEW STUDENT

by Regino Pedroso
(Cuban-Chinese)

Until yesterday I was polite and peaceful . . .

Last year I drank the yellow-leaved Yunnan tea
in fine cups of porcelain,
and deciphered the sacred texts of Lao-Tze,
of Mang-tze,
and of the wisest of the wise, Kung-fu-Tseu.

Deep in the shade of the pagodas
my life ran on, harmonious and serene,
white as the lilies in the pools,
gentle as a poem by Li Tai Po,
watching the loop-the-loop
of white storks at eve
against the screen of an alabaster sky.

But I have been awakened by the echo of foreign voices
booming from the mouths of mechanical instruments:
dragons setting ablaze with howls of grapeshot—
to the horror of my brothers
murdered in the night—
my bamboo houses
and my ancient pagodas.
And now, from the airplane of my new conscience,
I watch over the green plains of Europe,
and her magnificent cities
blossoming in stone and iron.

Before my eyes the western world is naked.
With the long pipe of the centuries
in my pale hands,
I am no longer enticed by the opium of barbarism;
and today I march toward the progress of the people,
training my fingers on the trigger of a Mauser.

Over the flame of today
impatiently I cook the drug of tomorrow;
I would breathe deep of the new era
in my great pipe of jade.
A strange restlessness has taken all sleep from my
      slanting eyes.
To gain a deeper view of the horizon
I leap up on the old wall of the past . . .

Until yesterday I was polite and peaceful . . .

DEAD SOLDIER

by Nicolás Guillén
(Cuba)

What bullet killed him?
      Nobody knows.
Where was he born?
      In Jovellanos, they say.

Why did they pick him up?
      He was lying dead in the road

And some other soldiers saw him.
What bullet killed him?

His sweetheart comes and kisses him.
His mother comes and cries.
When the Captain gets there
All he says is:
> Bury him!

> Rat-ta-tat-tat!
THERE GOES THE DEAD SOLDIER.

> Rat-ta-tat-tat!
THEY PICKED HIM UP IN THE ROAD.
> Rat-ta-tat-tat!
A SOLDIER AIN'T NOTHING.
> Rat-ta-tat-tat!
THERE'RE PLENTY OF SOLDIERS.

CHILDREN'S POETRY

CHILDREN AND POETRY

Children are not nearly so resistant to poetry as are grown-ups. In fact, small youngsters are not resistant at all. But in reading my poems to children from kindergarten to junior high school age, I sometimes think they might want to know *why* people write poetry. So I explain to them:

> If you put
> Your thoughts in rhyme
> They stay in folks' heads
> A longer time.

Since most people want others to remember what they say, poetry helps people to remember.

For instance, I say, "Does your mother ever send you to the store and you forget what she sent you after? Or you bring back the wrong thing? That often happened to me when I was a boy. But if my mother had told me in verse what she wanted, for example:

> Langston, go
> To the store, please,
> And bring me back
> A can of peas.

"I wouldn't have brought back a can of corn. *Please* and *peas* rhyme, which makes it easy to remember. Or if my mother had said:

> Sonny, kindly
> Do me a favor
> And go get a bottle
> Of vanilla flavor.

"Then I am sure I would not have gotten a bottle of vinegar. The word *flavor*, not simply *bottle*, would have stuck in my head because of its sound tag with *favor*. That is one reason why:

> To make words sing
> Is a wonderful thing—

145

> Because in a song
> Words last so long.

"Of course," I say, "there are other very good reasons for making rhymes or writing poetry. One is to share a beautiful or moving scene or experience that you have known. When I first saw the new high-arching bridges in San Francisco, one spanning the Golden Gate and the other leaping across the city's harbor, I made up a poem called, TRIP:

> I went to San Francisco.
> I saw the bridges high
> Spun across the water
> Like cobwebs in the sky.

"And when I saw the city all sparkling with lights at night—also remembering other cities like New York, Cincinnati, Chicago, Dallas, with tall cliff-like buildings—this is the song I wrote:

> In the morning the city
> Spreads its wings
> Making a song
> Of stone that sings.
>
> In the evening the city
> Goes to bed
> Hanging lights
> About its head.

"When the sun is hidden behind a sky of grey, soft and fluffy and dark, it seems as though the heavens had sort of wrapped up for bad weather, so it goes into rhyme like this:

> The clouds weave a shawl
> Of downy plaid
> For the sky to put on
> When the weather's bad.

"But here is a poem of much brighter cloth. All of us have seen gypsy women in gay, colorful clothes, wide skirts swinging as they stride. Maybe some of us have lived near a vacant lot where a gypsy family has stopped for a day or two to cook and wash. To see their vari-colored garments hanging on a line from tree to tree is a wonderful sight. I once tried to capture something of the gypsies in a poem:

Gypsies are picture-book people
Hanging picture-book clothes on a line.
The gypsies fill the vacant lots
With colors gay as wine.

The gypsies' skins are olive-dark,
The gypsies' eyes black fire.
The gypsies wear bright headcloths dyed
By some elfin dyer.

The gypsies wear gay glassy beads
Strung on silver threads
And walk as though forever
They've had suns about their heads.

"But poems need not always be about what one sees or thinks or feels oneself. During the war I was deeply moved by the plight of many poor people in Europe mistreated and enslaved by the Nazis suffering bombardments and hunger and cold. Some were fortunate enough to escape and get to the United States. There must have been great joy in their hearts when they saw our Statue of Liberty. And when those who are permitted to become citizens of our country take the Oath of Allegiance, they must feel a great emotion such as I have tried to capture in my poem, REFUGEE IN AMERICA:

There are words like *Freedom*
Sweet and wonderful to say.
On my heart-strings freedom sings
All day everyday.

There are words like *Liberty*
That almost make me cry.
If you had known what I knew
You would know why.

"To help us all remember what America is, and how its future belongs to all of us, recently I added two new lines to an old poem of mine—the last two lines to help us remember to walk together:

We have tomorrow
Bright before us
Like a flame.

Yesterday
A night-gone thing,

A sun-down name.
And dawn-today
Broad arch above
The road we came.

We march!
Americans together,
We march!

18 Poems for Children

THERE'S ALWAYS WEATHER

There's always weather, weather,
Whether we like it or not.
Some days are nice and sunny,
Sunny and bright and hot.

There's always weather, weather,
Whether we like it or don't.
Sometimes so cold and cloudy!
Will it soon snow, or won't?

If days were always just the same,
Out-of-doors would be so tame—
Never a wild and windy day,
Never a stormy sky of gray.

I'm glad there's weather, weather,
Dark days, then days full of sun.
Summer and fall and winter—
Weather is so much fun!

NEW FLOWERS

So many little flowers
Drop their tiny heads—
But newer buds come to bloom
In their place instead.

I miss the little flowers
That have gone away,
But the newly budding blossoms
Are equally gay.

YEAR ROUND

Summertime
Is warm and bright,
With light-bugs
At night.

Autumn time
Is not so sunny,
But Halloween
Is funny.

Winter
Changes most of all,
Bright, then gray,
Then snowflakes fall.

But Spring
I like the very best
When birds come back
To nest.

Also in the
Springtime rain
Flowers start
To bloom again.

COUNTRY

My mother said,
A house we'll buy
In the country where the sky
Is not hidden by tall buildings.

I said,
We'll have a hill
For coasting in the wintertime
Or climbing in the summertime—
        I love to coast!
        I love to climb!

GRANDPA'S STORIES

The pictures on the television
Do not make me dream as well
As the stories without pictures
Grandpa knows how to tell.

Even if he does not know
What makes a Spaceman go,
Grandpa says back in his time
Hamburgers only cost a dime,
Ice cream cones a nickle,
And a penny for a pickle.

PIGGY-BACK

My daddy rides me piggy-back.
My mama rides me, too.
But grandma says her poor old back
Has had enough to do.

SHEARING TIME

It must be nice to be a sheep
With nothing to do but graze and sleep.
But when it's time the wool to shear,
That poor old sheep bleats, "Oh, dear!"

BRAND NEW CLOTHES

My mama told me,
Kindly, please,
Do not get down
On your knees
With your brand new
Clothes on.

I said, Mom,
I'm already down.
Can't I stay
On the ground
With my brand new
Clothes on?

My mother said,
No, I say!
So my mother had her way—
That's why I'm so clean today
With my brand new
Clothes on.

PROBLEMS

2 and 2 are 4.
4 and 4 are 8.

But what would happen
If the last 4 was late?

And how would it be
If one 2 was me?

Or if the first 4 was you
Divided by 2?

NOT OFTEN

I seldom see
A kangaroo
Except in a zoo.

At a whale
I've never had a look
Except in a book.

Another thing
I never saw
Is my great-

Great-great-grandpa—
Who must've been
A family fixture,
But there's no
Picture.

GROCERY STORE

Jimmy, go
To the store, please,
And bring me back
A can of peas.

Also, get
A sack of flour,
And kindly do not
Stay an hour.

POOR ROVER

Rover was in clover
With a bone
On the front lawn—
But Rover's fun was over
When his bone
Was gone.
Poor Rover!

THE BLUES

When the shoe strings break
On *both* your shoes
And you're in a hurry—
That's the blues.

When you go to buy a candy bar
And you've lost the dime you had—

Slipped through a hole in your pocket somewhere—
That's the blues, too, *and bad!*

SILLY ANIMALS

The dog ran down the street
The cat ran up the drain
The mouse looked out and said,
 There they go again!

OLD DOG QUEENIE

 Old Dog Queenie
 Was such a meanie,
 She spent her life
 Barking at the scenery.

LITTLE SONG

Carmencita loves Patrick.
Patrick loves Si Lan Chen.
Xenophon loves Mary Jane.
Hildegarde loves Ben.

Lucienne loves Eric.
Giovanni loves Emma Lee.
Natasha loves Miguelito—
And Miguelito loves me.

Ring around the Maypole!
Ring around we go—
Weaving our bright ribbons
Into a rainbow!

FRIENDLY IN A FRIENDLY WAY

I nodded at the sun
And the sun said, *Howdy do!*
I nodded at the tree
And the tree said, *Howdy, too!*

I shook hands with the bush.
The bush shook hands with me.
I said to the flower,
Flower, how do you be?

I spoke to the man.
The strange man touched his hat.
I smiled at the woman—
The world is smiling yet.

Oh, it's a holiday
When everybody feels that way!
What way?—*Friendly*
In a friendly way.

SHEPHERD'S SONG AT CHRISTMAS

Look there at the star!
I, among the least,
Will arise and take
A journey to the East.
But what shall I bring
As a present for the King?
What shall I bring to the Manger?

I will bring a song,
A song that I will sing,
A song for the King
In the Manger.

Watch out for my flocks,
Do not let them stray.
I am going on a journey

Far, far away.
But what shall I bring
As a present for the Child?
What shall I bring to the Manger?

I will bring a lamb,
Gentle, meek, and mild,
A lamb for the Child
In the Manger.

I'm just a shepherd boy,
Very poor I am—
But I know there is
A King in Bethlehem.
What shall I bring
As a present just for Him?
What shall I bring to the Manger?

I will bring my heart
And give my heart to Him.
I will bring my heart
To the Manger.

SONG LYRICS

SONGS CALLED THE BLUES

"The Blues! Songs folks make up when their heart hurts, that's what the Blues are. Sad funny songs—too sad to be funny and too funny to be sad." Thus one of the characters in the Negro play, DON'T YOU WANT TO BE FREE?, at the Harlem Suitcase Theatre, defines the Blues.

Then he goes on to say that, "Colored folks made up the Blues. Now, everybody sings 'em. We made 'em out of being poor and lonely, and homes busted up, and desperate, and broke." For the Blues are genuine folk-songs born out of heartache. They are songs of the black South, particularly the city South. Songs of the poor streets and back alleys of Memphis and Birmingham, Atlanta and Galveston, out of black and beaten, but unbeatable throats, from the strings of pawn-shop guitars, and the chords of pianos with no ivory on the keys.

The Blues and the Spirituals are two great Negro gifts to American music. The Spirituals are group songs, but the Blues are songs you sing alone. The Spirituals are religious songs, born in camp meetings and remote plantation districts. But the Blues are *city* songs rising from the crowded streets of big towns, or beating against the lonely walls of hall bed-rooms where you can't sleep at night. The Spirituals are escape songs, looking toward heaven, tomorrow, and God. But the Blues are *today* songs, here and now, broke and broken-hearted, when you're troubled in mind and don't know what to do, and nobody cares.

There are many kinds of Blues. There are the family Blues, when a man and woman have quarreled, and the quarrel can't be patched up. There's the loveless Blues, when you haven't even got anybody to quarrel with. And there's the left-lonesome Blues, when the one you care for's gone away. Then there's also the broke-and-hungry Blues, a stranger in a strange town. And the desperate going-to-the-river Blues that says:

> I'm goin' down to de river
> And take ma rockin' chair—
> If the Blues overcome me,
> I'm gonna rock on away from here!

But it's not always as bad as that, because there's another verse
that declares:

> Goin' down to de railroad,
> Lay my head on de track,
> I'm goin' to de railroad,
> Lay my head on de track—
> But if I see de train a-comin'
> I'm gonna jerk it back!

For sad as Blues may be, there's almost always something humorous
about them—even if it's the kind of humor that laughs to keep from
crying. You know

> I went to de gypsy's
> To get ma fortune told.
> Went to de gypsy's
> To get ma fortune told,
> But the gypsy said, dog-gone your
> Un-hard-lucky soul!

In America, during the last quarter of a century, there have been
many great singers of the Blues, but the finest of all were the three
famous Smiths—no relation, one to another—Mamie Smith, Clara
Smith, and the astounding Bessie Smith. Clara and Bessie are both
dead now, and Mamie no longer sings, but thousands of Blues
collectors in the United States and abroad prize their records. Today
a girl named Georgia White carries on the old tradition of the
Blues in the folk manner. And Midge Williams, of the Louis Arm-
strong band, sings them in a more polished, but effective way. Of
the men, Lonnie Johnson is perhaps the finest living male singer of
the Blues, although there's a portly fellow named Jimmy Rushing
in Count Basie's orchestra who is a runner-up. And Lead Belly also
is to be considered.

The most famous Blues, of course, is the ST. LOUIS BLUES, that Mr.
W. C. Handy wrote down one night on the corner of a bar on a
levee street in St. Louis, and which has since gone all over the
world. The ST. LOUIS BLUES is sung more than any other song on
the air, is known in Shanghai and Buenos Aires, Paris and Berlin—
in fact, is heard so often in Europe that a great many Europeans
believe it to be the American National Anthem.

Less popular, but equally beautiful are the Blues, TROUBLE IN
MIND, MEMPHIS BLUES, YELLOW DOG BLUES, and the never to be sur-

passed GULF COAST BLUES which begins with one of the loneliest lines in all the realm of song:

> The mail man passed but
> He didn't leave no news. . . . . .

Blues are still being made. One of the newest authentic Blues to come up out of the South, by way of the colored boys in the government work camps, is the DUPREE BLUES, that sad story of a man who wanted to give his girl a diamond ring, but had none to give her, so he took his gun and went to the jewelry store where, instead of getting the diamond ring, he got the jewelry man, jail, and the noose.

The real Negro Blues are as fine as any folk music we have, and I'm hoping the day will come when Marion Anderson and Paul Robeson, famous concert singers, will include a group of Blues on their programs as well as the Spirituals which they now sing so effectively.

A young dancer in New York, Felicia Sorel, is already using the Blues as a background for the creation of new dance forms. I see no reason why great dances could not be born of the Blues, great American dances containing all the laughter and pain, hunger and heartache, search and reality of the contemporary scene—for the Blues have something that goes beyond race or sectional limits, that appeals to the ear and heart of people everywhere—otherwise, how could it be that in a Tokyo restaurant one night I heard a Louis Armstrong record of the ST. LOUIS BLUES played over and over for a crowd of Japanese diners there? You don't have to understand the words to know the meaning of the Blues, or to feel their sadness, or to hope their hopes:

> Troubled in mind, I'm blue,
> But I won't be blue always:
> The sun's gonna shine
> In my back door someday.

And for that sunshine, everybody waits.

L. H., 1940.

RED SUN BLUES

> Little birds, little birds,
> Ain't you gonna sing today?

Little birds, little birds,
Ain't you gonna sing this morn?
I feel so lonesome,
My baby's gone away.

Red sun, red sun,
Ain't you gonna shine today?
Red sun, red sun,
Ain't you gonna shine today?
I can't sleep, can't eat,
My baby's gone away.

Gray skies, gray skies,
Won't you let the sun shine through?
Gray skies, gray skies,
Won't you let that sun shine through.
My baby's left me,
I don't know what to do.

It's a mighty blues morning
When your sugar leaves your bed.
If you got no sugar
You might as well be dead.

*"Red Sun Blues," by Langston Hughes and Albert Hague, © Herb Reis
Music Corporation, reprinted by Permission of Reis Publications, Inc.*

FIVE O'CLOCK BLUES

I'm gonna take the Five O'Clock
And run down to K. C.
Gonna take the Five O'Clock,
Run down to K. C.
I want to find out what's the reason
Why my gal left me.

They tell that the Five O'Clock
Leaves 'bout half-past five.
They tell that the Five O'Clock
Leaves 'bout half-past five.
I'm gonna catch that Five O'Clock
If I'm still alive.

I'll pass the pawnshop,
See what that man has got
If he's got an Owl Head pistol,

I'll buy it on the spot.
I really love my gal,
But sometimes that gal ain't nice.
I don't want to kill her—
Just sting her once or twice.

I'm gonna catch that Five O'Clock
And run down to K. C.
Yes, sir, catch the Five O'Clock,
Run down to K. C.
Because my Kansas City baby
Has put a charm on me.

"Five O'Clock Blues," © *Langston Hughes and David Martin.*

LONELY HOUSE

At night when everything is quiet
This old house seems to breathe a sigh.
Sometimes I hear a neighbor snoring,
Sometimes I hear a baby cry,
Sometimes I hear a staircase creaking,
Sometimes a distant telephone.
Then the quiet settles down again,
The house and I are all alone.
Lonely house! Lonely me!
Funny with so many neighbors
How lonely it can be.
Oh, lonely street! Lonely town!
Funny you can be so lonely
With all these folks around.
I guess there must be something
I don't comprehend—
Sparrows have companions,
Even stray dogs find a friend.
The night for me is not romantic.
Unhook the stars and take them down.
I'm lonely in this lonely house
In this lonely town.

REQUIEM

Now love and death
Have linked their arms together
And gone away into another bourne,
Beyond the far-off sky,
Beyond forever
They have gone
And left us here to mourn.

The summer's bright
With warm and golden weather,
And all the children in the streets
Laugh as they run,
But love and death
Have gone away together
To find their morning in the sun.

I DREAM A WORLD

I dream a world where man
No other man will scorn,
Where love will bless the earth
And peace its paths adorn.
I dream a world where all
Will know sweet freedom's way,
Where greed no longer saps the soul
Nor avarice blights our day.
A world I dream where black or white,
Whatever race you be,
Will *share* the bounties of the earth
And every man is free,
Where wretchedness will hang its head,
And joy, like a pearl,
Attend the needs of all mankind.
Of such I dream—
Our world!

NOVELS
AND
HUMOR

Not Without Laughter

GUITAR

THROW yo' arms around me, baby,
Like de circle round de sun!
Baby, throw you' arms around me
Like de circle round de sun,
An' tell you' pretty papa
How you want yo' lovin' done!

Jimboy was home. All the neighborhood could hear his rich low baritone voice giving birth to the blues. On Saturday night he and Annjee went to bed early. On Sunday night Aunt Hager said: "Put that guitar right up, less'n it's hymns you plans on playin'. An' I don't want too much o' them, 'larmin' de white neighbors.

But this was Monday, and the sun had scarcely fallen below the horizon before the music had begun to float down the alley, over back fences and into kitchen-windows where nice white ladies sedately washed their supper dishes.

Did you ever see peaches
Growin' on a watermelon vine?
Says did you ever see peaches
On a watermelon vine?
Did you ever see a woman
That I couldn't get for mine?

Long, lazy length resting on the kitchen-door-sill, back against the jamb, feet in the yard, fingers picking his sweet guitar, left hand holding against its finger-board the back of an old pocket-knife, sliding the knife upward, downward, getting thus weird croons and sighs from the vibrating strings:

O, I left ma mother
An' I cert'ly can leave you.
Indeed I left ma mother
An' I cert'ly can leave you,

167

> For I'd leave any woman
> That mistreats me like you do.

Jimboy, remembering brown-skin mamas in Natchez, Shreveport, Dallas; remembering Creole women in Baton Rouge, Louisana:

> O, yo' windin' an' you' grindin'
> Don't have no effect on me,
> Babe, yo' windin' an' yo' grindin'
> Don't have no 'fect on me,
> 'Cause I can wind an' grind
> Like a monkey round a coconut-tree!

Then Harriett, standing under the ripening apple tree, in the back yard, chiming in:

> Now I see that you don't want me,
> So it's fare thee, fare thee well!
> Lawd, I see that you don't want me,
> So it's fare—thee—well!
> I can still get plenty lovin',
> An' you can go to—Kansas City!

"O, play it, sweet daddy Jimboy!" She began to dance.

Then Hager, from her seat on the edge of the platform covering the well, broke out: "Here, madam! Stop that prancin'! Bad enough to have all this singin' without turnin' de yard into a show-house." But Harriett kept on, her hands picking imaginary cherries out of the stars, her hips speaking an earthly language quite their own.

"You got it, kid," said Jimboy, stopping suddenly, then fingering his instrument for another tune. "You do it like the stage women does. You'd be takin' Ada Walker's place if you keep on."

"Wha! Wha! . . . You chillen sho can sing!" Tom Johnson shouted his compliments from across the yard. And Sarah, beside him on the bench behind their shack, added: "Minds me o' de ole plantation times, honey! It sho do!"

"Unhuh! Bound straight fo' de devil, that's what they is," Hager returned calmly from her place beside the pump. "You an' Harriett both—singin' an' dancin' this stuff befo' these chillens here." She pointed to Sandy and Willie-Mae, who sat on the ground with their backs against the chicken-box. "It's a shame!"

"I likes it," said Willie-Mae.

"Me too," the little boy agreed.

"Naturally you would—none o' you-all's converted yet," countered the old woman to the children as she settled back against the pump to listen to some more.

The music rose hoarse and wild:

> I wonder where ma easy rider's gone?
> He done left me, put ma new gold watch in pawn.

It was Harriett's voice in plaintive moan to the night sky. Jimboy had taught her that song, but a slight, clay-colored brown boy who had hopped bells at the Clinton Hotel for a couple of months, on his way from Houston to Omaha, discovered its meaning to her. Puppy-love, maybe, but it had hurt when he went away, saying nothing. And the guitar in Jimboy's hands echoed that old pain with an even greater throb than the original ache itself possessed.

Approaching footsteps came from the front yard.

"Lord, I can hear you-all two blocks away!" said Annjee, coming around the house, home from work, with a bundle of food under her left arm. "Hello! How are you, daddy? Hello, ma! Gimme a kiss Sandy.... Lord, I'm hot and tired and most played out. This late just getting from work! ... Here, Jimboy, come on in and eat some of these nice things the white folks had for supper." She stepped across her husband's outstretched legs into the kitchen. "I brought a mighty good piece of cold ham for you, hon', from Mis' Rice's."

"All right, sure, I'll be there in a minute," the man said, but he went on playing *Easy Rider,* and Harriett went on singing, while the food was forgotten on the table until long after Annjee had come outdoors again and sat down in the cool, tired of waiting for Jimboy to come in to her.

Off and on for nine years, ever since he had married Annjee, Jimboy and Harriett had been singing together in the evenings. When they started, Harriett was a little girl with braided hair, and each time that her roving brother-in-law stopped in Stanton, he would amuse himself by teaching her the old Southern songs, the popular rag-time ditties, and the hundreds of varying verses of the blues that he would pick up in the big dirty cities of the South. The child, with her strong sweet voice (colored folks called it alto) and her racial sense of rhythm, soon learned to sing the songs as well as Jimboy. He taught her the *parse me la,* too, and a few other movements peculiar to Southern Negro dancing, and sometimes together they went through the buck and wing and a few taps. It was all great fun, and innocent fun except when one stopped to think, as white folks did, that some of the blues lines had, not only double, but triple meanings, and some of the dance steps required very definite movements of the hips. But neither Harriett nor Jimboy soiled their minds by thinking. It was music, good exercise—and they loved it.

"Do you know this one, Annjee?" asked Jimboy, calling his wife's name out of sudden politeness because he had forgotten to eat her food, had hardly looked at her, in fact, since she came home. Now he glanced towards her in the darkness where she sat plump on a kitchen-chair in the yard, apart from the others, with her back to the growing corn in the garden. Softly he ran his fingers, light as a breeze, over his guitar strings, imitating the wind rustling through the long leaves of the corn. A rectangle of light from the kitchen-door fell into the yard striking sidewise across the healthy orange-yellow of his skin above the unbuttoned neck of his blue laborer's shirt.

"Come on, sing it with us, Annjee," he said.

"I don't know it," Annjee replied, with a lump in her throat, and her eyes on the silhouette of his long, muscular, animal-hard body. She loved Jimboy too much, that's what was the matter with her! She knew there was nothing between him and her young sister except the love of music, yet he might have dropped the guitar and left Harriett in the yard for a little while to come eat the nice cold slice of ham she had brought him. She hadn't seen him all day long. When she went to work this morning, he was still in bed—and now the blues claimed him.

In the starry blackness the singing notes of the guitar became a plaintive hum, like a breeze in a grove of palmettos; became a low moan, like the wind in a forest of live-oaks strung with long strands of hanging moss. The voice of Annjee's golden, handsome husband on the door-step rang high and far away, lonely-like, crying with only the guitar, not his wife, to understand; crying grotesquely, crying absurdly in the summer night:

> I got a mule to ride.
> I got a mule to ride.
> Down in the South somewhere
> I got a mule to ride.

Then asking the question as an anxious, left-lonesome girl-sweetheart would ask it:

> You say you goin' North.
> You say you goin' North.
> How 'bout you' . . . lovin' gal?
> You say you goin' North.

Then sighing in rhythmical despair:

> O, don't you leave me here.
> Babe, don't you leave me here.
> Dog-gone yo' comin' back!
> Said don't you leave me here.

On and on the song complained, man-verses and woman-verses, to the evening air in stanzas that Jimboy had heard in the pine-woods of Arkansas from the lumber-camp workers; in other stanzas that were desperate and dirty like the weary roads where they were sung; and in still others that the singer created spontaneously in his own mouth then and there:

> O, I done made ma bed,
> Says I done made ma bed.
> Down in some lonesome grave
> I done made ma bed.

It closed with a sad eerie twang.

"That's right decent," said Hager. "Now I wish you-all'd play some o' ma pieces like *When de Saints Come Marchin' In* or *This World Is Not Ma Home*—something Christian from de church."

"Aw, mama, it's not Sunday yet," said Harriett.

"Sing *Casey Jones,*" called old man Tom Johnson. "That's ma song."

So the ballad of the immortal engineer with another mama in the Promised Land rang out promptly in the starry darkness, while everybody joined in the choruses.

"Aw, pick it, boy," yelled the old man. "Can't nobody play like you."

And Jimboy remembered when he was a lad in Memphis that W. C. Handy had said: "You ought to make your living out of that, son." But he hadn't followed it up—too many things to see, too many places to go, too many other jobs.

"What song do you like, Annjee?" he asked, remembering her presence again.

"O, I don't care. Any ones you like. All of 'em are pretty." She was pleased and petulant and a little startled that he had asked her.

"All right, then," he said. "Listen to me:"

> Here I is in de mean ole jail.
> Ain't got nobody to go ma bail.
> Lonesome an' sad an' chain gang bound—
> Ever' friend I had's done turned me down.

"That's sho it!" shouted Tom Johnson in great sympathy. "Now, when I was in de Turner County Jail . . ."

"Shut up yo' mouth!" squelched Sarah, jabbing her husband in the ribs.

The songs went on, blues, shouts, jingles, old hits: *Bon Bon Buddy, The Chocolate Drop; Wrap Me in Your Big Red Shawl; Under the Old Apple Tree; Turkey in the Straw*—Jimboy and Harriett breaking the silence of the small-town summer night until Aunt Hager interrupted:

"You-all better wind up, chillens, 'cause I wants to go to bed. I ain't used to stayin' 'wake so late, nohow. Play something kinder decent there, son, fo' you stops."

Jimboy, to tease the old woman, began to rock and moan like an elder in the Sanctified Church, patting both feet at the same time as he played a hymn-like, lugubrious tune with a dancing overtone:

> Tell me, sister,
> Tell me, brother,
> Have you heard de latest news?

Then seriously as if he were about to announce the coming of the Judgment:

> A woman down in Georgia
> Got her two sweeet-men confused.

How terible! How sad! moaned the guitar.

> One knocked on de front do',
> One knocked on de back—

Sad, sad . . . sad, sad! said the music.

> Now that woman down in Georgia's
> Door-knob is hung with black.

O, play that funeral march, boy! while the guitar laughed a dirge.

> An' de hearse is comin' easy
> With two rubber-tired hacks!

Followed by a long-drawn-out, churchlike:

> Amen . . . !

Then with rapid glides, groans, and shouts the instrument screamed of a sudden in profane frenzy, and Harriett began to ball-the-jack, her arms flopping like the wings of a headless pigeon, the guitar strings whining in ecstasy, the player rocking gaily to the urgent music, his happy mouth crying: "Tack 'em on down, gal! Tack 'em on down, Harrie!"

But Annjee had risen.

"I wish you'd come in and eat the ham I brought you," she said as she picked up her chair and started towards the house. "And you, Sandy! Get up from under that tree and go to bed." She spoke roughly to the little fellow, whom the songs had set a-dreaming. Then to her husband: "Jimboy, I wish you'd come in."

The man stopped playing, with a deep vibration of the strings that seemed to echo through the whole world. Then he leaned his guitar against the side of the house and lifted straight up in his hairy arms Annjee's plump, brown-black little body while he kissed her as she wriggled like a stubborn child, her soft breasts rubbing his hard body through the coarse blue shirt.

"You don't like my old songs, do you, baby? You don't want to hear me sing 'em," he said, laughing. "Well, that's all right. I like you, anyhow, and I like your ham, and I like your kisses, and I like everything you bring me. Let's go in and chow down." And he carried her into the kitchen, where he sat with her on his knees as he ate the food she so faithfully had brought him from Mrs. J. J. Rice's dinner-table.

Outside, Willie-Mae went running home through the dark. And Harriett pumped a cool drink of water for her mother, then helped her to rise from her low seat, Sandy aiding from behind, with both hands pushing firmly in Aunt Hager's fleshy back. Then the three of them came into the house and glanced, as they passed through the kitchen, at Annjee sitting on Jimboy's lap with both dark arms tight around his neck.

"Looks like you're clinging to the Rock of Ages," said Harriett to her sister. "Be sure you don't slip, old evil gal!"

But at midnight, when the owl that nested in a tree near the corner began to hoot, they were all asleep—Annjee and Jimboy in one room, Harriett and Hager in another, with Sandy on the floor at the foot of his grandmother's bed. Far away on the railroad line a whistle blew, lonesome and long.

Simple Speaks His Mind

A WORD FROM "TOWN & COUNTRY"

"Have you seen Watermelon Joe?" asked Simple, looking around the bar.

"No, I have not," I said. "Why?"

"He owes me a quarter."

"Do you expect to get it back?"

"No."

"Then why did you lend it to him?" I asked.

"From some people you expect to get nothing back," explained Simple, "but you does for them right on."

"Why?" I pursued the question.

"Why do you do for a dog? Why do you do for a woman?"

"Surely you do not put women and dogs in the same class?" I asked.

"Sometimes both of them are b—," Simple began.

"Shsss-ss-s! That is not a polite word," I said. "It will get you in the doghouse with the ladies, and there are ladies in this bar."

"The word for a lady dog *is* a polite word," Simple said. "I have seen it in *Town & Country,* which my boss's wife reads."

"Harlem does not read *Town & Country*," I said. "Colored people think *bitch* is a bad word, not a female hound."

"But I were using it in its good way to mean a woman and a hound," said Simple.

"In polite company, you do not use it for a female unless you mean it to be a hound," I said.

"I do not mean it to be a hound now," said Simple. "I mean it to be a woman who acts like a hound."

"Then you are using it in its profane sense," I said, "and you are insulting womankind."

"My mother was a woman," said Simple indignantly, "and I would not insult her."

"But you would insult *my* mother," I said, "if you applied that term to womankind."

174

"I do not even know your mother," said Simple.

"Well, I would appreciate it if you did not talk about her now," I said, "in the same breath with female hounds."

"You must be drunk," said Simple. "I did not mention your mother."

"You just got through mentioning my mother," I said, "so how can you say that?"

"I did not say she was that word I saw in *Town & Country*," said Simple.

"You'd better not," I said.

"But women in general are," said Simple.

"My mother is a woman."

"I mean, not including *your mother and mine*," said Simple.

"You're still making it rather broad," I said. "I also know some other women whom I highly respect."

"I will leave them out," said Simple. "But you know what I mean. Women is women. When you do for them, it is just about the same as doing for Watermelon Joe. You do not expect to get anything back."

"What do you want back?" I asked. "The little bit of money you spend?"

"No," said Simple. "I want love, respect, attention, 'Here is your slippers, daddy,' when I come home. Not, 'Where is that pound of butter I told you to bring?' And I say, 'Aw, woman, I just forgot.' Then she says, 'It is funny you can remember your Cousin Josephine's birthday and send her a card which costs a quarter and you cannot remember to get a pound of butter for your own home. No, you neglect what is nearest to you. I am your wife! Remember?'

"Then I say, 'Of course, you are my wife, Isabel, and I did not forget you. I just forgot the butter. Do you want to make something out of it?'

" 'Yes,' she says, 'I want to make something out of it. You don't work no harder than me and yet you expects me to do the shopping, cooking, cleaning, and wash your filthy clothes, too, when I come home. Yes, I think you should remember that butter! You getting ready to go down to that old bar right now and eyeball them loose womens.' Only she didn't say *womens*. She said that word that was in *Town & Country*. And all I could think of to say back, 'It's a lie! You are the only (word that's in *Town & Country*) that I have gazed at all day—and you hurt my eyes.'

"Then it were on! That is why we did not stay together. A woman is evil. And when a man is tired, sometimes the only word he can think of to say is the one that white folks use for dogs. I don't know why we can't use it, too."

"Because it is disrespectful to women," I said, "that is why."

"But that is what they is," said Simple.

"Be careful! My mother is a woman," I said.

"I am *not* talking about *your* mother, neither about *my* mother," said Simple. "I am just talking about women."

"Your mother was not a man, was she?"

"I do not play the dozens when I am drinking," said Simple.

TEMPTATION

"When the Lord said, 'Let there be light,' and there was light, what I want to know is where was us colored people?"

"What do you mean, 'Where were we colored people?' " I said.

"We must *not* of been there," said Simple, "because we are still dark. Either He did not include me or else I were not there."

"The Lord was not referring to people when He said, 'Let there be light.' He was referring to the elements, the atmosphere, the air."

"He must have included some people," said Simple, "because white people are light, in fact, *white*, whilst I am dark. How come? I say, we were not there."

"Then where do you think we were?"

"Late as usual," said Simple, "old C. P. Time. We must have been down the road a piece and did not get back on time."

"There was no C. P. Time in those days," I said. "In fact, no people were created—so there couldn't be any Colored People's Time. The Lord God had not yet breathed the breath of life into anyone."

"No?" said Simple.

"No," said I, "because it wasn't until Genesis 2 and 7 that God 'formed man of the dust of the earth and breathed into his nostrils the breath of life and man became a living soul.' His name was Adam. Then He took one of Adam's ribs and made a woman."

"Then trouble began," said Simple. "Thank God, they was both white."

"How do you know Adam and Eve were white?" I asked.

"When I was a kid I seen them on the Sunday school cards," said Simple. "Ever since I been seeing a Sunday school card, they was white. That is why I want to know where was us Negroes when the Lord said, 'Let there be light'?"

"Oh, man, you have a color complex so bad you want to trace it back to the Bible."

"No, I don't. I just want to know how come Adam and Eve was white. If they had started out black, this world might not be in the fix it is today. Eve might not of paid that serpent no attention. I never did know a Negro yet that liked a snake."

"That snake is a symbol," I said, "a symbol of temptation and sin. And that symbol would be the same, no matter what the race."

"I am not talking about no symbol," said Simple. "I am talking about the day when Eve took that apple and Adam et. From then on the human race has been in trouble. There ain't a colored woman living what would take no apple from a snake—and she better not give no snake-apples to her husband!"

"Adam and Eve are symbols, too," I said.

"You are simple yourself," said Simple. "But I just wish we colored folks had been somewhere around at the start. I do not know where we was when Eden was a garden, but we sure didn't get in on none of the crops. If we had, we would not be so poor today. White folks started out ahead and they are still ahead. Look at me!"

"I am looking," I said.

"Made in the image of God," said Simple, "but I never did see anybody like me on a Sunday school card."

"Probably nobody looked like you in Biblical days," I said. "The American Negro did not exist in B.C. You're a product of Caucasia and Africa, Harlem and Dixie. You've been conditioned entirely by our environment, our modern times."

"Times have been hard," said Simple, "but still I am a child of God."

"In the cosmic sense, we are all children of God."

"I have been baptized," said Simple, "also anointed with oil. When I were a child I come through at the mourners' bench. I was converted. I have listened to Daddy Grace and et with Father Divine, moaned with Elder Lawson and prayed with Adam Powell. Also I have been to the Episcopalians with Joyce. But if a snake were to come up to me and offer *me* an apple, I would say, 'Varmint, be on your way! No fruit today! Bud, you got the wrong stud now, so get along somehow, be off down the road because you're lower than a toad!' Then that serpent would respect me as a wise man— and this world would not be where it is—all on account of an apple. That apple has turned into an atom now."

"To hear you talk, if you had been in the Garden of Eden, the world would still be a Paradise," I said. "Man would not have fallen into sin."

"Not *this* man," said Simple. "I would have stayed in that garden making grape wine, singing like Crosby, and feeling fine! I would not be scuffling out in this rough world, neither would I be in Harlem. If I was Adam I would just stay in Eden in that garden with no rent to pay, no landladies to dodge, no time clock to punch —and *my* picture on a Sunday school card. I'd be a *real gone guy* even if I didn't have but one name—Adam—and no initials."

"You would be *real gone* all right. But you were not there. So, my dear fellow, I trust you will not let your rather late arrival on our contemporary stage distort your perspective."

"No," said Simple.

FAMILY TREE

"Anybody can look at me and tell I am part Indian," said Simple.

"I see you almost every day," I said, "and I did not know it until now."

"I have Indian blood but I do not show it much," said Simple. "My uncle's cousin's great-grandma were a Cherokee. I only shows mine when I lose my temper—then my Indian blood boils. I am quick-tempered just like a Indian. If somebody does something to me, I always fights back. In fact, when I get mad, I am the toughest Negro God's got. It's my Indian blood. When I were a young man, I used to play baseball and steal bases just like Jackie. If the empire would rule me out, I would get mad and hit the empire. I had to stop playing. That Indian temper. Nowadays, though, it's mostly womens that riles me up, especially landladies, waitresses, and girl friends. To tell the truth, I believe in a woman keeping her place. Womens is beside themselves these days. They want to rule the roost."

"You have old-fashioned ideas about sex," I said. "In fact, your line of thought is based on outmoded economics."

"What?"

"In the days when women were dependent upon men for a living, you could be the boss. But now women make their own living. Some of them make more money than you do."

"True," said Simple. "During the war they got into that habit. But boss I am still due to be."

"So you think. But you can't always put your authority into effect."

"I can try," said Simple. "I can say, 'Do this!' And if she does something else, I can raise my voice, if not my hand."

"You can be sued for raising your voice," I stated, "and arrested for raising your hand."

"And she can be annihilated when I return from being arrested," said Simple. "That's my Indian blood!"

"You must believe in a woman being a squaw."

"She better not look like no squaw," said Simple. "I want a woman to look sharp when she goes out with me. No moccasins. I wants high-heel shoes and nylons, cute legs—and short dresses. But I also do not want her to talk back to me. As I said, I am the man. *Mine* is the word, and she is due to hush."

"Indians customarily expect their women to be quiet," I said.

"I do not expect mine to be *too* quiet," said Simple. "I want 'em to sweet-talk me—'Sweet baby, this,' and 'Baby, that,' and 'Baby, you's right, darling,' when they talk to me."

"In other words, you want them both old-fashioned and modern at the same time," I said. "The convolutions of your hypothesis are sometimes beyond cognizance."

"Cog hell!" said Simple. "I just do not like no old loud back-talking chick. That's the Indian in me. My grandpa on my father's side were like that, too, an Indian. He was married five times and he really ruled his roost."

"There are a mighty lot of Indians up your family tree," I said. "Did your granddad look like one?"

"Only his nose. He was dark brownskin otherwise. In fact, he were black. And the womens! Man! They was crazy about Grandpa. Every time he walked down the street, they stuck their heads out the windows and kept 'em turned South—which was where the beer parlor was."

"So your grandpa was a drinking man, too. That must be whom you take after."

"I also am named after him," said Simple. "Grandpa's name was Jess, too. So I am Jesse B. Semple."

"What does the *B* stand for?"

"Nothing. I just put it there myself since they didn't give me no initial when I was born. I am really Jess Semple—which the kids changed around into a nickname when I were in school. In fact, they used to tease me when I were small, calling me 'Simple Simon.' But I was right handy with my fists, and after I beat the 'Simon' out of a few of them, they let me alone. But my friends still call me 'Simple.' "

"In reality, you are Jesse Semple," I said, "colored."

"Part Indian," insisted Simple, reaching for his beer.

"Jess is certainly not an Indian name."

"No, it ain't," said Simple, "but we did have a Hiawatha in our family. She died."

"*She?*" I said. "Hiawatha was no *she*."

"She was a *she* in our family. And she had long coal-black hair just like a Creole. You know, I started to marry a Creole one time when I was coach-boy on the L. & N. down to New Orleans. Them Louisiana girls are bee-oou-te-ful! Man, I mean!"

"Why didn't you marry her, fellow?"

"They are more dangerous than a Indian," said Simple, "also I do not want no pretty woman. First thing you know, you fall in love with her—then you got to kill somebody about her. She'll make you so jealous, you'll bust! A pretty woman will get a man in trouble. Me and my Indian blood, quick-tempered as I is. No! I do not crave a pretty woman."

"Joyce is certainly not bad-looking," I said. "You hang around her all the time."

"She is far from a Creole. Besides, she appreciates me," said Simple. "Joyce knows I got Indian blood which makes my temper bad. But we take each other as we is. I respect her and she respects me."

"That's the way it should be with the whole world," I said. "Therefore, you and Joyce are setting a fine example in these days of trials and tribulations. Everybody should take each other as they are, white, black, Indians, Creole. Then there would be no prejudice, nations would get along."

"Some folks do not see it like that," said Simple. "For instant, my landlady—and my wife. Isabel could never get along with me. That is why we are not together today."

"I'm not talking personally," I said, "so why bring in your wife?"

"Getting along *starts* with persons, don't it?" asked Simple. "You *must* include my wife. That woman got my Indian blood so riled up one day I thought I would explode."

"I still say, I'm not talking personally."

"Then stop talking," exploded Simple, "because with me it is personal. Facts, I cannot even talk about my wife if I don't get personal. That's how it is if you're part Indian—everything is personal. *Heap much personal.*"

THERE OUGHT TO BE A LAW

"Look here at these headlines, man, where Congress is busy passing laws. While they're making all these laws, it looks like to me they ought to make one setting up a few Game Preserves for Negroes."

"What ever gave you that fantastic idea?" I asked.

"A movie short I saw the other night," said Simple, "about how the government is protecting wild life, preserving fish and game, and setting aside big tracts of land where nobody can fish, shoot, hunt, nor harm a single living creature with furs, fins, or feathers. But it did not show a thing about Negroes."

"I thought you said the picture was about 'wild life.' Negroes are not wild."

"No," said Simple, "but we need protection. This film showed how they put aside a thousand acres out West where the buffaloes roam and nobody can shoot a single one of them. If they do, they get in jail. It also showed some big National Park with government airplanes dropping food down to the deers when they got snowed under and had nothing to eat. The government protects and takes care of buffaloes and deers—which is more than the government does for me or my kinfolks down South. Last month they lynched a man in Georgia and just today I see where the Klan has whipped a Negro within a inch of his life in Alabama. And right up North here in New York a actor is suing a apartment house that won't even let a Negro go up on the elevator to see his producer. That is what I mean by Game Preserves for Negroes—Congress ought to set aside some place where we can go and nobody can jump on us and beat us, neither lynch us nor Jim Crow us every day. Colored folks rate as much protection as a buffalo, or a deer."

"You have a point there," I said.

"This here movie showed great big beautiful lakes with signs up all around:

NO FISHING—STATE GAME PRESERVE

But it did not show a single place with a sign up:

NO LYNCHING

It also showed flocks of wild ducks settling down in a nice green meadow behind a government sign that said:

NO HUNTING

It were nice and peaceful for them fish and ducks. There ought to be some place where it is nice and peaceful for me, too, even if I am not a fish or a duck.

"They showed one scene with two great big old longhorn elks locking horns on a Game Preserve somewhere out in Wyoming, fighting like mad. Nobody bothered them elks or tried to stop them from fighting. But just let me get in a little old fist fight here in this bar, they will lock me up and the Desk Sergeant will say, 'What are you colored boys doing, disturbing the peace?' Then they will give me thirty days and fine me twice as much as they would a white man for doing the same thing. There ought to be some place where I can fight in peace and not get fined them high fines."

"You disgust me," I said. "I thought you were talking about a place where you could be quiet and compose your mind. Instead, you are talking about fighting."

"I would like a place where I could do both," said Simple. "If the government can set aside some spot for a elk *to be a elk* without being bothered, or a fish *to be a fish* without getting hooked, or a buffalo *to be a buffalo* without being shot down, there ought to be some place in this American country where a Negro can be a Negro without being Jim Crowed. There ought to be a law. The next time I see my congressman, I am going to tell him to introduce a bill for Game Preserves for Negroes."

"The Southerners would filibuster it to death," I said.

"If we are such a problem to them Southerners," said Simple, "I should think they would want some place to preserve us out of their sight. But then, of course, you have to take into consideration that if the Negroes was taken out of the South, who would they lynch? What would they do for sport? A Game Preserve is for to keep people from bothering anything that is living.

"When that movie finished, it were sunset in Virginia and it showed a little deer and its mama lying down to sleep. Didn't nobody say, 'Get up, deer, you can't sleep here,' like they would to me if I was to go to the White Sulphur Springs Hotel."

" 'The foxes have holes, and the birds of the air have nests; but the Son of man hath not where to lay his head.' "

"That is why I want a Game Preserve for Negroes," said Simple.

INCOME TAX

" 'Taxation without representation is tyranny,' so the books say.
I don't see why Negroes down South should pay taxes a-tall. You
know Buddy Jones' brother, what was wounded in the 92nd in
Italy, don't you? Well, he was telling me about how bad them red-
necks treated him when he was in the army in Mississippi. He said
he don't never want to see no parts of the South again. He were
born and raised in Yonkers and not used to such stuff. Now his
nerves is shattered. He can't even stand a Southern accent no
more."

"Jim Crow shock," I said. "I guess it can be as bad as shell shock."

"It can be worse," said Simple. "Jim Crow happens to men every
day down South, whereas a man's not in a battle every day. Buddy's
brother has been out of the army three years and he's still sore about
Mississippi."

"What happened to him down there?"

"I will tell it to you like it was told to me," said Simple. "You
know Buddy's brother is a taxicab driver, don't you? Well, the other
day he was telling me he was driving his cab downtown on Broad-
way last week when a white man hailed him, got in, and then said
in one of them slow Dixie drawls, "Bouy, tek me ovah to Fefty-
ninth Street and Fefth Avahnue.'

"Buddy's brother told him, 'I ain't gonna take you nowhere.
Get outta my cab—and quick!'

"The white man didn't know what was the matter so he says,
'Why?'

"Buddy's brother said, 'Because I don't like Southerners, that's
why! You treated me so mean when I was in the army down South
that I don't never want to see none of you-all no more. And I *sure*
don't like to hear you talk. It goes all through me. I spent eighteen
months in hell in Mississippi.'

"The white man got red in the face, also mad, and called a cop
to make Buddy's brother drive him where he wanted to go. The cop
was one of New York's finest, a great big Irishman. The copper
listened to the man, then he listened to Buddy's brother. Setting
right there in his taxi at 48th and Broadway, Buddy's brother told
that cop all about Mississippi, how he was Jim Crowed on the train on
the way down going to drill for Uncle Sam, how he was Jim
Crowed in camp, also howwhenever he had a furlough, him and his

colored buddies had to wait and *wait* and WAIT at the camp gate for a bus to get to town because they filled the busses up with white soldiers and the colored soldiers just had to stand behind and wait. Sometimes on payday if there were a big crowd of white soldiers, the colored G.I.'s would never get to town at all.

" 'Officer, I'm telling you,' Buddy's brother said, 'that Mississippi is something! Down South they don't have no nice polices like you. Down South all them white cops want to do is beat a Negro's head, cuss you, and call you names. They do not protect Americans if they are black. They lynched a man five miles down the road from our camp one night and left him hanging there for three days as a warning, so they said, to us Northern Negroes to know how to act in the South, particularly if from New York.'

"Meanwhile the Southern white man who was trying to get the cop to make Buddy's brother drive him over to Fifth Avenue was getting redder and redder. He said, 'You New York Negras need to learn how to act.'

" 'Shut up!' says the cop. 'This man is talking.'

"Buddy's brother talked on. 'Officer,' he says, 'it were so bad in that army camp that I will tell you a story of something that happened to me. They had us colored troops quartered way down at one end of the camp, six miles back from the gate, up against the levee. One day they sent me to do some yard work up in the white part of the camp. My bladder was always weak, so I had to go to the latrine no sooner than I got there. Everything is separated in Mississippi, even latrines, with signs up WHITE and COLORED. But there wasn't any COLORED latrine anywhere around, so I started to go in one marked WHITE.

" 'A cracker M.P. yelled at me, *'Halt!'*

" 'When I didn't halt—because I couldn't—he drew his gun on me and cocked it. He threatened to shoot me if I went in that WHITE latrine.

" 'Well, he made me so mad, I walked all the way back to my barracks and got a gun myself. I came back and I walked up to that Southern M.P. I said, *'Neither you nor me will never see no Germans nor no Japs if you try to stop me from going in this latrine this morning.'*

" "That white M.P. didn't try to stop me. He just turned pale, and I went in. But by that time, officer, I was so mad I decided to set down and stay awhile. So I did. With my gun on my lap, I just sat—and every time a Southerner came in, I cocked the trigger. Ain't nobody said a word. They just looked at me and walked out. I stayed there as long as I wanted to—black as I am—in that WHITE latrine. Down in Mississippi a colored soldier has to have a gun even to go to the toilet! So, officer, that is why I do not want to ride this man—because he is one of them that wouldn't even let me go in their latrines down South, do you understand?'

" 'Understand?' says the cop, 'Of course, I understand. Be jeezus! It's like that exactly that the damned English did the Irish. Faith, you do not have to haul him. . . . Stranger, get yerself another cab. Scram, now! Quick—before I run you in.'

"That white man hauled tail! And Buddy's brother drove off saluting that cop—and blowing his horn for New York City.

SPRING TIME

"I wish that spring would come more often now that it is here," said Simple.

"How could it come more often?"

"It could if God had made it that-a-way," said Simple. "I also wish it would last longer."

"It looks as if you would prefer spring all the year around."

"Just most of the year," said Simple. "As it is now, summer comes too soon and winter lasts too long. I do not like real hot weather, neither cold. I like spring."

"Spring is too changeable for me—sometimes hot, sometimes cold."

"I am not talking about that kind of spring," said Simple. "I mean June-time spring when it is just nice and mellow—like a cool drink."

"Of what?"

"Anything," said Simple. "Anything that is strong as the sun and cool as the moon. But I am not talking about drinking now. I am talking about spring. Oh, it is wonderful! It is the time when flowers come out of their buds, birds come out of their nests, bees come out of their hives, Negroes come out of their furnished rooms, and butterflies out of the cocoons."

"Also snakes come out of their holes."

"They is little young snakes," said Simple, "else big old sleepy snakes that ain't woke up good yet till the sun strikes them. That is why I do not like summer, because the sun is so hot it makes even a cold snake mad. Spring is my season. Summer was made to give you a taste of what hell is like. Fall was made for the clothing-store people to coin money because every human has to buy a overcoat,

muffler, heavy socks, and gloves. Winter was made for landladies
to charge high rents and keep cold radiators and make a fortune off
of poor tenants. But spring! Throw your overcoat on the pawnshop
counter, tell the landlady to kiss your foot, open your windows,
let the fresh air in. Me, myself, I love spring!

"Why, if I was down home now, daddy-o, I would get out my
fishing pole and take me a good old Virginia ham sandwich and
go set on the banks of the river all day and just dream and fish and
fish and dream. I might have me a big old quart bottle of beer tied
on a string down in the water to keep cool, and I would just fish
and dream and dream and fish."

"You would not have any job?" I asked.

"I would respect work just like I respected my mother and not
hit her a lick. I would be far away from all this six A.M. alarm-clock
business, crowded subways, gulping down my coffee to get to the
man's job in time, and working all day shut up inside where you
can't even smell the spring—and me still smelling ether and wor-
ried about my winter hospital bill. If I was down home, buddy-o, I
would pull off my shoes and let my toes air and just set on the river-
bank and dream and fish and fish and dream, and I would not
worry about no job."

"Why didn't you stay down home when you were there?"

"You know why I didn't stay," said Simple. "I did not like them
white folks and they did not like me. Maybe if it wasn't for white
folks, I would've stayed down South where spring comes earlier
than it do up here. White folks is the cause of a lot of inconveniences
in my life."

"They've even driven you away from an early spring."

"It do not come as early in Harlem as it does down South," said
Simple, "but it comes. And there ain't no white folks living can
keep spring from coming. It comes to Harlem the same as it does
downtown, too. Nobody can keep spring out of Harlem. I stuck my
head out of the window this morning and spring kissed me bang in
the face. Sunshine patted me all over the head. Some little old
birds was flying and playing on the garbage cans down in the alley,
and one of them flew up to the Third Floor Rear and looked at me
and cheeped, 'Good morning!'

"I said, 'Bird, howdy-do!'

"Just then I heard my next-door roomer come out of the bath-
room so I had to pull my head in from that window and rush to get
to the toilet to wash my face before somebody else got there because
I did not want to be late to work this morning since today is pay-

day. New York is just rush, rush, rush! But, oh, brother, if I were down home."

"I know—you would just fish and dream and dream and fish."

"And dream and fish and fish and dream!" said Simple. "If spring was to last forever, as sure as my name is Jess, I would just fish and dream."

SEEING DOUBLE

"I wonder why it is we have two of one thing, and only one of others."

"For instance?"

"We have two lungs," said Simple, "but only one heart. Two eyes, but only one mouth. Two—"

"Feet, but only one body," I said.

"I was not going to say *feet*," said Simple. "But since you have taken the words out of my mouth, go ahead."

"Human beings have two shoulders but only one neck."

"And two ears but only one head," said Simple.

"What on earth would you want with two heads?"

"I could sleep with one and stay awake with the other," explained Simple. "Just like I got two nostrils, I would also like to have two mouths, then I could eat with one mouth while I am talking with the other. Joyce always starts an argument while we are eating, anyhow. That Joyce can talk and eat all at once."

"Suppose Joyce had two mouths, too," I said. "She could double-talk you."

"I would not keep company with a woman that had two mouths," said Simple. "But I would like to have two myself."

"If you had two mouths, you would have to have two noses also," I said, "and it would not make much sense to have two noses, would it?"

"No," said Simple, "I reckon it wouldn't. Neither would I like to have two chins to have to shave. A chin is no use for a thing. But there is one thing I sure would like to have two of. Since I have—"

"Since you have two eyes, I know you would like to have two faces—one in front and one behind—so you could look at all those pretty women on the street both going and coming."

"That would be idealistic," said Simple, "but that is *not* what I was going to say. You always cut me off. So you go ahead and talk."

"I know you wish you had two stomachs," I said, "so you could eat more of Joyce's good cooking."

"No, I do *not* wish I had two stomachs," said Simple. "I can put away enough food in one belly to mighty near wreck my pocket-book—with prices as high as a cat's back in a dogfight. So I do not need two stomachs. Neither do I need two navels on the stomach I got. What use are they? But there is one thing I sure wish I had two of."

"Two gullets?" I asked.

"Two gullets is *not* what I wish I had at all," said Simple. "Let me talk! *I wish I had two brains.*"

"Two brains! Why?"

"So I could think with one, and let the other one rest, man, that's why. I am tired of trying to figure out how to get ahead in this world. If I had two brains, I could think with one brain while the other brain was asleep. I could plan with one while the other brain was drunk. I could think about the Dodgers with one, and my future with the other. As it is now, there is too much in this world for one brain to take care of alone. I have thought so much with my one brain that it is about wore out. In fact, I need a rest right now. So let's drink up and talk about something pleasant. Two beers are on me tonight. Draw up to the bar."

"I was just at the bar," I said, "and Tony has nothing but bottles tonight, no draft."

"Then, daddy-o, they're on *you*," said Simple. "I only got two dimes—and one of them is a Roosevelt dime I do not wish to spend. Had I been thinking, I would have remembered that Roosevelt dime. When I get my other brain, it will keep track of all such details."

FOR THE SAKE OF ARGUMENT

When I came out of the house about midnight to get a bite to eat, there was Simple in one corner of Paddy's Bar arguing loudly with an aggregation of beer-drinkers as to who is the darker, Paul Robeson or Jackie Robinson. I sat down on the lunch-counter side of the bar and ordered a plate of shortribs. After a while Simple spotted me and took possession of the next stool, although he had no apparent intention of eating.

"You know Robeson is not as light as Robinson," he announced.

"To me it makes not the slightest difference what their gradations of complexion are," I said. "Furthermore, I do not comprehend how you can stand around for hours in bars and on corners just arguing about nothing. You will argue with folks about which railroad has the fastest trains, or if Bojangles could tap more taps per second than Fred Astaire. And none of it is of any importance."

"I do not see how you can sit around looking so smart all the time and saying practically nothing," countered Simple. "You are company for nobody but yourself."

"I do not like to argue," I said.

"I do! I will argue about whether or not two and two makes four just for the sake of argument."

"It has been proven so long ago that two and two make four that I do not see the sense in discussing it. If you were arguing about what to do with the Germans or how to reform the South, then I could go along with you. But I do not like to argue about things on which there is really no argument."

"I do—because my argument is that it is good for a man to argue, just argue," said Simple, walking to the door of the bar and gazing out. Suddenly he turned around. "But I could not argue if you did not argue back at me. It takes two to make an argument. A man cannot argue by his self."

"The trouble with you is that you always wish to *win* the argument," I said. "For me, just an exchange of views is sufficient. But you, you always want to win."

"Naturally, I want to win. Otherwise, why should I be arguing?"

"You are so often wrong, Jess, also loud. You cannot win an argument when you are wrong. There are two sides to every question."

"There are sometimes more than two sides," said Simple, "except to the race question. For white folks that don't have but one side."

"There you go bringing up the race question," I said. "How is it two Negroes can never get together without discussing the race question?"

"Because it is not even a question," said Simple. "It is a hammer over our heads and at any time it may fall. The only way I can explain what white folks does to us is that they just don't give a damn. Why, I once knowed a white man down South who were so mean he wouldn't give a sick baby a doctor's address."

"Where and when was that?" I asked.

"When I were a boy," said Simple. "I was hired out one summer on his plantation. He used to ride all around over the plantation watching everybody work. He rid on a little old girl-horse named

Betsy, and Betsy were as mean as he were. In fact, he had taught Betsy how to bite Negroes in the back. 'Boy, hist that there tree out of that ditch!'

"If you did not hist fast enough to suit him—'I can't Capt'n Boss!'—he would holler, 'Boy, you better, else I'll bull-whip your hide wide open!'

"Then if you still didn't hist, he would tell that little old horse, 'Get him, Betsy!' Betsy would gallop up and nip your right between the shoulder blades."

"You are lying now, I do believe," I said.

"You have never lived down South," said Simple, "so you do not know."

"I admit I am not really familiar with the South," I said, "but sometimes I think conditions are exaggerated. Certainly in recent years they are getting better."

"They've still got Jim Crow cars," said Simple. "And the last time I was down home on a trip, I went to pay a visit on the old white man my uncle used to work for. I had kinder forgot how it is down there, so I just walked up on the porch where he was setting and says, 'Howdy, Mr. Doolittle.'

"He says, 'Boy, take off your hat when you address a white man.' And that is how he greeted me. He says, 'You must have been up North so long you done forgot yourself.'

"You know that kinder hurt my feelings because he used to know me when I was a boy. But I am a man now. That is the trouble with the South. They do not want to treat a Negro like a man. It's always *boy*, no matter if you are ninety-nine years old. I know some few things is getting better, but even them is slow as molasses. Here, lemme show you a little poem I writ about that very thing last week."

Simple pulled a piece of tablet paper out of his pocket and proceeded to read. "Listen fluently:

> *Old Jim Crow's*
> *Just panting and a-coughing,*
> *But he won't take wings*
> *And fly.*
>
> *Old Jim Crow*
> *Is laying in his coffin,*
> *But he don't want*
> *To die.*

> *I have writ*
> *His obituary,*
> *Still and yet*
> *He tarry."*

"Not bad, old man, except that 'He tarry' is not grammatical," I said. "If you want to be literary, you ought to know grammar."

"Joyce knows grammar," said Simple. "She will fix it up for me. I just have not showed her this one yet."

"A writer should never depend on anyone else to fix thing for him. You ought to fix up your own things," I said.

"There are some things in life you cannot fix all by yourself," said Simple. "For me, poetries is one. And the race problem is another. Now you take for instant, we got two colored congressmen down in Washington. But they can't even stop a filibuster. Every time them Civil Rights Bills come up, them old white Southerners filibuster them to hell and gone. Why don't them colored congressmen start a filibuster, too?"

"Probably because they cannot talk as long or as loud as the Southerners," I said. "It takes Southerners to keep a filibuster going, and there are a great many of them in the House. Neither Adam Powell nor Dawson represents the South."

"They are colored and they represent me," said Simple. "If I was down yonder in Congress representing the colored race, I would start a filibuster all my own. In fact, I would filibuster to keep them filibusters from starting a filibuster."

"If you had no help," I said, "you would just have to keep on talking day and night, week after week, because once you sat down somebody else would get the floor. So how would you hold out?"

"How would I hold out?" yelled Simple. "With the fate of my Race at stake, you ask me how would *I* hold out! Why, for my people I would talk until my tongue hung out of my mouth. I would talk until I could not talk no more! Then, I would use sign language. When I got through with that, I would get down on my knees and pray in silence. And nobody better not strike no gavel while I am communing with my Maker. While I am on my knees, I would get some sleep. When I riz up, it would be the next day, so I would start all over again. I would be the greatest one-man filibuster of all time, daddy-o! But I am running dry now. Treat me to a beer."

"I will not," I said.

"O.K., then," said Simple, "you are setting there eating and drinking and here I am empty-handed. You are a hell of a buddy."

"I will lend you a dime to buy your own beer," I said, "but a treat should be an invitation, not a request."

"Just so I get the beer," said Simple. "Now, I will continue. As I were saying, there ain't but one side to this race question—the white folks' side. White folks are setting on top of the world, and I wouldn't mind setting up there myself. Just look around you. Who owns this bar? White folks. Who owns mighty near every shop and store all up and down this street? White folks. But what do I own? I'm asking you."

"As far as I know, you do not own a thing. But why don't you get a bar or a store?"

"Why don't you?"

"Let's consider the broader picture," I said.

"I asked you a question," said Simple. "Why don't *you* get a bar or a store?"

"I asked you first," I countered.

"I do not get a bar or a store for the same reason that you don't," said Simple. "I have nothing to get me one with. On Saturday I draws my wages. I pay my rent, I get out my laundry, I take Joyce to a show, I pay you back your Two Dollars, I drink a little beer. What have I got left to buy a store with?"

"Do you think Tony the Italian that owns this Paddy's Bar—with its Irish name—also two stores, and a bookie joint, had anything when he came to America twenty years ago in the steerage?"

"Columbus come before him and smoothed the way," said Simple. "Besides, if you are white, you can get credit. If you are white, you can meet somebody with money. If you are white, you can come up here to Harlem and charge double prices. If I owned a store and charged what they charge, folks would say, 'That Negro is no good.' I tell you, white folks get away with murder. They murder my soul every day and my pocketbook every night. They got me going and coming. They say, 'You can't have a good job. You're black.' Then they say, 'Pay double. You can't eat downtown. We got this grease-ball joint for you in Harlem where it's a dime more for a beef stew. Pay it or else!' A man can't else. That's the way they get ahead when they come to America. Columbus didn't start out with Jim Crow around his neck. Neither did the guy who owns this bar. Any foreigner can come here, white, and Jim Crow me, black, from the day he sets foot off the boat. Also overcharge. He *starts* on top of my head so no wonder he gets on top of the world. Maybe I ought to go to Europe and come back a foreigner."

"While you are over there, in order to change your complexion, you'd have to be born again."

"As colored as I am," said Simple, "I'd have to be born two or three times."

RACE RELATIONS

"Don't let's talk about it," he said when I asked him about Joyce. "Don't let's even mention her name. I can't stand it. I have tried every way I know to make up with that woman. But she must have a heart like a rock cast in the sea. I have also tried every way I know to forget her. But no dice. I cannot wear her off my mind. I've even taken up reading. This week I bought all the colored papers from the *Black Dispatch* to the *Afro-American,* trying to get a race-mad on, reading about lynchings, head-whippings, barrings-out, share-croppers, cheatings, discriminations, and such. No dice. I have drunk five bottles of beer tonight and I'm still sober. Nothing has no effect. So let's just not talk about Joyce.

"There is a question, anyhow, I want to ask you because I wish to change the subject," said Simple.

"Them colored papers are full of stuff about Race Relations Committees functioning all over the country, and how they are working to get rid of the poll tax and to keep what few Negroes still have jobs from losing them, and such. But in so far as I can tell, none of them committees is taking up the real problem of race relations because I always thought *relations* meant being related. Don't it? And to be related you have to have relations, don't you? But I don't hear nobody speaking about us being kinfolks. All they are talking about in the papers is poll taxes and jobs."

"By relations, I take it that you mean intermarriage? If that is what you mean, nobody wants to talk about that. That is a touchy subject. It is also beside the point. Equal rights and fair employment have nothing to do with intermarriage."

"Getting married," said Simple, "is also a equal right."

"You do not want to marry a white woman, do you?" I asked.

"I do not," said Simple, "but I figure some white woman might want to marry me."

"You'd better not let Joyce hear you talking like that," I said. "You know colored women do not like the idea of intermarriage at all."

"I know they don't," said Simple. "Neither do white men. But if the races are ever going to relate, they must also mate, then you will have race relations."

"Race relations do not necessarily have to be on so racy a basis," I said. "At any rate, speaking about them in such a manner only infuriates the South. It makes Southerners fighting mad."

"I do not see why it should infuriate the South," said Simple, "because the South has always done more relating than anybody else. There are more light-skinned Negroes in the South whose pappy was a white man than there is in all the rest of this whole American country."

"True," I said, "many colored people are related to white people down South. But *some* relationships are private matters, whereas things like equal job opportunities, an unsegregated army, the poll tax, and no more Jim Crow cars affect everybody, in bed or out. These are the things Race Relations Committees are trying to deal with all over the country. It would only complicate the issues if they brought up intermarriage."

"Issues are complicated already," said Simple. "Why, I even got white blood in me myself, dark as I am. And in some colored families I know personally down South, you can hardly tell high yellows from white."

"My dear fellow," I said, "the basic social issues which I am talking about are not to be dealt with on a family basis, but on a mass basis. All Negroes, with white blood in them or not, in fact, everybody of whatever parentage, ought to have the right to vote, to live a decent life, and to have fair employment."

"Also to relate," said Simple.

"I keep telling you, race relations do not have anything to do with that kind of relating!"

"If they don't," said Simple, "they are not relations."

"Absurd," I said. "I simply will not argue with you any more. You're just as bad as those Southerners who are always bringing up intermarriage as a reason for *not* doing anything. What you say is entirely beside the point."

"The point must have moved then," said Simple.

"We are not talking about the same thing at all," I said patiently. "I am talking about fair employment, and you are talking about..."

"Race relations," said Simple.

Simple Takes a Wife

SCIENCE SAYS IT'S A LIE

When I met him again, "It were wonderful," he said. "Soft lights, pretty womens, and a jam-up band. I really enjoyed my fool self. So did Joyce. And she looked like a dreamboat, jack! Brownskin, all in white, floating like a cloud. Like a sail in the sunset, like the Queen of Sheba, like Josephine Baker! She were righteous! From the minute we hit the floor, folks started making admiration over Joyce. And everything was going fine at the formal until Jimboy—who's gotten kind of famous lately as a jazz piano-player—brought his wife up to our box to introduce her to the ladies."

"What happened then?"

"The ladies friz up," said Simple.

"Why?"

"Jimboy's wife is white."

"That's right," I said, "he did marry a white girl, didn't he? I haven't run into him since he got married."

Dorothea is not only white, *she is pretty,*" said Simple. "There is nothing a colored woman hates more than to see a colored man married to a *pretty* white woman. If she's some old beat-up strumpet, they don't care much. But Jimboy's wife is a nice girl. So when he come up to our box with Dorothea, the womens just friz up, Joyce included."

"That was not very polite," I said.

"Of course it were not," said Simple, draining his beer. "It were right embarrassing. Besides, I wanted to ask Jimboy's wife for a dance, but I did not dare after I saw that *no-you-don't* look in Joyce's eyes.

"I just said, 'Excuse me, folks, I have got to go to the MEN'S ROOM.'

"When I come back Jimboy and his wife was gone, and Joyce and her women friends was talking like mad about them.

"'That little old white Southern hussy,' they says—because Jimboy's wife is from Arkansas. 'The idea of her coming up here to

195

Harlem and marrying a Negro! Why didn't she marry one of her own?'

" 'Why didn't he marry one of *his* own?' another one says. Man, they carried on just like Bilbo."

"It's too bad we have prejudices, too," I said.

"Too bad," nodded Simple. "But Jimboy's son is going to be a smart child. He is about six months old now, and he started to teaching his mama before he was born."

"What do you mean, started teaching his mama before he was born?"

"Ain't you heard that story about how Jimboy's son was born? Where have you been lately? That child refused to be born in Arkansas."

"Quit kidding," I said.

"I am not kidding," declared Simple. "What I am telling you is true. That baby knows a colored man married to a white woman is against the law in Dixie. Last fall Jimboy's wife wanted to be with her mother and the rest of her white folks when her first child was born. So she went down to Arkansas. Jimboy could not go because he were working. He knew if he gave up his job, he's liable not to get another one soon."

"So when her time were about come, Dorothea was put on the train by her colored husband and went on home—home being where mama is in Dixie. Me, myself, I would not marry a woman who thought home was where mama is. When a woman marries a man, like the Bible says, she should cleave unto *him*—not run looking for mama when his offspring is due. *My wife would stay with me.*"

"A lot of help you would be in childbirth," I said.

"There's a Medical Center with nurses, not midwives," said Simple. "But Jimboy does not have much influence over his wife, I reckon. Being blonde, I expect he is scared of her. So she left the free North and went back South to birth her child—her family being *liberals,* so she told her husband. She regretted it, likewise Jimboy. While he were waiting for the great event, looking each and every day for a telegram, '*It's a boy,*' else '*A girl,*' Jimboy grew twenty-two gray hairs, missed three nights at the club, lost his touch on the piano, and had heartburn."

"What happened?"

"A new page in history," said Simple, "which science would say was a lie."

"Don't keep me in suspense," I demanded. "Did his wife have the child or not?"

"Dorothea had the child, but not in Arkansas. When she got there, it were time. But nothing happened. One week went by, two weeks, three, an extra month—almost two."

"Then what?"

"Another month. By that time it were *too* long. Dorothea got worried herself. Jimboy in Harlem got gray-headed. He wired his wife in Arkansas to go to the hospital anyhow. It was way overdue. So she went—which is the story. When that white girl got in the hospital, naturally a white doctor proceeded to examine her. He had a thing with earphones they press on the belly of the mother-to-be to listen for the unborn child's heartbeats. Well, sir, the doctor pressed them earphones on Jimboy's wife—but what that doctor heard was not heartbeats at all. He heard Jimboy's unborn baby singing the blues in a real strong voice just like Sugar Chile Robinson. That brownskin baby was singing real loud:

> *I won't be born down here!*
> *No, sir, I won't be born down here!*
> *If you want to know*
> *What it's all about—*
> *As long as South is South,*
> *I won't come out!*
> *I won't be born down here!*"

"That is really a tall tale," I said.

"Ask Jimboy if it ain't so," said Simple. "Dorothea had to come on back to New York to have her baby. Their child were born in Harlem Hospital where he had no fear."

FANCY FREE

"Before spring is over, if I can't get no spring clothes, at least I would like to have me a real good mess of greens."

Simple stood at the bar and uttered this statement as though it were of great importance. Then he shook his head with a gesture of despair.

"But there is no place in New York to pick greens. Maybe that is why womens do not cook them much in big cities. Not even a dandelion do I see growing in Morningside Park. If there was, it wouldn't stay there long because some Negro would pull it and eat it."

"Greens *are* good," I said.

"Don't talk!" cried Simple. "All boiled down with a side of pork, delicious! Greens make my mouth water. I have eaten so many in my life until I could write a book on greenology—and I still would like to eat that many more. What I wouldn't give right now for a good old iron pot full! Mustard greens, collard greens, turnip greens, dandelions, dock. Beet-tops, lamb's tongue, pepper grass, sheepcress, also poke. Good old mixed greens! Spinach or chard, refined greens! Any kind of fresh greens. I wonder why somebody don't open a restaurant for nothing but greens? I should think that would go right good up North."

"I hear you always talking about going into business," I said. "Why don't you open one?"

"Where would I get the greens?" asked Simple. "They don't grow around here. Wild mustard has never been known to be found sprouting on Lenox Avenue. And was I to see poke in New York, I would swear it were a miracle. Besides, even if they did grow here, who would pick 'em? That is woman's work, but I would not trust it to Joyce. She might not know greens from poison weeds, nor pepper grass from bridal mist. Joyce were not raised on dandelions like me. I don't expect she would be caught with a basket picking greens. Joyce is cultural."

"She likes greens, though, doesn't she?"

"Eats them like a horse," said Simple, "when somebody else serves them. The same by chitterlings. Joyce tried to tell me once she did not eat pig ruffles, would not cook them, couldn't bear to clean them, and *loathed* the smell. But when my cousin in the Bronx invited us to a chitterling supper, I could hardly get near the pot for Joyce. I do not belive people should try to pass."

"What do you mean, *pass*?"

"Pass for non-chitterling eaters if they are chitterling eaters," said Simple. "What I like, I like, and I do not care who knows it. I also like watermelon."

"Why not?" I asked.

"Some colored folks are ashamed to like watermelon. I told you about that woman who bought one in the store once and made the clerk wrap it up before she would carry it home. She didn't want nobody to see her with a watermelon. Me, I would carry a watermelon unwrapped any day any where. I would eat one before the Queen of England."

"A pretty picture you would make, eating a slice of watermelon before the queen."

"I would give the queen a slice—and I bet she would thank me for it, especially if it was one of them light green round striped melons with a deep red heart and coal-black seeds. Man, juicy! Oh, my soul! Sweet, yes! And good to a fare-thee-well! I wish I had a pot of greens right now, a pitcher of buttermilk, and a watermelon."

"You would have a stomach ache."

"It would be worth it! But let's talk no more about such things. I would settle for a cold bottle of beer on you here."

"I see no reason why I should buy you a bottle of beer."

"I am broke and I have dreamed you up a beautiful dream," said Simple. "You know you like them things, too. If I had not dreamed them up, you might not of thought of watermelon or greens tonight—greens, greens, greens!"

"Thinking of greens is not the same as eating them," I said.

"No," said Simple, "but at least we can share the thought. It was my thought. Don't you intend to share the beer? O.K. Draw two, bartender! Pay the man—and let us wash down those greens we have thought up. Pass the corn bread. I thank you, daddy-o! Now, hand me the vinegar, also the baby onions."

"You are certainly indulging in a flight of fancy! In fact, your imagination is running riot. Beer is not free."

"No, but fancy is, and if I had my way," said Simple, seizing his beer, "I would be a bird in a meadow full of greens right now!"

"Why a bird? Why not a horse, or a sheep?"

"A bird can fly high, see with a bird's eye, and dig all that is going on down on earth, especially what people are doing in the springtime."

"Birds are not customarily interested in the doings of human beings," I said, "except to the point of keeping out of their way."

"I would keep out of people's way," said Simple, "but also I would observe everything they do."

"Suppose they captured you and put you in a cage?"

"No, I would not be a pretty bird, the kind anybody would want in a cage. I would be just a plain old ugly bird that caws and nobody would want. That way I would be free. I would sail over towns and cities and look down and see what is going on. I would ride on tops of cars in Italian weddings, on top of hearses in Catholic funerals, I would light on the back of fish-tail Cadillacs in Harlem, and when I wanted to travel without straining myself, I would ride the baggage rack of a Greyhound bus to California.

"Before I left I would build me a nest on top of the Empire State so that when I came home I could rest on top of the world. I would dig worms in Radio City's gardens and set underneath a White House bush when I visited Washington. I would wash my feet in every fountain from here to yonder, and eat greens in every meadow. Down South I would ignore FOR WHITE and FOR COLORED signs—I would drink water anywhere I wished. I would not be tied to no race, no place, nor fixed location.

"I would be the travelingest bird you ever met—because everywhere that Jackie went, I would go. Every time Robinson batted a ball over the fence, I would be setting on that fence. I would watch Joe Black daily, and caw like mad for Campanella. I would outfly the Dodgers from New York to St. Louis, and from Boston to Chicago. Everywhere they went, there would be old me. Ah, but I would fly! On summer evenings I would dip my wings in the sea at Southampton and in winter live on baby oranges in Florida —if I did not go further to the West Indies and get away from Jim Crow. In fact, come to think of it, I believe I would just fly *over* the South, stopping only long enough to spread my tail feathers and show my contempt.

"If I was a bird, daddy-o, I would sometimes fly so high I would not see this world at all. I would soar! Just soar way up into the blue where heaven is, and the smell of earth does not go, neither the noise of juke boxes nor radios, television or record shops. Up there, I would not hear anything but winds blowing. I would not see anything but space. I would not remember no little old tawmarble called the world rolling around somewhere with you on it and Joyce and my boss and my landlady and her hound-dog of a Trixie. There would not be no paydays up there, neither rent-days nor birthdays nor Sunday. There would not be nothing but blue sky—and wind—and space. So much space!

"But when I got real lonesome looking at space, I would head back towards earth. I would pierce old space with my beak and cleave the wind with my wings. Yes, I would! I would split the sky wide open to get back to earth. And when I come in sight of Lenox Avenue, man, I would caw once real loud. Everybody would look up and think it was a horn honking on the Chariot of God. But it wouldn't be nobody but me—coming back to Harlem.

"I would swoop down on Seventh Avenue at six P.M. in the evening like a bat out of hell, do two loop-the-loops over the Theresa, and land on 125th Street by the Chock-Full-O'-Nuts. Then I would change myself back into a human, take the bus to my corner, put my key in my old landlady's vestibule, go up to my Third Floor Rear, wash my face, change my clothes, lay my hair down, and go see Joyce, and tell her I am tired of eating raw greens—to cook me up some ham and collards. I could not stand to be no bird anyhow if Joyce were not with me. Also, I would miss my friends. I would see how lonesome it were all day long up there in the heavenly blue and I would come back to this earth and home. Two beers, bartender!"

THAT POWERFUL DROP

Leaning on the lamp post in front of the barber shop, Simple was holding up a copy of the *Chicago Defender* and reading about how a man who looks white had just been declared officially colored by an Alabama court.

"It's powerful," he said.

"What?"

"That one drop of Negro blood—because just *one* drop of black blood makes a man colored. *One* drop—you are a Negro! Now, why is that? Why is Negro blood so much more powerful than any other kind of blood in the world? If a man has Irish blood in him, people will say, 'He's *part* Irish.' If he has a little Jewish blood, they'll say, 'He's *half* Jewish.' But if he has just a small bit of colored blood in him, BAM!—'*He's a Negro!*' Not, 'He's *part* Negro.' No, be it ever so little, if that blood is black, '*He's a Negro!*' Now, that is what I do not understand—why our *one* drop is so powerful. Take paint—white will not make black *white*. But black will make white *black*. One drop of black in white paint—and the white ain't white no more! Black is powerful. You can have ninety-nine drops of white blood in your veins down South—but if that other *one* drop is black, shame on you! Even if you look white, you're black. That drop is really powerful. Explain it to me. You're colleged."

"It has no basis in science," I said, "so there's no logical explanation."

"Anyhow," said Simple, "if we lived back in fairy tale days and a good fairy was to come walking up to me and offer me three wishes, the very first thing I would wish would be:

THAT ALL WHITE FOLKS WAS BLACK

then nobody would have to bother about white blood and black blood any more. And my second would be:

THAT ALL POOR FOLKS WAS RICH

which would include my relatives—so I wouldn't have to worry about them any more. After that I'd wish:

THAT ALL SICK FOLKS WAS WELL

then nobody would suffer."

"Do you think things are that simple?" I asked. "If everybody in the world were the same color, nobody was poor, and everybody was well, do you really think there would be no more problems?"

"All *mine* would be solved," said Simple.

"There would still be the problems of the heart."

"Joyce is *my* heart and I can take care of her," said Simple. "But if I just had one more wish, my fourth and final wish would be:

THAT I HAD MY DIVORCE

—from Isabel, so I could marry Joyce."

"Your divorce is on the way, isn't it?"

"Somebody still has to make that final payment, I told you."

"Since you are making so free with your wishes," I said, "why don't you wish for a little foresight, so you wouldn't start so late doing what you should have done long ago. You have been courting Joyce five or six years. For the last two or three years you have been intending to marry her. And you still haven't saved enough money to pay for even one installment on a three-way divorce. Why is that?"

"You know why that is," said Simple. "I don't make enough money. Since the war plants closed down, who in Harlem has made any money—except politicians, number writers, and dope pushers? Have you? And you are colleged. People with an education should always have money. So if I had another wish, I would wish:

THAT YOU ALWAYS BE STANDING PAT

because you have been on the up and up with me. You are one of my few buddies who will always buy me a beer when I am broke. Naturally I include you in my wishes. In fact, I wish I had a Piel's right now."

"Do you realize this is the middle of the week, also that you've had four beers already, and that excess in anything is sin? Since you are changing the world by wishes tonight, why don't you wish that you were free from sin?"

"Sin ain't free," said Simple. "That costs money, too."

MIDSUMMER MADNESS

Pavement hot as a frying pan on Ma Frazier's griddle. Heat devils dancing in the air. Men in windows with no undershirts on—which is one thing ladies can't get by with if they lean out windows. Sunset. Stoops running over with people, curbs running over with kids. August in Harlem too hot to be August in hell. Beer is going up a nickel a glass, I hear, but I do not care. I would still be forced to say gimme a cool one.

"That bar's sign is lying—AIR COOLED—which is why I'd just as well stay out here on the sidewalk. Girl, where did you get them baby-doll clothes? Wheee-ee-oooo!" The woman did not stop, but you could tell by the way she walked that she heard him. Simple whistled. "Hey, Lawdy, Miss Claudy! Or might your name be Cleopatra?" No response. "Partner, she ig-ed me."

"She really ignored you," I said.

"Well, anyhow, every dog has its day—but the trouble is there are more dogs than there are days, more people than there are houses, more roomers than there are rooms, and more babies than there are cribs."

"You're speaking philosophically this evening."

"I'm making up proverbs. For instance: 'A man with no legs don't need shoes.' "

"Like most proverbs, that states the obvious."

"It came right out of my own head—even if I did hear it before," insisted Simple. "Also I got another one for you based on experience: 'Don't get a woman that *you* love. Get a woman that loves you!' "

"Meaning, I take it, that if a woman loves *you,* she will take care of you, and you won't have to take care of her."

"Something like that," said Simple, "because if you love a woman you are subject to lay down your all before her, empty your heart and your pockets, and then have nothing left. I bet if I had been born with a silver spoon in my mouth, some woman would of had my spoon before I got to the breakfast table. I always was weak for women. In fact, womens is the cause of my being broke tonight. After I buy Joyce her summer ice cream and Zarita her summer beer, I cannot hardly buy myself a drink by the middle of the week. At dinner time all I can do is walk in a restaurant and say, 'Gimme an order of water—in a clean glass.' "

"I will repeat a proverb for *you*," I said. " 'It's a mighty poor chicken that can't scratch up his own food.' "

"I am a poor rooster," said Simple. "Womens have cleaned me to the bone. I may give out, but I'll never give up, though. Neither womens nor white folks are going to get Jesse B. down."

"Can't you ever keep race out of the conversation?" I said.

"I am race conscious," said Simple. "And I ain't ashamed of my race. I ain't like that woman that bought a watermelon and had it *wrapped* before she carried it out of the store. I am what I am. And what I say is: 'If you're corn bread, don't try to be an angel-food cake! That's a mistake. . . . Look at that chick! Look at that de-light under the light! So round, so firm, so fully packed! But don't you be looking, too, partner. You might strain your neckbone."

"You had better take your own advice," I said, "or you might get your head cut off. A woman with a shape like that is bound to have a boy friend."

"One more boy friend would do her no harm," said Simple, "so it might as well be me. But you don't see me moving out of my tracks, do you? I have learned one thing just by observation: Midsummer madness brings winter sadness, so curb your badness. If you can't be good, be careful. In this hot weather with womens going around not only with bare back, but some of them with mighty near everything else bare, a man has got to watch his self. Look at them right here on the Avenue—play suits, sun suits, swim suits, practically no suits. I swear, if I didn't care for Joyce, I'd be turning my head every which-a-way, and looking every which-a-where. As it is, I done eye-balled a plenty. This is the hottest summer I ever seen—but the womens look cool. That is why a man has to be careful."

"Cool, too, you mean—controlled!"

"Also careful," said Simple. "I remember last summer seeing them boys around my stoop, also the mens on the corner jiving with them girls in the windows, and the young mens in the candy store buying ice cream for jail bait and beating bongos under be-bop windows. And along about the middle of the winter, or maybe it was spring, I heard a baby crying in the room underneath me, and another one gurgling in the third floor front. And this summer on the sidewalk I see *more* new baby carriages, and rattles being raised, and milk bottles being sucked. It is beautiful the way nature keeps right on producing Negroes. But the Welfare has done garnished some of these men's wages. And the lady from the Domestic Relations Court has been upstairs in the front room investigating twice as to where Carlyle has gone. When he do come home he will meet up with a summons."

"I take it Carlyle is a young man who does not yet realize the responsibilities of parenthood."

"Carlyle is old enough to know a baby has to eat. And I do not give him credit for cutting out and leaving that girl with that child—except that they had a fight, and Carlyle left her a note which was writ: 'Him who fights and runs away, lives to fight some other day.' The girl said Carlyle learned that in high school when he ought to have been learning how to get a good job that pays more than thirty-two dollars a week. When their baby were born, it was the coldest day in March. And my big old fat landlady, what always said she did not want no children in the house, were mad when the Visiting Health Nurse came downstairs and told her to send some heat up.

"She said, 'You just go back upstairs and tell that Carlyle to send me some money down. He is two weeks behind now on his rent. I told him not to be setting on my stoop with that girl last summer. Instead of making hay while the sun were shining, he were using his time otherwise. Just go back upstairs and tell him what I said.'

" 'All of which is no concern of mine,' says the Health Nurse. 'I am concerned with the welfare of mother and child. Your house is cold, except down here where you and your dog is at.'

" 'Just leave Trixie out of this,' says the landlady. 'Trixie is an old dog and has rheumatism. I love this dog better than I love myself, and I intends to keep her warm.'

" 'If you do not send some steam upstairs, I will advise your tenants to report you to the Board of Health,' says the Health Nurse.

"She were a real spunky little nurse. I love that nurse—because about every ten days she came by to see how them new babies was making out. And every time she came, that old landlady would steam up. So us roomers was warm some part of last winter, anyhow."

"Thanks especially to Carlyle and his midsummer madness," I said. "But where do you suppose the boy went when he left his wife?"

"To his mama's in the Bronx," said Simple. "He is just a young fellow what is not housebroke yet. I seen him last night on the corner of Lenox and 125th and he said he was coming back soon as he could find himself a good job. Fight or not fight, he says he loves that girl and is crazy about his baby, and all he wants is to find himself a Fifty or Sixty Dollar a week job so he can meet his responsibilities. I said, 'Boy, how much did you say you want to make a week?' And he repeated himself, Fifty to Sixty.

"So I said, 'You must want your baby to be in high school before you returns.'

"Carlyle said, 'I'm a man now, so I want to get paid like a man.'

" 'You mean a white man,' I said.

" 'I mean a *grown* man,' says Carlyle.

"By that time the Bronx bus come along and he got on it, so I did not get a chance to tell that boy that I knowed what he meant, but I did not know how it could come true. . . . Man, look at that chick going yonder, stacked up like the Queen Mary! . . . Wheee-ee-ooo! Baby, if you must walk away, walk straight—and don't shake your tail-gate."

"Watch yourself! Have you no respect for women?"

"I have nothing but respect for a figure like that," said Simple. "Miss, your mama must of been sweet sixteen when she borned you. Sixteen divided by two, you come out a figure 8! Can I have a date? Hey, Lawdy, Miss Claudy! You must be deaf—you done left! I'm standing here by myself.

"Come on, boy, let's go on in the bar and put that door between me and temptation. If the air cooler is working, the treat's on me. Let's investigate. Anyhow, I always did say if you can't be good, be careful. If you can't me nice, take advice. If you don't think once, you can't think twice."

STAGGERING FIGURES

"If you had a Million Dollars and no poor relatives, what would you do with your money—buy a saloon?" I asked Simple.

"First I'd marry Joyce," said Simple. "And I would not buy no saloon, since I can come in here and drink. I would buy a house. After I bought the house, I would set Joyce up in business, so she would not always be around the house."

"That's a strange thing to say," I said. "Most men want their wives to stay home and keep house."

"I like to drop ashes on the floor sometimes," said Simple, "so I would want Joyce to be home in the daytime only to cook because, if I had a Million Dollars, I would be home all the time myself I would not go out to work nowhere—I would just rest and get my strength back after all these years I been working. I could not rest with no woman around the house all day, not even Joyce. A woman is all the time saying, 'Do this' and 'Do that.' And 'Ain't you cut the grass yet?'

"I would say, 'No, I ain't, baby. Let it go till next week.'

"Then, if she's like the rest of the women, she would say, 'You don't take no pride in nothing. I have to do everything.' And she would go out and cut it herself, just to spite me.

"That is why, if I had a Million Dollars, first thing I would do if I was married would be to set my wife up in business so she wouldn't worry me. Womens like to be active. They *hate* to see a man set down. So I would give my wife some place else to be active other than around me."

"In other words, you would make your wife work," I said.

"I would rather make her work than to have her make *me* work. Of course, if she was the type that just liked to lounge around and eat chocolates, which I have never known no colored woman to do, that might be different. Colored women are so used to working that they can't stop when they get a chance to set down. And they hate to see a man do nothing. Why do you reckon this is?"

"You've supplied the answer yourself. Activity over a long period of time breeds intolerance to inactivity," I said. "One has to be accustomed to leisure to know how to enjoy it."

"I am not accustomed to it," said Simple, "but I really could enjoy it. Why, man, if I had a Million Dollars, I would not stir a peg nor lift a finger! Of course, I might tap my own beer keg. But I doubt if I would even do that. I would have a house-man to tap it for me. I would also have a butler serve it. And I would have a valet to press my clothes, so all I would have to do would be to get in my car and go downtown to see how my wife was running her business. If I found her with time on her hands, I might say, 'Baby, come on home and cook me some lunch.'"

"You certainly do have old-time ideas about women," I said.

"I cannot put them in force," said Simple. "Lend me a dime for that last beer so I can get home and see if F.D. is in the house. I am not only broke tonight, but beat. Buddy, you are heaven-sent! Any man who will lend me a dime is O.K. by me any time. Money talks! Big money hollers! I couldn't hear my ears if I had a Million Dollars! I don't like noise—so gimme *just* a dime, and we'll have a drink."

"No! I've set you up twice already. I do not intend to break a dollar, not having a million."

"Loan your dollar to me and I will break it. Buddy, I am as

free from money now as a Christian is from sin. Gimme the dollar. I will treat you."

"Calm down, calm down! What are you celebrating anyhow?"

"I'm celebrating just because it's Monday. Tuesday I'm always too broke to celebrate. Wednesday I'm too tired. Thursday I'm disgusted. Friday, exhausted. But Saturday, Sunday, and sometimes even Monday—whoopee! So let's have another one. If I go to sleep sober I might dream I'm handling money, and wake up screaming. I don't trust myself. My left hand might short change my right. Let's have one for the road. Go ahead and break your dollar. What difference do it make?"

"With my dollar intact," I said, "I'm only $999,999 away from having a million."

"Such figures staggers me," said Simple.

THAT WORD *BLACK*

"This evening," said Simple, "I feel like talking about the word *black*."

"Nobody's stopping you, so go ahead. But what you really ought to have is a soap-box out on the corner of 126th and Lenox where the rest of the orators hang out."

"They expresses some good ideas on that corner," said Simple, "but for my ideas I do not need a crowd. Now, as I were saying, the word *black*, white folks have done used that word to mean something bad so often until now when the N.A.A.C.P. asks for civil rights for the black man, they think they must be bad. Looking back into history, I reckon it all started with a *black* cat meaning bad luck. Don't let one cross your path!

"Next, somebody got up a *black-list* on which you get if you don't vote right. Then when lodges come into being, the folks they didn't want in them got *black-balled*. If you kept a skeleton in your closet, you might get *black-mailed*. And everything bad was *black*. When it came down to the unlucky ball on the pool table, the eight-rock, they made it the *black* ball. So no wonder there ain't no equal rights for the *black* man."

"All you say is true about the odium attached to the word *black*," I said. "You've even forgotten a few. For example, during the war if you bought something under the table, illegally, they said you were trading on the *black* market. In Chicago, if you're a gangster, the *Black Hand Society* may take you for a ride. And certainly if you don't behave yourself, your family will say you're a *black* sheep. Then if your mama burns a *black* candle to change the family luck, they call it *black* magic."

"My mama never did believe in voodoo so she did not burn no black candles," said Simple.

"If she had, that would have been a *black* mark against her."

"Stop talking about my mama. What I want to know is, where do white folks get off calling everything bad *black*? If it is a dark night, they say it's *black* as hell. If you are mean and evil, they say you got a *black* heart. I would like to change all that around and say that the people who Jim Crow me have got a *white* heart. People who sell dope to children have got a *white* mark against them. And all the white gamblers who were behind the basketball fix are the *white* sheep of the sports world. God knows there was few, if any, Negroes selling stuff on the black market during the war, so why didn't they call it the *white* market? No, they got to take me and my color and turn it into everything *bad*. According to white folks, black is bad.

"Wait till my day comes! In my language, bad will be *white*. Blackmail will be *white* mail. Black cats will be good luck, and *white* cats will be bad. If a white cat crosses your path, look out! I will take the black ball for the cue ball and let the *white* ball be the unlucky eight-rock. And on my blacklist—which will be a *white* list then—I will put everybody who ever Jim Crowed me from Rankin to Hitler, Talmadge to Malan, South Carolina to South Africa.

"I am black. When I look in the mirror, I see myself, daddy-o, but I am not ashamed. God made me. He also made F.D., dark as he is. He did not make us no badder than the rest of the folks. The earth is black and all kinds of good things comes out of the earth. Everything that grows comes up out of the earth. Trees and flowers and fruit and sweet potatoes and corn and all that keeps mens alive comes right up out of the earth—good old black earth. Coal is black and it warms your house and cooks your food. The night is black, which has a moon, and a million stars, and is beautiful. Sleep is black which gives you rest, so you wake up feeling good. I am black. I feel very good this evening.

"What is wrong with black?"

DEAR DR. BUTTS

"Do you know what has happened to me?" said Simple.

"No."

"I'm out of a job."

"That's tough. How did that come about?"

"Laid off—they're converting again. And right now, just when I am planning to get married this spring, they have to go changing from civilian production to war contracts, installing new machinery. Manager says it might take two months, might take three or four. They'll send us mens notices. If it takes four months, that's up to June, which is no good for my plans. To get married a man needs money. To stay married he needs more money. And where am I? As usual, behind the eight-ball."

"You can find another job meanwhile, no doubt."

"That ain't easy. And if I do, they liable not to pay much. Jobs that pay good money nowadays are scarce as hen's teeth. But Joyce says she do not care. She is going to marry me, come June, anyhow —even if she has to pay for it herself. Joyce says since I paid for the divorce, she can pay for the wedding. But I do not want her to do that."

"Naturally not, but maybe you can curtail your plans somewhat and not have so big a wedding. Wedlock does not require an elaborate ceremony."

"I do not care if we don't have none, just so we get locked. But you know how womens is. Joyce has waited an extra year for her great day. Now here I am broke as a busted bank."

"How're you keeping up with your expenses?"

"I ain't. And I don't drop by Joyce's every night like I did when I was working. I'm embarrassed. Then she didn't have to ask me to eat. Now she does. In fact, she insists. She says, 'You got to eat somewheres. I enjoy your company. Eat with me.' I do, if I'm there when she extends the invitation. But I don't go looking for it. I just sets home and broods, man, and looks at my four walls, which gives me plenty of time to think. And do you know what I been thinking about lately?"

"Finding work, I presume."

"Besides that?"

"No. I don't know what you've been thinking about."

"Negro leaders, and how they're talking about how great democracy is—and me out of a job. Also how there is so many leaders I don't know that white folks know about, because they are always in the white papers. Yet *I'm* the one they are supposed to be leading. Now, you take that little short leader named Dr. Butts, I do not know him, except in name only. If he ever made a speech in Harlem it were not well advertised. From what I reads, he teaches at a white college in Massachusetts, stays at the Commodore when he's in New York, and ain't lived in Harlem for ten years. Yet he's leading me. He's an article writer, but he does not write in colored papers. But lately the colored papers taken to reprinting parts of what he writes—otherwise I would have never seen it. Anyhow, with all this time on my hands these days, I writ him a letter last night. Here, read it."

Harlem, U.S.A.
One Cold February Day

Dear Dr. Butts,

I seen last week in the colored papers where you have writ an article for The New York Times *in which you say America is the greatest country in the world for the Negro race and Democracy the greatest kind of government for all, but it would be better if there was equal education for colored folks in the South, and if everybody could vote, and if there were not Jim Crow in the army, also if the churches was not divided up into white churches and colored churches, and if Negroes did not have to ride on the back seats of busses South of Washington.*

Now, all this later part of your article is hanging onto your but. *You start off talking about how great American democracy is, then you but it all over the place. In fact, the* but *end of your see-saw is so far down on the ground I do not believe the other end can ever pull it up. So me myself, I would not write no article for no* New York Times *if I had to put in so many buts. I reckon maybe you come by it naturally, though, that being your name, dear Dr. Butts.*

I hear tell that you are a race leader, but I do not know who you lead because I have not heard tell of you before and I have not laid eyes on you. But if you are leading me, make me know it, *because I do not read the* New York Times *very often, less I happen to pick up a copy blowing around in the subway, so I did not know you were my leader. But since you are my leader, lead on, and see if I will follow behind your* but—*because there is more behind that* but *than there is in front of it.*

Dr. Butts, I am glad to read that you writ an article in The New York Times, *but also sometime I wish you would write one in the colored papers and let me know how to get out from behind all these* buts *that are staring me in the face. I know America is a great country* but—*and it is that* but *that has been keeping me where I is all these years. I can't get over it, I can't get under it, and I can't get around it, so what am I supposed to do? If you are leading me, lemme see. Because we have too many colored leaders now that nobody knows until they get from the white papers to the colored papers and from the colored papers to me who has never seen hair nor hide of you. Dear Dr. Butts, are you hiding from me—and leading me, too?*

From the way you write, a man would think my race problem was made out of nothing but buts. *But* this, *but* that, *and, yes, there is Jim Crow in Georgia* but—. *America admits they bomb folks in Florida—but Hitler gassed the Jews. Mississippi is bad—but Russia is worse. Detroit slums are awful—but compared to the slums in India, Detroit's Paradise Valley is Paradise.*

Dear Dr. Butts, Hitler is dead. I don't live in Russia. India is across the Pacific Ocean. And I do not hope to see Paradise no time soon. I am nowhere near some of them foreign countries you are talking about being so bad. I am here! And you know as well as I do, Mississippi is hell. There ain't no but *in the world can make it out different. They tell me when Nazis gas you, you die slow. But when they put a bomb under you like in Florida, you don't have time to say your prayers. As for Detroit, there is as much difference between Paradise Valley and Paradise as there is between heaven and Harlem. I don't know nothing about India, but I been in Washington, D.C. If you think there ain't slums there, just take your* but *up Seventh Street late some night, and see if you still got it by the time you get to Howard University.*

I should not have to be telling you these things. You are colored just like me. To put a but *after all this Jim Crow fly-papering around our feet is just like telling a hungry man, "But Mr. Rockefeller has got plenty to eat." It's just like telling a joker with no overcoat in the winter time, "But you will be hot next summer." The fellow is liable to haul off and say, "I am hot now!" And bop you over your head.*

Are you in your right mind, dear Dr. Butts? Or are you just writing? Do you really think a new day is dawning? Do you really think Christians are having a change of heart? I can see you now taking your pen in hand to write, "But just last year the Southern Denominations of Hell-Fired Salvation resolved to work toward Brotherhood." In fact, that is what you already writ. Do you think Brotherhood means colored to them Southerners?

Do you reckon they will recognize you for a brother, Dr. Butts,
since you done had your picture taken in the Grand Ballroom of the
Waldorf-Astoria shaking hands at some kind of meeting with five
hundred white big-shots and five Negroes, all five of them Negro
leaders, *so it said underneath the picture? I did not know any of*
them Negro leaders by sight, neither by name, but since it says in
the white papers that they are leaders, I reckon they are. Anyhow, I
take my pen in hand to write you this letter to ask you to make your-
self clear to me. When you answer me, do not write no "so-and-so-
and-so but—." I will not take but for an answer. Negroes have been
looking at Democracy's but too long. What we want to know is how
to get rid of that but.

Do you dig me, dear Dr. Butts?

Sincerely very truly,
JESSE B. SEMPLE

Simple Stakes a Claim

BANG-UP BIG END

"I wonder how come they don't have lady pallbearers?" asked my friend.

"Lady pallbearers?"

"Yes," said Simple, "at funerals. I have never yet seen a lady carrying a coffin. Women do everything else these days from flying airplanes and driving taxis to fighting bulls. They might as well be pallbearers, too."

"Maybe it's because women are more emotional than men," I said. "They might break down from sorrow and drop the corpse."

"Whooping and hollering and fainting and falling out like they used to do at the old time funerals," said Simple, "has gone out of style now, leastwise in Harlem where the best undertakers has a nurse in attendance. If anybody faints at a funeral now, the nurses stick so much smelling salts up to your nose that you sneeze and come to right away. You better come to—else that ammonia will blow your wig off. They say undertakers' helpers get paid by the hour now, too. They are very busy people, also expensive, so they have no time for nobody holding up a funeral by fainting. And these modern educated ministers do not like their sermons interrupted by people screaming and yelling. Modern ministers is all Doctors of Divinities and such, so too cultured for hollering. But I remember a funeral I went to once down in Virginia where all the mourners delivered sermons, too, and talked and hollered louder than the preacher. And the widow of the deceased asked the dead man why did he leave her.

" 'Why did you leave me, Thomas?' she cried. 'Why?'

"She knew darned well the man drunk himself to death, also that she had put him out of the house more than once, and quit him twice. Yet there she was crying because he had relieved her of his burden once and for all. You could hardly hear the minister who was preaching the corpse to heaven instead of hell, so much racket did his wife and relatives keep up."

"Ways of grieving vary," I said. "In India, for example, the widow in some communities throws herself onto a flaming bier and perishes with her husband."

"Them widows must be right simple," said Simple.

"In some countries widows wear black all the rest of their lives after the husband dies."

"Which saves them cleaning bills," said Simple. "Dirt does not show on black."

"In Ireland they have wonderful wakes the night before a funeral and eat and drink all night."

"I wish I was in Ireland," said Simple. "I could really help drain a bottle."

"And in Haiti they play cards at the wake."

"No," said Simple, "*no cards!* I would not want to lose my money gambling, not even for my best friend. I would not play no cards at nobody's wake."

"In some parts of Asia, they bury the dead standing up."

"Which is better than being buried upside down," said Simple, "or cremated—burnt up before you gets to hell."

"Cremation is a sanitary process, I think. Besides, ashes takes up very little space. Just imagine all the acres and acres of land nowadays taken up by cemeteries. A person's ashes in a jar can be kept on the mantelpiece."

"What old mantelpiece? Where?" cried Simple. "Never no ashes of no deceased on my mantelpiece. Oh, no! When a person is dead and gone they should be where they belong, in the ground."

"Pure custom," I said. "In some countries folks are not buried in the ground at all. In certain primitive communities the dead are put on a mountaintop and left there. At sea you're dropped in the water. It's all according to what you are accustomed."

"Well, I have not been buried yet," said Simple, "but when the end comes and I am, I want to be decent buried, not dropped in no water, nor left on no mountain, neither burnt up. Also I want plenty of whooping and hollering and crying over me so the world will know I have been here and gone—a bang-up big end. I do not want no quiet funeral like white folks. I want people to hear my funeral through the windows. If not, I am liable to rise up in my coffin myself and holler and cry. I demand excitement when I leave this earth. Whoever inherits my insurance money, I want 'em to holler, moan, weep and cry for it. If they don't, I dead sure will come back and cut 'em out of my will. Negroes don't have much in this world, so we might as well have a good funeral."

BIG ROUND WORLD

"The other day a white man asked where is my home," said Simple. "I said, 'What do you mean, where is my home—as big and round as the world is? Do you mean where I live now? Or where I *did* live? Or where I was born?'

" 'I mean, where you *did* live,' the white man said.

" 'I did live every-which-a-where,' I told him.

" 'I mean, where was you born—North or South?' the white man said.

" 'I knowed that's what you mean,' I said, 'so why didn't you say so? I were born where you was born.'

" 'No, you weren't,' he declared, 'because I was born in Germany.'

" 'Some Negroes was born as far away as Africa,' I said.

" 'You weren't, were you?' he asked.

" 'Do I look like a Mau Mau?' I said.

" 'You look African, but you speak our language,' that white man told me.

" '*Your* language,' I hollered, 'and you was born in Germany! You are speaking *my* language.'

" 'Then you are an American?'

" 'I are,' I said.

" 'From what parts?' he kept on.

" 'All parts,' I said.

" 'North or South?' he asked me.

" 'I knowed you'd get down to that again,' I said. 'Why?'

" 'Curiosity,' he says.

" 'If I told you I was born in the South,' I said, 'you would believe me. But if I told you I was born in the North, you wouldn't. So I ain't going to say where I was born. I was just borned, that's all, and my middle name is Harlem.' That is what I told that white man. And that is all he found out about where I was borned," said Simple.

"Why did you make it so hard on him?" I asked. "I see no reason why you should not tell the man you were born in Virginia."

"Why should I tell him that? White folks think all Negroes should be born in the South," said Simple.

"There is nothing to be ashamed of about being born down South," I said.

"Neither about eating watermelon or singing spirituals," said

Simple. "I like watermelon and I love 'Go Down, Moses,' but I do not like no white man to ask me do I like watermelon or can I sing spirituals."

"I would say you are racially supersensitive," I said. "I am not ashamed of where I was born."

"Where was you borned?" asked Simple.

"Out West," I said.

"West of Georgia?" asked Simple.

"No," I said, "west of the Mississippi."

"I knowed there was something Southern about it," said Simple.

"You are just like that white man," I said. "Just because I am colored, too, do I *have* to be born down South?"

"I expect you was," said Simple. "And even if you wasn't, if that white man was to see you, he would think you was. They think all of us are from down in 'Bam."

"So what? Why are you so sensitive about the place of your birth certificate?"

"What old birth certificate? Where I was born they didn't even have no birth certificates."

"Then you could claim any nationality," I said, "East Indian, West Indian, Egyptian, German."

"I could even claim to be French," said Simple.

"Yes," I said, "or Swiss."

"No, no!" said Simple. "Not Swiss! Somebody might put *chitterling* in front of it. And I am not from Chitterling-Swiss! No, I am not from Georgia! And I have not traveled much, but I have been a few places. And one thing I do know is that if you go around the world, in the end you get right back to where you started from —which is really going around in circles. I wish the world was flat so a man could travel straight on forever to different places and not come back to the same place."

"In that case it would have to stretch to infinity," I said, "since nothing is endless except eternity. There the spirit lives and grows forever."

"Suppose man was like the spirit," said Simple, "and not only lived forever but kept on growing, too. How long do you suppose my hair would get?"

"Don't ask foolish questions," I said.

"Negroes who claim to have Indian grandmas always swear their grandma's hair was so long she could set on it. My grandma did not have so much hair in this world. But, no doubt, in the spirit world that is changed, also her complexion, since they say that up there we shall be whiter than snow."

"That, I think, refers to the *spirit*, not the body. You change and grow in holiness, not in flesh."

"I would also like to grow in the flesh," said Simple. "I would like to be bigger than Joe Louis in the spirit world. In fact, I would like to be a giant, a great big black giant, so I could look down on Dixie and say, 'Don't you dare talk back to me!' I would like to have hands so big I could pick up Georgia in one and Mississippi in the other, and butt them together, bam! And say, 'Now you-all get rid of this prejudice stuff.' I would also like to slap Alabama on the backsides just once, and shake Florida so bad until her teeth would rattle and she would abolish separate schools.

"As I grew taller, I would look over the edge of the big round world and grab England and shake her till she turns the Mau Maus free, and any other black parts of the world in her possession. I would also reach down in South Africa and grab that man, Malan, and roll him in mulberry juice until he is as dark as me. Then I would say, 'Now see how *you* like to be segregated your own self. Apart your own hide!'

"As I keep on growing bigger and taller I'll lean over the earth and blow my breath on Australia and turn them all Chinese-yellow and Japanese-brown, so they won't have a lily-white Australia any more. Then some of them other folks from Asia can get in there where there is plenty of room and settle down, too. Right now I hear Australia is like Levittown—NO COLORED ADMITTED. I would not harm a hair of Australian heads. I would just maybe kink their hair up a little like mine. Oh, if I was a giant in the spirit world, I would really play around!"

"You have an imagination *par excellence*," I said, "which is French for *great*."

"Great is right," said Simple. "I would be the coolest, craziest, maddest, baddest giant in the universe. I would sneeze—and blow the Klu Klux Klan plumb out of Dixie. I would clap my hands—and mash Jim Crow like a mosquito. I would go to Washington and rename the town—the same name—but after Booker T., not after George, because by that time segregation would be plumb and completely gone in the capital of the U.S.A. and Sarah Vaughn would be singing like a bird in Constitution Hall. With me the great American giant, a few changes would be made. Of course, there would be some folks who would not like me, but they would be so small I would shake them off my shoe tops like ants. I would take one step and be in California, another step to Honolulu, and one more to Japan, shaking a few ants off into the ocean each time I stepped. And wherever there was fighting and war, I would say, 'I don't care who started this battle, stop! But right now! Be at peace, so folks can settle down and plant something to eat again, particularly greens.' Then I would step on a little further to wherever else they are fighting and do the same. And anybody in this world who looked like they wanted to fight or drop atom bombs, I would snatch them up by their collars and say, 'Behave yourselves! Talk things out. Buy yourselves a glass of beer and argue. But he who fights will have *me* to lick!' Which I bet would calm them down, because I would be a real giant, the champeen, the Joe Louis of the universe, the cool kid of all time. This world would just be a marble in my pocket, that's all. I would not let nobody nick my marble with shells, bombs, nor rifle fire. I would say, 'Pay some attention to your religion, peoples, also to Father Divine, and shake hands. If you has no slogan of your own, take Father's, *Peace! It's truly wonderful!*' "

TWO SIDES NOT ENOUGH

"A man ought to have more than just two sides to sleep on," declared Simple. "Now if I get tired of sleeping on my left side, I have nothing to turn over on but my right side."

"You could sleep on your back," I advised.

"I snores on my back."

"Then why not try your stomach?"

"Sleeping on my stomach, I get a stiff neck—I always have to keep my head turned toward one side or the other, else I smothers. I do not like to sleep on my stomach."

"The right side, or the left side, are certainly enough sides for most people to sleep on. I don't know what your trouble is. But, after all, there are two sides to every question."

"That's just what I am talking about," said Simple. "Two sides are not enough. I'm tired of sleeping on either my left side, or on my right side, so I wish I had two or three more sides to change off on. Also, if I sleep on my left side, I am facing my wife, then I have to turn over to see the clock in the morning to find out what time it is. If I sleep on my right side, I am facing the window so the light wakes me up before it is time to get up. If I sleep on my back, I snores, and disturbs my wife. And my stomach is out for sleeping, due to reasons which I mentioned. In the merchant marine, sailors are always talking about the port side and the starboard side of a ship. A human should have not only a left side and a right side, but also a port side and a starboard side."

"That's what left and right mean in nautical terms," I said. "You know as well as I do that a ship has only two sides."

"Then ships are bad off as a human," said Simple. "All a boat can do when a storm comes up, is like I do when I sleep—toss from side to side."

"Maybe you eat too heavy a dinner," I said, "or drink too much coffee."

"No, I am not troubled in no digestion at night," said Simple. "But there is one thing that I do not like in the morning—waking up to face the same old one-eyed egg Joyce has fried for breakfast. What I wish is that there was different kinds of eggs, not just white eggs with a yellow eye. There ought to be blue eggs with a brown eye, and brown eggs with a blue eye, also red eggs with green eyes."

"If you ever woke up and saw a red egg with a green eye on your plate, you would think you had a hang-over."

"I would," said Simple. "But eggs *is* monotonous! No matter which side you turn an egg on, daddy-o, it is still an egg—hard on one side and soft on the other. Or, if you turn it over, it's hard on both sides. Once an egg gets in the frying pan, it has only two sides, too. And if you burn the bottom side, it comes out just like the race problem, black and white, black and white."

"I thought you'd get around to race before you got through. You can't discuss any subject at all without bringing in color. God help you! And in reducing everything to two sides, as usual, you over-simplify."

"What does I do?"

"I say your semantics make things too simple."

"My which?"

"Your verbiage."

"My what?"

"Your words, man, your words."

"Oh," said Simple. "Well, anyhow, to get back to eggs—which is a simple word. For breakfast I wish some other birds besides chickens laid eggs for eating, with a different kind of flavor than just a hen flavor. Whatever you are talking about with your *see-antics*, Jack, at my age a man gets tired of the same kind of eggs each and every day—just like you get tired of the race problem. I would like to have an egg some morning that tastes like a pork chop."

"In that case, why don't you have pork chops for breakfast instead of eggs?"

"Because there is never no pork chops in my icebox in the morning."

"There would be if you would put them there the night before."

"No," said Simple, "I would eat them up the night before—which is always the trouble with the morning after—you have practically nothing left from the night before—except the race problem."

DEPRESSION IN THE CARDS

"I really think another depression is coming back," said Simple.

"Why do you say that?" I asked.

"I see it in the cards," said Simple. "House-rent parties is returning to Harlem in a big way. I have collected me a whole cigar box full of house-rent party cards this winter, and still getting them. Look at these in my pocket now. Here's one that says:

"HOP, MISTER BUNNY,
SKIP, MISTER BEAR!
IF YOU DON'T DIG THIS PARTY
YOU AIN'T NOWHERE.
AROUND THE CORNER
AND UP ONE STAIR,
HEY STED, JIM DADDY,
THE ROCKING'S THERE!

"And last night when I stopped by this bar for my Friday beer, a fellow come handing me this card which says:

"WITH DIM LIGHTS ON
AND SHADES PULLED TIGHT,
LET'S CLOWN ON DOWN
TILL BROAD DAYLIGHT—
AT A SOCIAL GIVEN BY SNOOKS AND AMY
FRIDAY NIGHT—TEN—UNTIL!

"I asked Joyce did she want to go. Joyce said, 'With all the nice friends we got, why would you wish to be going to a party at somebody's house you don't even know?'

"I says, 'House-rent parties is fun, girl. Has you ever been to one?'

"Joyce said she has not and, what is more, is not going to none. She said I better not go neither. So I reckon I won't. But look here at this card which I have still got in my pocket from last week:

"DON'T MOVE TO THE
OUTSKIRTS OF TOWN.
JUST DROP AROUND

AND MEET A NEW BROWN

AT SUSIE SEALEY'S DO-RIGHT PARTY

SATURDAY NIGHT! TOO TIGHT! 50¢

"Naturally, I did not show that card to Joyce."

"Did you go to the party?" I asked.

"I were tempted," said Simple, "but I did not yield. And here is one sounds kinder good for next weekend. Do you want to come with me?"

"Where's it going to be?"

"Way up town, 154th Street, in the brown-sugar part of Sugar Hill. Listen to these poetries at the top of this card:

"NOT TOO SLOW

AND NOT TOO FAST

BUT A REAL GOOD TIME

WHILE THE DANCING LAST—

GIVEN BY PRETTY POLLY & SUNSHINE LENNIE—

PLENTY TO EAT, DRINK, AND BE MERRY WITH.

ENTRY: ONE SIMOLEON

"Don't you think we ought to go?"

"Well, maybe we should take it in," I said. "I haven't been to a house-rent party since the depression days of bathtub gin and wood alcohol."

"Now they serves Long Island corn," said Simple. "Supposed to be from the hills of West Virginia, but they make it right across the river in Brooklyn. It tastes like corn whiskey, though. You know, they can make anything in New York City."

"I rather hate to see bootlegging and pay-parties coming back," I said.

"Why?" asked Simple. "Sometimes you can have more fun at a pay-party than you do at a free one. At a free party to which you is invited, you has to behave yourself. At a paid one, you can clown down. Listen at this card:

"WE'LL HAVE OODLES OF GIRLS,

TALL, SLIPPERY AND SLIM.

THEY CAN DO THE MOMBO

TILL IT'S TOO BAD, JIM!

"And who will mombo right along with them is me, daddy-o! I know there'll be a kid setting back in the corner with a Calypso drum. You can smell the pigs' feet from the kitchen to the parlor, and hear folks laughing clean down on the first floor."

"Or screaming, 'Bloody Murder!' if a fight breaks out," I interposed.

"Negroes do not fight so much like they used to in the old days," said Simple, "not even at house-rent parties. Of course, now, if somebody puts it down too strong on somebody else's old lady—Help! But I do not goof off like that myself with strange women. I respect other men's property, pay-party or not. I do not like excitements. Now this card about the party tonight is pure mischief:

"ONE LIGHT'S BLUE AND
THE OTHER LIGHT'S RED.
YOU CAN STAY ALL NIGHT
BUT YOU CAN'T GO TO BED
AT TALL SLIM MAMIE'S PARLOR SOCIAL
WHERE AIN'T NO DEPRESSION—
JUST A LITTLE RECESSION!
SO PAY AS YOU GO!

"Should I go," asked Simple, "or not?"

"No," I said.

"If everybody said no, poor Mamie could not pay her rent. I believe I will run by for a few minutes and spend a dollar. I might need help myself someday should I throw a party. Who knows?"

OUT-LOUD SILENT

"When you smell smoke there's due to be fire," said Simple. "And when you see sawdust, the mill can't be far away."

"Just what you mean by all this, I do not know," I said.

"I mean with Negroes setting in the front seats of buses down South, something is bound to happen," said Simple. "Montgomery, Birmingham, Miami, Tallahassee—every bus seat must be a hot seat. Wood do burn!"

"Speaking of sawdust," I said, "the mills of the gods grind slowly."

"But grind some mills do," said Simple, "and not just sawdust. Some mills also grind muscle, bone, flesh, and soul."

"Which is exactly what I was commenting on," I answered.

"You are an off-beat commentator," said Simple, "and I do not always know what you mean. You can be a puzzlement. Sometimes with me I think you are, sometimes not."

"True," I said, "sometimes *yes,* sometimes *no* in regard to you. You are not a man with whom I can always agree."

"I cannot always agree with myself," said Simple. "And when I talk back to myself, sometimes, I talk too loud."

"Out loud?"

"I ain't that old yet," said Simple. "I do not go around talking really *out loud* to myself. What I do is I talks silent in my own brain —*out-loud silent*—and sometimes I say, 'Jesse B., listen! You are getting old enough to know better. Now, at times you do do better, but not better enough. Jesse B., you got a long ways to go, and you didn't start from so far back that you are not due to be a lot further along. If you had not stopped so often to enjoy your damn self so much on the way, Jesse B., just think! You might own your own house in Harlem now and not be dependent on no landlord, neither landlady for a place to lay your head, and Joyce's."

"True," I said.

"Now, take Joyce, my wife, who is a good woman—I owes her a better living than I am making. She tells me so herself every day. I get mad to hear it, but it is the truth. Joyce deserves the best. What I give her is the best she can *make* of it, but not the *best*. Take our kitchenette. We got a bed that folds up and makes like a couch, so our place won't look like a bedroom when company comes. A man and wife, white or colored, should not have to fold up their bed every morning when they get up, particularly on Sundays. You might want to jump in it again—and there it is all folded up in case company comes. Dog-gone company, I say! But a woman does not take that position. A woman, no matter what she is doing, wants to have things looking well if company comes. Women get all flustered. I say just let company knock until you get the bed folded up. You can be sure there's no white folks coming visiting—and most colored folks live just like us in New York. But Joyce says it looks like by now we could at least afford a house with a bedroom. She is right. If I had not spent so much time in so many barrooms before marriage, I could have a bedroom after marriage. Oh, well, daddy-o, such a lot of beer has gone over the bar that there is no use crying over spilt milk in a kitchenette. Me, I cry not, but sometimes I recalls. And the beer were good!"

"But the memory is bitter," I commented.

"Not too bitter," declared Simple. "The trouble about remembering the past is that so many *wrong* things were *so* good. It is hard to regret what were FINE! It is also hard to kick yourself in the behind for what you got a kick out of doing. There is no kicks in kicks for kicks, nor sense neither. If I kicked my gizzard out now, it will not bring back one glass of the beer that has gone through my gullet, nor restore nary wasted dime to my pocket. I regrets I has no regrets—but honestly I has none, not even when I think silent. But I agrees with that book I read on how to get ahead in the world— the time to start is NOW, daddy-o-boy, not then. THEN is dust that the wind has blowed away. Yesterday is leaves on old trees that too many winters has caught. Tomorrow is almost all that is, since today is nearly gone by the time you get started, and tomorrow is nearly here now. The two connects so close together, today and tomorrow. So close, so close! But what I really love is tomorrow.

"'But what if tomorrow never comes?' says Joyce.

"'Aw, baby,' says I, 'then couldn't we leave our bed down *just* for today—and, in case tomorrow comes, make it up then?'"

JIM CROW'S FUNERAL

"I wish there was some way of dying without dying," said Simple, "of getting rid of the bad things that afflicts mens, keeping the good —and still being alive. For instant, my old Aunt Lucy had arthritis, which made her kind of snappy at times, but she was a good soul, one of the best. Now if the *arthritis* would have just died, instead of her, that would have been like it should be. Look at President Roosevelt—if what ailed him could have died, but not *him* the world might have been different today."

"In other words," I said, "you mean if the ills of the flesh could pass on, but not the good people who have them, it would be a fine thing. Your fallacy there is that not *all* people are good to begin with. Some are ill—and evil, too."

"It is the bad in them that I wish would die," said Simple. "If I were a judge I would not put nobody to death. I would just sentence the bad in them to die."

"Unfortunately, mankind has devised no sure-fire way to separate the evil from man, or man from evil. The theory of capital punishment is that if the *whole* man is put to death, the evil will go with him—his particular evil, that is. It is a kind of legal assassination. But the trouble is that the patterns of evil are not individual, they are social. They spread among a great many people. Electrocute one murderer today, but someone else is committing murder some other place at that very moment. Killing a man doesn't kill the form of the crime. It just kills him. What we need to do is get at the basic roots of evil, just as a physician tries to get at the roots of disease."

"That is what I mean," said Simple. "It is the sick root that should go, not the whole green tree."

"Of course, there are arguments on both sides," I said. "Sometimes the illness has spread from the root to the whole green tree, as you put it. So the leaves are no longer green, but withered and dry, and the branches have no sap in them, in which case some say you might as well cut the tree down."

"I really started out talking about people being sick, not trees, not murder, not evil. Just plain old backache, headache, stomach-ache sick—which is what removes more people from this world than an electric chair. I am wishing, for instant, that I will never get nothing that will make me sick enough to die."

"In that case, you would just die of old age. Everybody dies of something."

"I do not want to catch old age, either," said Simple.

"Old age catches everyone sooner or later. No human is immortal on this earth. You were not meant to stay here forever."

"I'd *like* to stay here," said Simple.

"For what purpose?"

"To live to see the day when I would not have to hire a lawyer to go to the Supreme Court to eat in a restaurant in Virginia. I would like to live to see the day when I could eat anywhere in the U.S.A."

"That may not be long," I said.

"It will be longer than it takes for some germ to mow me down," said Simple. "If Jim Crow was only human, maybe Jim Crow would get sick, catch pneumonia, get knotted up with arthritis, have gallstones, a strain, t.b., cancer, else a bad heart—and die. I would not mind seeing Jim Crow die. If necessary, *put* to death. In fact, I would pay for Jim Crow's funeral—even send flowers. If the family requested, I would even rise and preach his funeral. Yes, I would! I would say, 'Jim Crow, Jim Crow, the Lord has taken you away! Thank God, Jim Crow, you will never again drink from no *white* water fountain while I go dry. Never again, Jim Crow, will you set up in front of the buses from Washington to New Orleans while I rides back over the wheels. Never again will you, Jim Crow, laying here dead, rise up and call me out of my name, *nigger*. I got you in my power now, and I will preach you to your grave.

"'You did not know a Negro was going to preach your funeral, did you, Jim Crow? Well, I is! Me, Jesse B. Semple, was made in the image of God from time eternal from the clay of the infinite into whom was breathed the Breath of Life *just to preach your funeral*, Jim Crow, and to consign you to the dust where you may rot in peace until the world stops spinning around in the universe and comes to a halt so all-of-a-sudden-hell-fired-quick that it will fling you, me and everybody through the A.M. and the P.M. of Judgment *wham* to the foot of the throne of God! God will say, *Jim Crow! Jim Crow! Get away! Hie yourself hence! Make haste—and take your place in hell!*

" 'I'm sorry, but that is what God will say, Jim Crow. So I might as well say it first.

" 'It gives me great pleasure, Jim Crow, to close your funeral with these words—as the top is shut on your casket and the hearse pulls up outside the door—and Talmadge, Eastland, and Byrnes wipe their weeping eyes—and every coach on the Southern Railroad is draped in mourning—as the Confederate flag is at half-mast—and the D.A.R. has fainted—*Jim Crow, you go to hell!*' "

REASON AND RIGHT

"Well, sir," said Simple, "did you see in the paper where they canceled that Brotherhood Week program down in Florida because a colored minister and a white minister was to speak together on the same program, and the choirs was to be mixed?"

"No," I said. "What happened?"

"They canceled it 'in the interest of brotherhood'! I'm telling you, white folks is something, particularly in Florida—barring out Negro Republicans from their own party dinner, barring Lena Horne out of that hotel at Miami Beach, and then canceling their Brotherhood Week programs—so they can have brotherhood!"

"That later action," I said, "certainly sounds like a contradiction in terms."

"It is a contradiction," said Simple. "White folks at times can certainly be contrary. That is no way to behave in our democratic day and age. If a white minister and a colored minister can't even preach together, and white choirs and colored choirs can't sing together, how in God's name are Christians ever going to *get* together? The paper says the old folks—the white old folks—even gave the children notes to take to school, saying they didn't want to be no part of a Brotherhood program with colored folks on it. Them white parents put ugly ideas into their children who might act right if they was let alone. Don't the Bible say, 'Unless ye become as little children . . . ,' which my Aunt Lucy always said meant *pure* as childrens are, unless which 'ye cannot enter into the kingdom of heaven'? I do not see how Florida folks are ever going to get into the kingdom."

"I don't either, unless they are born again."

"Well, if they are born again, they ought to be born old—and grow backwards, from old age to youth. Then maybe they would get smarter as they grow younger—like children are smart—because now as folks get older they get dumber. It would be nice anyhow for everybody to be born seventy years old, bald-headed with false teeth, then grow backwards into children, getting younger and younger, instead of older and older. By the time a Southern white man had growed backwards in age to be ten years old, he might by then be nice and pure and good like a child. Growing backwards, by the time he got to be a baby, he would not have to suffer and die. He could just go on back where he came from and wouldn't even know it, since a baby don't know here from yonder. So, at that age, dying wouldn't mean a thing."

"A fantastic idea," I said.

"But a good one," said Simple. "In fact, for anybody, white or colored, to be born old and grow young would be good, instead of like it is now, being born young and growing old. Just think, if I was growing younger every day instead of older, what I would have to look forward to! In reverse, I could look backwards to when I was forty and had drunk too much licker, smoked too many cigarettes, suffered too much rheumatism, had too many toothaches, too many hangovers, and too much backache. But I could say, 'All that is going, going, gone now. I'm getting younger everyday. I can look forward to not drinking at all soon because I'll be under age, sneezing if I inhale a cigarette, and never having toothache, backache, or any other kind of ache—not being married. I can look forward to being a boy again with nothing to worry about in the way of wives, even undivorcing myself from my first wife without having to pay a cent, just by growing backwards. Even growing out of owing you the five dollars which I do now—by growing backwards past all my debts. Oh, it would be wonderful to grow backwards instead of forwards, pal, younger instead of older.'

"For white folks, it would really be something, growing in reverse. Them old prejudiced crackers could outgrow all their prejudices just by growing backwards to childhood, before they knew any difference in color. They could grow right back to brotherhood, too, even in Florida. Then just think how wonderful it would be in Miami! White folks and colored folks all sun-tanning on the same beach together, children singing in the same choir in the same church, all integrated, with a fine young five-year-old minister, white, saying, 'It's truly wonderful!' And me, colored and four years old, saying, 'Thank you, father!' And over in Atlanta, Georgia, Talmadge, just two years old, making a speech, saying,

'We're all brothers—everybody, white and black—not just during Brotherhood Week, but every week.' To which I would say, 'Amen!' Then all of America would soon be a young nation again, like they was before they forgot what brotherhood means. I say, let's grow backwards."

"By growing backwards, you think we might solve the problems of race. But how do you feel about juvenile delinquency?"

"We old folks, white or black, *do* behave better than the young ones nowadays, don't we? We damn sure do! Take for example, when I was young," said Simple, "kids used to fight with their fists, wrestle and run, and maybe at a distance, throw stones. At the worst, the very worst, if you was *real* bad, a boy might draw a knife—but seldom use it. Nowadays, these teen-agers and children, too, shoot—and shoot to kill. Why do you reckon that is?"

"When we were young," I said, "wars were fought with rifles. Nowadays, wars are fought with atom bombs. Fighting has moved ahead for the worse."

"When I was young," said Simple, "if I got caught smoking just a plain old Piedmont cigarette, I were whipped. Nowadays, cigarettes ain't nothing. Kids smoke reefers and blow the smoke in their mama's face. Why you reckon that is?"

"When you were young," I said, "grownups were having a wild time if they went on a beer party and got home at midnight. Nowadays, if they don't have Scotch, bourbon, gin and vodka, it's a tame shindig. And midnight is just about the time to start. Everybody's gotten wilder since your generation."

"I were twenty-five years old," said Simple, "before I ever saw a dirty picture. Now, I read in the papers where they sell them naked in the schoolyards."

"When you were young," I said, "people hid *True Confessions* so their grandmothers wouldn't see it around the house. But that was before the days when grandmas read Mickey Spillane, and comic books are on every newsstand."

"Comics was really comic when I was a kid," said Simple. "You know 'Mutt and Jeff' and 'Bringing Up Father' and 'The Katzenjammer Kids.' Now the comics ain't even funny no more. They are all crime and stuff, and monsters and crazy people and spies and such. No wonder kids have stopped trying to be cute and are trying to be criminal. And the movies used to be all about piethrowers and love and vampires and Chicago gangsters who got shot in the end. Now, it's not just gangsters shooting up the show. Everybody carries a gun in pictures nowadays. This must be the Gun Age. I thought people had to have a license to carry a gun.

But I never see nobody pull out a license in the movies. They just pull out a gun. *Bam!* And somebody is dead! I seed six killings in one picture the last time I went to a movie. Same on TV. Same on the radio. A show is not a show without one killing at the beginning, two in the middle, and three on the end. Can you blame children? Kids think life ain't worth living, I reckon, if they ain't shooting."

"Certainly our entertainment media are full of violence," I said. "But after all, it's make-believe. I think even youngsters realize it is not real."

"It's so exciting, they want to make it real," said Simple.

"So you believe life imitates art? Personally, I think it is the other way around. The radio, TV and the movies are so violent nowadays because life itself has gotten so violent. Or maybe it's just a vicious circle."

"At least, thank God," said Simple, "it ain't just Negroes in the circle. Everybody is shooting and killing now. We are the least of it. On radio you never hear a Negro kill nobody, just white folks killing. And the biggest and best crimes on TV are committed by whites."

"No one race has a monopoly on crime. So why bring color in at all?"

"Because I am colored," said Simple. "My peoples was colored and my children will be colored. So why not bring in color?"

"To a sociological problem like crime," I said, "I consider color irrelevant."

"If I was an elephant, I would bring in elephants," said Simple. "Was I a lion, I would bring in lions. Beings I'm a Negro, I bring in Negroes. I do not want to be segregated, not even in crime, neither in life, the movies, nor on TV. I wants my rights—to which I stakes a claim."

"Violence and crime are wrong," I said. "Do you want the right to be wrong?"

"I want every right there is," yelled Simple. "Then I can pick out the right to be right. A man has to have the right to be *wrong* in order to have the right to be *right,* don't he?"

"Your logic defies reason," I said.

"Then you take reason, but give me right," said Simple. "Meanwhile, I intends to grow younger."

SIMPLE STASHES BACK

"When I stash back on my hind legs and really speak my mind," said Simple, "white folks better beware of what they are liable to hear."

"What do you mean, stash back?" I asked.

"I mean rear back and tell them off," said Simple. "I always did have bench legs, so I can stash back farther than you can."

"I believe you are double-jointed at the knees," I said, "since you can bend your legs almost as far backwards as you can forward."

"I got ball-bearing joints," said Simple, "so when I get ready to sound off, Jack, I really stashes back."

"But most of the sounding off you do is done in Harlem with not a white man in earshot, unless it is some Italian bar owner who has been selling you liquor for years—and bar owners are so used to Negroes sounding off that they pay you no mind."

"I wish I was in the United Nations," said Simple, "so the world could hear what I have to say. When I would rise in the Assembly and step to the podium, I would take my text from the word *Mississippi*—which is spelled M-i-s-s-i-s-s-i-p-p-i—and I would go right down the line from there, starting with *M*. I would say, 'Gentlemens of the United Nations and delegates, including Russians, the word *Mississippi* starts with an *M* which stands for *Murder,* which is what they have done there to Negroes for years just for being colored, with nobody sent to jail, let alone electrocuted. Mississippi murder did not just begin with little Emmett Till a few summers ago, nor with Rev. Lee who wanted to vote at Belzoni. It goes way back to slavery days when they whipped Negroes to death, and freedom days when the Klan drug us behind horses till we died, and on up to now when they shoot you for belonging to the N.A.A.C.P., so this evening I begin my talk with the word *murder,* and the first letter comes from Mississippi—not from behind nobody's Iron Curtain, but from M-i-s-s-i-s-s-i-p-p-i.

"I now continues with the next letter which is *I*—which means me. I, colored, am not even worth two hoots in hell in Mississippi, so therefore I myself do not give two hoots in hell about Mississippi. But I take that word for a text this evening just to let the world know how I feel. Wait! Correction! Strike *me* from the record. What that first *I* really means is *igaroot* from *ignoramus*—*I* for *igaroot.*

"S is the next letter, which stands for several things. Mississippi ain't from none of them, neither from double S, which is followed by an I meaning *imps*—imps of Satan—which is what Mississippians is. In spite of the fact that they claim to be Christians, they is devils. I is followed by double S again—*s-s*—which means I will not Soft Soap you into believing Mississippi is a part of the Free World because it is not. Mississippi is not from *Sugar*, nether from *Salt*, period! And it do not take a double S to spell what it is from neither. And I hope all you translators setting here at the United Nations with earphones to your ears translating into all foreign languages, has got an S in your language to spell what I mean that Mississippi ain't from.

"Let us continue with the next I after the double S. That I means *Idiots*—which some folks must be to behave the way they do in Mississippi. Now I will go on to the P—which is what I plan to do as soon as I reach heaven, attach my wings, and learn to fly. As soon as I get to be an angel, that *very* first day, I will fly over Mississippi and I will P all over the state. After which I will double the P, as it is in the spelling. Excuse the expression, but right over Jackson, which is the state capital, I will *P-P*. As I fly, I hope none of them Dixiecrats has time to get their umbrellas up.

"Now I come to the final letter which is I—I meaning *me*—who will spell as I fly, M-i-s-s-i-s-s—*yes*—I-P-P-i!"

AN AUTO-OBITUARY

"I will now obituarize myself," said Simple at the bar. "I will cast flowers on my own grave before I am dead. And I will tell people how good I were, in case nobody else has the same feeling. Even if you are good in this life, when you are gone, most people think it is a good riddance. So, before I become dust to dust and ashes to ashes, I will light my own light—and not hide it under no bushel. My light will be lit now."

"I believe you are well lit already," I said.

"I have not had a drink today," said Simple, "except these beers in this bar."

"Then what gives you this flow of morbid thoughts?" I asked. "And why is death so prevalent this evening in your conversation? You do not look like a man who is about to die."

"Cold weather has got me," said Simple. "I swear, when I went out to work this morning, I thought I would freeze to death. This cold wave is nothing to play with. Hawkins is talking like the rent man does on the fifteenth, when you should have paid your rent on the first. I have not done nothing to the weather, so I do not know why the weather should be so hard on me. But I am so ashy in that mirror I look like ashes, and so cold I feel like ice. That's why I'm talking about death this evening—because if I do die of cold, I want some FINE words said over my body—which is why I think I had better say them myself right now, then I know they will be said, because my wife may not have enough money to pay the minister to state what I want stated. I wants to be praised to the skies, even if I do go to hell."

"Such a desire is understandable," I said, "so go ahead, preach."

"I wants myself," said Simple, "a sermon preached by a good minister something like this: 'Jesse B. Semple, born in Virginia, married twice for better or for worse—the first time for worse, the last time for good. Jesse B. Semple, he were a good man. He were raised good, lived good, did good, and died good.'

"Whereupon, in my coffin, I would say, 'Rev, you have lied good. Keep on!'

"And my old minister would preach on: 'Jesse B. Semple deserves to rest in peace, deserves to pass on over to the other shores where there is light eternal, where darkness never comes, and where he will receive a crown upon his noble head, that head that thought such noble thoughts, that head that never studied evil in this world, that head that never harbored harm—that head, that head, oh, that head of Jesse B. Semple that receiveth his crown. And slippers! Golden slippers on his feet with heelplates of silver to make music up and down the golden streets. Oh, Jesse B. Semple, walking on the golden streets, hailing a celestial cab to go whirling through eternal space down the Milky Way to see can he find some old friends in the far-off parts of heaven! Angel after angel passes and he does not know any of them. He does not know this angel, nor that angel. But here, oh, here at last is an angel that knows him.'

" 'Rev! Rev!' I would whisper from my coffin, 'You will have to tell me the angel's name, because I don't recollect who it is. I think all my friends must have gone to hell.'

"Rev would preach on: ' 'Tis an angel from your youthhood, Semple, a young angel you grew up with, but whom you cannot recognize since this angel died before the age of sin, but is now whiter than snow, as all are here in heaven. No matter how dark on earth you may be, in heaven you are whiter than snow, Jesse B. Semple, whiter than snow!'

" 'Aw, now Rev,' I would say, 'with me you do not need to go that far.'

"But old Rev would keep on, because that sermon would be getting good to him by now: 'Though your sins be as scarlet, in heaven, I say, Jesse B. Semple, old earthly Semple, down-home Semple is whiter than snow. White! White! White! White! Oh, yes, you are whiter than snow!'

" 'Then, Rev,' I would have to holler, 'I would not know my own self in the mirror, were I to look.'

" 'In God's mirror all are white,' says Rev, 'white wings, white robe, white face, white neck, white shoulders, white hips, white soul! Oh, precious soul of Jesse B., worth more than words can tell! Worth more than tongues can fabulate, worth more than speech can spatulate, than throat can throttle, than human mind can manipulate! This soul, this Jesse B. of a soul! This simple soul, this Semple! Gone to glory, gone to his great reward of milk and honey, manna and time unending, and the fruit of the tree of eternity.'

" 'Rev,' I would be forced to say laying there in my coffin thirsty, 'your words are as dry as popcorn and rice. You have mentioned neither beer nor wine—and I am *paying* you to preach this sermon.'

" 'The juice! Sweet, sweet juice of the wine! Juice, juice, juice,' Rev would say. 'Oh, yes, Jess Semple is partaking today of the juice of the vine, and the fruit of the tree, and the manna of time unending, and the milk and honey of the streets of gold, and the wine of the vine of timeless space in that blessed place beneath his crown of gold, wrapped in the white robes of his purity, with white wings flapping, and his immortal soul winging its way through immortal space into that eternal place where time shall be no more, and he shall rest in peace forever and forever, ever and forever—for Semple were born good! He were raised good! He lived good, did good, and lied—I mean, *died*—good. Amen!' "

CHIPS ON THE SHOULDER

"Take that chip off your shoulder," I said.

"I will not," said Simple. "And suppose I did? There's always some chip to weigh a colored shoulder down. I remove this one, white folks will put another chip up there tomorrow. All you have to do is read the newspapers—Montgomery, Clinton, Miami, New

Orleans, Citizens Councilors, John Kasper, the Ku Klux Klan, the New York School Board! Man, each and all of them is piling chips on my shoulder daily. So many chips I have to shift from the left to the right shoulder."

"You live in such a limited world," I said. "Broaden your horizons—get away from race."

"With my face?" asked Simple. "Dark as I be, you can't mean me? Or do you?"

"Suppose an Italian-American did not think about anything but Italy," I said.

"He'd still be Joe Di Maggio," said Simple, "or Costello."

"Suppose an Irish-American did not pay any attention to anything but Ireland."

"He'd still be a cop or a politicianer."

"Suppose the Jews were interested in nothing but Israel."

"My groceryman would still be in business in Harlem," said Simple. "So why can't I be interested in the Negro race without somebody like you calling my time? And you are as colored as me, too."

"But you have me beat on racialness," I said. "You talk about almost nothing but the race problem day in, night out."

"And women," said Simple.

"For a married man, you let your mind stray too often," I said.

"For a friend, you criticize too much," declared Simple. " 'Take the mote out of your own eye before you start to take the chip off my shoulder.' That's what the Bible says."

"You're misquoting now," I said. "It does not."

"I growed up on the Bible," declared Simple, "and sometimes I live by it, too. My Aunt Lucy were a Bible lover. In fact, it were her Rock. And I still respects its word. The Bible says take the mote out of your own eye before you start talking about me. I might not be snow-white, but you are not snow-white yourself—and I am not talking about complexion in neither case."

"Forget and forgive then," I said. "Let's change the subject."

"What shall we talk about?" asked Simple. "How there ain't no white children hardly in Harlem schools? How we don't have integration up North, let alone down South?"

"You're picking up that chip again," I said.

"I don't have to *pick* it up, it falls from above. My head is beat with chips right now this evening, right here in this bar where I come for a quickie. If I had not run into you, man, I would be home in my bed by now enjoying my wife's dreams. Buy me a beer, buddy-boy-baby-daddy-o, old kid."

"I will not," I said. "You buy me one."

"I runs on a budget since I been married," explained Simple, "and my budget does not include beers for *myself*, let alone you. Of course, meet me on payday before I contributes to the budget, and I will see you go. Today is not payday. Come on, let's order up."

"Who—let's?"

"You—let's. Else no let's. Then the conversation is ended right now. I will take my chips and go home."

"Good night."

"But not before we have one for the road."

"See if your chips will pay for a beer."

"Man, you know this Italian bartender ain't interested in Negroes."

PLAYS

Soul Gone Home

A One-Act Play*

CHARACTERS

The MOTHER
Her SON
TWO MEN

SETTING: *Night. A tenement room, bare, ugly, dirty. An unshaded electric-light bulb. In the middle of the room a cot on which the body of a negro youth is lying. His hands are folded across his chest. He is a soul gone home.*

As the curtain rises: his MOTHER, *a large middle-aged woman in a red sweater, kneels weeping beside the cot.*

MOTHER: (*Loudly*) Oh, Gawd! Oh, Lawd! Why did you take my son from me? Oh, Gawd, why did you do it? He was all I had! Oh, Lawd, what am I gonna do? (*Looking at the dead boy and stroking his head*) Oh, son! Oh, Rannie! Oh, my boy, speak to me! Rannie, say something to me! Son, why don't you talk to your mother? Can't you see she's bowed down in sorrow? Son, speak to me, just a word! Come back from the spirit world and speak to me! Rannie, come back from the dead and speak to your mother!

SON: (*Lying there dead as a door-nail. Speaking loudly*) I wish I wasn't dead, so I *could* speak to you. You been a hell of a mama!

MOTHER: (*Falling back from the cot in astonishment, but still on her knees*) Rannie! Rannie! What's that you say? What you sayin' to your mother? (*Wild-eyed*) Is you done opened your mouth and spoke to me? What you said?

* Originally published in the *One-Act Play* Magazine, Vol. 1, No. 3, July 1937. Copyright 1937, by Langston Hughes.

SON: I said you a hell of a mama!

MOTHER: (*Rising suddenly and backing away, screaming loudly*) Awo-OOO-o! Rannie, that ain't you talkin'!

SON: Yes, it is me talkin', too! I say you been a no-good mama.

MOTHER: What you talkin' to me like that, Rannie? You ain't never said nothin' like that to me before.

SON: I know it, but I'm dead now . . . and I can say what I want to say. (*Stirring*) You done called on me to talk, ain't you? Lemme take these pennies off my eyes so I can see. (*He takes the coins off his eyes, throws them across the room, and sits up in bed. He is a very dark boy in a torn white shirt. He looks hard at his* MOTHER) Mama, you know you ain't done me right.

MOTHER: What you mean, I ain't done you right? (*She is rooted in horror*) What you mean, huh?

SON: You know what I mean.

MOTHER: No, I don't neither. (*Trembling violently*) What you mean comin' back to hant your poor old mother? Rannie, what does you mean?

SON: (*Leaning forward*) I'll tell you what I mean! You been a bad mother to me.

MOTHER: Shame! Shame! Shame, talkin' to your mama that away. Damn it! Shame! I'll slap your face. (*She starts towards him, but he rolls his big white eyes at her, and she backs away*) Me, what bored you! Me, that suffered the pains o' death to bring you into this world! Me, what raised you up, what washed your dirty didies. (*Sorrowfully*) And now I'm left here mighty nigh prostrate 'cause you gone from me! Rannie, what you mean talkin' to *me* like that . . . what brought you into this world?

SON: You never did feed me good, that's what I mean! Who wants to come into the world hongry and go out the same way?

MOTHER: What you mean hongry? When I had money, ain't I fed you?

SON: (*Sullenly*) Most the time you ain't had no money.

MOTHER: 'Twarn't my fault then.

SON: 'Twarn't *my* fault neither.

MOTHER: (*Defensively*) You always was so weak and sickly, you couldn't earn nothin' sellin' papers.

SON: I know it.

MOTHER: You never was no use to me.

SON: So you just lemme grow up in the street, and I ain't had no manners nor morals, neither.

MOTHER: Manners and morals? Rannie, where'd you learn all them big words?

SON: I learnt 'em just now in the spirit-world.

MOTHER: (*Coming nearer*) But you ain't been dead no more'n an hour.

SON: That's long enough to learn a lot.

MOTHER: Well, what else did you find out?

SON: I found out that you was a hell of a mama puttin' me out in the cold to sell papers soon as I could walk.

MOTHER: What? You little liar!

SON: If I'm lyin', I'm dyin'! And lettin' me grow up all bowlegged and stunted from undernourishment.

MOTHER: Under-nurse-mint?

SON: Undernourishment. You heard what the doctor said last week?

MOTHER: Naw, what'd he say?

SON: He said I was dyin' o' undernourishment, that's what he said. He said I had T.B. 'cause I didn't have enough to eat never when I were a child. And he said I couldn't get well, nohow, eating nothin' but beans ever since I been sick. Said I needed milk and eggs. And you said you ain't got no money for milk and eggs, which I know you ain't. (*Gently*) We never had no money, mama, not ever since you took to hustlin' on the streets.

MOTHER: Son, money ain't everything.

SON: Naw, but when you got T.B. you have to have milk and eggs.

MOTHER: (*Advancing sentimentally*) Anyhow, I love you, Rannie!

SON: (*Rudely*) Sure you love me . . . but I am dead.

MOTHER: (*Angrily*) Well, damn your hide, you ain't even decent dead. If you was, you wouldn't be sittin' there jawin' at your mother when she's sheddin' ever' tear she's got for you tonight.

SON: First time you ever did cry for me, far as I know.

MOTHER: Tain't! You's a lie! I cried when I bored you . . . you was such a big child . . . ten pounds.

SON: Then I did the cryin' after that, I reckon.

MOTHER: (*Proudly*) Sure, I could of let you die, but I didn't. Naw, I kept you with me . . . off and on. And I lost the chance to marry many a good man, too . . . if it weren't for you. No man wants to take care o' nobody else's child. (*Self-pityingly*) You been a burden to me, Randolph.

SON: (*Angrily*) What did you have me for then, in the first place?

MOTHER: How could I help havin' you, you little bastard? Your father ruint me . . . and you's the result. And I been worried with you for sixteen years. (*Disgustedly*) Now, just when you get big enough to work and do me some good, you have to go and die.

SON: I sure am dead!

MOTHER: But you ain't decent dead! Here you come back to hant your poor old mama, and spoil her cryin' spell, and spoil the mournin'. (*There is the noise of an ambulance gong outside. The* MOTHER *goes to the window and looks down into the street. Turns to* SON) Rannie, lay down quick! Here comes the city's ambulance to take you to the undertaker's. Don't let them white men see you dead, sitting up here quarrelin' with your mother. Lay down and fold your hands back like I had 'em.

SON: (*Passing his hand across his head*) All right, but gimme that comb yonder and my stocking cap. I don't want to go out of here with my hair standin' straight up in front, even if I is dead. (*The* MOTHER *hands him a comb and his stocking cap. The* SON *combs his hair and puts the cap on. Noise of* MEN *coming up the stairs*)

MOTHER: Hurry up, Rannie, they'll be here in no time.

SON: Aw, they got another flight to come yet. Don't rush me, ma!

MOTHER: Yes, but I got to put these pennies back on your eyes, boy! (*She searches in a corner for the coins as her* SON *lies down and folds his hands, stiff in death. She finds the coins and puts them nervously on his eyes, watching the door meanwhile. A knock*) Come in.

(*Enter* TWO MEN *in the white coats of City Health employees*)

MAN: Somebody sent for us to get the body of a Rannie Bailey?

MOTHER: Yes, sir, here he is! (*Weeping loudly*) He's my boy! Oh, Lawdy, he's done gone home! His soul's gone home! Oh, what am I gonna do? Mister! Mister! The Lawd's done took him home. (*As the* MEN *unfold the stretchers, she continues to weep hysterically. They place the* BOY'S *thin body on the stretchers and cover it with a rubber cloth. Each* MAN *takes his end of the stretcher silently. They walk out the door as the* MOTHER *wails*)

MOTHER: Oh, my son! Oh, my son! Come back, come back, come back! Rannie, come back! (*One loud scream as the door closes*) Awo-OOO-o! (*As the footsteps of the* MEN *die down on the stairs, the* MOTHER *becomes suddenly quiet. She goes to a broken mirror and begins to rouge and powder her face. In the street the ambulance gong sounds fainter and fainter in the distance. The* MOTHER *takes down an old fur coat from a nail and puts it on. Before she leaves, she smooths back the quilts on the cot from which the dead boy has been removed. She looks in the mirror again, and once more whitens her face with powder. She dons a red hat. From a handbag she takes a cigarette, lights it, and walks slowly out the door. At the door she switches off the light. The hallway is dimly illuminated. She turns before closing the door, looks back in the room, and says)* Tomorrow, Rannie, I'll buy you some flowers . . . if I can pick up a dollar tonight. You was a hell of a no-good son, I swear!

THE CURTAIN FALLS

Simply Heavenly

A New Musical Folk Comedy

BASED ON THE NOVEL "SIMPLE TAKES A WIFE"
BOOK AND LYRICS BY LANGSTON HUGHES
MUSIC AND ORCHESTRATION BY DAVID MARTIN
DIRECTED BY JOSHUA SHELLEY
SETTING AND LIGHTING BY RAYMOND SOVEY

THE CAST
(In order of appearance)

Simple	Melvin Stewart
Madam Butler	Wilhelmina Gray
Boyd	Stanley Greene
Mrs. Caddy	Dagmar Craig
Joyce Lane	Marilyn Berry
Hopkins	Duke Williams
Bar Pianist	Willie Pritchett
Mamie	Claudia McNeil
Bodiddly	Charles A. McRae
Character	Allegro Kane
Melon	John Bouie
Gitfiddle	Brownie McGhee
Zarita	Anna English
Arcie	Josephine Woods
John Jasper	Charles Harrigan
Big Boy, Cop	Maxwell Glanville
Nurse, Party Guest	Dagmar Craig

SIMPLY HEAVENLY *premiered on Broadway at The Playhouse, Tuesday, August 20, 1957.*

CHARACTER NOTES FOR "SIMPLY HEAVENLY"

General: The characters in "Simply Heavenly" are, on the whole, ordinary, hard-working lower-income bracket Harlemites. Paddy's Bar is like a neighborhood club, and most of its patrons are not drunkards or bums. Their small kitchenette rooms or overcrowded apartments cause them to seek the space and company of the bar. Just as others seek the church as a social center, or the poolhall, or dancehall, these talkative ones seek the bar.

SIMPLE: Simple is a Chaplinesque character, slight of build, awkwardly graceful, given to flights of fancy, and positive statements of opinion—stemming from a not so positive soul. He is dark with a likable smile, ordinarily dressed, except for rather flamboyant summer sport shirts. Simple tries hard to succeed, but the chips seldom fall just right. Yet he bounces like a rubber ball. He may go down, but he always bounds back up.

JOYCE: Joyce is a quiet girl more inclined toward club work than bars, toward "culture" rather than good-timing. But she is not snobbish nor cold. She is tall, brownskin, given to longish ear-rings, beads, scarfs, and dangling things, very feminine, and cries easily. Her charm is her sincerity.

BOYD: Hopkins has probably been half-way through college before his army service in Europe. Serious-minded, pleasant-looking, trying to be a writer, perhaps taking English courses at New York University on the last of his G. I. money. Almost every Harlem bar has such a fellow among its regular customers, who acts sometimes as a kind of arbiter when "intellectual" discussions come up.

ZARITA: Zarita is a lively bar-stool girl wearing life, like a loose garment, but she is *not* a prostitute. Brassy-voiced, good-hearted, good-looking, playing the field for fun and drinks, she lives a come-day-go-day existence, generous in accepting or giving love, money, or drinks. A good dancer.

MISS MAMIE: Mamie is a hard-working domestic, using biting words to protect a soft heart and a need for love too often betrayed.

GITFIDDLE: Gitfiddle is a folk artist going to seed, unable to compete with the juke box, TV, and the radio, having only his guitar and his undisciplined talents.

MADAM BUTLER: Madam Butler has a bark that is worse than her bite—but her bark is bad enough. Large, fat, comical and terrible, she runs her rooming house as Hitler ran Germany.

CHARACTERS

JESSE B. SEMPLE	*Harlemite*
MADAM BUTLER	*Simple's Landlady*
ANANAIS BOYD	*Simple's Neighbor*
MRS. CADDY	*Joyce's Landlady*
JOYCE LANE	*Simple's Girl*
HOPKINS	*A Genial Bartender*
PIANIST	*A Barfly*
MISS MAMIE	*A Plump Domestic*
BODIDDLY	*A Dock Worker*
CHARACTER	*A Snob*
MELON	*A Fruit Vendor*
GITFIDDLE	*A Guitar Player*
ZARITA	*A Glamorous Goodtimer*
ARCIE	*Bodiddly's Wife*
JOHN JASPER	*Her Son*
BIG BOY	*A Root Doctor*
A NURSE	
A POLICEMAN	

TIME: *The Present*
PLACE: *Harlem, U. S. A.*
MOOD: *Of the moment*

SCENES

ACT I

1. SIMPLE' ROOM
2. JOYCE'S ROOM
3. PADDY'S BAR
4. HOSPITAL ROOM
5. PADDY'S BAR

MUSICAL NUMBERS

ACT I

ACT II

ACT I

A lonely guitar is
playing in the darkness—
it's the blues . . .

Scene 1

Simple's room. Early spring evening. SIMPLE, *just coming home from work, removes his jacket as he enters, but before he can hang it up, the voice of* MADAM BUTLER, *his* LANDLADY, *is heard calling up the stairs. Through the half-open door.*

LANDLADY: Mr. Semple! Oh, Mr. Semple!

SIMPLE: Yes'm?

LANDLADY: I heard you come in! Mr. Semple, would you mind taking Trixie out for a walk? My arthritis is bothering me.

SIMPLE: Madam Butler, please! I've got no time to walk no dog tonight. Joyce is waiting for me.

LANDLADY: From all I've heard, that girl's been waiting for you to marry her for years! A few minutes of waiting for you to show up tonight won't hurt.

SIMPLE: Madam, my private affairs ain't none of your business.

LANDLADY: Um-hum! Well, you don't need to take Trixie to no tree—just the nearest fireplug.

(BOYD, *a fellow-roomer, peers in*)

SIMPLE: Aw, I ain't hardly got home from work good, yet . . . Hello, Boyd. Come on in. Landladies is a bodiddling! How come she never make none of the other roomers—or you—to walk her dog?

BOYD: She knows I won't do it, that's why.

SIMPLE: Don't you ever get behind in your rent?

BOYD: Not to the point of walking dogs. But you seem to walk Trixie pretty often.

SIMPLE: Mostly always.

LANDLADY: Did you say you would take the dog?

SIMPLE: Oh, hell, lemme go walk the bitch.

LANDLADY: No profanity in my house.

SIMPLE: Madam, that's a perfectly good word meaning a fine girl dog—bitch—for female dog.

LANDLADY: There'll be no bitches in my house—and that goes for your girl friend, Zarita, too.

SIMPLE: I'll thank you to leave my friends out of this.

LANDLADY: I'll thank you to keep your profanity to yourself. This is a decent house. Now, come on and walk my dog—else pay me my rent.

SIMPLE: I'll walk your dog—because I love Trixie, though, that's what! If I had a dog, I wouldn't keep it penned up in the house all day neither. Poor old thing, airless as she is.

LANDLADY: She's not hairless.

SIMPLE: I said *airless*, Madam! Shut up airtight, wonder Trixie don't get arthritis, too. Dogs and womans, dogs and womens! Damn! What am I gonna do?

BOYD: Good luck pal.

(SIMPLE *and* BOYD *exit.* BLACKOUT. *in the darkness, Trixie's bark is heard. Auto horns, street noises.* SIMPLE'S *voice addresses the barking dog*)

SIMPLE: Now Trixie, come on now. Come on Trixie, do your duty. Leave that other dog alone, Trixie! Hound, get away from here! O.K., O.K., let's head on in the house.

(Bark)

Now, go on to your madam. I guess you love her. Well, I love somebody, too! My choice, Joyce! She's the one I found—and that's where I'm bound. Trixie, that's where I am bound.

(The music of "SIMPLY HEAVENLY" rises happily as the lights come up to reveal Joyce's room)

Scene 2

Joyce's room a bit later. JOYCE *is singing as, in a frilly dressing gown, she is putting her clothes away.*

JOYCE:

> LOVE IS SIMPLY HEAVENLY!
> WHAT ELSE COULD IT BE?
> WHEN LOVE'S MADE IN HEAVEN
> AND YOU ARE MADE FOR ME.
> LOVE IS SIMPLY HEAVENLY!
> WHAT ELSE CAN I SAY?
> WHEN LOVE SENDS AN ANGEL
> TO HOLD ME CLOSE THIS WAY.
> LOVE IS LIKE A DREAM
> THAT'S TOO GOOD TO BE TRUE,
> BUT WHEN YOUR LIPS KISS MINE
> THE DREAM TURNS INTO YOU.
> YES, IT'S SIMPLY HEAVENLY!
> OUR LOVE'S JUST DIVINE—
> FOR LOVE IS MADE IN HEAVEN
> AND YOU, MY LOVE, ARE MINE!
>
> LOVE IS SIMPLY HEAVENLY . . .

(Voice of her LANDLADY *calls from below stairs)*

MRS. CADDY: Oo-oo-oo-oo! Miss Lane!

JOYCE: Yes?

MRS. CADDY: I'm letting Mr. Semple come up. OK?

JOYCE: Yes, indeed, Mrs. Caddy, I'm expecting him.

(SIMPLE *knocks lightly and enters grinning*)

SIMPLE: Hey, Baby!

(*He closes the door, to which* JOYCE *objects*)

JOYCE: Jess! No! Just a crack . . .

SIMPLE: Aw, your old landlady's worse than mine. At least I can shut my door when I got company.

JOYCE: You're a man. I'm a . . .

(SIMPLE *hugs* JOYCE)

SIMPLE: Lady! Which is what I like about you. Joyce, morals is your middle name. But you can still be a lady behind closed doors.

JOYCE: I know, Jess, those are the landlady's rules. Besides, I respect Mrs. Caddy.

SIMPLE: She don't respect you if she thinks soon as the door is shut—

JOYCE: Sshhss! Come on, rest your jacket, honey. It's warm.

SIMPLE: I knowed there was something! I forgot to bring your ice cream! I passed right by the place, too!

JOYCE: We can walk out for a soda.

SIMPLE: Or a beer?

JOYCE: Tomorrow's communion Sunday, and I do not drink beer before communion.

SIMPLE: You just don't drink beer, period! Gimme a little sugar and we'll skip the beer.

JOYCE: Don't think I'll skip the ice cream.

SIMPLE: Let's set on the—

(*He dances toward the studio bed*)

JOYCE: There's a chair.

SIMPLE: Baby, what's the matter? Don't you trust me yet?

JOYCE: I don't mind you being close to me. But when you get close to a bed, too—

SIMPLE: Then you don't trust yourself.

JOYCE: Have you ever known me to—

SIMPLE: That's the trouble . . .

JOYCE: That goes with marriage, not courtship. And if you don't move on from courtship to engagement soon, Jess Semple, and do something about that woman in Baltimore.

SIMPLE: My wife! Isabel—she run me out—but she would claim I left her. She could find some grounds to get a divorce.

JOYCE: Since you're not together: why don't you get one?

SIMPLE: Joyce, I don't want to pay for no woman's divorce I don't love. And I do not love Isabel. Also, I ain't got the money.

JOYCE: I would help you pay for it.

SIMPLE: One thing I would not let you do, Joyce, is pay for no other woman's divorce. No!

JOYCE: Well, if you and I just paid for half of it, you'd only be paying for your part of the divorce.

SIMPLE: That woman wants me to pay for it all! And, Joyce, I don't love her. I love you. Joyce, do you want me to commit bigamy?

JOYCE: Five years you've been away from your wife—three years since you met me! In all that time you haven't reached a point yet where you can ask for my hand without committing bigamy. I don't know how my love holds out so long on promises. But now my friends are all asking when I'm going to get married. Even my landlady's saying it's a mighty long time for a man to just be "coming around calling," just sitting doing nothing.

SIMPLE: I agree, baby—when there ain't no action, I get kinder drowsy.

JOYCE: Well, to me, a nice conversation is action.

SIMPLE: Conversationing makes me sleepy.

JOYCE: Then you ought to go to bed early instead of hanging over Paddy's Bar until all hours. You have got to go to work just like I do.

SIMPLE: When I sleep, I sleeps fast. Anyhow, I can't go to bed early just because you do, Joyce, until—unless—

JOYCE: Until what?

SIMPLE: Until we're married *Joyce!* Simple! But, listen! It's Saturday night, fine outside. Spring in Harlem! Come on, let's us get some ice cream.

JOYCE: O.K., but Jess, are you coming to church in the morning to see me take communion?

SIMPLE: You know I'll be there. We'll just take a little stroll down Seventh Avenue now and catch some air, heh?

JOYCE: And you'll bring me home early, so we can both get our rest.

SIMPLE: In a jiffy, then I'll turn in, too.

JOYCE: You don't mean into a bar?

SIMPLE: Baby, one thing I *bar* is bars.

JOYCE: Turn your back so I can dress.

SIMPLE: Don't stand over there. Anybody could be looking in.

JOYCE: There are no peeping-toms in this house.

(SIMPLE *turns his back as she dresses, but drops his pack cigarettes on the floor, bends down to get it, then remains that way, looking at Joyce from between his legs*)

Baby, is your back turned?

SIMPLE: Yes'm.

    (JOYCE *glances his way, clutches her dress to her bosom and screams*)

JOYCE: Oh, Simple!

SIMPLE: I love it when you call me Simple.

    (*Head still down, he proceeds to turn a somersault, coming up seated on the floor with his back toward her*)

    Now say my back ain't turned.

JOYCE: I didn't mean you had to turn inside out.

SIMPLE: That's the way you've got my heart—turned in . . .

    (*He turns his eyes to look at her*)

JOYCE: Then turn your head so I can dress.

SIMPLE: O.K. Joyce. Now, is everything all right?

JOYCE: Everything is all right.

SIMPLE: So you feel O.K.?

JOYCE: Simply heavenly! Oh, Jess, it's wonderful to be in love.

SIMPLE: Just wonderful—wonderful—wonderful—

    (*As* JOYCE *dresses, they sing*)

BOTH:

> LOVE IS SIMPLY HEAVENLY!
> WHAT ELSE COULD IT BE?
> WHEN LOVE'S MADE IN HEAVEN
> AND YOU ARE MADE FOR ME.
> LOVE IS SIMPLY HEAVENLY!
> WHAT ELSE CAN I SAY?
> WHEN LOVE SENDS AN ANGEL
> TO HOLD ME CLOSE THIS WAY.
> LOVE IS LIKE A DREAM
> THAT'S TOO GOOD TO BE TRUE,
> BUT WHEN YOUR LIPS KISS MINE
> THE DREAM TURNS INTO YOU.
> YES, IT'S SIMPLY HEAVENLY!
> OUR LOVE'S JUST DIVINE—
> FOR LOVE IS MADE IN HEAVEN
> AND YOU, MY LOVE, ARE MINE!

SIMPLE:

> LOVE IS SIMPLY HEAVENLY!
> WHAT ELSE COULD IT BE?
> WHEN LOVE IS MADE IN HEAVEN
> AND YOU ARE MADE FOR ME

JOYCE:

> LOVE IS SIMPLY HEAVENLY!
> WHAT ELSE CAN I SAY?

> WHEN LOVE SENDS ME AN ANGEL
> TO HOLD ME CLOSE THIS WAY.

SIMPLE:

> LOVE IS LIKE A DREAM
> THAT'S TOO GOOD TO BE TRUE,

(*Dressed now,* JOYCE *emerges and* SIMPLE *rises to embrace her*)

JOYCE:

> BUT WHEN YOUR LIPS KISS MINE
> THEN DREAM TURNS INTO YOU.

BOTH:

> YES, IT'S SIMPLY HEAVENLY!
> OUR LOVE'S JUST DIVINE—
> FOR LOVE IS MADE IN HEAVEN
> AND YOU, MY LOVE, ARE MINE!

BLACKOUT

Scene 3

Paddy's Bar. Midnight. At a battered old piano in the corner a roustabout PIANIST *is playing a Calypso while the* BARTENDER *beats on the bar with his hands as if playing bongos. They sing and the* OTHERS *in bar join in on the choruses.*

PIANIST:

> CALYPSO! CALYPSO! CALYPSO!

HOPKINS:

> BEAT IT OUT, MON, FOR ME!

PIANIST:

> CALYPSO! CALYPSO! CALYPSO!

HOPKINS:

> BEAT IT OUT, MON, FOR ME.

BOTH:

> BRINGS ME BACK TO ME ISLAND
> WHEN I HEAR SWEET MELODY.

HOPKINS:

> I HAVE MADE A STUDY OF WOMEN
> AND I HAVE A FEW THINGS TO SAY:
> IN THE NIGHT SOME GALS SO PRETTY,
> BUT LOOK LIKE A WITCH BY DAY.
> I TOOK UP THE PROBLEM OF WOMEN
> SO HER CUSTOMS I HAVE DOWN FINE:

SHE AT MIDNIGHT WHISPERS SWEETLY—
AND AT NOONTIME, ROAR LIKE LION.

ALL:

CALYPSO! CALYPSO! CALYPSO!
BEAT IT OUT, MON, FOR ME!
CALYPSO! CALYPSO! CALYPSO!
BEAT IT OUT, MON, FOR ME.
BRINGS ME BACK TO ME ISLAND
WHEN I HEAR SWEET MELODY.

HOPKINS:

I HAVE MADE A STUDY OF LOVIN'
AND THERE'S ONE THING THAT I DO KNOW:
NEVER PAYS A MON GO RUSHIN'—
WITH FEMALE, JUST TAKE IT SLOW.
SINCE I MADE A PROJECT OF KISSIN'
NOW I REALLY KNOW WHAT IS TRUE:
IT IS BETTER WHEN YOU'RE KISSIN'
MAKE A *LONG* KISS DO FOR TWO.

ALL:
CALYPSO! CALYPSO! CALYPSO!

HOPKINS:

IT LOOKS LIKE YOU YOUNG GALS THINK MONEY
MUST BE GROWIN' LIKE LEAVES ON TREES.
IF YOU DON'T RESPECT ME, HONEY,
JUST RESPECT MY BANKROLL, PLEASE.
YOU EAT UP ME PEAS AND RICE NOW,
THEN YOU GOIN' ON HOME TO HE.
IF YOU EAT ME PEAS AND RICE, GAL,
LET YOUR LEGAL HUSBAND BE.

ALL:
CALYPSO! CALYPSO! CALYPSO! . . . . . *etc.*

HOPKINS:

WHEN YOU COME TO SEE ME WHY CAN'T YOU
EVER LEAVE MY GOOD RUM ALONE?
YOU DONE DRUNK MY HEALTH SO OFTEN
YOU ALMOST HAVE RUINT YOUR OWN.
I NOTICE WHEN HEARIN' THE BONGOS
YOU JUST SHAKE AND YOU SHAKE YOURSELF.
YOU HAVE SHOOK SO MUCH CALYPSO
TILL YOU AIN'T GOT NO SHAKE LEFT.

ALL:
CALYPSO! CALYPSO! CALYPSO! . . . . . *etc.*

(MISS MAMIE, *a large but shapely domestic servant enters and sits at her usual table*)

HOPKINS: Good evening Miss Mamie. How's tricks?

MAMIE: Hopkins, them white folks over in Long Island done like to worked me to death. I'm just getting back to town.

PIANIST: You ought to have a good man to take care of you, Miss Mamie—like me.

MAMIE: Huh! Bill, from what I see of you, you can hardly take care of yourself. I got a mighty lot of flesh here to nourish.

PIANIST: Big woman, big appetite.

MAMIE: Right—which is why I like to work for rich folks. Poor folks ain't got enough to feed me.

PIANIST: I never eat much. But I sure am thirsty.

MAMIE: Stay that way! Hopkins, gimme a gin.

(BODIDDLY, *a dock worker, leaps in shouting*)

BODIDDLY: Hey, now, anyhow!

MAMIE: Anyhow, what?

BODIDDLY: Anyhow, we's here! Who's setting up tonight?

(*Dead silence. No one answers*)

Well, Hop, I'll take a short beer.

MAMIE: It ain't nobody's payday in the middle of the week, Bodiddly. And the only man in this bar who manages to keep a little change in his pocket is Mr. Boyd here, drawing his G.I. pension.

(BODIDDLY *points at* BOYD *proudly*)

BODIDDLY: My boy!

BOYD: Hi, Bo!

MAMIE: Huh! There's as much difference between you and Ananias Boyd as between night and day.

BODIDDLY: Yeah, I know! His predilect's toward intellect—and mine's toward womens.

HOPKINS: And beer.

BODIDDLY: Boyd's the only man around here who's colleged.

BOYD: For all the good it does me. You dockworkers make more a week than I ever see writing these stories.

BODIDDLY: But none of us gets pensions.

MAMIE: None of you-all in the war and got wounded neither. But if I was a man, I would have gone to war so I could get me a pension.

PIANIST: They had lady soldiers.

BODIDDLY: Whacks and Wavers.

MAMIE: By that time, I were too big.

(*A* LITTLE MAN *in nose glasses, carrying an umbrella, enters with*

*an armful of highbrow papers and magazines. Noticing no one,
he takes a table and begins to remove his gloves*)

There comes that character trying to make people think he's
educated. One thing I like about Boyd here, even if he is a
writer, he ain't always trying to impress folks. Also he speaks
when he comes in a public place.

(*The* LITTLE MAN *goes to end of the bar*)

CHARACTER: A thimble of Scotch, please.

BODIDDLY: A *thimble* of Scawtch!

(ALL *laugh but* BOYD)

CHARACTER: And a tumbler of plain water, no ice.

HOPKINS: Right, sir! Like the English.

(*As if to show her derision,* MAMIE *orders loudly*)

MAMIE: Hopkins, gimme some more gin.

HOPKINS: Coming up, Miss Mamie!

(*A* VENDOR'S CRY *is heard outside. Carrying a watermelon, a
jovial fellow,* WATERMELON JOE, *enters*)

MELON:

> WATERMELONS! JUICY SWEET!
> WATERMELONS! GOOD TO EAT!
> RIPE AND RED—
> THAT'S WHAT I SAID—
> WATERMELONS!

MAMIE: Joe, you better shut up all that catterwalling! You ain't
working this time o' night?

MELON: Yes I is. I done sold all but one watermelon. Who wants it?
Sweet as pie! No lie! My, my, my!

(MAMIE *inspects the melon*)

MAMIE: Hmmm! It do look good. Thumps good, too. Leave it for
me behind the bar. I'll take it.

MELON: Thank you, Miss Mamie.

BODIDDLY: Better tie your pushcart to the curb 'fore somebody steals
it.

MELON: I'm ahead of you, Diddly—got it locked to the lamp post.
Boy, when I cry "Watermelon!" do you-all know what happens
to womens?

BODIDDLY: What?

MELON: Their blood turns to water and their knees start to shake
—cause they know I'm a man, and no mistake! Why I sold a
woman a watermelon one day and moved in and stayed three
years.

BODIDDLY: That's nothing. I just spoke to a strange lady once setting on a stoop—and went upstairs and ain't come down yet. That was in 1936.

MELON: Diddly, you lying. Your wife done run you out twice with a kitchen knife.

BODIDDLY: I mean, excusing temporary exits.

MAMIE: Well, I been buying watermelons, Joe, for two summers, and I finds your fruits sweeter than you.

MELON: That's because you don't know me well, baby. Besides, I do not use my professional voice in your personal presence:

> WA—TER—MELONS!
>
> MELONS! MELONS! MELONS!
>
> SWEET AS THEY CAN BE!
>
> SWEET, GOOD LORD!
>
> BUT THEY AIN'T AS SWEET AS ME!
>
> WATERMELON JOE HAS GOT YOUR
>
> WA—TER—MELONS!

(*He eases up to her cheek*)

> ME—LAWNS! . . . ME—LOANS! . . . ME—LOONS!

MAMIE: Man, you better get away from me! You know I got a husband, Watermelon Joe.

MELON: Where's he at?

MAMIE: I don't know where he's at, but I got one. And if I ain't, I don't want you.

(*He croons in her ear*)

MELON: Watermelons. Wa—ter—mel—ons. . . . .

MAMIE: I sure do like your watermelons, though.

MELON: Nice red melons. . . .

(*The* LITTLE MAN *rises indignantly*)

CHARACTER: Stereotypes! That's all both of you are. Disgraceful stereotypes!

(MAMIE *turns on him furiously*)

MAMIE: Mister, you better remove yourself from my presence before I stereo your type! I like watermelons, and I don't care who knows it. That's nothing to be ashamed of, like some other colored folks are. Why, I knowed a woman once was so ashamed of liking watermelons that she'd make the clerk wrap the melon up before she'd carry it out of the store. I ain't no pretender, myself, neither no passer.

BODIDDLY: What do you mean, passer?

MAMIE: Chitterling passer—passing up chitterlings and pretending I don't like 'em when I do. I like watermelon and chitterlings both, and I don't care who knows it.

CHARACTER: Just stereotypes, that's all. (*He shakes his head*)

MAMIE: Man, get out of my face!

CHARACTER: Stereotypes. . . . stereotypes. . . . stereo. . . . (*He retreats muttering*)

MAMIE: Why, it's getting so colored folks can't do nothing no more without some other Negro calling you a stereotype. Stereotype, hah! If you like a little gin, you're a stereotype. You got to drink Scotch. If you wear a red dress, you're a stereotype. You got to wear beige or chartreuse. Lord have mercy, honey, do-don't like no blackeyed peas and rice! Then you're a down-home Negro for true—which I is—and proud of it!

(MAMIE *glares around as if daring somebody to dispute her. Nobody does*)

I didn't come here to Harlem to get away from my people. I come here because there's more of 'em. I loves my race. I loves my people. Stereotype!

CHARACTER: That's what I said, Stereotypes!

MAMIE: You better remove yourself from my presence, calling me a stereotype.

CHARACTER: Tch-tch-tch!

(*Clicking his tongue in disgust, the* LITTLE MAN *leaves the bar as* MAMIE *rises and threatens him with her purse. The* PIANIST *rushes over to congratulate her*)

PIANIST: Gimme five, Miss Mamie, gimme five!

(*They shake hands*)

MAMIE: Solid!

PIANIST: You and me agree! I could drink on that.

MAMIE: You go right back where you was and set down.

BODIDDLY: Who agrees is me! Bartender set up the bar—this far—from Mamie to me. What'll you have Cleopatra, a beer?

MAMIE: You know I drinks gin, Bodiddly. And I needs another one. That character done got me all upset. Where's all the decent peoples tonight? Where's Jess Simple?

BODIDDLY: I seen old Simp a couple of hours ago walking down Lenox Avenue with his girl. But Joyce turns in early. And when she turn in, she turns him out.

MAMIE: That's what I call a decent woman.

MELON: Damn if I do.

MAMIE: And that Simple is a good man. He needs himself a decent woman—instead of gallivanting around with chippies like Zarita that keeps a bar door flapping all night long. I never seen a woman could run in and out of a bar so much and so fast.

BODIDDLY: Ah, but that Zarita, she's sure a fine looking chick.

MAMIE: She wears her morals like a loose garment. Ain't no woman's man safe with her around.

MELON: She sure will drink a body up. Zarita damn near drunk me out of a whole car load of melons one night.

MAMIE: You sure is weak for young womens.

MELON: Miss Mamie, I could be weak for you.

MAMIE: Melon, scat! I done told you, get from over me! Scat!

GITFIDDLE: Hey, Hop!

(*The door flies open and a seedy looking fellow rushes in calling to the bartender*)

Hey, Hop! Lend me my guitar from behind the bar there, please. Hurry up, man! I'll bring it back.

HOPKINS: What's the hurry?

GITFIDDLE: There's a big party of folks in the Wonder Bar down the street spending money like water.

HOPKINS: Here you are, Git.

GITFIDDLE: Thank you, man! (*He takes guitar and exits*)

HOPKINS: I sure hope he can play up a few dollars—that man has been broke so long, it just ain't fair.

MAMIE: A good musicianer—doing nothing but playing for quarters folks throw him!

MELON: They say a woman brought old Gitfiddle low.

MAMIE: Getting high brought him low! Womens helps more mens than they don't.

MELON: I sure wish you'd help me.

MAMIE: Wish again, honey, because I ain't coming. I likes a man who works in one place, with one job, not all up and down the streets where he's subject to temptation. And as for me, I don't need nobody to help me.

(MELON *shrugs*)

MELON: Well, so that's that!

(SIMPLE *enters*)

SIMPLE: Good!

MAMIE: We been missing you. Excusing Boyd there, this bar's full of nothing but characters.

BOYD: Thank you, Miss Mamie.

MAMIE: Where you been, Simple?

SIMPLE: Eating ice cream.

CROWD: What?

SIMPLE: And I had my picture took.

BODIDDLY: With your lady fair.

SIMPLE: For my lady fair. All posed like this.
  (SIMPLE *assumes an attitude*)
HOPKINS: She must've fell out laughing at that pose.
SIMPLE: She did not. That's one thing about Joyce. She never laughs at nothing about me, never does, which is why I loves that girl.
BOYD: You can find more reasons for liking a woman, Jess. Every time, a different woman, it's a different reason.
HOPKINS: Pay him no mind, Mr. Boyd. Zarita laughs with him and at him.
SIMPLE: Zarita's different. I do not, never will, can't—won't, and don't love no jumping jack of a Zarita. A man can't hardly keep Zarita in his arms, let alone in his heart.
HOPKINS: So we know, Jess Simple!
SIMPLE: But I have kept Joyce in my heart ever since I met her— and she is there to stay. Dog-gone it, I wish I had my divorce from Isabel. But at last, it looks like I am making some headway. They say a man's life changes every seven years. I sure hope I am going through the change.
HOPKINS: Mr. Change, what are you drinking?
  (SIMPLE *takes an envelope from his pocket*)
SIMPLE: Give me and Boyd a couple of beers. Then I want you to read something. Didn't even show it to Joyce yet—not to get her hopes up too high. It's from my wife.
BOYD: I don't want to read your personal letters, Jess.
SIMPLE: Here, pal, read it—because I can't believe my eyes.
BOYD: Um-mmmm! Well, here goes: "Dear Mr. Simple: Jess, at last I have found a man who loves me enough to pay for my divorce. This new man is a mail clerk, his first wife being dead, so he want me for his second."
SIMPLE: Thank you, Father!
BOYD: "He knows I been married and am still married in name only to you, as you have not been willing to pay for the legal paper which grants freedom from our entanglement. This man is willing to pay for it. He says he will get a lawyer to furnish me grounds unless you want to contest. I do not want no contest, you hear me! All I want is my divorce. I am writing to find out if you will please not make no contest out of this. Let me hear from you tonight as my husband-to-be has already passed the point where he could wait. Once sincerely yours, but not now, ISABEL."
SIMPLE: Sounds just like my wife!
HOPKINS: I suppose you've no intention of cross-filing.
SIMPLE: I would not cross that wife of mine no kind of way. My last contest with that woman was such that the police had to pro-

tect me. So that man can have her. I do not even want a copy of the diploma. I told Isabel when we busted up that she had shared my bed, my board, my licker, and my hair oil, but that I did not want to share another thing with her from that day to this, not even a divorce. Let that other man pay for it—they can share it together. Me, I'll be married again before the gold seal's hardly out from under the stamper.

HOPKINS: Good! Perhaps you'll settle down, stop running around, and stay home nights with Joyce.

SIMPLE: Married, I'll get somewhere in the world, too. Let's drink to it. And that man in Baltimore better pay for my wife's divorce! If he don't, I'll fix him. Here's my toast.

(*He lifts his glass of beer*)

> In a horserace, Daddy-o
> One thing you will find—
> There ain't NO way to be out in front
> Without showing your tail
> To the horse behind . . .

(ZARITA *enters glittering*)

ZARITA: Hey now! Hi, all and sundry!

SIMPLE: Zarita!

ZARITA: Excuse me folks for being in a hurry.

MAMIE: I told you so!

ZARITA: Jess, I'm going to Jersey! Come on! Coleman and his girl've got their car outside.

SIMPLE: The one with the top down?

ZARITA: That's the chariot—and I got nobody to ride back there with me.

MAMIE: Don't that child just bring you to tears?

SIMPLE: Is Coleman sober?

ZARITA: Just feeling a little groovy that's all! Come on!

BODIDDLY: Woman, shut that outside door! It's chilly. You know it ain't official summer yet.

ZARITA: Your blood's thin. My, it's hot in here! Come on, Jess. The motor's running.

SIMPLE: The motor might be running, but I ain't. Come here, girl, I got something to say to you. Zarita, you know I'm almost engaged to be married. I can't be running around with you.

ZARITA: You really got yourself tangled up. Well, anyhow, we'll just ride over the bridge to a little after-hours spot in Jersey for a few drinks, and come right back. There's no harm in that.

SIMPLE: You sure you coming right back? And Coleman is gonna drive me right to my door?

ZARITA: Or mine! Your room is kinder little and small and cold. Sugar, is you is, or is you ain't?

(*She moves toward the door*)

SIMPLE: Zarita, it's chilly out there, and I ain't got my top coat.

ZARITA: Oh, Knuckle-Nose, we got a fifth of licker in the car to keep us warm. And there's some fine bars just across the George Washington Bridge. You does or you don't?

SIMPLE: Aw, Zarita!

ZARITA: Old Simple Square, do I have to beg and plead with you? Listen! I've got my own money. I'll even treat you to a couple of drinks. Come on.

(*She entices him in song*)

> LET ME TAKE YOU FOR A RIDE.
> LET THE BREEZE BLOW THROUGH YOUR HAIR.
> LET ME CUDDLE BY YOUR SIDE.
> LET ME SHOW YOU THAT I CARE.
> LET ME TAKE YOU FOR A RIDE.
> MAKE YOUR HEARTSTRINGS HUM LIKE MAD.
> LET ME GAZE INTO YOUR EYES
> WHILE YOU MAKE LIKE ALAN LADD.
> EVEN THOUGH IT'S JUST PRETENDING—
> I KNOW YOU DON'T BELONG TO ME—
> COME ON, KID, LET'S MAKE PRETENDING
> FULL OF FANCY FREE.
> SINCE I FIND YOUR SHOULDER SOFT
> AND YOUR EAR SWEET TO CONFIDE,
> BABY, GRANT MY LITTLE WISH—
> LET ME TAKE YOU FOR A RIDE.

(*Softly she pleads*)

> WON'T YOU TAKE ME FOR A RIDE?

SIMPLE:

> LET THE BREEZE BLOW THROUGH *MY* HAIR?

ZARITA:

> LET ME CUDDLE BY YOUR SIDE.

SIMPLE:

> THAT'S JUST SO MUCH WEAR AND TEAR.

ZARITA:

> WON'T YOU TAKE ME FOR A RIDE?

SIMPLE:

> ALL THAT SCENERY, I DONE SEEN.

ZARITA:

> LET ME GAZE INTO YOUR EYES
> WHILE YOU MAKE LIKE BENZEDRINE.

SIMPLE:
> EVEN THOUGH IT'S JUST PRETENDING—
> I KNOW YOU DON'T BELONG TO ME—
> COME ON, KID, LET'S MAKE PRETENDING
> FULL OF FANCY FREE!

BOTH:
> SINCE I FIND YOUR SHOULDER SOFT
> AND YOUR EAR SWEET TO CONFIDE,
> BABY, GRANT MY LITTLE WISH—
> COME ON, KID, LET'S RIDE!
> COME ON, KID, LET'S RIDE!

"LET ME TAKE YOU FOR A RIDE," Copyright 1956 BOURNE, INC., New York, N. Y. Copyright 1957 BOURNE, INC., New York, N. Y. Reprinted by Permission of BOURNE, INC.

(THEY *exit gaily*)

MAMIE: There goes a lamb to slaughter again. Ain't it a shame the kind of a deal a good woman gets when she goes to bed early!

BODIDDLY: Huh?

MAMIE: I ain't talking about a man like you with seventeen children. I'm talking about Joyce.

BODIDDLY: Oh!

MAMIE: She goes to bed early, leaving Simple to yield to temptation.

MELON: I'd never yield, Miss Mamie. But if I did, I'd yield with you.

MAMIE: Melon, I say, get out of my face. It's mighty near midnight. Lemme go home.

MELON: If I didn't have my pushcart to wheel, I would 'scort you, Miss Mamie.

MAMIE: Watermelon Joe, with you at the handle, I might have to jump out and walk—or roll out, one—wild as you is with womens. Hopkins, hand me my watermelon and let me go to my virtuous couch. Goodnight all, goodnight!

(MAMIE *exits with her watermelon under her arm*)

MELON: Huh, so she don't trust me to 'scort her home. Anyhow, I think I'll truck along after her and see can't I tote her melon to a taxi. Watermelons! Nice red ones!

(MELON *exits*)

BODIDDLY: Gimme a sherry, man. What'll you have, Boyd?

BOYD: Nothing, thanks.

(ARCIE *enters bustling*)

BODIDDLY: Arcie, my love, what you doing out this time of night?

ARCIE: I come out looking for you—and done looked in seven bars.

(HOPKINS *automatically pours Arcie some sherry*)

BODIDDLY: And had a drink in each and every one!

ARCIE: Naturally! A lady don't go in a bar and not buy nothing. Diddly, lover, listen, there ain't but five of our children home —which means an even dozen is still out in the streets.

BODIDDLY: The children's big enough to take care of themselves.

ARCIE: If you was any kind of a father—If you was any kind of . . .

BODIDDLY: Woman, hush! And put that sherry wine down—before you be walking sidewise to keep from flying. Let's be getting upstairs—before some more of our children don't get home. Be seeing you, folks!

ARCIE: That man!

(*The bar is empty except for* BOYD *who rises to leave*)

HOPKINS: Say, Boyd, as a writer, would you say them folks are stereotypes?

BOYD: In the book I'm writing they're just folks. Goodnight, Hop.

(GITFIDDLE *comes reeling into the bar as* BOYD *exits*)

GITFIDDLE: Got-dog it! I done broke another string!

HOPKINS: Well, did you make any money?

GITFIDDLE: They paid me off in drinks. I had nothing to eat all day. Here, Hop, lend me another half for a sandwich—and keep this for security.

(GITFIDDLE *offers his guitar to Hopkins*)

HOPKINS: You must think Paddy's Bar is a bank. I lent you two dollars and a quarter already this week. Here's. Here's fifty cents more.

GITFIDDLE: Thanks, Hop! But wait a minute, Hop—lemme play you just one more blues.

(*The woebegone* GITFIDDLE *strums his guitar*)

> I GOT SOMETHING TO TELL YOU,
> IF IT'S NEWS TO YOU.
> IF YOU AIN'T GOT FIVE STRINGS,
> MAKE FOUR STRINGS DO.
> IF YOU AIN'T GOT FOUR STRINGS,
> PLAY IT ON THREE.
> THAT IS WHAT THE BLUES
> HAS TAUGHT TO ME.
> IF YOU AIN'T GOT THREE STRINGS,
> PLUNK ON TWO,
> THAT IS WHAT THE BLUES
> WILL DO TO YOU.
> IF YOU AIN'T GOT TWO STRINGS,
> PLAY IT ON ONE,
> AND WHEN YOU AIN'T GOT ONE,
> THEN HUM IT WITH NONE!

THAT IS WHAT THE BLUES
HAS DONE! DONE DONE!
THAT IS WHAT THE BLUES
HAS DONE! DONE DONE!

"BROKEN STRINGS," Copyright 1956 BOURNE, INC., New York, N. Y. Reprinted by Permission of BOURNE, INC.

(*The lights fade as his last note dies.* BLACKOUT)

Scene 4

Hospital room. Next day. SIMPLE *is propped up in a very white, very clean bed, very quiet. Both his legs are up in traction. A* NURSE *all in white tiptoes in and calls softly. He answers with a groan.*

NURSE: Mr. Semple.

SIMPLE: Aw-um-mmm-mm-m!

NURSE: Such groaning! You aren't that bad off.

SIMPLE: When I suffers, Nurse, I like to suffer loud.

NURSE: There's a gentleman to see you.

(*She beckons the caller*)

Here he is, sir.

MELON: Thank you, Nurse.

(MELON *enters.* NURSE *exits*)

Oh, man! You're all packed for shipping!

SIMPLE: Strung, hung, and slung's what I am. Melon, this is the most! Um-mmm-mm-m!

MELON: All I heard was, you was in an accident.

SIMPLE: It were an accident, all right. Got-dog that Zarita! My mind told me—

MELON: Never mind what your mind told you, Daddy-o, just gimme the details. Here.

SIMPLE: What's that?

MELON: I brought you some books.

SIMPLE: I wish you'd of brought me a quart of beer and some pigs feet. I ain't much on books.

MELON: Comic books, man.

SIMPLE: Oh! *Horror in Hackensack. Terror in Trenton.*

MELON: Man, that's the crazy history of New Jersey.

SIMPLE: This makes me feel better already. Thanks, Melon.

MELON: Now, tell me what happened.

SIMPLE: The car tried to climb the George Washington Bridge, instead of going *across* it—turned half over—Coleman, his girl, and Zarita and me. But I was the *only* one that got throwed out, and on my—bohunkus. Melon, I'm all bruised up on my sit-downer.

MELON: I told you, you should stop balling, and take care of yourself.

SIMPLE: If I had took care of myself, I would not have these pretty nurses taking care of me now.

MELON: But look at the big hospital bill when you get out.

SIMPLE: Lemme hit one number, I'll settle it. But what worries me is when I'm going to get out.

MELON: You will never get out if you don't observe the rules and stop telling folks to bring you beer and pigs feet and things you are not supposed to have.

SIMPLE: But alcohol had nothing to do with it.

MELON: Oh, no?

SIMPLE: Womens aggravate a man, drunk or sober. Melon, I hope Joyce knows Zarita ain't nothing to me, even if I do accidentally go riding with her. But I don't want to discuss how come I'm in this hospital. You know, no matter what a man does, sick or well, something is always liable to happen—especially if he's colored. In this world, Melon, it's hard for a man to live until he dies.

(The NURSE *enters)*

MELON: I think you'll make it.

NURSE: There's a Miss Joyce Lane to see you.

(A look of great helplessness comes over SIMPLE. *He appeals to his friend)*

SIMPLE: Melon. . . .

MELON: It's Joyce.

SIMPLE: Just like a man has to face his Maker alone, the same goes for facing a woman.

MELON: You want to see her, don't you?

SIMPLE: Worse than anything, I want to see Joyce, Melon. Also, I—I—I—

MELON: Also, you don't want to see her. I know. Good luck, old man.

(The NURSE *shows* MELON *out. As they exit,* JOYCE *enters)*

JOYCE: Jess!

(Tears come, and she takes out her handkerchief)

SIMPLE: Baby, please don't cry. I'm all right.

JOYCE: But your legs! Are they broken?

SIMPLE: Doc says they ain't. But they sure are bent.

JOYCE: Then why are they all trussed up that way?

SIMPLE: Because I can't lay on my hine, that's why.

JOYCE: Your what?

SIMPLE: My hindparts is all skint up, Joyce. I hope that's a polite word for saying it.

JOYCE: But aren't you hurt badly?

SIMPLE: No.

JOYCE: I am.

SIMPLE: Baby, don't you want to set down? Here on the bed. Then pull your chair up close, please.

JOYCE: Oh, Jess!

SIMPLE: I know, Joyce, I know. I hadn't ought to done it.

JOYCE: With a drunken driver, too—and Zarita.

SIMPLE: You know I love you.

JOYCE: And that's the way you show it? With your legs tied up in the air—on account of a—

SIMPLE: Auto wreck—

JOYCE: Woman.

SIMPLE: Just a little old innocent joy ride.

JOYCE: Oh, stop it!

SIMPLE: Baby, did you take communion this morning?

JOYCE: Yes, Jess, I did. I was almost late. I waited for you to go with me.

SIMPLE: Did they sing, "Jesus Knows Just How Much I Can Bear"?

JOYCE: Not today.

SIMPLE: I used to like that song. You know how I feel now? Just like I felt the last time Aunt Lucy whipped me. Did I ever tell you about that, Joyce?

JOYCE: No.

SIMPLE: It were a girl caused that whipping.

JOYCE: I'm not surprised, Jess.

SIMPLE: Aunt Lucy is dead and gone to glory, Joyce. But it were Aunt Lucy taught me right from wrong. When I were a little young child, I didn't have much raising. I knocked around every-which-where, pillar to post. But when Aunt Lucy took me, she did her best to whip me and *raise* me, too—'cause Aunt Lucy really believed in her Bible. "Spare the rod and spoil the child." I were *not* spoiled. But that last whipping is what did it—made me the man I am today . . . I could see that whipping coming Joyce, when I sneaked out of the henhouse one of Aunt Lucy's best hens and give it to that girl to roast for her Sunday School picnic, because that old girl said she was aiming to picnic *me*—except that she didn't have nothing much to put in her basket. I was trying to jive that girl, you know. Anyhow, Aunt Lucy found out about it and woke me up the next morning with a switch in her hand. . . . But I got all mannish that morning, Joyce. I said, "Aunt Lucy, you ain't gonna whip me no more. I'se a man now—and you ain't gonna whip me." Aunt Lucy said, "You know you had no business snatching my best laying hen right off her nest." Aunt Lucy was angry. And big as I was, *I* was scared. . . . Yet I was meaning not to let her whip me, Joyce. But, just when I was aiming to snatch that switch out of her hand, I seed Aunt Lucy was crying. I said, "What you crying for?" She said, "I'm crying 'cause here you is a man and don't know how to act right *yet*, and I done did my best to raise you so you'll grow up to be a good man. I wore out so many switches on your back—still you tries my soul. But it *ain't* my soul I'm thinking of, son, it's you. Jess, I wants you to carry yourself right. You understand me? I'm getting too old to be using my strength up like this. Here!" Aunt Lucy hollered, "Bend over and lemme whip you one more time!" . . . Big as I was, Joyce, you know I bended. When I seen her crying, I would have let Aunt Lucy kill me before I raised a hand. When she got through, I said, "Aunt Lucy, you ain't gonna have to whip me no more—I'm going to do my best to do right from now on, and not try your soul. And I am sorry about that hen . . ." Joyce, from that day to this, I have tried to behave myself. Aunt Lucy is gone to Glory, now, but if she's looking down, she knows that's true. That was my last whipping. But it wasn't the whipping that taught me what I needed to know. It was because she cried and cried. When peoples care for you and cry for you—and *love* you—Joyce, they can straighten out your soul.

(SIMPLE *lost in his story, had not been looking at Joyce. Instead, as he finishes, he is looking at the ceiling. Suddenly* JOYCE *turns to bury her head on the back of her chair, sobbing aloud.* SIMPLE, *forgetting that his legs are tied and that he cannot get out of bed, tries to rise*)

Joyce! . . . Joyce! . . . Joyce!

(*If he could, he would go to her and take her in his arms*)

Joyce, you're crying for me!

JOYCE: I'm not! I'm crying for your grandmother.

SIMPLE: It wasn't my grandmother I was telling you about, Joyce, it were my Aunt Lucy.

JOYCE: Well, whoever it was, she had her hands full with you.

SIMPLE: She loved me, Joyce, just like I love you . . . Come here, feel my heart—now it's beating just for you . . . Joyce, please come here.

(SIMPLE *reaches out his hand and* JOYCE *comes. She takes it, and* HE *pulls her toward him*)
Feel my heart.
(*He puts her hand on his heart. But suddenly* JOYCE *buries her head on his chest and sobs violently.* SIMPLE *puts an arm about her and smiles, quietly happy*)

BLACKOUT

SCENE 5

Paddy's bar. Saturday night. The joint is jumping. GITFIDDLE *is plunking his guitar.* ARCIE *is in the middle of the floor, curring up as if she were a young woman.* JOHN JASPER, *one of her teenage jitterbug sons comes in, hits a few steps himself, whirls around, then taps her on the shoulder.*

JOHN JASPER: Mama! Hey, Mama!
ARCIE: Get away from me, son! Can't you see your mama is having a good time and don't want to be bothered with no children? Stop that dancing! Where's all my children? Arcilee and Melinda and Mabel and Johnny and Little Bits and Cora? Also Lilac? Huh?
JOHN JASPER: They all in the street, gone to Saturday night parties and things. Mama, lend me a quarter. I want to take the bus down to 96th Street to the Swords and Sabres dance.
ARCIE: Ask your daddy. He ain't paid me off yet. Got his pockets just full of wages—I hope. Hey! Hey! Hey!
(ARCIE *continues dancing as the* BOY *approaches* BODIDDLY *at the bar*)
JOHN JASPER: Hey, Daddy, gimme a quarter.
BODIDDLY: Scram! You too young to be in this bar, John Jasper. Here take this quarter, boy, and scram! Children all under a man's feet!
JOHN JASPER: Thanks, Dad!
(*He skips off.* MISS MAMIE *and* MELON *do a slow Lindy hop to the music*)
ARCIE: Bartender, another sherry—on my husband there.
BODIDDLY: Woman, you better stop spending my money before you get it. Is you done your Saturday night shopping yet?
ARCIE: Can I do it on credit? Hand it over, Diddly, lover!

BODIDDLY: Many mouths as you got to feed, you better get to the stores before they close.

ARCIE: Them's your children, too. Ain't you gonna help me carry the grits?

BODIDDLY: Woman, you know I'm tired. Go do your shopping.

ARCIE: Treat me first.

BODIDDLY: Hop, give this woman a glass of Domesticated Sherry. (HOPKINS *laughs and pours her another glass of sherry before* SHE *exits.* ZARITA *enters*)

ZARITA: Simple hasn't been in yet tonight, has he, Hop?

HOPKINS: Not yet.

BODIDDLY: But if he's able to walk, he'll be here before it's over.

ZARITA: He's been back at work three or four days, and I haven't seen him. You know, Hop, when I went by Harlem Hospital, he acted like he was mad at me.

HOPKINS: No wonder—you took him riding and got him all banged up.

ZARITA: He didn't have to go. Nobody forced him. I just said, "Come on." Say, Hop, what you doing this morning when you get off from work?

HOPKINS: I'm going home, Zarita.

ZARITA: There's a nice new after-hours spot opened down on Seventh Avenue.

HOPKINS: I said, I am going home.

ZARITA: You didn't always go home so early after work, Mr. Hopkins.

HOPKINS: Do you call three o'clock in the morning early?

ZARITA: Real early! Don't you remember that night you drove me over to Newark?

HOPKINS: I remember.

ZARITA: And we didn't get back early either.

HOPKINS: Zarita, this is one morning I'm turning in. Maybe Simple'll take you to this new Bottle club.

ZARITA: Maybe he will—if he ain't still mad. Anyhow, if you see him, tell him I'll be back. I will be back.

HOPKINS: Cool, Zarita, cool.

(ZARITA *exits in rhythm to* GITFIDDLE'S *guitar*)

MELON: Hey, Git, you sounds mighty good plunking over there in the corner. C'mon, Miss Mamie, let's dance.

MAMIE: Yes, you ought to be on the juke box.

GITFIDDLE: Juke boxes is the trouble now, Miss Mamie. Used to be, folks liked to hear a sure-enough live guitar player. Now, I start playing, somebody puts a nickel in the piccolo, drowns me out. No good for musicianers any more, but I got to make the rounds, try to hustle. See you later, Miss Mamie.

MAMIE: Git, I'd rather hear you than records any day. When you come back, I'm gonna throw you a dollar just to pick a blues for me.

GITFIDDLE: I won't be long, Miss Mamie, won't be long.

(GITFIDDLE *exits as* JOHN JASPER *runs in*)

JOHN JASPER: Papa!

BODIDDLY: John Jasper, now what you want? A man can't . . .

JOHN JASPER: Ronnie Belle. . . .

BODIDDLY: A man can't enjoy his self. . . .

JOHN JASPER: Ronnie Belle. . . .

BODIDDLY: . . . . without some child stuck up in his face.

(JOHN JASPER *dances as he talks*)

JOHN JASPER: Ronnie Belle says she won't stay home and mind the babies, and it's my turn to go out this Saturday night. She says if I go, she's going.

BODIDDLY: You tell Ronnie Belle I'll come up there and fan her good, if she don't do what she's supposed to. I declare to goodness, these young folks nowadays! You get upstairs, John Jasper, and tell your sister what I said.

JOHN JASPER: Yes, sir, Papa!

(JOHN JASPER *exits*)

MAMIE: Diddly, you sure got some fine children.

BODIDDLY: And every one of them born in New York City, Harlem. When I left the South, I never did go back.

(JOHN JASPER *returns*)

JOHN JASPER: I forgot.

BODIDDLY: Lord, that boy's back again. John Jasper now what do you want?

JOHN JASPER: Mama says for you to come on upstairs and bring her a pint of cooking sherry.

BODIDDLY: You know your mama ain't gonna do no cooking this time of the night! Tell Arcie to come down here and get her own wine. Scat, boy, scat!

(JOHN JASPER *dances out*)

MAMIE: Diddly, that's the cutest one of your children. I'll give him a dime myself.

BODIDDLY: Lemme get way back in the corner so's no more of my kin folks can find me—not even my wife.

(*He goes into a corner as* SIMPLE *enters*)

MAMIE: Look who's coming there!

PIANIST: Hy, Jess!

MELON: Jess Simple!

(THE BARTENDER *lifts a bottle of beer*)

HOPKINS: It's on the house!

MAMIE: Welcome home!

BODIDDLY: To the land of the living!

MAMIE: Amen! Bless Jess!

HOPKINS: Zarita was just looking for you.

(*Happily the* CUSTOMERS *retire to tables with the drinks as* SIMPLE *remains leaning stiffly on the bar*)

SIMPLE: Don't mention Zarita, please, Hop! She's near about ruint me. Joyce is treating me cool, cool, cool, since I come out the hospital and I explained to her over and over I was just out riding. Hop, oh Hop! Oh, man, have I got a worried mind! You know when I reached home my old landlady come handing me a Special Delivery from my wife which stated that the Negro in Baltimore has only made one payment on our divorce, leaving two payments to go. Hop, you're educated. How much is one payment on $400, leaving two payments to go?

HOPKINS: $133.33 and one-third cents.

SIMPLE: Now I could just about pay one-third cents.

HOPKINS: I thought you said that man in Baltimore loved your wife so much he was willing to pay for the whole divorce.

SIMPLE: Inflation's got him—so he just made one down payment. Isabel writ that if I would make one payment now, she would make one, then everybody could marry right away. But I cannot meet a payment now—with the hospital bill, rent up, food up, phones up, cigarettes up—everything up—but my salary. Divorces are liable to go up, too, if I don't hurry up and pay up. Lord! Women, women, women!

(*He paces the floor*)

MELON: Don't let women get you excited, man! Sit down and take it easy.

(*Offered a seat,* SIMPLE *protects his haunches with his palms*)

SIMPLE: The last thing I want to do is set down!

MAMIE: Then stand up to it like a man! You made your own bed hard. What you drinking?

SIMPLE: Whiskey.

VOICES: Whiskey.

MELON: And you're usually a beer man!

SIMPLE: Tonight I want whiskey. Hop, I said, whiskey! I'm broke, busted, and disgusted. And just spent mighty near my last nickle for a paper—and there ain't no news in it about colored folks. Unless we commit murder, robbery or rape, or are being chased by a mob, do we get on the front page, or hardly on the back. Take flying saucers. For instance according to the DAILY NEWS, everybody has seen flying saucers in the sky. Everybody but a Negro. They probably won't even let flying saucers fly over Harlem, just to keep us from seeing one. Not long ago, I read where some Karl Krubelowski had seen a flying saucer, also Giovanni Battini saw one. And way out in Pennsylvania mountains some Dutchman named Heinrich Armpriester seen one. But did you read about Roosevelt Johnson or Ralph Butler or Henry Washington or anybody that sounded like a Negro seeing one? I did not. Has a flying saucer ever passed over Lenox Avenue yet? Nary one! Not even Daddy Grace has glimpsed one, nor Ralph Bunche. Negroes can't even get into the front page news no kind of way. I can't even see a flying saucer. When I do, that will be a great day.

HOPKINS: It would probably scare you to death—so you wouldn't live to see your name in the papers.

SIMPLE: Well, the—I could read about it in the other world then—and be just as proud—me, Jess Semple, kilt by a flying saucer.

(ARCIE *enters yelling tipsily*)

ARCIE: Bodiddly! Bodiddly! Why don't you come on upstairs?

BODIDDLY: Aw, woman, hush! Every time I turn around there's families under my feet. Set down and leave me be.

ARCIE: I did not come to set down. It's past midnight. I come to get you to go to bed.

BODIDDLY: I know when to go to bed my own self.

ARCIE: Then come on, you great big no-good old bull-necked son-of-a-biscuit eater!

BODIDDLY: Sit down, I'll buy you a sherry wine. Hop!

(ZARITA *enters with an enormous well-dressed* FELLOW *in a turban*)

ZARITA: Hellow, you-all! Hey, Jess Semple! Folks, dig this champion roots-herbs-and-numbers-seller from south of the border. I just come by to show you my new man I met at the Baby Grand. Don't he look like a sultan? But we got business. Come on! We're gonna do the town ain't we, Ali Baba?

MAMIE: Ali Baba?

ZARITA: Sugar Hill, Smals, and every place! Come on Texas Tarzan, come on! Jess, I'm glad you came out of that little accident O.K. Bye, all!

(ZARITA *kisses the* BIG BOY. *He sneezes.* MELON *ducks. As* ZARITA *and her new* MAN *exit,* SIMPLE *looks sheepish*)

BODIDDLY: She don't need us tonight.

HOPKINS: She's got her a two-ton Sugar Daddy.

MELON: She's got her a human shower.

MAMIE: Paddy's Bar is small-time to Zarita this evening. She'll be in here Monday all beat out, though—and looking for Jess Semple.

SIMPLE: Or somebody else simple—but it won't be me.

MELON: Where have I heard that before?

SIMPLE: Where have I heard that before?

(They glare at each other)

MELON: Where have I heard that before?

(SIMPLE's *feelings are hurt*)

SIMPLE: I'm going and see Joyce. ~~I need to see somebody that loves me.~~

(*A* POLICEMAN's VOICE *is heard in the street*)

POLICEMAN: Hey, you! Stay off the street with that noise box. Don't you know it's against the law, out here hustling for dimes? Next time I hear that racket, I'll run you in.

GITFIDDLE: Yes, sir, Officer!

(GITFIDDLE *enters crestfallen*)

A man can't play music nowhere no more. Juke box drowns him out in the bars, cops run him off the streets, landlady won't let you play in your own room. I might as well break this damn box up!

MAMIE: Gitfiddle, I told you, you can play for me.

BODIDDLY: Me too.

ARCIE: Sure, Git.

MELON: And me, Git.

MAMIE: Come on, now! Let's have some music like you feels it Gitfiddle.

MELON:

    DID YOU EVER HEAR THE BLUES?
    ON A BATTERED OLD GUITAR:
    DID YOU EVER HEAR THE BLUES
    OVER YONDER, LORD, HOW FAR?
    DID YOU EVER HEAR THE BLUES
    ON A SATURDAY NIGHT?
    DID YOU EVER HEAR THE BLUES
    ABOUT SOME CHICK AIN'T DONE YOU RIGHT?
    BABY, DID YOU EVER HEAR THE BLUES?

MAMIE:

    DID YOU EVER HEAR THE BLUES

ON AN OLD HOUSE-RENT PIANO?
DID YOU EVER HEAR THE BLUES
LIKE THEY PLAY 'EM IN SAVANNAH?
DID YOU EVER HEAR THE BLUES
IN THE EARLY, EARLY MORN?
WONDERING, WONDERING, WONDERING
WHY YOU WAS EVER BORN?
BABY, DID YOU EVER HEAR THE BLUES?

MELON:

WHEN THE BAR IS QUIET
AND THE NIGHT IS ALMOST DONE.
THEM OLD BLUES OVERTAKE YOU
AT THE BOTTOM OF YOUR FUN.
OH, LORD, THEM BLUES!
ECHO . . . ECHO . . . ECHO . . . OF THE BLUES!

MAMIE:

GOOD MORNING BLUES! GOOD MORNING!
GOOD MORNING BLUES, I SAY!
GOOD MORNING BLUES, GOOD MORNING!
YOU DONE COME BACK TO STAY?
YOU COME BACK TO BUG ME
LIKE YOU DRUG ME YESTERDAY?

MELON:

BLUES, I HEARD YOU KNOCK LAST NLGHT,
BUT I WOULD NOT LET YOU IN.
KNOCK, KNOCK, KNOCK, LAST NIGHT
BUT I WOULD NOT LET YOU IN.
I TRIED TO MAKE BELIVE
IT WEREN'T NOTHING BUT THE WIND.

ALL:

BLUES, BLUES, BLUES!
IT WERE THE BLUES!
MAYBE TO SOME PEOPLE
WHAT THE BLUESES SAY IS NEWS
BUT TO ME IT'S AN OLD, OLD STORY.

MAMIE:

DID YOU EVER HEAR THE BLUES
ON A BATTERED OLD GUITAR?
DID YOU EVER HEAR THE BLUES
OVER YONDER, LORD, HOW FAR?
DID YOU EVER HEAR THE BLUES
ON A SATURDAY NIGHT?

BOTH:

> DID YOU EVER HEAR THE BLUES
> ABOUT SOME CHICK AIN'T DONE YOU RIGHT?

ALL:

> BABY, DID YOU EVER HEAR THE BLUES?

BLACKOUT

Scene 6

Joyce's room. Sunday evening. JOYCE *is sewing. The bell rings seven times. The* LANDLADY *calls.*

MRS. CADDY: I'll answer it, Miss Lane. I'm right here in the hall.

JOYCE: Oh, thank you, Mrs. Caddy. You're about the nicest landlady I know.

MRS. CADDY: Are you decent? Do you want to see Mr. Semple? He's kinda cripple—so down here or up there?

JOYCE: I'm sewing, so let him come up here, please—if he can make it.

*(*SIMPLE *enters and closes the door)*

SIMPLE: I've made it. Well, I'm back on my feet, up, out, and almost at it.

JOYCE: I see. You may come in. Remember the door—Mrs. Caddy's rules.

(He opens the door a crack)

SIMPLE: Dog-gone old landlady! Joyce, I knew I'm a black sheep. But I explained it all to you the last time you come by the hospital.

JOYCE: I accepted your explanation.

SIMPLE: But you don't seem like you're glad to see me, now I'm out—the way you didn't say almost nothing when I come by Friday.

JOYCE: I'm glad to see you.

SIMPLE: Then lemme kiss you. Ouch! My back!

JOYCE: Oh!

SIMPLE: I think my veterbrays is disconnected.

JOYCE: What did the x-rays show?

SIMPLE: Nothing but a black mark. The doctor says I'm O.K. Just can't set down too suddenly for a while.

JOYCE: Then have a slow seat.

SIMPLE: Joyce, is you my enemy? You sound so cool. Am I intruding?

JOYCE: Oh, no. I'm just having a nice peaceful Sunday evening at home—which I must say, I haven't had too often since I've been knowing you.

SIMPLE: Baby darling, I'm sorry if I'm disturbing you, but I hope you're glad to see me. What you making?

JOYCE: Just lingerie for a girl friend who's getting married.

SIMPLE: Step-ins or step-outs?

JOYCE: Slips, Jess, slips. Jess Semple, stop breathing down my neck. The way you say things sometimes, you think I'm going to melt again, don't you? Well, instead you might get stuck with this needle. Listen, hand me that pattern book over there. Let me see how I should insert this lace.

SIMPLE: What're you doing with all those timetables and travel books, baby?

JOYCE: Just in case we ever should get married, maybe I'm picking out a place to spend our honeymoon—Niagara Falls, the Grand Canyon, Plymouth Rock . . .

SIMPLE: I don't want to spend no honeymoon on no rock. These books is pretty, but, baby, we ain't ready to travel yet.

JOYCE: We can dream, can't we?

SIMPLE: Niagara Falls makes a mighty lot of noise falling down. I likes to sleep on holidays.

JOYCE: Oh, Jess! Then how about the far West? Were you ever at the Grand Canyon?

SIMPLE: I were. Facts, I was also at Niagara Falls, after I were at Grand Canyon.

JOYCE: I do not wish to criticize your grammar, Mr. Semple, but as long as you have been around New York, I wonder why you continue to say, I were, and at other times, I was?

SIMPLE: Because sometimes I were, and sometimes I was, baby. I was at Niagara Falls and I were at the Grand Canyon—since that were in the far distant past when I were a coachboy on the Santa Fe. I was more recently at Niagara Falls.

JOYCE: I see. But you never were "I were"! There is no "I were." In the past tense, there is only "I was." The verb to be is declined, "I am, I was, I have been."

SIMPLE: Joyce, baby, don't be so touchous about it. Do you want me to talk like Edward R. Murrow?

JOYCE: No! But when we go to formals I hate to hear you saying for example "I taken" instead of "I took." Why do colored people say, "I taken," so much?

SIMPLE: Because we are taken—taken until we are undertaken, and, Joyce, baby, funerals is high!

JOYCE: Funerals are high.

SIMPLE: Joyce, what difference do it make?

JOYCE: Jess! What difference does it make. Does is correct English.

SIMPLE: And do ain't?

JOYCE: Isn't—not ain't.

SIMPLE: Woman, don't tell me *ain't* ain't in the dictionary.

JOYCE: But it ain't—I mean—it isn't correct.

SIMPLE: Joyce, I give less than a small damn! What if it aren't? *(In his excitement he attempts to sit down, but leaps up as soon as his seat touches the chair)*

JOYCE: You say what if things aren't. You give less than a damn. Well, I'm tired of a man who gives less than a damn about "What if things aren't." I'm tired! Tired! You hear me? Tired! I have never known any one man so long without having some kind of action out of him. You have not even formally proposed to me, let alone writing my father for my hand.

SIMPLE: I did not know I had to write your old man for your hand.

JOYCE: My father, Jess, not my old man. And don't let it be too long. After all, I might meet some other man.

SIMPLE: You better not meet no other man. You better not! Do and I will marry you right now this June in spite of my first wife, bigamy, your old man—I mean your father. Joyce, don't you know I am not to be trifled with? I'm Jesse B. Semple.

JOYCE: I know who you are. Now, just sit down and let's spend a nice Sunday evening conversing, heh?

(SIMPLE sits down, but it hurts him)

SIMPLE: Ouch!

JOYCE: Oh, sweety! Let me make you a nice cool drink. Lemonade?

SIMPLE: Yes, Joyce, lemonade.

(JOYCE exits. Suddenly SIMPLE realizes what he has agreed to drink and cries in defeat)

Lemonade!

BLACKOUT

Scene 7

Simple's room. A month later. MR. BOYD *comes down the hall and see Simple's door ajar. He looks in.*

BOYD: Hey, fellow, what you doing home on Saturday night?

SIMPLE: Boyd, man, come on in. Joyce is gone to some gal's wedding shower—and damn if I'm going out to any bar. Still and yet, Boyd, I'm in a good mind to take that money I been saving and blow it all in, every damn penny, because man, it looks hopeless. Push done come to shove on that divorce, I got to pay for my part of it. So last month I started saving. But, damn, I got so far to go!

BOYD: How much do you have to save in all?

SIMPLE: One hundred thirty-three dollars and thirty-three cents. I'm as far as Leviticus.

BOYD: What do you mean, Leviticus?

SIMPLE: Aunt Lucy always said, "The Bible is the Book. Put your trust therein." So that's where I'm putting my money. I got to save $133.33. If I put a ten dollar bill in each chapter every week from Genesis on, in 18½ weeks I will have it—and I'll only have to go as far as Nahum.

BOYD: Nahum?

SIMPLE: That's a book in the Bible, somewhere down behind Ezekiel. If I ever get to Nahum that's it. I done put ten in Genesis, ten in Exodus, and five in Levi.

BOYD: I thought you said *ten* every week.

SIMPLE: I were a little short this past week. Anyhow, I got twenty-five.

BOYD: Come on, let's go around to Paddy's.

SIMPLE: Thanks, Daddy-o! I will not yield to temptation! No! Not especially since I done got another letter from that used-to-be wife of mine, Isabel. Sit down, Boyd. Listen. "Jesse B. Semple, you are less than a man. You marry a girl, neglect her, ignore her, and won't help her divorce herself, not even when your part ain't only but one-third of the payment. You can go to hell! You do not deserve no gold seal on your decree, because you have not put a cent into it. Therefore, since I am going to pay for this divorce myself, your paper may not be legal. From now on, you kiss my foot! Isabel Estherlee Jones. P.S. I have taken back my maiden name, as I want no parts of you attached to me any longer. MISS JONES."

BOYD: She's angry.

SIMPLE: Seems like it, Boyd, I will not let Isabel get the last word on me. I'll send that lawyer my part of the money next week, even if I have to put my whole paycheck in to do it. Right now I got twenty-five in the Bible. When I add my old check, that won't leave but about ah-er-a sixty to go. I can pawn a suit, one overcoat, and my radio—which might still leave about fifty. Boyd, can you lend me fifty?

BOYD: Fellow, are you out of your mind?

SIMPLE: This is an emergency. I need a gold seal on my divorce, too—so I got to pay for it. I got to have that gold seal, Boyd! I got to have it! It's got to be legal for Joyce. But then it's up to me to get that money, ain't it, Boyd? It ain't up to you nor nobody else—it's just up to me.

BOYD: Yes, Simple, I'm afraid it is. Get hold of yourself, make a man out of yourself. You got to live up to your obligations.

SIMPLE: You done said a big word, Boyd.

BOYD: And it's a big thing you've got to do, fellow, facing up to yourself. You're not the first man in the world to have problems. You've got to learn how to swim, Jess, in this great big ocean called the world.

SIMPLE: This great big old white ocean—and me a colored swimmer.

BOYD: Aw, stop feeling sorry for yourself just because you're colored. You can't use race as an excuse forever. All men have problems. And even if you are colored, you've got to swim beyond color, and get to that island that is you—the human you, the man you. You've got to face your obligations, and stand up on that island of you, and be a man.

SIMPLE: Obligations! That's a word for you, Boyd! Seems like to me obligations is just a big old rock standing in a man's way.

BOYD: Then you've got to break that rock, fellow. Or, maybe I should say rocks.

SIMPLE: I know what you mean—like the beer rock, huh, Boyd?

BOYD: Um-hum!

SIMPLE: And the licker-rock—only I don't drink much whiskey.

BOYD: Well, say the bar-rock in general.

SIMPLE: That night-owl rock.

BOYD: Out until four A.M.

SIMPLE: Yes, the chick-chasing rock.

BOYD: Zarita!

SIMPLE: Not mentioning no names! But, man I done shook that chick. But then there's always that old trying-to-save-money rock.

BOYD: You mean putting-it-off-until-tomorrow rock.

SIMPLE: Which has really been my stumbling rock.

BOYD: You got to bust it, man. You know about John Henry, don't you?

SIMPLE: Sure I do.

BOYD: He was the champion rock-buster of them all.

SIMPLE: My Uncle Tige used to sing about him. Boyd, I been making up my mind to break through my rocks, too.

(BOYD *smiles*)

Yes, I is, Boyd, I is.

BOYD: You just got to bust 'em, fellow, that's all.

(BOYD *exits.* SIMPLE *takes off his shirt and changes into a ragged pajama top*)

SIMPLE: Bust 'em! I got to bust 'em. Like that song of Uncle Tige's. That old man sure could sing—made up songs, too.

(SIMPLE *sits on bed to take off his shoes*)

Made his own about John Henry which went—lemme see.

(He tries to remember)

How did it go? Something about—

> THEY SAY JOHN HENRY WAS A MAN.
>
> AND THEY SAY HE TOOK A HAMMER IN HIS HAND—

(He uses one shoe as a hammer)

That's it!

> AND BUSTED A ROCK
>
> SO HARD HE GAVE THE WORLD A SHOCK!
>
> YES, THEY SAY JOHN HENRY WAS A MAN.

(SIMPLE *rises*)

> THEY SAY JOHN HENRY WON A PRIZE,
>
> AND THEY SAY HE GAVE HIS LIFE TO WIN THAT PRIZE.

(He comes forward)

> YES, THEY SAY HE HAMMERED ON
>
> UNTIL HIS BREATH WAS GONE!

(As if speaking to himself)

> THEY SAY JOHN HENRY WON A PRIZE.

(He reaches toward his back pocket)

> WELL, THERE'S A PRIZE I'M GONNA WIN,
>
> AND THE TIME'S LONG GONE I SHOULD BEGIN.

(From his wallet he shakes his last five dollar bill, opens the Bible, and puts it in between the pages)

> BUT IT'S BETTER LATE THAN NEVER,
>
> AND NO TIME AIN'T FOREVER.

(He clasps the Bible to his chest)

> SO RIGHT NOW, I'M GONNA START TO WIN.

(He turns forward resolutely, putting Bible down)

> IT TAKES A LONG HAUL TO GET THERE, SO THEY SAY,
>
> AND THERE'S GREAT BIG MOUNTAINS IN THE WAY.
>
> BUT I'M GONNA MAKE IT THROUGH
>
> IF IT'S THE LAST DAMN THING I DO.

(He bangs his head on the Bible)

> I'M GONNA BE JOHN HENRY, BE JOHN HENRY,
>
> I'M GONNA BE JOHN HENRY, TOO.

(Chorus rises in background, and as light fades on Simple a distant male voice is heard repeating last phrases)

VOICE:

> GONNA BE JOHN HENRY, BE JOHN HENRY,—

CHORUS:

> GONNA BE JOHN HENRY, TOO!

"(I'M GONNA BE) JOHN HENRY," Copyright 1957 BOURNE, INC., New York, N. Y. Reprinted by Permission of BOURNE, INC.

BLACKOUT

ACT II

> *The music of the blues on the guitar, slow haunting, syncopated, precedes the rise of the curtain . . .*

Scene 1:

Paddy's bar. A week later. Evening. ARCIE *is sitting alone at a table drinking sherry wine and working a crossword puzzle in the paper.* BOYD *is writing in a notebook at another table. The* PIANIST *lazily runs his fingers over the keys as* HOPKINS, *behind the bar, stifles a yawn.*

HOPKINS: Blue Monday night, no money, and I feel like hell. What you writing, Boyd?

BOYD: Just making some notes for a story I might write—after observing life in Harlem over the weekend.

HOPKINS: You didn't go to Philly Sunday to see that young lady?

BOYD: She's vacationing in Paris, which is O.K. by me, because when we get ready to honeymoon, I won't have to take her to Europe.

HOPKINS: Far as I could take a chick on a honeymoon would be the Theresa Hotel.

BOYD: That's about as far as I *could* take one, unless I sell some of this stuff I've been writing.

(MAMIE *enters, panting*)

HOPKINS: Hey, Mamie! What's the matter?

MAMIE: I'm seeking escape — — — that Melon — —

(MELON *enters with a hangdog air*)

Man, if you would just stop following me! Now that you're so bold as to call at my house every night, at least let me have a little peace when I take a walk, without you at my heels.

MELON: Aw, Miss Mamie, you know I'm drawn to you.

MAMIE: When I get home from work, man, *I am tired.* I just want to set down, and rest, and read my paper. But Tang-a-lang-lang! You ring the bell! It looks like here lately, at home, in the bar, anywhere, every time — — —

WHEN I'M IN A QUIET MOOD, HERE YOU COME.

WHEN I'M DEEP IN SOLITUDE, HERE YOU COME.

WHEN I FEEL LIKE SETTLING DOWN — — —

MELON:

THERE I ARE:

MAMIE:

WHEN I'M GAZING AT THE MOON — —

MELON:

IN FALLS YOUR STAR!

MAMIE:

MY DIAL IS SET, THE TONE IS LOW,

THERE'S NICE SWEET MUSIC ON MY RADIO.

I TAKE A BOOK, THE STORY'S FUN — —

BUT WHEN YOU RING MY BELL I NEVER GET MY READING DONE.

WHEN I'M IN A QUITE MOOD, UP YOU POP.

WHEN I'M PLAYING SOLITAIRE, IN YOU DROP.

MELON:

THE WAY YOU UPSET ME MAKES MY HEARTSTRING HUM — —

MAMIE:

WHEN I'M IN A QUIET MOOD

BOTH:

HERE YOU (I) COME!

MAMIE:

IT'S RAINING OUTSIDE. IT'S NICE IN THE HOUSE.

EVERYTHING IS COOL — —QUIET AS A MOUSE.

THE DOORBELL RINGS. WHO CAN IT BE?

MY SOLITUDE IS ENDED, LORD YOU'RE LOOKING FOR ME!

SLIPPERS ON MY FEET, IN MY BOUDOIR CHAIR,

F-M ON THE DIAL, "THE LONDONDERRY AIR."

THE TELEPHONE RINGS, YOU SAY YOU'RE COMING BY.

WHEN YOU GET TO MY DOOR — —

BOTH:

MY! OH, MY!

(MAMIE *walks away,* MELON *follows*)

MELON:

OH, YOU ACT SO CUTE AND YOU SWITCH SO COY — —

MAMIE, I WAS MEANT TO BE YOUR PLAYBOY.

I DIAL YOUR PHONE, HEAR YOU YELL, "DAMN SAM!"

WHICH MEANS THAT YOU KNOW I'M YOUR HONEY LAMB.

WITH HANKERING HEART, I JUST FOLLOW YOU.

YOUR KISSES ARE AS SWEET AS SWEET MOUNTAIN DEW.

I RING YOUR BELL, IT'S JUST OLD ME. — —

I COME AROUND TO TRY TO KEEP YOU COMPANY.

I'VE SAMPLED LOTS OF MELONS WHOSE FLAVOR'S FINE,

BUT YOU ARE THE SWEETEST MELON ON MY VINE.

I KNOW THAT YOU LOVE ME BY THE LOOK IN YOUR EYE.

WHEN I KNOCK AT YOUR DOOR — —

BOTH:

MY! OH, MY!

MAMIE:

WHEN I'M IN A QUIET MOOD, UP YOU POP.

WHEN I'M PLAYING SOLITAIRE, IN YOU DROP.

MELON:

THE WAY YOU UPSET ME MAKES MY HEARTSTRINGS HUM.

MAMIE:

WHEN I'M IN A QUIET MOOD — —

BOTH:

HERE YOU (I) COME!

MAMIE:

WHEN THE NIGHT IS FREE TO GET MY BEAUTY SLEEP,

I CANNOT SLEEP, SO I'M COUNTING SHEEP.

THE DOORBELL RINGS—I SHOOT THE SHEEP—BAM! BAM!

'CAUSE THERE IN THE DOOR STANDS SOME OLD MOTH-EATEN LAMB.

I COULD SCREAM! IT'S NOT A DREAM—

HERE YOU COME—TO UPSET ME! . . . AND HONEY, I'M LEAVING.

HERE I GO! . . . AND I MEAN IT!

MELON: Well, I guess this time she really means it.

MAMIE: Well, if you're coming, come on!

MELON: I'M GOING TO FOLLOW—HERE I COME!

> *"WHEN I'M IN A QUIET MOOD," Copyright 1951 BOURNE, INC., New York, N. Y. Copyright 1957 BOURNE, INC., New York, N. Y. Reprinted by Permission of BOURNE, INC.*

(MAMIE *and* MELON *exeunt.* SIMPLE *bursts in exuberantly*)

SIMPLE: Hey, now, moo-cow! Gimme a little milk. Barman, untap your keg. Suds us up! Let's drink to it, even if it is my last dollar.

HOPKINS: Your last dollar, didn't you get paid this week?

SIMPLE: I did, but I took that money—all of it—and added it to what was in the Bible and sent it off to Baltimore — — — $133.34. Being last on payments, I had to pay that extra penny to change Divorce Pending to Divorce Ending!

HOPKINS: Congratulations!

SIMPLE: Joyce knows I love her. But to get a woman to make his

bed down, a man has to make his mind up. Joyce is sweet, I
mean! My queen—my desire, my fire, my honey—the only
woman who ever made me save my money!

ARCIE: Simple.

SIMPLE: Yes, ma'am?

ARCIE: What's a four-letter word for damn?

SIMPLE: Arcie, do you see that sign?
(He points to: "No Profanity in Here")
Well, I do not repeat no four-letter words in public.

ARCIE: Damn!
(ZARITA enters briskly switching)

ZARITA: Hi, folks! I thought I'd stop by and have a quick one. Mr.
Semple, how do you do? Set me up, Hop.
(She approaches Simple)
How are you Sugar?

SIMPLE: Zarita, could I have a word with you, private?

ZARITA: Of course! It won't be the first time.

ARCIE: Hummmmm-mm-m! I thought so. That girl is like a magnet
to that man.
(HOPKINS pours Arcie a drink as SIMPLE and ZARITA go aside)

HOPKINS: Stay out of other people's business, Arcie.

ARCIE: OK! OK!

ZARITA: So you're not even going to speak to me again?

SIMPLE: What I do say is, I ain't gonna talk to you. Good-evening—
and Good-bye! Excuse me.

ZARITA: Aw, not like that, Jess, listen . . .
(ZARITA puts an arm around SIMPLE)

ARCIE: Hey there, you writer, Boyd. What is the path in the field
which a plow makes called?

BOYD: Furrow.

ARCIE: Six letters, just right. Now, wait a minute. Tell me, what is
a hole with just one opening?

BOYD: How many letters?

ARCIE: Six. Starts with D.

HOPKINS: Dugout?

ARCIE: Just fits. A dead general. A God-damn dead general?
(SIMPLE pulls away from ZARITA)

ZARITA: But Jess, you know you and me together always has fun.

SIMPLE: Zarita, I'm the same as about to get married. I got respon-
sibilities.

ZARITA: I am a lady, Jess Semple. Don't worry, I'll stay out of your
life. I'm tired of paying you a sometime call when I'm feeling
lonely. Anyhow, I always did bring my own licker. You never
had none.

SIMPLE: But I always treat you when I meet you—when I can. Zarita, you know I'd give you the shirt off my back.

ZARITA: And I'd gladly give you mine. Go on and get your rest, Jess. You never turned in this early before.

SIMPLE: I still got to make a week's work before that lay-off comes.

ZARITA: I guess you'll say goodnight, even if you wouldn't say hello.

SIMPLE: Goodnight.

ZARITA: Goodnight.

SIMPLE: Going my way, Boyd?

BOYD: I might as well, it's getting late. So long, folks!

ARCIE: And I ain't finished this puzzle.

BOYD: Hop'll help you. Goodnight.

(SIMPLE *and* BOYD *exit, as the* PIANIST *ripples the key*)

ARCIE: It ain't but a quarter to twelve. What's happening to Simple?

ZARITA: He's getting domesticated. You know, Arcie, I wish someone would feel about me the way Simple feels about Joyce, and she about him, even if they do have their ups and downs. I guess a little trouble now and then just helps to draw people together. But you got to have somebody to come together with. *(The notes on the piano rise hauntingly)*

Gee, Bill, you play pretty sometimes.

PIANIST: I studied to be a concert pianist, but the concert never came off.

ZARITA: What's that you're playing now? Sounds familiar.

PIANIST: Some new piece a colored boy wrote, I heard on the radio:

> JUST A LITTLE SHADE AND SHADOW
> MIXED IN WITH THE LIGHT
> HELPS TO MAKE THE SUNSHINE BRIGHTER
> WHEN THINGS TURN OUT RIGHT.

(ZARITA *leans on the piano and takes up the song*)

ZARITA:

> JUST A LITTLE PAIN AND TROUBLE
> MIXES IN WITH THE FAIR.
> HELPS TO MAKE YOUR JOYS SEEM DOUBLE
> WHEN CLOUDS ARE NOT THERE.
> LOOK FOR THE MORNING STAR
> SHINNING IN THE DAWN:
> LOOK FOR THE RAINBOW'S ARCH
> WHEN THE RAIN IS GONE!
> DON'T FORGET THEY'RE BLUEBIRDS
> SOMEWHERE IN THE BLUE.
> LOVE WILL SEND A BLUEBIRD
> FLYING STRAIGHT TO YOU.

(The light fades as she sings)

LOOK FOR THE MORNING STAR

SHINE, SHINE, SHINING IN THE DAWN!

RAINBOW, RAINBOW, RAINBOW'S ARCH

WHEN THE RAIN IS GONE.

DON'T FORGET YOU'LL FIND BLUEBIRDS

SOMEWHERE IN THE BLUE.

LOVE WILL SEND A LITTLE BLUEBIRD

FLYING STRAIGHT TO YOU.

"LOOK FOR THE MORNING STAR," Copyright 1957 BOURNE, INC., New York, N. Y. Reprinted by Permission of BOURNE, INC.

(BLACKOUT *as the melody continues into the next scene*)

Scene 2

Joyce's room. Two weeks later. JOYCE *has served* SIMPLE *some sandwiches. They are eating, but* SIMPLE *looks very serious. The music of "Look For the Morning Star" comes softly over Joyce's radio.*

SIMPLE: Shades and shadows, just like that song says. Listen, Joyce, I got to tell you something, much as I don't want to.

JOYCE: About our divorce?

SIMPLE: No. Sugar, that's all filed, paid for. I just didn't tell you— I'm being laid off my job.

JOYCE: Oh, Jess! Not fired!

SIMPLE: No, not fired, just temporary, three or four months till after New Year's while they converts. Converting! And us planning to get married. Every time a Negro plans something—

JOYCE: Aw, come now! We'll get married, Jess.

SIMPLE: I can't even get my laundry out—let alone put my dirty shirts in.

JOYCE: Jess, I'll do your laundry. Bring me a bundle tomorrow and I'll bring them back to you—rub-a-dub-dub—white as snow.

SIMPLE: You're a doll, Joyce, you almost never come to my room.

JOYCE: Well, this'll give me a chance to see the curtains I made for you.

SIMPLE: Come see.

JOYCE: I will—when I bring this laundry, and if you need it, Jess, I can let you have a little money.

SIMPLE: I couldn't take no money from you.

JOYCE: But you can have it.

SIMPLE: I'd be embarrassed.

JOYCE: Have you got enough to eat?

SIMPLE: Oh, sure, I'll make out.

JOYCE: Well, on the weekend, Mr. Semple, you're going to dine with me. Make up your mind to that. And don't say one word about being embarrassed. Everything is going to be all right, I know. I talk to the Lord every night on my knees and I know.

SIMPLE: How long exactly it'll be before that job opens up again, to tell the truth, I don't know. Joyce, what are we going to do? We wants to get married, and all these years I have not saved a thing. Baby, have you figured up how much our wedding is going to cost?

JOYCE: There's no need to worry about that now. You've got enough on your mind tonight, darling. I just want you to know that I'm behind you.

SIMPLE: But, Joyce, baby, look! I ain't got nothing put away. I don't know if our plans are gonna go through or not.

JOYCE: Look, Jess, don't worry. If you ain't got the money to buy no license, well, when we get ready to get married we gonna get that license.

SIMPLE: But, Joyce, honey, I don't want you to be building no castles in the sand.

JOYCE: Jess, I have built my castles in my heart. They're not in no sand. No waves is gonna beat them down. No wind is gonna blow them apart. Nothing can scatter my castles. I tell you, nothing! Their bricks are made out of love and their foundations are strong. And you, Jess Semple, you are the gate-keeper of my castle—which is in my heart. You are the gate-keeper of my castle.

(She sits on the floor at his feet and lays her head in his lap)

You know, Jess, when I was in school, I used to like to read stories about the Middle Ages.

SIMPLE: Middle Ages? Baby, we ain't middle-aged.

JOYCE: I mean about ancient times, Jess—King Arthur and Gwenivere, and all back in there. Listen:

(She sings)

IN DAYS OF OLD WHEN LADIES FAIR

WERE WOOED BY KNIGHTS OF HIGH ESTATE,

EACH CASTLE TALL HAD A WINDING STAIR,

A WALL OUTSIDE, AND A GREAT LOCKED GATE — — —

AND A SQUIRE WHO GUARDED THE GATE. NOW. . . .

YOU'RE THE GATE KEEPER OF MY CASTLE,

THE GATE KEEPER OF MY HEART.

YOUR LOVE WILL ALWAYS GUARD ME,

EVEN THOUGH WE'RE FAR APART.

SIMPLE:

> I'M THE GATE KEEPER OF YOUR CASTLE,
> YOUR GUARDIAN BY DAY AND NIGHT.

JOYCE:

> YOUR LOVE IS LIKE A BEACON — — —
> I'M GUIDED BY ITS LIGHT.
> ONCE I WAS LOST AND LONELY.

SIMPLE:

> ONCE I HAD NO ONE TO CARE.

JOYCE:

> NOW I'M NOT LOST AND LONELY — — —
> FOR YOU MY LOVE, ARE THERE.

SIMPLE:

> I'M THE GATE KEEPER OF YOUR CASTLE.

JOYCE:

> SWEET DREAMER WHERE MY DREAMS START.
> YOU ARE MY LOVE!

SIMPLE:

> I LOVE YOU!

JOYCE:

> I TRUST YOU WITH MY HEART.

(Now they sing both together)

BOTH:

> ONCE I WAS LOST AND LONELY,
> ONCE I HAD NO ONE TO CARE.
> NOW I'M NOT LOST AND LONELY — — —
> FOR YOU, MY LOVE, ARE THERE.
> I'M (YOU'RE) THE GATE KEEPER OF YOUR (MY) CASTLE,
> SWEET DREAMER WHERE OUR DREAMS START.
> YOU ARE MY LOVE! I LOVE YOU!
> I TRUST YOU WITH MY HEART.

"GATEKEEPER OF MY CASTLE," Copyright 1957 BOURNE, INC., New York, N. Y. Reprinted by Permission of BOURNE, INC.

BLACKOUT

Scene 3

SIMPLE's *room. Early evening.* SIMPLE *is lying on his bed, shoes off and shirt tail out, dozng. A doorbell is heard ringing madly. Commotion downstairs and in the hallway.* ZARITA *busts in on a startled* SIMPLE.

ZARITA: It's my birthday, Jess! And I brought my friends around to

celebrate—since you're broke these days and don't come out
no more.

(SIMPLE *leaps up and begins to tuck his shirt in and put on a
shoe. Voices are heard on the stairs*)

BODIDDLY: What floor is it on?

HOPKINS: You're sure he's expecting us?

MAMIE: We rung the bell.

MELON: I been here before.

ARCIE: I'm having trouble with these steps.

(BOYD *is seen outside Simple's door*)

BOYD: Shsss-ss-sss! Be quiet. What the hell s going on? You want to
get us in trouble with the landlady?

(*By now the* CROWD *has pushed* BOYD *into the room as all the
Paddy's Bar set center*)

ZARITA: I tell you, it's my birthday, Jess! Come on in, everybody.

MELON: Happy birthday!

PIANIST: Happy birthday, Zarita!

(GITFIDDLE *begins to play*)

SIMPLE: Zarita, your birthday ain't mine. And I don't want — — —

ZARITA: But I want to share it with you, Daddy! We brought our
own liquor. When it runs out, we'll send and get some more.
Won't we, Melon?

MELON: Liquor's about gone now, Whoopee-ee-ee!

ARCIE: Have some o' my sherry, Simple. I got my own bottle.

ZARITA: Jess, honey, I forgot to tell you I'd be twenty-some odd
years old today. We started celebrating this morning and we're
still going strong.

BODIDDLY: The ball is on!

ZARITA: Let the good times roll!

BODIDDLY: Let the good times roll in "D".

MELON: Whoopee!

(ZARITA *begins to sing*)

ZARITA:

> IF YOU AIN'T GOT NOTHING
> AND THERE'S NOTHING TO GET,
> WHO CARES LONG AS YOU'RE DOING IT?
> IF YOU AIN'T GOT ANYTHING
> BETTER TO DO,
> WHY NOT DO WHAT'S GOOD TO DO?

MELON: What's that?

ZARITA:

> BALL, BALL, LET'S BALL AWHILE!

BALL, BALL, HONEY CHILE!
SING! SHOUT! BEAT IT OUT!

ALL:

DANCE! PRANCE! TAKE A CHANCE!
GRAB THE BLUES AND GET THEM TOLD—
WHEN YOU'RE HAPPY IN YOUR SOUL.
START THE MUSIC PLAYING
LET THE GOOD TIMES ROLL.

ALL:

WHAIL! SAIL! LET IT FLY!

ZARITA:

COOL FOOL: WE'RE RIDING HIGH!

ALL:

BALL, BALL, LET'S BALL AWHILE!

(EVERYBODY *dances wildly with a dazed* SIMPLE *in their midst,
one shoe still off*)

ZARITA:

BALL, BALL, LET'S BALL AWHILE!
BALL, BALL, HONEY CHILE!
SING! SHOUT! BEAT IT OUT!
DANCE! PRANCE! TAKE A CHANCE!
GRAB THE BLUES AND GET THEM TOLD—
WHEN YOU'RE HAPPY IN YOUR SOUL.
START THE MUSIC PLAYING,
LET THE GOOD TIMES ROLL.
WHAIL! SAIL! LET IT FLY!
COOL FOOL: WE'RE RIDING HIGH!
BALL, BALL, LET'S BALL AWHILE!

(ZARITA *forces* SIMPLE *to dance*)

ALL:

BALL, BALL, LET'S BALL AWHILE!
BALL, BALL, HONEY CHILE!
SING! SHOUT! BEAT IT OUT!
DANCE! PRANCE! TAKE A CHANCE!
GRAB THE BLUES AND GET THEM TOLD—
WHEN YOU'RE HAPPY IN YOUR SOUL.

ZARITA:

START THE MUSIC PLAYING
LET THE GOOD TIMES ROLL!

(*The whole room starts rocking*)

ALL:

WHAIL! SAIL! LET IT FLY!

COOL FOOL: WE'RE RIDING HIGH!
BALL! BALL! LET'S BALL AWHILE!

BODIDDLY: Hey, now!

ZARITA: Ow! It's my birthday! We're balling!

HOPKINS: Happy birthday, Zarita!

MELON: Dog-gone it! This bottle is empty.

ARCIE: Mine, too. Diddly, go get some more.

BODIDDLY: Send Melon. Here's fifty cents.

(*He tosses* MELON *a coin*)

ZARITA: Play that agin, Git, "Let's Ball Awhile."

MAMIE:

BALL! BALL! HONEY CHILE!
BALL! BALL! LET'S BALL AWHILE!

ARCIE: Yippeee-ee-ee-e! Diddly, shake yourself!

(ZARITA'S *big red pocketbook is swinging wildly on her arms as
the* CROWD *stops dancing and moves back to let her and* SIMPLE
*cavort madly together in a fast and furious jitterbug, each try-
ing to outdo the other in cutting capers*)

Aw, do it, Zarita!

(ZARITA *spins around and around with her purse in her hand
swirling high above her head. Suddenly the clasp comes open—
the innumerable and varied contents of her enormous pocket-
book fly all over the room, cascading everywhere: compact,
lipstick, handkerchief, pocket mirror, key ring with seven
keys, scattered deck of cards, black lace gloves, bottle opener,
cigarette case, chewing gum, bromo quinine box, small change,
fountain pen, sun glasses, address books, fingernail file, blue
poker chips, matches, flask and a shoe horn*)

ZARITA: Oh, ooo-oo-o! My bag! Stop the music! Stop, Git, stop!

ARCIE: Girl, your perfume done broke!

ZARITAS My *Night in Egypt!*

BODIDDLY: If you broke your mirror, it's seven years bad luck.

PIANIST: Help her pick her things up, man.

BODIDDLY: I'm helping. But what's this?

(*Holding up a red brassiere*)

BOYD: Lord, women sure can have a lot of stuff in their pocketbooks!

MAMIE: She's even got poker chips!

ZARITA: Jess, you help me, baby. The rest of you-all stay where you
are. I don't know some of you folks, and I don't want to lose
nothing valuable.

ARCIE: You ain't got nothing I want, child.

ZARITA: Where's my *China Girl* lipstick in the jade-studded holder? I don't want to lose that lipstick! Jess, you reckon it rolled outside?

SIMPLE: Might could be. Lemme look.

(Just then the doorbell rings nine times)

SIMPLE *(cont'd)*: My ring!

ZARITA: My lipstick! Where's my lipstick? Help me, sugar.

(ZARITA pulls SIMPLE down with her on the floor to search for the lipstick in the doorway as the bell continues to ring)

ARCIE: Somebody let Melon in with that licker.

BODIDDLY: Let that man in.

HOPKINS: The door's still open. He ought to have sense enough to come in.

BODIDDLY: I say to hell with the bell, and help Zarita find her stuff. Whee! Smell that "Night in Egypt"!

(SIMPLE finds the lipstick and ZARITA kisses him)

SIMPLE: Here it is!

ZARITA: Aw, goody!

(GITFIDDLE starts the music again and ALL dance)

Aw, Simple, just because we're dancing, you don't have to keep on kissing me.

SIMPLE: Who's kissing who, Zarita? *You're* kissing me.

BODIDDLY: Come up for air, you two! Come up for air! Aw, play it, Git.

(The music soars. But suddenly the room becomes dead silent as EVERYONE stops still, except SIMPLE and ZARITA who are embracing. JOYCE is standing in the doorway. Drunkenly ARCIE speaks)

ARCIE: Come on in, girl, and join the fun!

PIANIST: Slappy Slirthday!

(JOYCE can hardly believe her eyes)

JOYCE: This *is* Mr. Semple's room, isn't it?

PIANIST: We're having a ball.

(Her back to the door, ZARITA hollers)

ZARITA: Play it again, Git! Come on—"Let's Ball A While!" Where's Melon with the licker? . . . . . Oh!

(Suddenly both she and SIMPLE see JOYCE. SIMPLE is astounded)

SIMPLE: Joyce!

JOYCE: Jess, I brought your laundry I washed for you. I thought you might want to wear one of the shirts Sunday.

ZARITA: Tip on in, Joyce, and enjoin my birthday. We don't mind.

I'm Zarita. Just excuse my stuff all over the place. We been
having a ball, Simp and me and—

JOYCE: I did not know you had company, Jess.

(WATERMELON JOE *arrives with his arms full of bottles and
pushes past* JOYCE)

MELON: Gangway! The stuff is here and it's mellow! Get out of the
door, woman! Make room for Watermelon Joe—and the juice
with the flow.

(JOYCE *hands* SIMPLE *his bundles as* MELON *distributes bottles*)

JOYCE: Excuse me for being in your guests' way. Here, please take
your laundry.

(*The loud voice of* SIMPLE's LANDLADY *is heard calling angrily as
she enters in kimona and curlers*)

LANDLADY: Wait a minute! I'm the landlady here, and what I want
to know is, who is this strange man walking in my house with
his arms full of bottles? And *who* left my front door open? Did
you, Jesse Semple? This is a respectable house. What's going
on here? Do you hear me, Mr. Semple?

(*Meekly* SIMPLE *answers*)

SIMPLE: Yes'm. These is just some guestests, that's all.

LANDLADY: Well, get 'em out of here—raising sand in my house!
Get 'em out I say!

(*She exits in a huff*)

JOYCE: I'm going—as quick as I can.

(JOYCE *starts to pass Simple*)

SIMPLE: Joyce! . . . . . Joyce! You know she don't mean you. I
wants a word with you, Joyce.

(JOYCE *turns on him furiously, fighting back her tears*)

JOYCE: With me? You don't need to explain to me, Jesse Semple.
Now I have seen that Zarita woman with my own eyes in your
bedroom. No wonder you're giving a birthday party to which
I am not invited. I won't be in your way tonight, Jess—nor
ever—any more.

(*She looks back into the room as she leaves*)

Enjoy yourselves. Goodnight!

(JOYCE *rushes down the hall and out of the house*)

SIMPLE: Joyce! . . . . . . Joyce! . . . . . . Joyce!

ZARITA: Huh! Who does that old landlady think she is? You pay
your rent, don't you, Simple? Come on, folks, let's ball awhile.

PIANIST: Happy Slirthday!

(SIMPLE *stands holding his parcel of laundry*)

SIMPLE: I'm sorry, Miss Arcie, Boyd, Diddly! . . . . . *To hell with your
birthday,* Zarita! . . . . Folks, I'm sorry. Will you all go?

(ARCIE *scurries out. The* OTHERS *follow.* MELON *retrieves several of the bottles and takes them with him.* ZARITA *picks up her red bag and swaggers out with* MAMIE *behind her*)

ZARITA: I know where we can ball, folks—at my house! Come on!

MAMIE: I been throwed out of better places than this.

(GITFIDDLE *turns at the door and looks at Simple as if to say he's sorry, but* SIMPLE *does not look up.* BOYD, *the last to go, closes the door.* ALL *exit down the stairs leaving* SIMPLE *in the middle of the floor. He feels his cheek, looks in the mirror, then takes his handkerchief and violently tries to wipe Zarita's lipstick from his jaw. He throws the handkerchief on the dresser and sinks down on the bed, his head in his hands.*)

SIMPLE: Oh, my God!

(GITFIDDLE's *guitar is heard going down the stairs*)

SIMPLE *(cont'd)*: Oh, my God! .... My God! ... Oh, God!

(*The lights dim to a single spot on the forlorn figure. There is the snapping of a broken string on the distant guitar*)

CURTAIN

Scene 4

Paddy's Bar. A quiet Sunday evening. SIMPLE *enters and gloomily begins taking articles from his pockets and putting them on the bar.*

SIMPLE: Hop, is you seen Zarita?

HOPKINS: Nope. Guess she's still recovering from her birthday.

SIMPLE: If you do see her, give her this junk.

HOPKINS: Looks like to me you've snatched her purse.

SIMPLE: I'd snatch her head if I could! That woman has ruint me now—Joyce is out of my life.

HOPKINS: Have a drink, fellow, on me.

SIMPLE: This is one time I do not want a drink, Hop. I feel too bad. I have phoned her seventeen times, and Joyce will not answer the phone. I rung her bell four nights straight. Nobody would let me in. I sent Joyce eight telegrams, which she do not answer.

HOPKINS: And Zarita?

SIMPLE: I don't never want to see Zarita no more. The smell of that "Night in Egypt" is still in my room.

HOPKINS: A man should not fool around with a bad woman when he's got a good woman to love.

SIMPLE: Don't I know that now!

HOPKINS: Have you tried to see Joyce today? Sunday, she might be home.

SIMPLE: Tried? Are you kidding? That's all I've done. These is my bitter days! Hop, what shall I do?

HOPKINS: I don't know, Jess.

SIMPLE: Negroes never know anything important when they need to. I'm going to walk by her house again now. I just want to know if Joyce got home safe from church.

HOPKINS: She's been getting home safe all these years.

SIMPLE: Hop, I'm nearly out of my head. I got to talk to her. I'll stand in front of her house all night if I have to.

(ZARITA *enters, cool, frisky, and pretty as ever*)

HOPKINS: Uh-oh!

ZARITA: Hel-lo! Jess, I'm glad I caught you. I was a little shy about coming around to your place for my things.

SIMPLE: I brought your things here, Zarita.

(HOPKINS *puts them on the bar*)

ZARITA: I thought you might, you're so sweet, sugar. Lemme treat you to a drink, and you, too, Hop.

SIMPLE: No thank you.

ZARITA: Don't be that way. Set us up here, Hopkins.

SIMPLE: I'm not drinking no more myself.

ZARITA: What? Just because you're out of work, you don't have to put down all the pleasures. Say, listen, Jess, if you're broke, I can let you have a little money.

HOPKINS: Zarita!

ZARITA: But no jive, Jess. Because you're wifeless and workless, a nice little old guy like you don't have to go hungry, never. I cook stringbeans and ham almost every day.

SIMPLE: I don't like stringbeans.

ZARITA: I'll fry you some chicken, then.

SIMPLE: Forget it, please.

ZARITA: O.K. If you're that proud.

(ZARITA *opens her purse*)

Anyhow, here honey-boy, take this ten—in case you need it.

SIMPLE: Um-um! No! Thanks, Zarita, no!

(SIMPLE *backs away*)

ZARITA: I meant no harm. I'm just trying to cheer you up. Like that party which I brought around to your house. Knowing you wasn't working, thinking maybe you'd be kinder embarrassed to come to my place for my birthday and not bring a present, I brought the party to you. Meant no harm—just to cheer you up.

SIMPLE: Please don't try to cheer me up no more, Zarita. Hop, I'm cutting out. I'm going by—you know where I told you, one more time.

(SIMPLE *starts out*)

HOPKINS: Don't try to break her door down.

SIMPLE: I'm just gonna stand on the sidewalk and look up at her window.

(*He exits*)

ZARITA: That Simple! Hop, of all the men in my life, he's the toughest to handle.

HOPKINS: I don't get you.

ZARITA: I usually know what to do with men, now:

JUST SUPPOSE I INVITED SAMMY DAVIS UP TO DINE

IT MIGHT BE HARD TO START A MAN LIKE SAMMY TO SWINGING

WITH JUST PLAIN OLE PORK CHOPS AND WINE.

BUT TO HAVE MR. WONDERFUL, WOULD BE SO—SO!

I'D JUST TELL SAMMY, SAMMY OLD BOY, PUT ON YOUR ONE-MAN SHOW:

OH, THE MEN IN MY LIFE,

ONCE THEY START TO PET ME,

EVEN IF THEY HAVE A WIFE,

CAN NEVER FORGET ME.

I TRY TO SUPPLY

WHAT I THINK A POOR GUY NEEDS.

TO SAMMY I'D COO,

I KNOW YOU DO A LOT OF IMITATIONS.

I'M EVE—

CAN YOU DO ONE OF ADAM WITH NO LIMITATIONS?

OH, THE MEN IN MY LIFE!

THE MEN IN MY LIFE!

OH! OH! OH! OH!

THE MEN IN MY LIFE!

(HOPKINS *sits at a table and* ZARITA *sits on his knee*)

NOW WHAT IF I INVITED ADAM POWELL UP SOME DAY

IT MIGHT BE HARD TO GET A MAN LIKE ADAM DELIGHTED

SINCE IN MY PANTRY I'VE NO POLITICAL HAY.

SO I'D SKIP OVER THE BUDGET AND CONGRESSIONAL CHORES—

AND SIMPLY SIGH, ADAM, I'M YOURS.

OH, THE MEN IN MY LIFE,

ONCE THEY STARTED TO PET ME,

EVEN IF THEY HAVE A WIFE,

CAN NEVER FORGET ME.

I TRY TO SUPPLY

WHAT I THINK A POOR GUY NEEDS.

TO A MAN LIKE ADAM,
WHO IS JUST MY TYPE,
I'D SAY, I LOVE A DEMOCRAT
WITH A REPUBLICAN STRIPE.
OH, THE MEN IN MY LIFE!
THE MEN IN MY LIFE!
OH! OH! OH! OH!
THE MEN IN MY LIFE!
     (ZARITA *approaches the Pianist*)
JUST SUPPOSE I INVITED JACKIE ROBINSON UP FOR A CHAT,
IT WOULD BE HARD TO GET A MAN LIKE JACKIE GOING
NOW THAT HE'S NO LONGER AN ACTIVE PLAYER.
BUT IF HIS BASES GOT LOADED, HERE'S WHAT I'D SAY—
JACKIE, OLD BOY, LET'S MAKE A SQUEEZE PLAY!
OH, THE MEN IN MY LIFE,
ONCE THEY START TO PET ME—
EVEN IF THEY HAVE A WIFE—
CAN NEVER FORGET ME.
I TRY TO SUPPLY
WHAT I THINK THE POOR GUY NEEDS.
SO WITH A MAN LIKE JACKIE
THERE BE NO IFS, ANDS, AND BUTS.
I'D TELL HIM RIGHT OFF,
I JUST LOVE CHOCK FULL O' NUTS.
OH, THE MEN IN MY LIFE!
THE MEN IN MY LIFE!
OH! OH! OH! OH! OOOOH!
THE MEN IN MY LIFE!

"THE MEN IN MY LIFE," Copyright 1957 BOURNE, INC., New York, N. Y. Reprinted by Permission of BOURNE, INC.

BLACKOUT

Scene 5

Simple's room. Late evening. SIMPLE *is lighting a cone of incense in a saucer on his dresser as* BOYD *pokes his head in the door, sniffs, and enters.*

BOYD: Hy, fellow! What's that burning on the dresser?
SIMPLE: Incense. I lit it to keep warm. I really hates winter.
BOYD: Oh, man, cold weather makes you get up and go, gives you
         vim, vigor, vitality!

SIMPLE: It does not give me anything but a cold and all that snow outside!

BOYD: Perhaps you are just not the right color for winter, being dark. In nature you know, animals have protective coloration to go with their environment. Desert toads are sand-colored. Tree lizards are green. Ermine, for example, is the color of the snow country in which it originates.

SIMPLE: Which accounts for me not having no business wading around in snow, then. It and my color do not match. But, please, let's stop talking about snow, Boyd.

BOYD: Agreed— as cold as it is in this icebox!

SIMPLE: Landladies has no respect for roomers a-tall, Boyd. In fact, ours cares less for her roomers than she does for her dog. She will put a roomer out—dead out in the street—when he does not pay his rent, but she does not put out that dog. Trixie is her heart! She keeps Trixie warm. But me, I has nothing to keep warm by, but incense. I'm sick of this kind of living, Boyd. Maybe if I just had a little something, a place to live, some money, I could win Joyce back. If I don't get her back, Boyd, I don't know! I just don't know!

BOYD: I can lend you a small amount, Jess, if you need it—you know, five or ten.

SIMPLE: But I borrows only when I *hope* I can pay back, Boyd.

(A creaking sound is heard on the steps. The LANDLADY'S VOICE *is heard outside)*

LANDLADY: I do believes somebody's smoking marijuana in my house.

SIMPLE: Listen! Don't I hear a elephant walking?

(She knocks loudly on Simple's door)

Come in!

LANDLADY: Mr. Semple, I am forced to inform you that I allows no reefer smoking in my home.

SIMPLE: I allows none in my room, neither.

LANDLADY: Then what do I smell?

SIMPLE: Chinese incense from Japan.

LANDLADY: Is you running a fast house?

SIMPLE: Madam, you have give me a idea!

LANDLADY: I am not joking, Jess Semple. Tell me, how come you burning that stuff in my house? Is it for bad luck or good?

SIMPLE: I don't believe in no lucky scents. I am just burning this for fun. It also gives out heat. Here, I will give you a stick to perfume up your part of the house.

LANDLADY: Thank you, I'll take it, even if it do smell like a good-time house to me. And that nude naked calendar you got hang-

ing on your wall ain't exactly what I'd call decent. Don't your
licker store give out no respectable girls on their calendars?

SIMPLE: They do, but they got clothes on.

LANDLADY: Naturally! Never would I pose in a meadow without
my clothes on.

SIMPLE: I hope not, Madam.

LANDLADY: Meaning by that . . . . ?

SIMPLE: Meaning you have such a beautiful character you do not
have to show your figure. There is sweetness in your face.

LANDLADY: I appreciates that, Mr. Semple.

(She shivers)

Wheel! It *is right chilly* up here.

SIMPLE: It's a deep freeze.

LANDLADY: If you roomers would go to bed on time—and your
guests would go home—including Mr. Boyd—I would not have
to keep heat up until all hours of the night.

SIMPLE: Has the heat been up tonight?

LANDLADY: You know it were warm as toast in this house at seven
P.M. Funny where *your* heat disappears to. Downstairs I fails
to notice any change myself.

SIMPLE: Madam, science states that heat is tied in with fat.

LANDLADY: Meaning. . . . ?

SIMPLE: You're protected.

LANDLADY: I don't study ways of insulting roomers, Jess Semple and
that is the second sly remark you made about me tonight. I'll
thank you to regret it.

SIMPLE: Madam, I does regret it!

LANDLADY: To my face—fat! Huh! You heard him, Mr. Boyd.

(She exits muttering)

Elephant, huh? Behind in your rent, huh!

BOYD: Now our landlady's angry.

SIMPLE: I tell you, something's always happening to a colored man!
Stormy weather! Boyd, I been caught in some kind of riffle
ever since I been black. All my life, if it ain't raining, it's blow-
ing. If it ain't sleeting, it's snowing. Man, you try to be good,
and what happens? You just don't be good. You try to live right.
What happens? You look back and find out you didn't live
right. Even when you're working, and you try to save money,
what happens? Can't do it. Your shoes is wore out. Or the
dentist has got you. You try to save again. What happens? You
drunk it up. Try to save another time. Some relative gets sick
and needs it. What happens to money, Boyd? What happens?

BOYD: Come on, man, snap out of it! Let's go down to Paddy's and

have a drink. At least we can sit up in the bar and get warm—
and not think about what happens.

SIMPLE: You go, Boyd. What happens has done already happened
to me.

(*Slowly* BOYD *leaves. Half through the door suddenly a bright
thought comes to him. He smiles and snaps his fingers, then
exits closing the door, leaving* SIMPLE *alone as the LIGHT
FADES SLOWLY TO DARKNESS*)

BLACKOUT

Scene 6

Sidewalk on Lenox Avenue. Early evening. BOYD *walks briskly down
the street as if on a mission. Exits. Following him,* JOHN JASPER *comes
dancing along the sidewalk selling papers and stopping to hit a step
now and then.*

JOHN JASPER: Paper! . . . Amsterdam News! . . . Read all about it!
Get your paper!

(*He dances off.* BODIDDLY *enters followed by* ARCIE *hobbling
along behind him.* BODIDDLY *turns, stops*)

BODIDDLY: Woman, you better stop tagging *behind* me on the street,
and walk *beside* me, like a wife should—before I lose my im-
patience.

ARCIE: Diddly, those new shoes hurt my feet.

BODIDDLY: I paid $20 for them for you! Arcie, ain't you read in the
Bible where Moses walked for forty years in the wilderness
barefooted? Now, here you can't walk a block without com-
plaining!

ARCIE: But Diddly, lover, I ain't Moses.

BODIDDLY: Aw, come on, woman!

(*Exeunt. Enter* MAMIE, *trailed by* MELON)

MAMIE: Melon, you got more nerve than Liberace's got sequins.
You ain't gonna get nowhere, so there's no need of you trailing
me through the streets like this.

MELON: I can't help it, Miss Mamie. I'm marked by a liking for you!

You're my sugar,
You're my spice,
You're my everything
That's nice.

MAMIE: Melon, I done told you—

You *ain't* my sugar
You *ain't* my spice.
If you was a piece of cheese
I'd throw you to the mice.

(*She moves on with* MELON *in pursuit*)

MELON: Miss Mamie—

Your words are bitter
But your lips are sweet.
Lemme kiss you, baby—
And give you a treat.

MAMIE: Melon—

When cows start playing numbers
And canary birds sing bass,
That is when you'll stick your
Big mouth in my face.

(MAMIE *exits indignantly with* MELON *pleading as he follows*)

MELON: Aw, Miss Mamie, listen!

Wait a minute now!
I ain't no canary bird,
And you sure ain't no cow.
But . . . .

(*Exit* MELON)

BLACKOUT

Scene 7

Joyce's room. Same evening. BOYD *stands at the door as* JOYCE *opens it.*

BOYD: I hope you'll pardon me, Miss Lane,—and maybe it's none of my business at all—but I was just walking down Lenox Avenue when the idea came to me and I felt like I ought to come and talk to you.

(*He stands awkwardly*)

JOYCE: You may sit, Mr. Boyd.

(*She takes his hat*)

BOYD: Thank you. I—I—

JOYCE: Yes?

BOYD: Well, it's about Simple. You know, I mean Jess Semple. He didn't ask me to come to see you. In fact he doesn't know I'm here at all. But he's been rooming right next to me quite a while now, and I—well—Well, I never saw him like he is before.

(JOYCE *begins to freeze*)

JOYCE: You know him well?

BOYD: Very well.

JOYCE: Are you one of his drinking buddies of the Paddy's Bar set?

BOYD: I'm not much of a drinking man, Miss Lane. I'm a writer.

JOYCE: A writer! What do you write?

BOYD: Books.

JOYCE: Books!

BOYD: About Harlem.

JOYCE: Harlem! I wish I could get away from Harlem.

BOYD: Miss Lane, I'm worried about Simple.

JOYCE: You're worried about Simple. He never seems to worry about himself.

BOYD: I think maybe you really don't know about that birthday party.

JOYCE: There's really nothing I want to learn.

BOYD: Except that it wasn't Simple's party. He didn't plan it, and didn't know anything about it until it descended on him.

JOYCE: Just like that—from above.

BOYD: They came to surprise us.

JOYCE: You too? You don't look like the type of man to attract that conglamoration of assorted humans. If you're going to tell me something, Mr. Boyd, tell me the truth.

BOYD: Well, everybody just likes Simple. That's his trouble. He likes people, so they like him. But he's not going with all those women. He wasn't even going with Zarita.

(JOYCE *does not believe him*)

JOYCE: You can have your hat, Mr. Boyd, if you will.

(*As he takes his hat he continues talking*)

BOYD: I mean, not lately, not for two or three years, since he's met you—why, he doesn't talk about anybody but you, hasn't for a long time—Joyce, Joyce, Joyce! Now, he's even talking to himself in the night, trying to explain to you. I room next door, and sometimes I can hear him crying late in the night. Nobody likes to hear a grown man crying, Miss Lane.

(*Sternly she dismisses him*)

JOYCE: Thank you very much, Mr. Boyd.

BOYD: Miss Lane!

(*She closes the door as he backs out.* JOYCE *comes toward the center of the room, stops, thinks, then rushes to the closet and begins to put on her coat)*

BLACKOUT

Scene 8

Simple's room. Same evening. SIMPLE *is alone, standing beside his dresser turning the pages of the Bible.*

SIMPLE: My old Aunt Lucy always said, "The Bible is the Rock, and the Rock is the Truth, and the Truth is the Light." Lemme see.
   (He reads from Job)
   It says here, "Let thy day be darkness. Let no God regard it from above, neither let the light shine upon it . . . Man is born unto trouble." Lemme turn over!
   (He tries the next page)
   Uh-huh! This is just as bad. "They meets with darkness in the daytime and grope in the noonday like as in the night." Great Gordon Gin! What part of the Bible am I reading out of? *Job!* No wonder! He's the one what suffered everything from boils to blindness. But it says here the Lord answered Job. Looks like don't nobody answer me. Nobody!
   (He shuts the Bible and goes to the window. JOYCE *comes up the stairs and down the hall. Outside his door she calls)*
JOYCE: Jess!
   (His body stiffens)
SIMPLE: Am I hearing things?
JOYCE: Jess!
SIMPLE: I must be going crazy! Can't be that voice.
   (She knocks softly and enters)
JOYCE: Jess!
SIMPLE: Why are you here?
JOYCE: To see you, Jess. There's something maybe I ought to tell you.
SIMPLE: There's nothing for you to tell me, Joyce.
JOYCE: But, Jess—
   (After a long silence he speaks)
SIMPLE: You've come to *me*, Joyce.
JOYCE: Yes, Jess.

SIMPLE: Every time something's happened between us, in the end you come to me. It's my turn to come to you now.

JOYCE: You tried. I wouldn't let you in. I got those messages. I heard you ringing my bell. It's my fault, Jess.

SIMPLE: It's not your fault, Joyce. I had no business trying to see you *then*. But I wasn't man enough not to try.

JOYCE: Jess, you were at my door and I wouldn't let you in.

SIMPLE: All my life I been looking for a door that will be just mine—and the one I love. Joyce, I been looking for *your* door. But sometimes you let the wrong *me* in, not the me I want to be. This time, when I come through your door again, it's gonna be the *me* I ought to be.

JOYCE: I know, Jess—we've had problems to solve. But—

SIMPLE: The problem to solve is me, Joyce—and can't no one solve that problem but me. Until I get out of this mud and muck and mire I been dancing in half my life, don't you open your door to the *wrong* me no more. *Don't open your door.* And don't say nothing good to me, Joyce. Don't tell me nothing a-tall.

(He has already risen. Now she rises, embracing him, but he pushes her away)

Joyce, baby, darling, no . . . .

(He wants to call her all the sweet names he knows, to take her in his arms, to keep her then and there and always. But instead he speaks almost harshly)

No! don't say nothing—to me—Joyce.

(He opens the door. As JOYCE *turns to go, she looks at Jess, lifts her head, and smiles the most beautiful smile a man has ever seen—a smile serene and calm and full of faith. The lights dim to a spot on her face as she turns and leaves without a word. Suddenly there is a great burst of music, wild, triumphant, wonderful and happy)*

BLACKOUT

Scene 9

Paddy's Bar on a winter night. BODIDDLY, BOYD, GITFIDDLE, *and the* PIANIST *are scattered about.* MELON *leans over Miss Mamie's table and emits a playful howl.*

MELON: Ow-ooo-oo-o! Miss Mamie, you're a killer, that you is! Sweet my lands! You-oo-O!

MAMIE: Melon: I don't want no wolf-howling compliments. I just
come here to set in peace. I don't want to be bothered with you
drunken Negroes.

MELON: Who is drunk?

MAMIE: You!

BODIDDLY: She's right, you is.

MELON: Listen here! Diddly and Mamie, both of you-all belong to
my church—the Upstairs Baptist—yet you go around talking
about me like a dirty dog.

MAMIE: Well, you do drink—guzzle, guzzle, guzzle!

MELON: I don't get drunk!

MAMIE: I say you do!

MELON: Woman, listen! Miss Mamie, I respects you too much to
dispute your word. If you say I do, I does.

MAMIE: Now that that's settled, come and have a drink on me. A
little eye-opener in the morning, a bracer at noon, and a
night-cap at night, never hurt nobody.

MELON: Mamie, you got money?

MAMIE: I always get me some money, been had money, and always
will have money. And one reason I do is, I'm a lone wolf, I
runs with no pack.

MELON: I would pack you on my back if you would let me.

MAMIE: I don't intend to let you. To tell the truth, I doubt your
intentions. And, Melon, I wants you to know:

(*She sings:*)

> I BEEN MAKING MY WAY FOR A LONG, LONG TIME,
> I BEEN MAKING MY WAY THROUGH THIS WORLD.
> I KEEP ON TRYING TO BE GOOD
> 'CAUSE I'M A GOOD GIRL.
> I BEEN MAKING MY WAY WITH A BOOT AND A SHOE.
> IN NO OYSTERS HAVE I FOUND A PEARL.
> I TRUST MYSELF—SO I'VE GOT LUCK OO
> 'CAUSE I'M A GOOD OLD GIRL.
> SOMETIMES THE DEVIL BECKONS
> I LOOK AT THE DEVIL AND SAY,
> stop that!
> DEVIL, DEVIL, DEVIL—
> DEVIL BE ON YOUR WAY!
> I BEEN MAKING MY WAY THROUGH THICK AND THIN
> 'SPITE O' DEVILISH MEN IN THIS WORLD.
> THERE AIN'T NO MAN CAN GET ME DOWN
> Not even Harry Belafonte,
> 'CAUSE I'M A GOOD OLD GIRL.

(MAMIE *rises and addresses the entire bar*)

I MAKE FIVE OR TEN DOLLARS, SOMETIMES MORE A DAY.
YOU MEN WHAT AIN'T WORKING KNOW THAT THAT AIN'T HAY.
DON'T LET NO STRANGE MAN GET HIS HANDS ON YOU—
THERE'S NO TELLING, BABY, WHAT A STRANGE CAT WILL DO.
IT TAKES ALL KINDS OF FOLKS TO SPIN THIS GLOBE AROUND,
BUT ONE BAD ACTOR TEARS YOUR PLAYHOUSE DOWN.
DON'T EVER LET NO BAD ACTOR COME AROUND—
THERE'S NO TELLING, BABY, WHAT THAT CAT'S TRYING
    TO LAY DOWN!
SOMETIMES THE DEVIL BECKONS.
I LOOK AT THE DEVIL AND SAY,
Ain't you got enough trouble?
DEVIL, DEVIL, DEVIL—
DEVIL, BE ON YOUR WAY!
I BEEN MAKING MY WAY THROUGH THICK AND THIN
'SPITE O' DEVILISH MEN IN THIS WORLD.
THERE'S NO MAN CAN GET ME DOWN
'CAUSE I'M A GOOD OLD GIRL.
MY NAME IS MAMIE—
I'M A GOOD OLD GIRL!
Like Mamie Eisenhower,
I'M A GOOD OLD GAL!

(*To shouts of approval from the* BAR CROWD, *she continues*)

I BEEN MAKING MY WAY FOR A LONG, LONG TIME!
Now listen, Punchy: I've been making my way:
I've been making my very own way for a long, long time.
I don't need you, Melon.
I've been making my way through this world.
Who needs that face?
I keep on trying to be good.
You think I'm a doll?
I'm a good old girl—
Might be a human doll! Anyhow—
I BEEN MAKING MY WAY THROUGH THICK AND THIN
'SPITE O' DEVILISH MEN IN THIS WORLD,
You always been this ugly, Melon?
THERE AIN'T NO MAN CAN GET ME DOWN—
'CAUSE I'M A GOOD OLD GIRL!
I KEEP REPEATING—I'M A GOOD OLD GIRL!

Now, what's the sense of going on with this?

BODIDDLY: Melon, I guess you realize there's nothing more independent than an independent woman. You'd better stop worrying Miss Mamie or she'll floor you and stomp on your carcass.

MELON: Diddly, if you don't have some respect for my personal conversation, I'm going to bust a watermelon over your head.

BODIDDLY: Take it easy, man. See you later. Hi, Simp!

(SIMPLE *enters shivering, passing* BODIDDLY *as he exits*)

SIMPLE: Hi, Bo! Hop! Man, this bar is the warmest place I know in winter. At least you keep steam up here.

HOPKINS: Cold as it is, do you mean to tell me you haven't got any steam in your room?

SIMPLE: I done beated on my radiator pipe six times today to let my old landlady know I was home—freezing.

HOPKINS: And what happened?

SIMPLE: Nothing—she just beat back on the pipes at me. Which is why I come down here, to get warm, just like Boyd.

HOPKINS: Want a drink?

SIMPLE: I sure could use one.

HOPKINS: Coming up.

SIMPLE: Hey, Boyd! I got something to tell you. I'm working part-time, back down at the plant as a helper—helping reconvert.

BOYD: That's wonderful!

SIMPLE: With a good job and a good wife, man, it'll be like Joyce used to say when I kissed her—"Simply Heavenly." And when we get married, Boyd, you're gonna be standing there beside me at my wedding. You're gonna hand me the ring. Ain't that what the best man does?

MAMIE: Yeah, that's right. Melon, ain't you got no home?

BOYD: Hey, this is the first time you've sprung this on me, about being your best man. After all we've only known each other for a few years. A best man is usually somebody you grew up with, or something.

SIMPLE: I didn't grow up with nobody, Boyd. So I don't know anybody very well. So, will you please be my best man?

BOYD: Best man, eh? Then I'll have to start buying me a brand new suit. And a best man is due to give a bachelor's party for the groom a night or two before the ceremony. Your wedding's going to cost me a lot of dough, Jess.

SIMPLE: Just a keg of beer. I mean a private one—with my name on it.

BOYD: You got it lad. I live to see the day!

SIMPLE: Where you going, Boyd?

BOYD: Listen, Jess: Hot or cold, I've got to bust that book-writing rock and I've got to get home to my typewriter. Good-night, all.

SIMPLE: Well, that's settled. Thank God, I don't have to worry about Zarita. I ain't seen her for months.

HOPKINS: Zarita's getting ready to fly to Arizona for Christmas. That Big Boy, Ali Baba, sent her a ticket. She's all set to go. I think they're going to get married.

SIMPLE: I wishes her all the luck in the world. But I sure wish I could understand a woman.

HOPKINS: Socrates tried, he couldn't. What makes you hold such hopes?

SIMPLE: Long as I live, Hop, I lives in hopes.

(*Loud weeping is heard outside*)

Damn, there's some woman hollering now.

HOPKINS: I wonder what's wrong.

(ARCIE *enters crying and sinks at a table*)

What's wrong, Arcie?

ARCIE: Gimme a sherry, Hopkins, quick! Gimme a sherry.

HOPKINS: What's the matter, Arcie?

ARCIE: Abe Lincoln is going to the army.

SIMPLE: The army?

ARCIE: My oldest son, Abraham Lincoln Jones.

SIMPLE: Well, why didn't you say so?

ARCIE: I'm trying to! Abe got his draft call.

SIMPLE: Don't cry, Arcie. The army'll do the boy no harm. He'll get to travel, see the world.

ARCIE: The first one of my children to leave home!

SIMPLE: As many as you got, you shouldn't mind *one* going somewhere.

ARCIE: I does mind. Abe is my oldest, and I does mind. Fill it up again, Hop.

SIMPLE: That boy Abe is smart, Arcie. You'll be proud of him. He's liable to get to be an officer.

HOPKINS: At least a sergeant—and come back here with stripes on his sleeve.

SIMPLE: Else medals on his chest. Now, me, if I was to go in the army today—now that we's integrated—I would come back a general.

HOPKINS: Quit your kidding.

SIMPLE: I would rise right to the top today and be a general—and be in charge of white troops.

MELON: Colored generals never command white troops.

SIMPLE: The next war will be integrated. In fact, I'd like to command a regiment from Mississippi.

HOPKINS: Are you drunk?

SIMPLE: No, sir.

MELON: Then why on earth would you want to be in charge of a white regiment from Mississippi?

SIMPLE: In the last war, they had white officers in charge of Negroes. So why shouldn't I be in charge of whites? Huh? General Simple! I would really make 'em toe the line. I know some of them Dixiecrats would rather die than left face for a colored man, but they would left face for me.

MELON: Man, you got a great imagination.

SIMPLE: I can see myself now, in World War III, leading white Mississippi troops into action. Hop, I would do like all the other generals do, and stand way back on a hill somewhere and look through my spy-glasses and say, "Charge on! Mens, charge on!" Then I would watch them Dixiecrats boys go—like true sons of the Old South, mowing down the enemy. When my young white lieutenants from Vicksburg jeeped back to headquarters to deliver their reports in person to me, they would say, "Captain General, sir, we have taken two more enemy positions." I would say, "Mens, return to your companies—and tell 'em to keep on charging on!" Next day, when I caught up to 'em, I would pin medals on their chest for bravery. Then I would have my picture taken in front of all my fine white troops—me—the first *black* American general to pin medals on white soldiers from Mississippi. Then, Hop, —man, oh, man— then when the war be's over, I would line my companies up for the last time and I would say, "Men, at ease. Gentlemen of the Old South, relax. Put down your fighting arms and lend me your ears—because I am one of you, too, borned and bred in Dixie.

(GITFIDDLE *begins to play a syncopated march—a blend of* "Dixie," "Sewanee River," *and* "Yankee Doodle")

And I'm willing to let bygones be bygones, and forget how you failed to obey my orders in the old days and right faced-ted when I said, "Left," because you thought I was colored. Well, I is colored. I'll forget that. You are me—and I am you—and we are one. And now that our fighting is done, let's be Americans for once, for fun. Colonels, captains, majors, lieutenants, sergeants, and Hopkins open up a keg of nails for the men— let's all drink to you, brave sons of the South! Drink, mens, drink! And when we all stagger back to peace together, let

there be peace—between you, Mississippi, and me! Company
—'tention! Right shoulder arms! . . . Forward, march! . . .
come on, boys, I'm leading you! Come on! By the left flank
march!

(SIMPLE *proudly inspects his troops as they pass in review.*
OTHERS *in the bar, except* MISS MAMIE, *applaud and cheer*)

HOPKINS: March, fellows, march!

SIMPLE: By the right flank, march!

HOPKINS: March, fellows, march!

ARCIE: Ain't that fine!

HOPKINS: March, march, march!

SIMPLE: Forward! March!

HOPKINS: March! March! March!

*"YANKEE DIXIE MARCH," Copyright 1957 BOURNE, INC., New York, N. Y.
Reprinted by Permission of BOURNE, INC.*

(SIMPLE *exits. There is a long pause. Finally* MISS MAMIE *turns
to Hopkins. As if an entire army is following him,* SIMPLE *leads
his soldiers out of the bar*)

MAMIE: You know something—that boy is sick!

BLACKOUT

Scene 10

*A phone booth. Christmas Eve. Chimes are softly tolling "Jingle
Bells" as* SIMPLE *speaks excitedly into the phone.*

SIMPLE: Joyce? . . . Joyce? Is this Joyce? . . . Yes, it's Jesse B. . . .
It's Simple, honey! . . . What? You say I sound like a new
man? I *am* a new man! And I got something for you, Joyce.
It's Christmas Eve and, you know, well—like it says in the
Bible, "Wise men came bringing gifts." . . . tree . . . Sure, I
got a few little gifts for you on my Christmas tree . . . Sure, I
got a tree! What's on it for you? . . . I don't want to tell you,
Joyce. I want to show you. You say you're coming right over?
. . . . . Oh, baby!

(*With the receiver still in his hand, he rises excitedly and
starts out, but is jerked back by the cord. Quickly he hangs
up and leaves as the music of "Jingle Bells" fills the air*)

BLACKOUT

Scene 11

Simple's room. Christmas Eve. A star shines in the darkness. The lights come up revealing SIMPLE *and* JOYCE *standing before a tiny Christmas tree. The star glows atop this tree hung with tinsel and little balls of colored glass. On the tree there are four gifts tied with ribbonss one is a letter, one a roll of paper, one a long parchment, and one is a tiny box.* JOYCE *rushes in.*

JOYCE: Jess!

SIMPLE: Look.

> (*He shows her the tree*)

JOYCE: Oh! It's beautiful.

SIMPLE: May I take your coat? Won't you sit down?

> (*He hands her the parchment*)

JOYCE: Jess, what is it? A picture of some kind? Maybe a map? Why it's all in Roman letters. It's a divorce!

SIMPLE: With a gold seal on it, too.

JOYCE: Free! Jess, you're free! Like in Uncle Tom's Cabin!

SIMPLE: Yes, baby, I'm free. That's the paper.

JOYCE: It's dated a whole month ago. Jess, why didn't you tell me you had your divorce?

SIMPLE: I was waiting for something else to go with it. Here, this is for you, too.

> (*He hands her an envelope*)

JOYCE: My father's writing!

SIMPLE: Read it. You see, your ole—your father—gimme your hand.

> (*While she reads the letter,* SIMPLE *opens the little box on the tree and polishes a ring on his coat lapel*)
>
> Now, can I take your hand?
>
> (*He slips the ring on her finger*)
>
> For you—if you'll wear it?

JOYCE: Forever!

> (*She starts to rise, but gently he pushes her down and returns to the tree*)

SIMPLE: This is something only married people can have. And it's not ready, yet, either. They just about now digging the first hole in the ground—busting that first rock. We both got to sign our names—if you're willing.

JOYCE: An apartment! Oh, Jess! A place to live! An apartment!

SIMPLE: Can we both sign our names, Joyce?

JOYCE: Yes, Jess!

> (JOYCE *rises, scattering papers, and flings her arms about him*)

SIMPLE: Now we can get ready for that wedding in June.
JOYCE: Oh, Jess! Jess, baby! Jess!
    (*Singing, they embrace*)
SIMPLE:

        JUST FOR YOU THESE CHRISTMAS TOKENS
        ON OUR CHRISTMAS TREE—

JOYCE:

        HELP TO MAKE ME KNOW THAT YOU ARE
        SANTA CLAUS TO ME.

SIMPLE:

        JUST A LITTLE PAIN AND TROUBLE
        MIXED IN WITH THE PAST

BOTH:

        HELP TO MAKE OUR JOYS DOUBLE
        WHEN WE'RE SURE THEY'LL LAST.

JOYCE:

        WONDERFUL THE MORNING STAR
        SHINING IN THE DAWN!

BOTH:

        WONDERFUL THE RAINBOW'S ARCH
        WHEN THE RAIN IS GONE.

    (*The bar is revealed as the entire* COMPANY *enters singing and form tableaux, some around the piano,* MAMIE *at her table with* MELON, BODIDDLY, ARCIE, *and* JOHN JASPER *making a family group at another table. The entire chorus of "Look for the Morning Star" is repeated as* ALL *come forward for bows*)
ALL:

        DON'T FORGET THERE'RE BLUEBIRDS
        SOMEWHERE IN THE BLUE.
        LOVE WILL SEND A LITTLE BLUEBIRD
        FLYING STRAIGHT TO YOU.

CURTAIN

AUTOBIOGRAPHY

The Big Sea

BEYOND SANDY HOOK

Melodramatic maybe, it seems to me now. But then it was like throwing a million bricks out of my heart when I threw the books into the water. I leaned over the rail of the S.S. *Malone* and threw the books as far as I could out into the sea—all the books I had had at Columbia, and all the books I had lately bought to read.

The books went down into the moving water in the dark off Sandy Hook. Then I straightened up, turned my face to the wind, and took a deep breath. I was a seaman going to sea for the first time—a seaman on a big merchant ship. And I felt that nothing would ever happen to me again that I didn't want to happen. I felt grown, a man, inside and out. Twenty-one.

I was twenty-one.

Four bells sounded. As I stood there, whiffs of salt spray blew in my face. The afterdeck was deserted. The big hatches were covered with canvas. The booms were all tied up to the masts, and the winches silent. It was dark. The old freighter, smelling of crude oil and garbage, engines pounding, rolled through the pitch-black night. I looked down on deck and noticed that one of my books had fallen into the scupper. The last book. I picked it up and threw it far over the rail into the water below, that was too black to see. The wind caught the book and ruffled its pages quickly, then let it fall into the rolling darkness. I think it was a book by H. L. Mencken.

You see, books had been happening to me. Now the books were cast off back there somewhere in the churn of spray and night behind the propeller. I was glad they were gone.

I went up on the poop and looked over the railing toward New York. But New York was gone, too. There were no longer any lights to be seen. The wind smelt good. I was sleepy, so I went down a pair of narrow steps that ended just in front of our cabin— the mess boys' cabin.

Inside the hot Cabin, George lay stark naked in a lower bunk,

317

talking and laughing and gaily waving his various appendages around. Above him in the upper bunk, two chocolate-colored Puerto Rican feet stuck out from one end of a snow-white sheet, and a dark Puerto Rican head from the other. It was clear that Ramon in the upper bunk didn't understand more than every tenth word of George's Kentucky vernacular, but he kept on laughing every time George laughed—and that was often.

George was talking about women, of course. He said he didn't care if his Harlem landlady pawned all his clothes, the old witch! When he got back from Africa, he would get some more. He might even pay her the month's back rent he owed her, too. Maybe. Or else here he waved one of his appendages around—she could have what he had in his hand.

Puerto Rico, who understood all the bad words in every language, laughed loudly. We all laughed. You couldn't help it. George was so good-natured and comical you couldn't keep from laughing with him—or at him. He always made everybody laugh—even when the food ran out on the return trip and everybody was hungry and mad.

Then it was ten o'clock, on a June night, on the S.S. *Malone,* and we were going to Africa. At ten o'clock that morning I had never heard of the S.S. *Malone,* or George, or Ramon, or anybody else in its crew of forty-two men. Nor any of the six passengers. But now, here were the three of us laughing very loudly, going to Africa.

I had got my job at a New York shipping office. Ramon got his job at another shipping office. But George just simply walked on board about supper time. A Filipino pantry boy got mad and quit at the last moment. Naturally, the steward didn't want to sail short-handed. He saw George hanging around the entrance to the pier, watching the stevedores finish loading. The Filipino steward said: "Hey, colored boy! You, there! You want a job?" And George said: "Yes," so he walked on board, with nothing but a shirt and a pair of overalls to his back, and sailed.

Now, he lay there in his bunk, laughing about his landlady. He said she intended to put him out if he didn't find a job. And now that he had found a job, he wouldn't be able to tell her for six months. He wondered if she knew Africa was six months away from Harlem.

"*Largo viaje,*" said Ramon.

George commented in pig-Latin—which was the only "foreign" language he knew.

I might as-well tell you now what George and Ramon were like.

Everybody knew all about George long before we reached the coast of Africa. But nobody ever knew much about Ramon.

George was from Kentucky. He had worked around race horses. And he spoke of several white gentlemen out of his past as "Colonel." We were all about the same age, George, Ramon, and I.

After Kentucky, George had worked in a scrap-iron yard in St. Louis. But he said the work wasn't good for his back, so he quit. He went and got a job in a restaurant near the station in Springfield, Illinois, washing dishes. A female impersonator came through with a show and took George with him as his valet. George said he got tired of being maid to the female impersonator, so as soon as he got a new suit of clothes, he quit in Pittsburgh. He found a good job in a bowling alley, but had a fight with a man who hit him with one of the balls because he set the pins up wrong. George claimed he won the fight. But he lit out for South Street in Philadelphia to avoid arrest. And after that, Harlem.

George had a thousand tales to tell about every town he'd ever been in. And several versions of each tale. No doubt, some of the stories were true—and some of them not true at all, but they sounded true. Sometimes George said he had relatives down South. Then, again, he said he didn't have anybody in the whole world. Both versions concerning his relatives were probably correct. If he did have relatives they didn't matter—lying there as he was now, laughing and talking in his narrow bunk on a hot night, going to Africa.

But Ramon of the upper bunk didn't talk much, in English or Spanish. He simple did his work in the morning. Then he got in bed and slept all the afternoon till time to set up the sailors' mess hall for supper. After supper, he got in bed and laughed at George until George went to sleep.

Ramon told us once that his mother was a seamstress in Ponce. Ernesto, the Puerto Rican sailor aboard, said "seamstress" was just another name for something else. Anyhow, Ramon was decent enough as a cabin mate, and practically always asleep. He didn't gamble. I saw him drunk only once. He seldom drew any money, and when he did he spent it on sweets—seldom on a woman. The only thing that came out of his mouth in six months that I remember is that he said he didn't care much for women, anyway. He preferred silk stockings—so halfway down the African coast, he bought a pair of silk stockings and slept with them under his pillow.

George, however, was always saying things the like of which you never heard before or since, making up fabulous jokes, playing pranks, and getting in on all the card games or fights aboard. George and I became pretty good pals. He could tap dance a little, shuffle a lot, and knew plenty of blues. He said he could play a guitar, but no one on the *Malone* possessed a guitar, so we never knew.

I had the petty officers' mess to take care of and their staterooms to make up. There was nothing hard about a mess boy's work. You got up at six in the morning, with the mid-Atlantic calm as a sunpool, served breakfast, made up the rooms, served luncheon, had all the afternoon off, served dinner, and that was all. The rest of the time you could lie on deck in the sun, play cards with the sailors, or sleep. When your clothes were dirty, you washed them in a bucket of soapsuds and lye. The lye made the washing easy because it took all of the dirt out quick.

When we got to Africa we took on a full African crew to supplement the regular crew who weren't supposed to be able to stand the sun. Then I had an African boy to do my washing, my cleaning, and almost all my work—as did everybody on board. The Africans stood both work and sun without difficulty, it seems.

Going over, it was a nice trip, warm, calm, the sea blue-green by day, gold-green at sunset. And at night phosphorescent stars in the water where the prow cut a rift of sparkling foam.

The S.S. *Malone* had been built during the war. It was a big, creaking, old freight boat, two or three years in the African trade now. It had cabins for a half dozen passengers. This trip the passengers were all Nordic missionaries—but one. That one was a colored tailor, a Garveyite who had long worshipped Africa from afar, and who had a theory of civilization all his own. He thought that if he could just teach the Africans to wear proper clothes, coats and pants, they would be brought forward a long way toward the standards of our world. To that end, he carried with him on his journey numberless bolts of cloth, shears, and tailoring tools, and a trunk full of smart patterns. The missionaries carried Bibles and hymnbooks. The Captain carried invoices and papers having to do with trade. We sailors carried nothing but ourselves.

At Horta, our only port of call in the Azores, we anchored at sea some distance from the rocky shore. Everybody went ashore in rowboats or motor launches. Some of the boys made straight for women, some for the wine shops. It depended on your temperament which you sought first. Nobody had much money, because the Captain didn't permit a draw. I had an American dollar, so George and I bought a big bottle of cognac, walked up a hill to the top of the town, and drank it. The sun was setting. The sea and the palm trees and the roofs of Horta were aglow. On the way down the hill in the amber dusk, George smashed the cognac bottle against the wall of a blue house and said: "I wants to holler."

"George, don't holler right here on the main street," I cautioned.

George said: "This town's too small to holler in, but I got to holler, anyhow." And he let out a tremendous "Yee-hoo-oo-o!" that sent children rushing to their mothers' arms and women scurrying into doorways. But a sleepy-looking cop, leaning against a wall with a lantern, must have been used to the ways of sailors, because he paid George no mind. In fact, he didn't even stir as we went on to the center of the village, where there were lots of people and lights.

We came across the bo'sun and some sailors in a bar, emptying their pockets, trying to get enough together to pay for a round of drinks that Slim—who didn't have a penny—had ordered for all. I had four cents to contribute. Chips had a quarter. But, all told, it didn't make enough to pay for the drinks, so the bartender said they should give him the rest when the S.S. *Malone* came back to Horta in five months. So everybody agreed they would settle then. Whereupon, the bartender set up another round of drinks for nothing.

The *Malone's* whistle began to blow. The bo'sun said: "Come on, you bloody so-and-so's, the Old Man's calling you!" We went down to the wharf. Some other boys were there. An Irish kid from Brooklyn and his cousin had two girls on their arms, and the wireless man, Sparks, was in the middle between the two girls. Sparks said they were the best two girls in town and that he always traded with them. The Irish kid said his was the best girl he ever had.

His cousin said: "Aw, nuts! You never had one before!" (The Irish kid was just out of high school and this was his first trip to sea. He looked like a choirboy, except that he couldn't sing.) We waited for the launch that we had paid to take us back. Finally it came. At seven bells we went on toward Africa, the engines chugging soft and serene.

The next day was Sunday and the missionaries wanted everybody to come to prayers in the saloon, but nobody went except the Captain and the Chief Mate. The bo'sun said he'd go if the missionaries had any communion wine, but the missionaries didn't have any, so he didn't go.

When we got to Teneriffe, in the Canary Islands, it was mid-afternoon and very bright. The Canaries looked like fairy islands, all sharp peaks of red rock and bright sandy beaches and little green fields dropped like patchwork between the beaches and the rocks, with the sea making a blue-white fringe around.

The Captain let us draw money—so Las Palmas seemed a gay city indeed. Ashore, three or four of us, including Ernesto and a Norwegian boy named Sven, had supper at a place with very bright lights, where they served huge platters of delicious mixed fish with big bottles of cool, white wine. Then we all went to a white villa by the sea, called *El Palacio de Amor* and stayed all night. In the morning very early, when the sun was just coming up, we drove back to the wharf in an open carriage. We kept thinking about the girls, who were Spanish, and very young and pretty. And Sven said he would like to take one of them with him.

But all those days I was waiting anxiously to see Africa. And finally, when I saw the dust-green hills in the sunlight, something took hold of me inside. My Africa, Motherland of the Negro peoples! And me a Negro! Africa! The real thing, to be touched and seen, not merely read about in a book.

That first morning when we sighted the coast, I kept leaving my work to lean over the rail and look at Africa, dim and far away, off on the horizon in a haze of light, then gradually nearer and nearer, until you could see the color of the foliage on the trees.

We put in at the port of Dakar. There were lots of Frenchmen, and tall black Senegalese soldiers in red fezes, and Mohammedans in robes, so that at first you couldn't tell if the Mohammedans were men or women.

The next day we moved on. And farther down the coast it was more like the Africa I had dreamed about—wild and lovely, the people dark and beautiful, the palm trees tall, the sun bright, and the rivers deep. The great Africa of my dreams!

But there was one thing that hurt me a lot when I talked with the people. The Africans looked at me and would not believe I was a Negro.

NEGRO

You see, unfortunately, I am not black. There are lots of different kinds of blood in our family. But here in the United States, the word "Negro" is used to mean anyone who has *any* Negro blood at all in his veins. In Africa, the word is more pure. It means *all* Negro, therefore *black*.

I am brown. My father was a darker brown. My mother an olive-yellow. On my father's side, the white blood in his family came from a Jewish slave trader in Kentucky, Silas Cushenberry, of

Clark County, who was his mother's father; and Sam Clay, a distiller of Scotch descent, living in Henry County, who was his father's father. So on my father's side both male great-grandparents were white, and Sam Clay was said to be a relative of the great statesman, Henry Clay, his contemporary.

On my mother's side, I had a paternal great-grandfather named Quarles—Captain Ralph Quarles—who was white and who lived in Louisa County, Virginia, before the Civil War, and who had several colored children by a colored housekeeper, who was his slave. The Quarles traced their ancestry back to Francis Quarles, famous Jacobean poet, who wrote *A Feast for Wormes*.

On my maternal grandmother's side, there was French and Indian blood. My grandmother looked like an Indian—with very long black hair. She said she could lay claim to Indian land, but that she never wanted the government (or anybody else) to give her anything. She said there had been a French trader who came down the St. Lawrence, then on foot to the Carolinas, and mated with her grandmother, who was a Cherokee—so all her people were free. During slavery, she had free papers in North Carolina, and traveled about free, at will. Her name was Mary Sampson Patterson, and in Oberlin, Ohio, where she went to college, she married a free man named Sheridan Leary.

She was with child in Oberlin when Sheridan Leary went away, and nobody knew where he had gone, except that he told her he was going on a trip. A few weeks later his shawl came back to her full of bullet holes. He had been killed following John Brown in that historic raid at Harper's Ferry. They did not hang him. He had been killed that first night in the raid—shot attacking, believing in John Brown. My grandmother said Sheridan Leary always did believe people should be free.

She married another man who believed the same thing. His name was Charles Langston, my grandfather. And in the 70's the Langston's came out to Kansas where my mother was born on a farm near Lawrence.

My grandfather never made much money. But he went into politics, looking for a bigger freedom than the Emancipation Proclamation had provided. He let his farm and his grocery store in Lawrence run along, and didn't much care about making money. When he died, none of the family had any money. But he left some fine speeches behind him.

His brother, John Mercer Langston, left a book of speeches, too, and an autobiography, *From a Virginia Plantation to the National Capital*. But he was much better than Charles at making money, so he left a big house as well, and I guess some stocks and bonds. When I was small, we had cousins in Washington, who lived a lot better than we did in Kansas. But my grandmother never wrote them for anything. John Mercer Langston had been a Congressman from Virginia, and later United States Minister to Haiti, and Dean of the first Law School at Howard University. He had held many high positions—very high positions for a Negro in his day, or any day in this rather difficult country. And his descendants are still in society.

We were never very much "in society" in Kansas, because we were always broke, and the families of the Negro doctors and lawyers lived much better than we did. One of the first things I remember is my grandmother worrying about the mortgage on our house. It was always very hard for her to raise the money to pay the interest. And when my grandmother died, the house went right straight to the mortgage man, quickly.

I was born in Joplin, Missouri, in 1902, but I grew up mostly in Lawrence, Kansas. My grandmother raised me until I was twelve years old. Sometimes I was with my mother, but not often. My father and mother were separated. And my mother, who worked, always traveled about a great deal, looking for a better job. When I first started to school, I was with my mother a while in Topeka. (And later, for a summer in Colorado, and another in Kansas City.) She was a stenographer for a colored lawyer in Topeka, named Mr. Guy. She rented a room near his office, downtown. So I went to a "white" school in the downtown district.

At first, they did not want to admit me to the school, because there were no other colored families living in that neighborhood. They wanted to send me to the colored school, blocks away down across the railroad tracks. But my mother, who was always ready to do battle for the rights of a free people, went directly to the school board, and finally got me into the Harrison Street School— where all the teachers were nice to me, except one who sometimes used to make remarks about my being colored. And after such remarks, occasionally the kids would grab stones and tin cans out of the alley and chase me home.

But there was one little white boy who would always take up for me. Sometimes others of my classmates would, as well. So I learned early not to hate *all* white people. And ever since, it has seemed to me that *most* people are generally good, in every race and every country where I have been.

The room my mother lived in in Topeka was not in a house. It was in a building, upstairs over a plumbing shop. The other rooms on that floor facing a long hall were occupied by a white architect and a colored painter. The architect was a very old man, and very kind. The colored painter was young, and used to paint marvelous lions and tigers and jungle scenes. I don't know where he saw such things in Topeka, but he used to paint them. Years later, I saw him paint them on the walls of cheap barrooms in Chicago and New York. I don't know where he is now.

My mother had a small monkey-stove in our room for both heating and cooking. You could put only one pot on the stove at a time. She used to send me through the downtown alleys every day after the stores closed to pick up discarded boxes to burn in our stove. Sometimes we would make a great racket, cutting kindling with a hatchet in our room at night. If it was a tough box we could not break up, we would put a whole piece of board in the stove, and it would stick out through the top, and my mother would call it "long-branch kindling." When she would go away and leave me alone, she would warn me about putting "long-branch kinding" in the stove, because it might burn until it broke off, and fall, and catch the rug on fire.

My mother used to take me to see all the plays that came to Topeka like *Buster Brown, Under Two Flags,* and *Uncle Tom's Cabin.* We were very fond of plays and books. Once we heard *Faust.*

When I was about five or six years old, my father and mother decided to go back together. They had separated shortly after I was born, because my father wanted to go away to another country, where a colored man could get ahead and make money quicker, and my mother did not want to go. My father went to Cuba, and then to Mexico, where there wasn't any color line, or any Jim Crow. He finally sent for us, so we went there, too.

But no sooner had my mother, my grandmother, and I got to Mexico City than there was a big earthquake, and people ran out from their houses into the Alameda, and the big National Opera House they were building sank down into the ground, and tarantulas came out of the walls—and my mother said she wanted to go back home at once to Kansas, where people spoke English or something she could understand and there were no earthquakes. So we went. And that was the last I saw of my father until I was seventeen.

When I was in the second grade, my grandmother took me to Lawrence to raise me. And I was unhappy for a long time, and very lonesome, living with my grandmother. Then it was that books began to happen to me, and I began to believe in nothing but books and the wonderful world in books—where if people suffered,

they suffered in beautiful language, not in monosyllables, as we did
in Kansas. And where almost always the mortgage got paid off, the
good knights won, and the Alger boy triumphed.

Our mortgage never got paid off—for my grandmother was not
like the other colored women of Lawrence. She didn't take in
washing or go out to cook, for she had never worked for anyone.
But she tried to make a living by renting rooms to college students
from Kansas University; or by renting out half her house to a
family; or sometimes she would move out entirely and go to live
with a friend, while she rented the whole little house for ten or
twelve dollars a month, to make a payment on the mortgage. But
we were never quite sure the white mortgage man was not going
to take the house. And sometimes, on that account, we would have
very little to eat, saving to pay the interest.

I remember one summer a friend of my mother's in Kansas City
sent her son to pass a few week with me at my grandmother's
home in Lawrence. But the little boy only stayed a few days, then
wrote his mother that he wanted to leave, because we had nothing
but salt pork and wild dandelions to eat. The boy was right. But
being only eight or nine years old, I cried when he showed me the
letter he was writing his mother. And I never wanted my mother
to invite any more little boys to stay with me at my grandmother's
house.

You see, my grandmother was very proud, and she would never
beg or borrow anything from anybody. She sat, looking very much
like an Indian, copper-colored with long black hair, just a little
gray in places at seventy, sat in her rocker and read the Bible, or
held me on her lap and told me long, beautiful stories about peo-
ple who wanted to make the Negroes free, and how her father had
had apprenticed to him many slaves in Fayetteville, North Caro-
lina, before the War, so that they could work out their freedom
under him as stone masons. And once they had worked out their
purchase, he would see that they reached the North, where there
was no slavery.

Through my grandmother's stories always life moved, moved
heroically toward an end. Nobody ever cried in my grandmother's
stories. They worked, or schemed, or fought. But no crying. When
my grandmother died, I didn't cry, either. Something about my
grandmother's stories (without her ever having said so) taught me
the uselessness of crying about anything.

She was a proud woman—gentle, but Indian and proud. I re-
member once she took me to Osawatomie, where she was honored
by President Roosevelt—Teddy—and sat on the platform with him

while he made a speech; for she was then the last surviving widow of John Brown's raid.

I was twelve when she died. I went to live with a friend of my grandmother's named Auntie Reed. Auntie Reed and her husband had a little house a block from the Kaw River, near the railroad station. They had chickens and cows. Uncle Reed dug ditches and laid sewer pipes for the city, and Auntie Reed sold milk and eggs to her neighbors. For me, there have never been any better people in the world. I loved them very much. Auntie Reed let me set the hens, and Uncle Reed let me drive the cows to pasture. Auntie Reed was a Christian and made me go to church and Sunday school every Sunday. But Uncle Reed was a sinner and never went to church as long as he lived, nor cared anything about it. In fact, he washed his overalls every Sunday morning (a grievous sin) in a big iron pot in the back yard, and then just sat and smoked his pipe under the grape arbor in summer, in winter on a bench behind the kitchen range. But both of them were very good and kind— the one who went to church and the one who didn't. And no doubt from them I learned to like both Christians and sinners equally well.

SALVATION

I was saved from sin when I was going on thirteen. But not really saved. It happened like this. There was a big revival at my Auntie Reed's church. Every night for weeks there had been much preaching, singing, praying, and shouting, and some very hardened sinners had been brought to Christ, and the membership of the church had grown by leaps and bounds. Then just before the revival ended, they held a special meeting for children, "to bring the young lambs to the fold." My aunt spoke of it for days ahead. That night I was escorted to the front row and placed on the mourners' bench with all the other young sinners, who had not yet been brought to Jesus.

My aunt told me that when you were saved you saw a light, and something happened to you inside! And Jesus came into your life! And God was with you from then on! She said you could see and hear and feel Jesus in your soul. I believed her. I had heard a great many old people say the same thing and it seemed to me they ought to know. So I sat there calmly in the hot, crowded church, waiting for Jesus to come to me.

The preacher preached a wonderful rhythmical sermon, all moans and shouts and lonely cries and dire pictures of hell, and then he sang a song about the ninety and nine safe in the fold, but one little lamb was left out in the cold. Then he said: "Won't you come? Won't you come to Jesus? Young lambs, won't you come?" And he held out his arms to all us young sinners there on the mourners' bench. And the little girls cried. And some of them jumped up and went to Jesus right away. But most of us just sat there.

A great many old people came and knelt around us and prayed, old women with jet-black faces and braided hair, old men with work-gnarled hands. And the church sang a song about the lower lights are burning, some poor sinners to be saved. And the whole building rocked with prayer and song.

Still I kept waiting to *see* Jesus.

Finally all the young people had gone to the altar and were saved, but one boy and me. He was a rounder's son named Westley. Westley and I were surrounded by sisters and deacons praying. It was very hot in the church, and getting late now. Finally Westley said to me in a whisper: "God damn! I'm tired o' sitting here. Let's get up and be saved." So he got up and was saved.

Then I was left all alone on the mourners' bench. My aunt came and knelt at my knees and cried, while prayers and songs swirled all around me in the little church. The whole congregation prayed for me alone, in a mighty wail of moans and voices. And I kept waiting serenely for Jesus, waiting, waiting—but he didn't come. I wanted to see him, but nothing happened to me. Nothing! I wanted something to happen to me, but nothing happened.

I heard the songs and the minister saying: "Why don't you come? My dear child, why don't you come to Jesus? Jesus is waiting for you. He wants you. Why don't you come? Sister Reed, what is this child's name?"

"Langston," my aunt sobbed.

"Langston, why don't you come? Why don't you come and be saved? Oh, Lamb of God! Why don't you come?"

Now it was really getting late. I began to be ashamed of myself, holding everything up so long. I began to wonder what God thought about Westley, who certainly hadn't seen Jesus either, but who was now sitting proudly on the platform, swinging his knickerbockered legs and grinning down at me, surrounded by deacons and old women on their knees praying. God had not struck Westley dead for taking his name in vain or for lying in the temple. So I decided that maybe to save further trouble, I'd better lie, too, and say that Jesus had come, and get up and be saved.

So I got up.

Suddenly the whole room broke into a sea of shouting, as they saw me rise. Waves of rejoicing swept the place. Women leaped in the air. My aunt threw her arms around me. The minister took me by the hand and led me to the platform.

When things quieted down, in a hushed silence, punctuated by a few ecstatic "Amens," all the new young lambs were blessed in the name of God. Then joyus singing filled the room.

That night, for the last time in my life but one—for I was a big boy twelve years old—I cried. I cried, in bed alone, and couldn't stop. I buried my head under the quilts, but my aunt heard me. She woke up and told my uncle I was crying because the Holy Ghost had come into my life, and because I had seen Jesus. But I really crying because I couldn't bear to tell her that I had lied, that I had deceived everybody in the church, that I hadn't seen Jesus, and that now I didn't believe there was a Jesus any more, since he didn't come to help me.

THE MOTHER OF THE GRACCHI

My Auntie Reed cooked wonderful salt pork and greens with corn dumplings. There were fresh peas and young onions right out of the garden, and milk with cream on it. There were hoe-cake, and sorghum molasses, and apple dumplings with butter sauce. And she and Uncle Reed owned their own home without a mortgage on it, clear.

In the spring I used to collect maple seeds and sell them to the seed store. I delivered papers for a while and sold the *Saturday Evening Post*. For a few weeks I also sold the *Appeal to Reason* for an old gentleman with a white beard, who said his paper was trying to make a better world. But the editor of the local daily told me to stop selling the *Appeal to Reason,* because it was a radical sheet and would get colored folks in trouble. Besides, he said I couldn't carry his papers and that one, too. So I gave up the *Appeal to Reason.*

On Saturdays I went to football games at the University of Kansas and heard the students yelling:

Walk-Chalk!
Jay Hawk! K. U.!

And I felt bad if Nebraska or Missouri beat Kansas, as they usually did.

When I was in the seventh grade, I got my first regular job, cleaning up the lobby and toilets of an old hotel near the school I attended. I kept the mirrors and spittoons shined and the halls scrubbed. I was paid fifty cents a week, with which I went to see Mary Pickford and Charlie Chaplin and Theda Bara on the screen. Also Pearl White in *The Clutching Claw,* until the theater (belonging to a lady named Mrs. Pattee) put up a sign: No COLORED ADMITTED. Then I went to see road shows like *The Firefly* and *The Pink Lady* and Sothern and Marlowe when they came to town, sitting up in the gallery of the Opera House all by myself, thrilled at the world across the footlights.

But there was a glamour in the real world, too. For a while there had been a poet in Lawrence who had left his mark on the town. I remember my mother, when I was a small child, pointing him out to me on the street. His name was Harry Kemp, but I don't remember clearly how he looked.

The great Negro actor, Nash Walker, of "Bon Bon Buddy, the Chocolate Drop" fame, had lived in Lawrence, too. And my Uncle Nat (before he died) had taught him music, long before I was born. I saw Nash Walker only once, because he was off in the East with the great Williams and Walker shows, since he was a partner of Bert Williams, but I often heard the local people speak of him. And I vaguely remember that he brought to Lawrence the first phonograph I had ever seen, when he came back ill to his mother at the end. He gave a concert at my aunt's church on the phonograph, playing records for the benefit of the church mortgage fund one night. I remember my mother said she had had dinner with Nash Walker and his mother, while he was ill, and that they ate from plates with gold edging. Then Nash (George Walker, as he was known in the theater) died and there was a big funeral for him and I got my hand slapped for pointing at the flowers, because it was not polite for a child to point.

When I went to live with Auntie Reed, whose house was near the depot, I used to walk down to the Santa Fe station and stare at the railroad tracks, because the railroad tracks ran to Chicago, and Chicago was the biggest town in the world to me, much talked of by the people in Kansas. I was glad when my mother sent for me to come to Lincoln, Illinois, where she was then living, not far from Chicago. I was going on fourteen. And the papers said the Great War had begun in Europe.

My mother had married again. She had married a chef cook named Homer Clark. But like so many cooks, as he got older he couldn't stand the heat of the kitchen, so he went to work at other things. Odd jobs, the steel mills, the coal mines. By now I had a little brother. I liked my step-father a great deal, and my baby brother, also; for I had been very lonesome growing up all by myself, the only child, with no father and no mother around.

But ever so often, my step-father would leave my mother and go away looking for a better job. The day I graduated from grammar school in Lincoln, Illinois, he had left my mother, and was not there to see me graduate.

I was the Class Poet. It happened like this. They had elected all the class officers, but there was no one in our class who looked like a poet, or had ever written a poem. There were two Negro children in the class, myself and a girl. In America most white people think, of course, that *all* Negroes can sing and dance, and have a sense of rhythm. So my classmates, knowing that a poem had to have rhythm, elected me unanimously—thinking, no doubt, that I had some, being a Negro.

The day I was elected, I went home and wondered what I should write. Since we had eight teachers in our school, I thought there should be one verse for each teacher, with an especially good one for my favorite teacher, Miss Ethel Welsh. And since the teachers were to have eight verses, I felt the class should have eight, too. So my first poem was about the longest poem I ever wrote—sixteen verses, which were later cut down. In the first half of the poem, I said that our school had the finest teachers there ever were. And in the latter half, I said our class was the greatest class ever graduated. So at graduation, when I read the poem, naturally everybody applauded loudly.

That was the way I began to write poetry.

It had never occurred to me to be a poet before, or indeed a writer of any kind. But my mother had often read papers at the Inter-State Literary Society, founded by my grandfather in Kansas. And occasionally she wrote original poems, too, that she gave at the Inter-State. But more often, she recited long recitations like "Lasca" and "The Mother of the Gracchi," in costume. As Lasca she dressed as a cowgirl. And as Cornelia, the mother of the Gracchi, she wrote a sheet like a Roman matron.

On one such occasion, she had me and another little boy dressed in half-sheets as her sons—jewels, about to be torn away from her by a cruel Spartan fate. My mother was the star of the program and the church in Lawrence was crowded. The audience hung on her words: but I did not like the poem at all, so in the very middle of it I began to roll my eyes from side to side, round and round in my head, as though in great distress. The audience tittered. My mother intensified her efforts, I, my mock agony. Wilder and wilder I mugged, as the poem mounted, batted and rolled my eyes, until the entire assemblage burst into uncontrollable laughter.

My mother, poor soul, couldn't imagine what was wrong. More fervently than ever, she poured forth her lines, grasped us to her breast, and begged heaven for mercy. But the audience by then couldn't stop giggling, and with the applause at the end, she was greeted by a mighty roar of laughter. When the program was over and my mother found out what had happened, I got the worst whipping I ever had in my life. Then and there I learned to respect other people's art.

Nevertheless, the following spring, at a Children's Day program at my aunt's church, I, deliberately and with malice aforethought, forgot a poem I knew very well, having been forced against my will to learn it. I mounted the platform, said a few lines, and then stood there—much to the embarrassment of my mother, who had come all the way from Kansas City to hear me recite. My aunt tried to prompt me, but I pretended I couldn't hear a word. Finally I came down to my seat in dead silence—and I never had to recite a poem in church again.

The only poems I liked as a child were Paul Lawrence Dunbar's. And *Hiawatha*. But I liked any kind of stories. I read all of my mother's novels from the library: *The Rosary, The Mistress of Shenstone, Freckles, Edna Ferber,* all of Harold Bell Wright, and all of Zane Grey. I thought *Riders of the Purple Sage* a wonderful book and still think so, as I remember it.

In Topeka, as a small child, my mother took me with her to the little vine-covered library on the grounds of the Capitol. There I first fell in love with librarians, and I have been in love with them ever since—those very nice women who help you find wonderful books! The silence inside the library, the big chairs, and long tables, and the fact that the library was always there and didn't seem to have a mortgage on it, or any sort of insecurity about it—all of that made me love it. And right then, even before I was six, books began to happen to me, so that after a while, there came a time when I believed in books more than in people—which, of course, was wrong. That was why, when I went to Africa, I threw all the books into the sea.

CENTRAL HIGH

I had no sooner graduated from grammar school in Lincoln than we moved from Illinois to Cleveland. My step-father sent for us. He was working in a steel mill during the war, and making lots of money. But it was hard work, and he never looked the same afterwards. Every day he worked several hours overtime, because they paid well for overtime. But after a while, he couldn't stand the heat of the furnaces, so he got a job as caretaker of a theater building, and after that as janitor of an apartment house.

Rents were very high for colored people in Cleveland, and the Negro district was extremely crowded, because of the great migration. It was difficult to find a place to live. We always lived, during my high school years, either in an attic or a basement, and paid quite a lot for such inconvenient quarters. White people on the east side of the ctiy were moving out of their frame houses and renting them to Negroes at double and triple the rents they could receive from others. An eight-room house with one bath would be cut up into apartments and five or six families crowded into it, each two-room kitchenette apartment renting for what the whole house had rented for before.

But Negroes were coming in in a great dark tide from the South, and they had to have some place to live. Sheds and garages and store fronts were turned into living quarters. As always, the white neighborhoods resented Negroes moving closer and closer—but when the whites did give way, they gave way at very profitable rentals. So most of the colored people's wages went for rent. The landlords and the banks made it difficult for them to buy houses, so they had to pay the exorbitant rents required. When my step-father quit the steel mill job, my mother went out to work in service to help him meet expenses. She paid a woman four dollars a week to take care of my little brother while she worked as a maid.

I went to Central High School in Cleveland. We had a magazine called the *Belfry Owl*. I wrote poems for the *Belfry Owl*. We had some wise and very good teachers, Miss Roberts and Miss Weimer in English, Miss Chesnutt, who was the daughter of the famous colored writer, Charles W. Chesnutt, and Mr. Hitchcock, who taught geometry with humor, and Mr. Ozanne, who spread the whole world before us in his history classes. Also Clara Dieke, who painted beautiful pictures and who taught us a great deal about many things that are useful to know—about law and order in art and life, and about sticking to a thing until it is done.

Ethel Weimer discovered Carl Sandburg for me. Although I had read of Carl Sandburg before—in an article, I think, in the *Kansas City Star* about how bad free verse was—I didn't really know him until Miss Weimer in second-year English brought him, as well as Amy Lowell, Vachel Lindsay, and Edgar Lee Masters, to us. Then I began to try to write like Carl Sandburg.

Little Negro dialect poems like Paul Lawrence Dunbar's and poems without rhyme like Sandburg's were the first real poems I tried to write. I wrote about love, about the steel mills where my step-father worked, the slums where we lived, and the brown girls from the South, prancing up and down Central Avenue on a spring day.

One of the first of my high school poems went like this:

> *Just because I loves you—*
> *That's de reason why*
> *My soul is full of color*
> *Like de wings of a butterfly.*
>
> *Just because I loves you*
> *That's de reason why*
> *My heart's a fluttering aspen leaf*
> *When you pass by.*

I was fourteen then. And another of the poems was this about the mills:

> *The mills*
> *That grind and grind,*
> *That grind out steel*
> *And grind away the lives*
> *Of men—*
> *In the sunset their stacks*
> *Are great black silhouettes*
> *Against the sky.*
> *In the dawn*
> *They belch red fire.*
> *The mills—*
> *Grinding new steel,*
> *Old men.*

And about Carl Sandburg, my guiding star, I wrote:

> *Carl Sandburg's poems*
> *Fall on the white pages of his books*
> *Like blood-clots of song*

From the wounds of humanity.
I know a lover of life sings
When Carl Sandburg sings.
I know a lover of all the living
Sings then.

Central was the high school of students of foreign-born parents—until the Negroes came. It is an old high school with many famous graduates. It used to be long ago the high school of the aristocrats, until the aristocrats moved farther out. Then poor whites and foreign-born took over the district. Then during the war, the Negroes came. Now Central is almost entirely a Negro school in the heart of Cleveland's vast Negro quarter.

When I was there, it was very nearly entirely a foreign-born school, with a few native white and colored American students mixed in. By foreign, I mean children of foreign-born parents. Although some of the students themselves had been born in Poland or Russia, Hungary or Italy. And most were Catholic or Jewish.

Although we got on very well, whenever class elections would come up, there was a distinct Jewish-Gentile division among my classmates. That was perhaps why I held many class and club offices in high school, because often when there was a religious deadlock, a Negro student would win the election. They would compromise on a Negro, feeling, I suppose, that a Negro was neither Jew nor Gentile!

I wore a sweater covered with club pins most of the time. I was on the track team, and for two seasons, my relay team won the city-wide championships. I was a lieutenant in the military training corps. Once or twice I was on the monthly honor roll for scholarship. And when we were graduated, Class of '20, I edited the Year Book.

My best pal in high school was a Polish boy named Sartur Andrzejewski. His parents lived in the steel mill district. His mother cooked wonderful cabbage in sweetened vinegar. His rosy-cheeked sisters were named Regina and Sabina. And the whole family had about them a quaint and kindly foreign air, bubbling with hospitality. They were devout Catholics, who lived well and were very jolly.

I had lots of Jewish friends, too, boys named Nathan and Sidney and Herman, and girls named Sonya and Bess and Leah. I went to my first symphony concert with a Jewish girl—for these children of foreign-born parents were more democratic than native white Americans, and less anti-Negro. They lent me *The Gadfly* and *Jean-Christophe* to read, and copies of the *Liberator* and the *Socialist Call*. They were almost all interested in more than basketball and the glee club. They took me to hear Eugene Debs. And when the Russian Revolution broke out, our school almost held a celebration.

Since it was during the war, and Americanism was being stressed, many of our students, including myself, were then called down to the principal's office and questioned about our belief in Americanism. Police went to some of the parents' homes and took all their books away. After that, the principal organized an Americanism Club in our school, and, I reckon, because of the customary split between Jews and Gentiles, I was elected president. But the club didn't last long, because we were never quite clear about what we were supposed to do. Or why. Except that none of us wanted Eugene Debs locked up. But the principal didn't seem to feel that Debs fell within the scope of our club. So the faculty let the club die.

Four years at Central High School taught me many invaluable things. From Miss Dieke, who instructed in painting and lettering and ceramics, I learnt that the only way to get a thing done is to start to do it, then keep on doing it, and finally you'll finish it, even if in the beginning you think you can't do it at all. From Miss Weimer I learnt that there are ways of saying or doing things, which may not be the currently approved ways, yet that can be very true and beautiful ways, that people will come to recognize as such in due time. In 1916, the critics said Carl Sandburg was no good as a poet, and free verse was no good. Nobody says that today—yet 1916 is not a lifetime ago.

From the students I learnt that Europe was not so far away, and that when Lenin took power in Russia, something happened in the slums of Woodlawn Avenue that the teachers couldn't tell us about, and that our principal didn't want us to know. From the students I learnt, too, that lots of painful words can be flung at people that aren't *nigger*. *Kike* was one; *spick,* and *hunky,* others.

But I soon realized that the kikes and the spicks and the hunkies —scorned though they might be by the pure Americans—all had it on the niggers in one thing. Summer time came and they could get jobs quickly. For even during the war, when help was badly needed, lots of employers would *not* hire Negroes. A colored boy had to search and search for a job.

My first summer vacation from high school, I ran a dumb-waiter at Halle's, a big department store. The dumb-waiter carried stock from the stock room to the various departments of the store. I was continually amazed at trays of perfume that cost fifty dollars a bottle, ladies' lace collars at twenty-five, and useless little gadgets like gold cigarette lighters that were worth more than six months' rent on the house where we lived. Yet some people could afford to buy such things without a thought. And did buy them.

The second summer vacation I went to join my mother in Chicago. Dad and my mother were separated again, and she was working as cook for a lady who owned a millinery shop in the Loop, a very fashionable shop where society leaders came by appointment and hats were designed to order. I became a delivery boy for that shop. It was a terrifically hot summer, and we lived on the crowded Chicago South Side in a house next to the elevated. The thunder of the trains kept us awake at night. We could afford only one small room for my mother, my little brother, and me.

South State Street was in its glory then, a teeming Negro street with crowded theaters, restaurants, and cabarets. And excitement from noon to noon. Midnight was like day. The street was full of workers and gamblers, prostitutes and pimps, church folks and sinners. The tenements on either side were very congested. For neither love nor money could you find a decent place to live. Prof-iteers, thugs, and gangsters were coming into their own. The first Sunday I was in town, I went out walking alone to see what the city looked like. I wandered too far outside the Negro ditsrict, over beyond Wentworth, and was set upon and beaten by a group of white boys, who said they didn't allow niggers in that neighborhood. I came home with both eyes blacked and a swollen jaw. That was the summer before the Chicago riots.

I managed to save a little money, so I went back to high school in Cleveland, leaving my mother in Chicago. I couldn't afford to eat in a restaurant, and the only thing I knew how to cook myself in the kitchen of the house where I roomed was rice, which I boiled to a paste. Rice and hot dogs, rice and hot dogs, every night for dinner. Then I read myself to sleep.

I was reading Schopenhauer and Nietzsche, and Edna Ferber and Dreiser, and de Maupassant in French. I never will forget the thrill of first understanding the French of de Maupassant. The soft snow was falling through one of his stories in the little book we used in school, and that I had worked over so long, before I really felt the snow falling there. Then all of a sudden one night the beauty and the meaning of the words in which he made the snow fall, came to me. I think it was de Maupassant who made me really want to be a writer and write stories about Negroes, so true that people in far-away lands would read them—even after I was dead.

But I did not dare write stories yet, although poems came to me now spontaneously, from somewhere inside. But there were no stories in my mind. I put the poems down quickly on anything I had at hand when they came into my head, and later I copied them in a notebook. But I began to be afraid to show my poems to anybody, because they had become very serious and very much a part of me. And I was afraid other people might not like them or understand them.

However, I sent some away to a big magazine in New York, where nobody knew me. And the big magazine sent them right back with a printed rejection slip. Then I sent them to one magazine after another—and they always came back promptly. But once Floyd Dell wrote and encouraging word across one of the rejection slips from the *Liberator.*

ABRUPT ENCOUNTER

Eleven years had gone by and I had not seen my father. Suddenly, one day in the spring of 1919, a letter came from Mexico saying:

> My Dear Langston:
>   I am going to New York for a few days on a business trip in June. On the way back I will send you a wire to be ready to meet me as the train comes through Cleveland. You are to accompany me to Mexico for the summer.
>
> Affectionately,
your father,
James N. Hughes.

This letter made my mother very angry. She said it was just like my devilish, evil father—when I got big enough to work and help her earn a living, he wanted to come and take me off to Mexico. Then she began to cry. She said after all she had done for me, if I wanted to go away and leave her, to go ahead, go ahead!

I said I wanted to go to Mexico for the summer to see what the country was like—and my father. Then I would be back in the fall.

My mother was a waitress in a restaurant on Central Avenue, and she and my step-father were back together. My mother wouldn't be alone if I went to Mexico, so I began to get ready to go. My step-father thought it would be a good thing and said: "Sure, go on."

That spring I had got my track letter for the high-jump and the 440-relays, but I didn't have the money to buy a new sweater, so I packed the track letter away in my suitcase to show to my father.

James N. Hughes, my father! I vaguely remembered him carrying me in his arms the night of the big earthquake in Mexico City, when I was six years old. Since then he had always been in Mexico and I had been in the States growing up while my grandmother died and the house went to the mortgage man, my mother traveled about the country looking for my step-father or for a better job, always moving from one house to another, where the rent was cheaper or there was at least a bathroom or a backyard to hang out clothes. And me growing up living with my grandmother, with aunts who were really no relation, with my mother in rented rooms, or alone trying to get through high school—always some kind of crisis in our lives. My father, permanently in Mexico during all those turbulent years, represented for me the one stable factor in my life. He at least stayed put.

"Your father is a devil on wheels," my mother said. "As mean and evil a Negro as ever lived!"

And when I displeased her, she declared I was just like my father.

I didn't believe her. In my mind I pictured my father as a kind of strong, bronze cowboy, in a big Mexican hat, going back and forth from his business in the city to his ranch in the mountains, free—in a land where there were no white folks to draw the color line, and no tenements with rent always due—just mountains and sun and cacti: Mexico!

That spring, I was anxious to see my father.

Then an unfortunate thing happened in Cleveland. We moved on the first of June. But I left word with the landlady, that, should any messages come for me, she should send them directly to the new place where we lived. And every morning, to make sure, I went out to our old lodgings to see if there was any word from my father, now in New York.

But his telegram came late one afternoon, when our former land-lady was not at home, so the delivery boy simply stuck it in the mail box, and the woman did not notice it there until the next morning.

The telegram said: "PASSING THROUGH TEN-FIFTY TONIGHT BE READY BOARD TRAIN AT STATION JAMES N. HUGHES"

That was the night before! The landlady found the wire, when I went out there the following morning. My heart stopped beating. Had my father gone on to Mexico without me, when he did not find me on the station platform? There was no further message from him. Had he, maybe, got off the train and stayed the night in Cleveland? Then where would he be?

I went to the telephone and called up the various colored hotels. The second one I called said, yes, there was a James Hughes stopping there, but that he had gone out to breakfast. I told them to tell him when he came back that his son would be right down.

The hotel was on Central Avenue, a block and a half from the restaurant where my mother worked as a waitress. I began to walk down Central Avenue as fast as I could. When I was about three blocks above the hotel, I saw a little, bronze man with a moustache, coming rapidly up the street toward me. We looked closely at each other as we passed. Then we turned and looked back.

The man said: "Are you Langston?"

I said: "Yes. Are you my father?"

"Why weren't you at the train last night?" he asked.

"We moved, and I didn't get your wire till this morning."

"Just like niggers," he spat out. "Always moving! Are you ready to go?"

"Soon as I tell my mother good-bye."

"I just saw your mother," he said, "waiting table in a restaurant. If she's stayed with me, she'd have been wearing diamonds."

I didn't know what to say about that, so I just stood there.

"I'm going to a barber shop," my father said. "Meet me at the hotel in half an hour. We'll leave on the noon train."

He turned and went up the street. He never said a word about being glad to see me.

That morning, by accident, he had been for breakfast to the very restaurant where my mother was working. When they recognized each other, he said: "How are you?"

All my mother said was: "What's your order?"

She served him ham and eggs and he left her a dime tip. She told the woman who ran the restaurant to throw the dime in the street.

When I came in, my mother was very angry as she told me this. "But go on if you want to! Go on! Go to Mexico if you want to go."

"Gee, ma! Don't be mad at me," I said. "I didn't pick him out for a father."

"Go with him!" she cried over the counter. "Go on—and leave me! Go ahead!"

"I might as well go," I said. "I haven't got any job in Cleveland."

"Sure, go on!" she said. "Hard as I've worked and as little as you care about me!"

By now, some customers came in and my mother had to wait on them. I sat on a stool at the counter a long time, but she kept walking by me silently to the coffee urns, the steam table, or to the kitchen. I wanted her to say something to me. But finally it was time to go. So I went.

FATHER

That summer in Mexico was the most miserable I have ever known. I did not hear from my mother for several weeks. I did not like my father. And I did not know what to do about either of them.

My father was what the Mexicans called *muy americano,* a typical American. He was different from anybody I had ever known. He was interested only in making money.

My mother and step-father were interested in making money, too, so they were always moving about from job to job and from town to town, wherever they heard times were better. But they were interested in making money to *spend.* And for fun. They were always buying victrolas and radios and watches and rings, and going to shows and drinking beer and playing cards, and trying to have a good time after working hours.

But my father was interested in making money to *keep.*

Because it is very hard for a Negro to make money in the United States, since so many jobs are denied him, so many unions and professional associations are barred to him, so many banks will not advance him loans, and so many insurance companies will not insure his business, my father went to Cuba and Mexico, where he could make money quicker. He had had legal training in the South, but could not be admitted to the bar there. In Mexico he was admitted to the bar and practised law. He acquired property in Mexico City and a big ranch in the hills. He lent money and foreclosed on mortgages.

During the revolutions, when all the white Americans had to flee from the Toluca district of Mexico, because of the rising nationalism, my father became the general manager of an electric light company belonging to an American firm in New York. Because he was brown, the Mexicans could not tell at sight that he was a Yankee, and even after they knew it, they did not believe he was like the white Yankees. So the followers of Zapata and Villa did not run him away as they did the whites. In fact, in Toluca, the Mexicans always called my father *el americano,* and not the less polite *el gringo,* which is a term that carries with it distrust and hatred.

But my father was certainly just like the other German and English and American business men with whom he associated in Mexico. He spoke just as badly about the Mexicans. He said they were ignorant and backward and lazy. He said they were exactly like the Negroes in the United States, perhaps worse. And he said they were very bad at making money.

My father hated Negroes. I think he hated himself, too, for being a Negro. He disliked all of his family because they were Negroes and remained in the United States, where none of them had a chance to be much of anything but servants—like my mother, who started out with a good education at the University of Kansas, he said, but had sunk to working in a restaurant, waiting on niggers, when she wasn't in some white woman's kitchen. My father said he wanted me to leave the United States as soon as I finished high school, and never return—unless I wanted to be a porter or a red cap all my life.

The second day out from Cleveland, the train we were on rolled across Arkansas. As we passed through a dismal village in the cotton fields, my father peered from the window of our Pullman at a cluster of black peons on the main street, and said contemptuously: "Look at the niggers."

When we crossed into Mexico at Laredo, and started south over the sun-baked plains, he pointed out to me a cluster of brown peons watching the train slow down at an adobe station. He said: "Look at the Mexicans!"

My father had a great contempt for all poor people. He thought it was their own fault that they were poor.

In Mexico City we went to the Grand Hotel. Then my father took me to call on three charming middle-aged Mexican ladies who were his friends—three unmarried sisters, one of whom took care of his rents in the city. They were very Latin and very Catholic, lived in a house with a charming courtyard, and served the most marvelous dishes at table—roast duck stuffed with pears and turkey with *mole* sauce, a sauce that takes several days to prepare, so complex is its making. And always there were a pile of steaming-hot tortillas, wrapped in a napkin, at one corner of the table.

In their youth, they were very lovely ladies to look at, I vaguely remembered from my trip there as a child. And they still wore their shawls of black lace with dignity and grace. They were all three the color of parchment, a soft, ivory-yellow—the blood of Spain overcast just a little by the blood of Mexico—for they were not Indians. And they were not revolutionists. They had adored the former dictator-president, Porfirio Diaz, and when they wanted to speak of some as uncouth, they said: *"Muy indio."* Very Indian!

These three aging ladies were, I think, the only people in the whole world who really ever liked my father. Perhaps that was because his property helped to provide them with an income. And perhaps also because they shared many of his aristocratic ideas regarding the peons.

Their only worry about my father concerned his soul. He was not Catholic and never went to mass. The first thing they gave me as a present was a little amulet of the Virgin of Guadalupe. But my father laughed when we got back to the hotel and said he hoped I did not believe in that foolishness. He said greasers and niggers would never get anywhere because they were too religious, always praying.

The following morning, we left for Toluca. I wanted to see my father's tenement houses in Mexico City, but he said I could see them some other time. He was anxious to get back to the plant in Toluca.

Off the big trunk line between the capital and the border, railroad travel in Mexico then was slow and uncomfortable. Many of the coaches had been burned or bullet-ridden in the revolts, so the trains were very crowded. They had a parlor car coach between Mexico City and Toluca, in which one could reserve a seat, but my father was too frugal with money to use this service. So we rode in a crowded second-class coach, with people standing in the aisles, and all over one's feet, and bundles and baskets hanging from everywhere. My father said: "Be careful of pickpockets and thieves. Mexicans steal."

The train wound up and up into the mountains, and finally came down into one of the most beautiful valleys in the world, all lush, green fields and lakes, where water lilies floated, with a snow-capped volcano in the distance, La Nevada de Toluca. We were in the highest inhabitable valley in Mexico. The air was very cool and sweet and the sky a brilliant blue.

We reached Toluca in time for luncheon. My father's *mozo* met us at the station. He was an Indian boy named Maximiliano, with a broad, brown face and black hair that fell into his eyes. He wore the common white trousers and shirt you see all over Mexico, and *huaraches* on his feet. He put all our baggage on his back and secured it in a sort of leather thong about his neck, and trotted on ahead of us toward the house.

My father's house faced a small park near the station. It was a low, blue-white house of one story, all spread out and surrounded by a blue-white wall. As you approached the house, you could see only high adobe walls, rimmed with dull red tile at the top. At one end of the wall, there was a big double door for the horses. At the other end, a small door that led into the patio and the house.

The patio would have been nice, had my father bothered to keep the grass and flowers tended. But he took much better care of the corral at the back of the house, where the horses and chickens were, and the cow.

He had recently foreclosed on the cow. But some shrewd Mexicans must have got the best of him that time, because the cow was ill. She had something hard in her udders; she gave bitter milk, and finally stopped giving milk altogether, as her udders began to petrify. A few weeks after I arrived, she was dead.

But there were two beautiful horses in the corral, and about a hundred large, healthy American chickens, not at all like the scrawny Mexican chickens other people had. My father said he could trade a pair of his chickens any day for a calf or a sheep, and it was true.

My father's housekeeper was a tall Mexican woman with a kind tan-brown face, and two children approaching their teens, whom my father would not permit to eat at our house. But she used to take food home to them at night. My father lived on a rather meagre diet of beef and beans. But the cook and I soon teamed up against him, and when he was away at the ranch, we would order all kinds of good things to eat from the shops where he traded, and put them on his bill. I would take the blame. My father stormed and said I was just like my mother, always wasting money. So he would usually make a scene whenever he came home from the country, sending the cook flying from the kitchen in tears. But, nevertheless, he would always eat whatever good things were set before him.

Maximiliano, the *mozo, took care of the horses and the chickens,* swept the patio and the corral, and saddle the horses for me or my father. He was a silent boy who spoke but little Spanish, his being an Indian language from the hills. He slept on a pile of sacks in the tool shed, so I asked my father why he didn't give Maximiliano a bed, since there were several old beds around.

He said: "Never give an Indian anything. He doesn't appreciate it."

But he was wrong about that. I gave Maximiliano my spare centavos and cigarettes, and we became very good friends. He taught me to ride a horse without saddle or stirrups, how to tell a badly woven serape from a good one, and various other things that are useful to know in that high valley beneath the white volcanos.

My father paid Maximiliano and the cook almost nothing, but he gave me ten pesos a week allowance, which I used to share with the two servants. There was nothing much to spend money for in Toluca. At least, not knowing any one and not yet being able to speak Spanish, I found nothing to spend money for, except the movies once a week, on Sundays.

The weekly movie show was a gala occasion for the whole town. Society and its pretty daughters attended and sat in the horseshoe of circular boxes, running from one side of the stage to the other around the ancient auditorium. The young blades and unmarried males of the better families sat in the orchestra proper, and between each reel of bad Hollywood movies, or arty German ones, practically all the males would rise and sweep the circle of boxes with their eyes until they found the girl each liked. Then they would stare at her until the house went dark again. The shows commenced at four o'clock and lasted an ungodly long time, because they had only one projector and had to show each picture reel by reel. When the sun went down, it got very cold in Toluca, and the old theater had no heat, but you gathered your coat about you and stuck it out until the last cowboy had killed the last redskin and smothered the heroine in a kiss. Then you came home through the badly lighted streets, where the meek Indian policemen, huddled in blankets to the eyebrows, slept leaning against adobe corners, a lantern on the ground at their feet.

I began to get very tired of Toluca. My father did not take me to the ranch with him, because he said the roads were infested with bandits, and I could not yet ride well enough. Instead of letting me go about with him to the country or to Mexico City, he put me to learning bookkeeping. I was never very good at figures, and I got hopelessly tangled up in the problems he gave me. My stupidity disgusted him immeasurably, and he would rail at me about the need of acquiring a good business head. "Seventeen and you can't add yet!" he'd cry. Then he would bend over the ledger and show me all over again how to balance the spoiled page, and say: "Now, hurry up and do it! Hurry up! Hurry up!"

"Hurry up!" was his favorite expression in Spanish or in English. He was always telling the employees under him at the electric light company, the cook at home, or Maximiliano, or me, to hurry up, hurry up and do whatever we were doing—so that we could get through and do something else he always had ready to be done.

Hurry up! My father had tremendous energy. He always walked fast and rode hard. He was small and tough, like a jockey. He got up at five in the morning and worked at his accounts or his mail or his law books until time to go to the office. Then until ten or eleven o'clock at night he would be busy at various tasks, stopping only to eat. Then, on the days he made the long trek to the ranch, he rose at three-thirty or four, in order to get out there early and see what his workers were doing. Every one else worked too slowly for him, so it was always, "Hurry up!"

As the weeks went by, I could think of less and less to say to my father. His whole way of living was so different from mine, his attitude toward life and people so amazing, that I fell silent and couldn't open my mouth when he was in the house. Not even when he barked: "Hurry up!"

I hadn't heard from my mother, even by July. I knew she was angry with me because I had gone to Mexico. I understood then, though, why she had been unable to live with my father, and I didn't blame her. But why had she married him in the first place, I wondered. And why had they had me? Now, at seventeen, I began to be very sorry for myself, in a strange land in a mountain town, where there wasn't a person who spoke English. It was very cold at night and quiet, and I had no money to get away, and I was lonesome. I began to wish I had never been born—not under such circumstances.

I took long rides on a black horse named Tito to little villages of adobe huts, nestled in green fields of corn and alfalfa, little villages, each with a big church with a beautiful tower built a hundred years ago, a white Spanish tower with great bells swinging in the turret.

I began to learn to read Spanish. I struggled with bookkeeping. I took one of the old pistols from my father's desk and fired away in the afternoon at a target Maximiliano had put up in the corral. But most of the time I was depressed and unhappy and bored. One day, when there was no one in the house but me, I put the pistol to my head and held it there, loaded, a long time, and wondered if I would be any happier if I were to pull the trigger. But then, I began to think, if I do, I might miss something. I haven't been to the ranch yet, nor to the top of the volcano, nor to the bullfights in Mexico, nor graduated from high school, nor got married. So I put the pistol down and went back to my bookkeeping.

My father was very seldom at home, but when he was, he must have noticed my silence and my gloomy face, because if I looked the way I felt, I looked woebegone, indeed. One day in August, he told me he was going to Mexico City for a week, and would take me with him for the trip. He said I could see the summer bullfights and Xochimilco. The trip was ten days off, but I began to dream about it, and to press my clothes and get ready.

It seemed that my father couldn't resist saying, "Hurry up," more and more during those ten days, and giving me harder and harder bookkeeping problems to have worked out by the time he got home from the office. Besides, he was teaching me to typewrite, and gave me several exercises to master each evening. "Hurry up and type that a hundred times before you go to bed. Hurry up and get that page of figures done so I can check on it. Hurry up and learn the verb, *estar*."

Hurry up . . . hurry up . . . hurry up . . . hurry up, began to ring in my ears like an obsession.

The morning came for us to go to Mexico City. The train left at seven, but unless you reserved parlor-car seats, you had to be in line at the station before dawn to be sure of getting on the train, for the coaches were crowded to capacity. My father did not wish to spend the extra money for parlor-car seats, so he woke me up at four-thirty. It was still dark.

"Hurry up and get dressed," he said through the dark.

At that hour of the morning it is bitter cold in Toluca's high mountain valley. From the well Maximiliano brought us water for washing that was like ice. The cook began to prepare breakfast. We sat down to eat. At the table my father gulped his food quickly, looked across at me, and barked for no reason at all: "Hurry up!"

Suddenly my stomach began to turn over and over. And I could not swallow another mouthful. Waves of heat engulfed me. My eyes burned. My body shook. I wanted more than anything on earth to hit my father, but instead I got up from the table and went back to bed. The bed went round and round and the room turned dark. Anger clotted in every vein, and my tongue tasted like dry blood.

My father stuck his head in the bedroom door and asked me what was the matter.

I said: "Nothing."

He said: "Don't you want to go to Mexico City?"

I said: "No, I don't want to go."

I don't know what else he said, but after a while I heard him telling Maximiliano in Spanish to hurry up with his bags. Then the outside door closed, and he was gone to the train.

The housekeeper came in and asked me what I wanted.

I said: "Nothing."

Maximiliano came back from the station and sat down silently on the tile floor just inside my door, his blanket about him. At noon the cook brought me a big bowl of warm soup, but I couldn't drink it. My stomach kept turning round and round inside me. And when I thought of my father, I got sicker and sicker. I hated my father.

They sent for the doctor. He came and gave me a prescription. The housekeeper took it herself and had it filled, not trusting the *mozo*. But when my father came back after four days in the city,

I still hadn't eaten anything. I had a high fever. He sent for the doctor again, and the doctor said I'd better go to the hospital.

This time my father engaged seats in the parlor car and took me to the American Hospital in Mexico City. There, after numberless examinations, they decided I had better remain several weeks, since they thought I had a stomach infection.

The three middle-aged Mexican sisters came to see me and brought a gift of guava jelly. They asked what on earth could have happened to make me so ill. I must have had a great shock, they said, because my eyes were a deep yellow. But I never told them or the doctors that I was sick because I hated my father.

For two or three weeks I got pushed around in a wheel chair in the charming gardens of the American Hospital. When I learned that it was costing my father twenty dollars a day to keep me there, I made no effort to get better. It pleased me immensely to have him spending twenty dollars a day. In September, I went back to Cleveland without having seen Xochimilco, or a bullfight.

BACK HOME

On the way back to Cleveland an amusing thing happened. During the trip to the border, several American whites on the train mistook me for a Mexican, and some of them even spoke to me in Spanish, since I am of a copper-brown complexion, with black hair that can be made quite slick and shiny if it has enough pomade on it in the Mexican fashion. But I made no pretense of passing for a Mexican, or anything else, since there was no need for it—except in changing trains at San Antonio in Texas, where colored people had to use Jim Crow waiting rooms, and could not purchase a Pullman berth. There, I simply went in the main waiting room, as any Mexican would do, and made my sleeping-car reservations in Spanish.

But that evening, crossing Texas, I was sitting alone at a small table in the diner, when a white man came in and took the seat just across the table from mine. Shortly, I noticed him staring at me intently, as if trying to puzzle out something. He stared at me a long time. Then, suddenly, with a loud cry, the white man jumped up and shouted: "You're a nigger, ain't you?" And rushed out of the car as if pursued by a plague.

I grinned. I had heard before that white Southerners never sat down to table with a Negro, but I didn't know until then that we frightened them that badly.

Something rather less amusing happened at St. Louis. The train pulled into the station on a blazing-hot September afternoon, after a sticky, dusty trip, for there were no air-cooled coaches in those days. I had a short wait between trains. In the center of the station platform there was a news stand and soda fountain where cool drinks were being served. I went up to the counter and asked for an ice cream soda.

The clerk said: "Are you a Mexican or a Negro?"

I said: "Why?"

"Because if you're a Mexican, I'll serve you," he said. "If you're colored, I won't."

"I'm colored," I replied. The clerk turned to wait on some one else. I knew I was home in the U.S.A.

I'VE KNOWN RIVERS

That November the First World War ended. In Cleveland, everybody poured into the streets to celebrate the Armistice. Negroes, too, although Negroes were increasingly beginning to wonder where, for them, was that democracy they had fought to preserve. In Cleveland, a liberal city, the color line began to be drawn tighter and tighter. Theaters and restaurants in the downtown area began to refuse to accommodate colored people. Landlords doubled and tripled the rents at the approach of a dark tenant. And when the white soldiers came back from the war, Negroes were often discharged from their jobs and white men hired in their places.

The end of the war! But many of the students at Central kept talking, not about the end of the war, but about Russia, where Lenin had taken power in the name of the workers, who made everything, and who would now own everything they made. "No more pogroms," the Jews said, "no more race hatred, no more landlords." John Reed's *Ten Days That Shook the World* shook Central High School, too.

The daily papers pictured the Bolsheviki as the greatest devils on earth, but I didn't see how they could be that bad if they had done away with race hatred and landlords—two evils that I knew well at first hand.

My father raised my allowance that year, so I was able to help my mother with the expenses of our household. It was a pleasant

year for me, for I was a senior. I was elected Class Poet and Editor
of our Year Book. As an officer in the drill corps, I wore a khaki
uniform and leather puttees, and gave orders. I went calling on a
little brownskin girl, who was as old as I was—seventeen—but only
in junior high school, because she had just come up from the poor
schools of the South. I met her at a dance at the Longwood Gym.
She had big eyes and skin like rich chocolate. Sometimes she wore
a red dress that was very becoming to her, so I wrote a poem about
her that declared:

> *When Susanna Jones wears red*
> *Her face is like an ancient cameo*
> *Turned brown by the ages.*
>
> *Come with a blast of trumpets,*
> *Jesus!*
>
> *When Susanna Jones wears red*
> *A queen from some time-dead Egyptian night*
> *Walks once again.*
>
> *Blow trumpets, Jesus!*
> *And the beauty of Susanna Jones in red*
> *Burns in my heart a love-fire sharp like pain.*
>
> *Sweet silver trumpets,*
> *Jesus!*

I had a whole notebook full of poems by now, and another one
full of verses and jingles. I always tried to keep verses and poems
apart, although I saw no harm in writing verses if you felt like it,
and poetry if you could.

June came. And graduation. Like most graduations, it made you
feel both sorry and glad: sorry to be leaving and glad to be going.
Some students were planning to enter college, but not many, be-
cause there was no money for college in most of Central's families.

My father had written me to come to Mexico again to discuss
with him my future plans. He hinted that he would send me to
college if I intended to go, and he thought I had better go.

I didn't want to return to Mexico, but I had a feeling I'd never
get any further education if I didn't, since my mother wanted me
to go to work and be, as she put it, "of some use to her." She
demanded to know how I would look going off to college and she
there working like a dog!

I said I thought I could be of more help to her once I got an education than I could if I went to work fresh out of high school, because nobody could do much on the salary of a porter or a bus boy. And such jobs offered no advancement for a Negro.

But about my going to join my father, my mother acted much as she had done the year before. I guess it is the old story of divorced parents who don't like each other, and take their grievances out on the offspring. I got the feeling then that I'd like to get away from home altogether, both homes, and that maybe if I went to Mexico one more time, I could go to college somewhere in some new place, and be on my own.

So I went back to Toluca.

My mother let me go to the station alone, and I felt pretty bad when I got on the train. I felt bad for the next three or four years, to tell the truth, and those were the years when I wrote most of my poetry. (For my best poems were all written when I felt the worst. When I was happy, I didn't write anything.)

The one of my poems that has perhaps been most often reprinted in anthologies, was written on the train during this trip to Mexico when I was feeling very bad. It's called "The Negro Speaks of Rivers" and was written just outside St. Louis, as the train rolled toward Texas.

It came about in this way. All day on the train I had been thinking about my father and his strange dislike of his own people. I didn't understand it, because I was a Negro, and I liked Negroes very much. One of the happiest jobs I had ever had was during my freshman year in high school, when I worked behind the soda fountain for a Mrs. Kitzmiller, who ran a refreshment parlor on Central Avenue in the heart of the colored neighborhood. People just up from the South used to come in for ice cream and sodas and watermelon. And I never tired of hearing them talk, listening to the thunderclaps of their laughter, to their troubles, to their discussions of the war and the men who had gone to Europe from the Jim Crow South, their complaints over the high rent and the long overtime hours that brought what seemed like big checks, until the weekly bills were paid. They seemed to me like the gayest and the bravest people possible—these Negroes from the Southern ghettos— facing tremendous odds, working and laughing and trying to get somewhere in the world.

I had been in to dinner early that afternoon on the train. Now it was just sunset, and we crossed the Mississippi, slowly, over a long bridge. I looked out the window of the Pullman at the great muddy river flowing down toward the heart of the South, and I began to think what that river, the old Mississippi, had meant to Negroes in the past—how to be sold down the river was the worst fate that could overtake a slave in times of bondage. Then I remembered reading how Abraham Lincoln had made a trip down the Mississippi on a raft to New Orleans, and how he had seen slavery at its worst, and had decided within himself that it should be removed from American life. Then I began to think about other rivers in our past—the Congo, and the Niger, and the Nile in Africa—and the thought came to me: "I've known rivers," and I put it down on the back of an envelope I had in my pocket, and within the space of ten or fifteen minutes, as the train gathered speed in the dusk, I had written this poem, which I called "The Negro Speaks of Rivers":

I've known rivers:
I've known rivers ancient as the world and older than the flow of
    human blood in human veins.

My soul has grown deep like the rivers.

I bathed in the Euphrates when dawns were young.
I built my hut near the Congo and it lulled me to sleep.
I looked upon the Nile and raised the pyramids above it.
I heard the singing of the Mississippi when Abe Lincoln went down
    to New Orleans, and I've seen its muddy bosom turn all golden
    in the sunset.
I've known rivers:
Ancient, dusky rivers.

My soul has grown deep like the rivers.

No doubt I changed a few words the next day, or maybe crossed out a line or two. But there are seldom many changes in my poems, once they're down. Generally, the first two or three lines come to me from something I'm thinking about, or looking at, or doing, and the rest of the poem (if there is to be a poem) flows from those first few lines, usually right away. If there is a chance to put the poem down then, I write it down. If not, I try to remember it until I get to a pencil and paper; for poems are like rainbows: they escape you quickly.

MEXICO AGAIN

That summer in Mexico, I wrote a great many poems, because I was very unhappy, in spite of the fact that it was a much more varied summer than the previous one. Even my father seemed kinder and less difficult. He had a new housekeeper now, a German woman named Frau Schultz, whom he later married. She helped to make the house much pleasanter.

Frau Schultz had just come from Germany, where she said people were starving. She was a widow with several children, the youngest of whom, Lottie, a child of ten, she had brought with her. She came with a big boatload of other Germans voyaging to the new world, to Cuba, Mexico, and South America, to start all over again. Her husband had been killed in the war, and when you mentioned war to her, she would say: *"Mensch!"* and spit.

She was a portly, kindly woman, with dull blue eyes and chestnut hair. Her little girl was very lively and very German-looking. What German I know I learned from Frau Schultz and Lottie, for they could speak neither English nor Spanish then, and I had to learn German to say anything at all to them. It was because my father had studied German for years, and was a great admirer of the German people, that he had employed her as his housekeeper. And Frau Schultz was happy to have work, because she had arrived in Mexico with only a few pesos, and had had to depend on the kindness of fellow-countrymen to whom she had letters.

Since Frau Schultz did not know a word of Spanish in which to give orders, she was unable to keep our Mexican cook, so she did all the cooking herself. And good it was, too, for a while—until my father felt that the butcher's bills were too high. Then for weeks at a time, we would revert to Mexican beans, except on days when he was at the ranch. Then Frau Schultz and I would often kill one of his prize American hens and she would stew the hen with dumplings and we would have a grand meal. Or else I would take the responsibility for running the grocery bills up, and would go to the store with Maximiliano and a gunny sack, and come back with all sorts of cheeses and sausages and good imported German things that Frau Schultz liked, and several cans of sardines, salmon, fruit, and American corn.

Once I came back with a delicious kind of white meat in a can with a Spanish label that neither of us could read. The meat was so good that I went back to the store and bought three or four cans more, and Frau Schultz made sandwiches of it at coffee time in the afternoons. Finally, one day it occurred to me to look up the delicacy's name in my Spanish-English dictionary. It turned out to be eel. I didn't mind, since I have no prejudice against eels. But when, in the English-German dictionary, Frau Schultz saw the frightful word in her own tongue, she almost died, declaring she'd as soon have eaten a snake! But by then we had both consumed several pounds of eel.

My father was away at the ranch a great deal of the summer. But when he was at home in town, he spoke German all the time at the table. And Spanish all the time elsewhere. So I began to learn Spanish fairly well, at least well enough to get about and meet people, and to read the novels of Blasco Ibáñez, whose *Cuentos Valencianos* I liked very much. And the terrific realism of *Caños y Barro* still sticks in my head.

I didn't do much that summer but read books, ride my horse, Tito, eat Frau Schultz's apple cake, feel lonesome, and write poems when I felt most lonesome. I began to wish for some Negro friends to pal around with. With my bad Spanish, I was still shy about making friends with the Mexicans. And I was worried about the days to come. My father hadn't yet got around to having a talk with me about college, and it was now already late July.

That summer my father was doubly busy, because the electric light company was in process of liquidation. Its main plant in the mountains had been destroyed by the revolutionists, who hated gringoes for the airs they put on, and the low wages they paid. The revolutionists had also taken off all the cattle and sheep on my father's ranch, and left it bare. The road to the ranch was infested with bandits, and since they had twice robbed my father, stopping him on the road and taking everything, from his boots to his horse, and leaving him standing in a pine forest in nothing but his underwear—since then my father never went to the ranch alone, but always with a party of other ranchers, or else German mining investors who were then making frequent trips to the silver mines in that region.

My father's ranch was most valuable for timber, he said. Now the mines were flooded, but should they ever open again, he would make thousands of dollars from his timber lands, since the mines would all have to be reshafted, and new barracks and houses built for the men.

When my father felt that I could ride rapidly enough and shoot straight enough to take care of myself in case of danger, he let me go with him to the ranch one weekend, in company with a party of German mine owners and Mexican rancheros. We started out at dawn. It was a good day's ride over rocky roads and mountain trails, through majestic scenery. The way was temporarily safe, since the Federal troops had recently been over the road and, appropriately enough, on a high pass called *Las Cruces* (the Crosses) they had hanged three bandits, and left them hanging there as examples to others. They were still there the day we passed, three poor Indian bandits with bare feet, strung from scrubby pine trees near the road, their thin dirty-white trousers flapping in the cold mountain wind. One had long black hair that lashed across his face. Their bodies swayed slowly in the high wind at the top of the pass, like puppets stiff against the sky.

That afternoon we passed through a large ruined village, destroyed, my father said, several years before by the Zapatistas. Now wild grass grew between the cobblestones of the main street, and nobody lived in the tumbled-down houses. The church stood roofless, with its tall bell-tower of carved stone lording it above the desolation of what had once been a town.

"The Zapatistas were bandits," my father said. "They loved to destroy property."

"I read somewhere that Zapata was a poor shoemaker, who wanted to get the land back for the peons," I answered.

"Lies!" my father cried. "Zapata, Villa, all of 'em dirty bandits!"

We got to the ranch at sundown. We had been delayed on the road because Tito, the horse I was riding, became enamoured of a mare belonging to the Germans. In a sudden burst of affection, Tito made a flying leap for the mare. The mare bolted, broke her bridle and threw her German rider to the ground, then dashed off down the road. It was all I could do to hold Tito, who acted like a bronco in a rodeo, as all the horses began to wheel and whinny and neigh.

Several of the men galloped off in pursuit of the mare. The rest of us went to the aid of the deposed German, who had landed in a rocky gully, six feet below the road. He was somewhat shaken up, but when he got himself together, he seemed none the worse for his fall, except a few stone bruises, and a tear in his trousers.

We were in a wild and lonesome-looking country as the shadows grew long in the late afternoon, and the mountains hid the sun. The party began to break up, some going to the abandoned mines, others to a ranch farther on. Those who were returning to Toluca shortly agreed to meet at dawn two days later to make the trip together.

My father's ranch seemed to take in a whole mountain side and on over the rim beyond that. Little fires were glowing on his mountain, as we rode upward in the dusk toward a cluster of peasant huts, half-hidden in the foliage at the far edge of a broad, slanting field. It was cold and the peons had lighted bonfires outside their doors, and were sitting about the fires, wrapped in blankets. A withered old woman fixed us a meal of tortillas and red beans that were very good. Then we slept on the floor inside one of the mud huts.

The next day I went with my father to a flooded mine shaft nearby. The German, who had fallen off the horse the day before, was there. He and my father did a great deal of talking and figuring, while Tito and the mare champed and neighed and rolled their eyes at each other from the respective trees where they were tied, yards apart.

On the way back to the ranch, my father suddenly announced that he had made up his mind to have me study mining engineering.

"In another five or six years," he said, "these mines will be open and there will be plenty of work for you here, near the ranch."

"But I can't be a mining engineer, I'm no good at mathematics," I said, as we walked the horses.

"You can learn anything you put your mind to," my father said. "And engineering is something that will make you some money. What do you want to do, live like a nigger all your life? Look at your mother, waiting table in a restaurant! Don't you want to get anywhere?"

"Sure," I said. "But I don't want to be a mining engineer."

"What do you want to be?"

"I don't know. But I think a writer."

"A writer?" my father said. "A writer? Do they make any money?"

"Some of them do, I guess."

"I never heard of a colored one that did," said my father.

"Alexandre Dumas," I answered.

"Yes, but he was in Paris, where they don't care about color. That's what I want you to do, Langston. Learn something you can make a living from anywhere in the world, in Europe or South America, and don't stay in the States, where you have to live like a nigger with niggers."

"But I like Negroes," I said. "We have plenty of fun."

"Fun!" my father shouted. "How can you have fun with the color line staring you in the face? I never could."

We were riding in a bowl of pine trees, with the distant rim of the mountains all around and the sky very blue. For once, my father did not seem to be in a hurry. He let his horse mosey along, biting at the wayside grass. As we rode, my father outlined a plan he had made up in his mind for me, a plan that I had never dreamed of before. He wanted me to go to Switzerland to college, perhaps to Basle, or one of the cantons where one could learn three languages at once, French, German, and Italian, directly from the people.

Then he wanted me to go to a German engineering school. Then come back to live in Mexico.

The thought of trigonometry, physics, and chemistry in a *foreign* language was more than I could bear. In English, they were difficult enough. But as a compromise to Switzerland and Germany, I suggested Columbia in New York—mainly because I wanted to see Harlem.

My father wouldn't hear of it. But the more I thought of it, the better I liked the idea myself. I had an overwhelming desire to see Harlem. More than Paris, or the Shakespeare country, or Berlin, or the Alps, I wanted to see Harlem, the greatest Negro city in the world. *Shuffle Along* had just burst into being, and I wanted to hear Florence Mills sing. So I told my father I'd rather go to Columbia than to Switzerland.

My father shut up. I shut up. Our horses went on down the mountain into the blue shadows. We didn't talk much for days. At home he gave me several involved problems in bookkeeping to do and told me to stop spending so much time with the Mexicans, promenading in the Portales in the evening. But his advice went in one ear and out the other. I liked the Portales, but I didn't like bookkeeping.

PROMENADE

In Toluca, the evening promenade was an established institution for the young people of the town and, on band concert nights, for the older people, too. Toluca's business district consisted largely of three sides of a square, with a cloistered walk running around the three sides. An enormous and very old church formed the fourth side of the square. The covered walkway had tall arched portals open to the cobblestoned street, hence its name, *Los Portales*.

The leading shops were along the Portales. The post office was there as well. And the biggest hotel. And a very appetizing chocolate and sweet shop, displaying enormous layer cakes, dripping with syrupy icings and candied fruits. Once a week, the town band gave a concert in the Portales. But every evening, concert or no concert, the young people of the town, between six and seven o'clock, took their evening stroll there.

I had become acquainted with Tomas, son of a dry goods merchant who had business dealings with my father, and Tomas took me to walk with the other young men of the town in the

Portales, at the hour when all the girls were out walking, too. But not walking with young men. Oh, no! Not at all. That was unheard of in Toluca. The girls of the better Mexican families merely strolled slowly up and down with their mothers or married sisters, or old aunts, or the family servants, but never unchaperoned or alone.

The boys promenaded in groups of three or four, usually, slowing down when you passed a particular girl you wanted to make an impression on. The girls would always pretend not to notice any of the boys, turning their heads away and giggling and looking in the shop windows. It was not considered polite for a nice girl really to notice boys, although it was all right for the boys to turn and stare at the girls as they went by. So the boys would pause and look and then walk on, turning at the end of the walk to retrace their steps until they had covered the three-sided promenade of the Portales perhaps fifteen or twenty times an evening. Then suddenly, it would be supper time, and the sidewalks would be deserted. The shops would begin to pull down their zinc shutters, and everybody would go home through the cool mountain darkness to a hot *merienda* of steaming chocolate, tamales, goat's cheese, and buns. And maybe some of the sticky and very sweet cake you had seen in the shop window on the Portales.

In Toluca, if a boy fell in love with a girl, he could not visit the young lady in her home until he had become engaged to her. He could only go to call on her outside the iron grilles of her front window, for all the houses in Toluca had iron grilles at the windows to keep lovers and bandits out. Within the living room, back in the shadows somewhere, the chaperon sat, and the lovers would have to speak very low indeed for that attentive female not to hear every word. The boy could hold the girl's hand, and maybe kiss her finger tips, but not very often would he be tall enough to steal a kiss from her lips, for most of the windows had a fairly high sill. And even if the girl sat on the floor, it is not easy to achieve a real kiss through grilled bars and with a vigilant chaperon in the offing.

Good girls in Toluca, as is the custom in very Catholic and very Latin countries, were kept sheltered indeed, both before and after marriage. They did not go into the street alone. They did not come near a man unchaperoned. Girls who worked, servants, typists, and waitresses, and others who ran the streets free, were considered fair game for any man who could make them. But good girls—between them and the world stood the tall iron bars of *la reja,* those formidable grilled windows of the Latin countries. Sometimes groups of boys in love got together with guitars and went from house to house serenading their sweethearts. And lots of boys wrote poems to their girls and handed the poems, in carefully folded little notes, through the grilles for the beloved to read at night in her bed.

But when the mother, or the old aunt, or the family servant decided it was time to close the shutters of *la reja,* the suitor would move on up the street in the dusk, for the shutters were usually closed early. Perhaps he would go home, or perhaps he would play a game of *carambola* in the town's one billiard hall. Or perhaps, if he could afford it, he would go to Natcha's house. There were in Toluca, two houses of love—one for gentlemen and army officers, the other for laborers and common soldiers. Natcha's house was for gentlemen and officers.

MEANS OF ESCAPE

September approached and still I had made no headway with my father about going to college. He said Europe. I said New York. He said he wouldn't spend a penny to educate me in the United States. I asked him how long I had to stay in Mexico. He said until I decided to act wisely. Not caring what that meant, I made up my mind to see about getting away myself.

I had no money, but Tomas' father had asked me if I would teach his son English, so I accepted, receiving a modest fee. Probably bcause Tomas proved an apt pupil (and we pal'd around together quite a little, too), others heard of his rapid progress in speaking *at* English, and I soon found myself with more applicants for classes than I could accept. I raised my fee. When the schools opened, I was offered two positions as an English instructor—one in Señor Luis Tovar's business college, another in Señorita Padilla's private finishing school for girls. I was able to take them both, since Señorita Padilla's classes were in the mornings and Señor Tovar's in the afternoon and early evening.

I used the Berlitz method, all instruction entirely in English, and I found that it worked very well. My students really did learn something, and we had lots of fun together, besides. Very shortly, the mayor of the town sent for me and asked if I would give private lessons to his son and daughter at home.

The daughter was about sixteen and very beautiful, but the son was as bad a fifteen-year-old youngster as ever decided *not* to learn a word of anything. Result, neither girl nor boy got much beyond the words *door* and *chair* that winter, and I don't think they cared. They were rather spoiled, cream-colored children, who played tennis with a doctor's family, browner and more Indian-looking—one of the few Indian families considered "aristocracy" in Toluca, where Spanish blood still prevailed in the best circles and the exaltation of things Indian had not yet triumphed—for Diego Rivera was still in Paris.

As a teacher of English to the "best" families, I met a great many interesting people and my funds for escape grew apace. For the first time in my life, I had my own money to spend in decent amounts, to send my mother, and to save. All that winter I did not ask my father for a penny. And I knew by summer I would have enough to go to New York, so I began to plan my trip long before the winter was over. I dreamt about Harlem.

CARD FROM CUERNAVACA

Six months anywhere is enough to begin to complicate life. By that time, if you stay in one place, you are bound to know people too well for things to be any longer simple. Well, that winter one of my pupils fell in love with me. She was a woman in her thirties, to whom I had been giving lessons two afternoons a week. She lived a secluded life with her old aunt, no doubt on a small income. And she had never been married because, since childhood, she had suffered with a heart ailment. She was a very delicate little woman, ivory-tan in color, with a great mass of heavy black hair and very bright but sad eyes. I always thought perhaps she was something like Emily Dickinson, shut away and strange, eager and lonesome, as Emily must have been.

But I had no way of knowing she was going to fall in love with me. She read and spoke a little English, but she wanted to be able to read big novels like Scott's and Dicken's. Yet she didn't pay much attention to her lessons. When I read aloud, she would look at me, until I looked at her. Then her eyes would fall. After several weeks of classes, shyly, in a funny little sentence of awkward English, she finally made me realize she must be in love.

She began to say things like: "Dear Mister, I cannot wait you to come back so long off Friday."

"But you have to learn your verbs," I'd say. "And it will take until Friday."

"The verbs is not much difficult. It's you I am think about, Mister."

She seemed almost elderly to me then, at eighteen. I was confused and didn't know what to say. After a few such sentences in English, she'd blush deeply and take refuge in Spanish. And all I could think of to tell her was that she mustn't fall in love with me, because I was going to New York as soon as I had saved the fare.

The little lady's eyes widened and her face went white when I said it. I thought for a moment she was surely going to faint. And one day she did faint, but it was not, I suppose, for love. It was while we were going over conditionals, sentences like, "I would write if I could," when she simply keeled over in her chair.

Her old aunt and the servants had told me that that might happen almost any time. Strains and excitement upset her. So after that I was never sure as to the safe thing to do when I found her looking at me. She might faint if I held her hand—or she might faint if I didn't.

But all things end in time. When I came to her house one afternoon at the class hour, I was very sorry (and ashamed at my feeling of relief) to learn that she was quite ill with a heavy cold. She remained in bed several days. I took her flowers and sat with her, surrounded by little bottles and boxes of pills. When she was better, her aunt carried her away to a lower and warmer climate to convalesce. I never saw her any more. But she wrote me a card once from Cuernavaca, and signed it just, "Maria."

BULLFIGHTS

Almost every week-end that winter, now that I was earning my own money, I went to the bullfights in Mexico City. Rudolfo Gaona was the famous Mexican matador of the day, a stocky Indian of great art and bravery. Sanchez Mejias was there from Spain that season, greatly acclaimed, as well as Juan Silveti, and a younger fighter called Juan Luis de la Rosa, who did not win much favor with the crowd. One afternoon, in the sunset, at the end of a six-bull corrida, (bulls from the Duque de Veragua) I saw de la Rosa trying to kill his final bull amidst a shower of cushions, canes, paper bags, and anything else throwable that an irate crowd could hurl at him. But he stuck it out, and finally the enormous animal slid to his knees, bleeding on the sand. But the matador was soundly hissed as he left the ring.

At the annual festival bullfight for the charities of la Cavadonga, when the belles of Mexico City, in their lace mantillas, drove about the arena in open carriages preceding the fight, and the National

Band played, and the *Presidente de la Republica* was there, and
Sanchez Mejias made the hair stand on your head and cold chills
run down your back with the daring and beauty of his *veronicas,*
after the fight there was a great rush into the ring on the part of
many of the young men in the crowd, to lift the famous fighters on
their shoulders or to carry off a pair of golden banderillas as a souve-
nir, with the warm blood still on them. I dived for the ring, too, the
moment the fight was over. In leaping the *barrera,* I tore my only
good trousers from knee to ankle—but I got my banderillas.

After the fights, I would usually have supper with the three
charming and aging Mexican sisters, the Patiños, friends of my
father's, who lived near the Zocalo, just back of the cathedral, and
who always invited me to vespers. To please them, I would go to
vespers, and I began to love the great, dusky, candle-lighted interiors
of the vast Mexican churches, smoky with incense and filled with
sad virgins and gruesome crucifixes with real thorns on the Christ-
head, and what seemed to be real blood gushing forth from His
side, thick and red as the blood of the bulls I had seen killed in the
afternoon. In the evenings I might go to see Margarita Xirgu, or
Virginia Fabregas in some bad Spanish play, over-acted and sticky
like the cakes in our Toluca sweet shop.

Meanwhile, ambitiously, I began to try to write prose. I tried
to write about a bullfight, but could never capture it on paper. Bull-
fights are very hard things to put down on paper—like trying to
describe the ballet.

Bullfights must be seen in all their strength of vigorous and grace-
ful movement and glitter of sun on sleek hides and silken suits
spangled with gold and silver and on the sharp points of the
banderillas and on the thin blades of the swords. Bullfights must be
heard, the music barbaric and Moorish, the roar of the crowd, the
grunt of the bull, the cry of the gored horse, the trumpets signalling
to kill, the silence when a man is gored. They must be smelt, dust
and tobacco and animals and leather, sweat and blood and the scent
of death. Then the cry of glory when a great kill is made and the
flutter of thousands of handkerchiefs, with roses thrown at the
feet of the triumphant matador, as he is awarded the tail and ears
of the bull. Or the hiss of scorn when the fighter has been cowardly
or awkward.

Then the crowd pouring out into the sunset, and the fighters
covered with sand and spattered with blood, gliding off to their
hotels in swift, high-powered cars; the women on the street selling
lottery tickets; beggars; and men giving out cards to houses of
pleasure; and the police clearing a passage for the big Duesenbergs

of the rich; and the naked bulls hanging beneath the arena, skinned, ready for the market.

A bullfight is like a very moving play—except that the fight is real, unrehearsed, and no two *corridas* are ever the same. Of course, the bull gets killed. But sometimes, the man dies first. It is not a game or a sport. It's life playing deliberately with death. Except that death is alive, too, taking an active part.

TRAGEDY IN TOLUCA

I could not put the bullfights down, so, wanting to write prose, I wrote instead an article about Toluca, and another about the Virgin of Guadalupe, and a little play for children called, *The Gold Piece.* I sent them to the *Brownie's Book,* a magazine for Negro children, just begun in New York by Dr. DuBois and the *Crisis* staff. These pieces of mine were accepted, and encouraging letters came back from Jessie Fauset, who was managing editor there. So I sent her my poem written on the train, "The Negro Speaks of Rivers." And in June, 1921, it appeared in the *Crisis,* the first of my poems to be published outside Central High School.

My father reacted to my published work with two questions: "How long did it take you to write that?" And next: "Did they pay you anything?"

Neither the *Crisis* nor the *Brownie's Book* paid anything, but I was delighted to be published. For the next few years my poems appeared often (and solely) in the *Crisis.* And to that magazine, certainly, I owe my literary beginnings—insofar as publication is concerned.

Finally my father gave in and said, yes, he would send me to Columbia. So I wrote for registration and dormitory space. I was admitted, and planned to leave for New York late in the summer. But that spring the block which our house occupied, facing the little park, was the scene of several weird and depressing happenings. I began to wish I had gone away sooner.

It began with my seeing an Indian at our corner get both his legs cut off by the bouncing little street car (on a Ford chassis) that wound from the center of the town to the station. Shortly after that, one early morning, I opened the big doors in the wall of the corral to let my father through, bound for the ranch. His horse dashed out, but suddenly balked for no reason in the middle of the road and threw him head-over-heels in the dust. My father got up, rubbed his head, grabbed the horse, and went on to the ranch. But Maximiliano declared the horse had seen the poor Indian's ghost walking through our park in the sunrise, with no legs.

A week or two later, one Sunday morning, leaving the house early to catch the seven o'clock train for Mexico City, I noticed a small crowd of Indians in their serapes, standing around the shallow basin of the fountain in the center of the park. As I passed, I looked down and there in scarcely three feet of water, lay the body of a young woman, curled about the base of the fountain. She was nicely dressed, and obviously of a decent family. The police found a suicide note. She was one of the good girls whose grilled *rejas* had not protected her from the step that in Mexico brings ruin and disgrace. But *what* will power it must have taken—to drown one's self in a shallow fountain of water hardly as deep as your knees!

In Mexico City, I told the three kind maiden ladies of the strange happenings on our plaza in Toluca, and they looked distressed and worried. They said they would pray that nothing happened to my father or me. And they begged me to go to mass with them. Perhaps their prayers worked. For, although tragedy soon descended in a most unexpected manner upon our house itself, neither my father nor I was home when that strange explosion of passion and of violence took place.

Our German housekeeper, Frau Schultz, had an old friend from Berlin in Mexico City, whose husband was not well and whose income was therefore reduced. This friend had several children, the oldest, a daughter of seventeen or eighteen in need of work.

That winter in Toluca, the wife of the German brewery-master died, and so he began looking about for a housekeeper. The brewery-master was sixty-five years old, and merely wanted someone to manage his Mexican servants and see that he got something to eat, German-style, once in a while. Frau Schultz immediately thought of her friend's daughter for the job. Although a young girl, she was nevertheless sober and industrious in her habits, and a very good cook, to boot.

She sent for the girl. Her name was Gerta Kraus. She was a very plain girl, awkward, shy and silent, with stringy ashen hair and a long face. She spoke no Spanish beyond *Buenos Dias,* so that was all we ever said to each other as long as I knew her. The old German gave her the job as his housekeeper. And as the winter went on, Frau Schultz reported that the girl was doing very well, that she kept the brewery-master's home spotless, and sent her wages to her parents in Mexico City.

Perhaps twice a week, Gerta would come down to our house and spend a few hours in the afternoon with Frau Schultz. Occasionally, I would come home from my various English classes and find them chattering away in German at a great rate, over a big pot of coffee and a platter of cakes. But I seldom joined them. My pupils' parents gave me chocolate, or sweetmeats, or something to eat or drink almost every time I taught a class, so I was seldom hungry until dinner time.

In the spring, Frau Kraus came up from Mexico City to spend a week with Frau Schultz and see her daughter, whom she hadn't seen all winter. That week the outdoor brick oven in our corral was always full of long loaves of bread and yellow cakes. All the German friends of Frau Schultz in Toluca came to call on Frau Kraus from Mexico City—that is all the Germans in *their* circle—for the wealthier Germans, like the brewery-master, did not move in such poor society.

My father had gone to the ranch, so the women had the house to themselves. Because I found Frau Schultz very kind and amiable, I was glad she was having a holiday week with her friends. Every day, Gerta came down to our house to be with her mother, and things were very lively and the patio was filled with feminine voices speaking German. Most of the time, I kept out of the way, since we couldn't understand one another, the Germans and I.

Then Friday came. The week was almost over and Frau Kraus would return to Mexico City on Sunday. But on Friday the terrible thing happened. Fortunately, there were no guests in the house that afternoon. Only Frau Schultz and her little girl, Lotte, Frau Kraus and her daughter, Gerta. It was a chilly, dismal afternoon, so they were all seated at the table in the dining room just off the warm kitchen. The coffee was hot, and the apple-cakes almost like the cakes at home in Germany, where the ovens were not built of adobe brick in dusty corrals. They were having a good time, the two women talking of days before the war in their suburb of Berlin, and of their children, and how ten-year-old Lotte was learning Spanish and becoming Catholic already in that Catholic school, and of how well Gerta had done with her job under the tall, cranky old brewery-master.

Just then someone knocked commandingly at the street entrance. Ten-year-old Lotte went down the corridor and across the patio to answer the door. There stood the brewery-master, tall with iron-white hair and a big white mustache. He did not say a word to Lotte. He came in and strode slowly along the corridor that skirted the patio, looking into each room as he passed. He came to the dining-room, which was at the end of the corridor. Hearing voices, he pushed open the door and walked in.

No one had time to say a word, to rise to greet him, or to offer him a chair. For the brewery-master took a pistol from his pocket and, without warning, began to fire on the women. First he fired on Gerta point-blank, sending a bullet through her head, another through her jaw, another through her shoulder, before she slumped unconscious to the floor beneath the table. In panic, the two women tried to run, but the old man, blocking the door, fired again, striking Frau Schultz in the right arm and breaking it. Then he went all through the patio looking for me, looking, looking, out into the corral and through the stables.

Lotte, wild-eyed, reached the street and called the neighbors. Frau Krau lay in a dead faint in the kitchen. Frau Schultz crouched, stunned, in a corner against the wall, afraid to move. A crowd of Indians assembled, but were wary of entering the house.

Finally the old German walked past the men on the sidewalk, with his pistol still in hand, and no one stopped him. He went directly to the police station and gave himself up. He had two bullets left in his gun, and he told the police he had intended them for me. He said he thought Gerta had been coming to our house to be with me. He said he was in love with Gerta and he wanted to kill her and to kill me.

When I got home a half-hour after the shooting, the ambulance had just taken every one to the hospital. The police would not let me in until they had completed their inspection. When I finally did get into the house, I found the dining room floor a pool of blood, a chair splintered by a bullet, and the tiles of the corridor spotted with red.

Since my father was at the ranch, I went in search of a German friend of his, a buyer of mines, who saw to it that proper hospitalization was provided for the women. Then we went to visit the jail. The old brewery-master sat in his cell, not saying a word, except that he was glad he had killed the girl. He was glad, he mumbled, glad!

But strangely enough, Gerta did not die! She was unconscious for six weeks, and remained in the hospital almost a year—but she didn't die. She finally got well again, with the marks of three bullets on her face and body. The court gave the old man twenty years in prison.

Had I arrived at home that afternoon a half-hour earlier, I probably would not be here today.

DEPARTURE

In the late summer I began to make ready to leave for Columbia. In Toluca the schools had vacation at odd times, so most of my English classes continued throughout the summer. I hated to leave them, but I told Señorita Padilla and Professor Tovar that they would have to find someone else.

A short time later, Professor Tovar told me he had learned that a new American couple had come to Toluca, a road engineer and his wife, and that the woman was willing to take over my English classes. I was glad, because the two Mexican teachers of English I had met there had a good knowledge of grammar, but atrocious pronunciation.

While I went for a final trip to the ranch with my father, Professor Tovar and Señorita Padilla called on the American woman and made final arrangements with her to take over the girls' school and business school classes. They set a day for her to come to the business school in the Portales to go over the lessons with me, and to visit the commercial classes.

Professor Tovar had neglected to tell the new teacher that I was an *americano de color*, brown as a Mexican, and nineteen years old. So when she walked into the room with him, she kept looking around for the American teacher. No doubt she thought I was one of the students, chalk in hand, standing at the board. But when she was introduced to me, her mouth fell open, and she said: "Why, Ah-Ah thought you was an American."

I said: "I am American!"

She said: "Oh, Ah mean a white American!" Her voice had a southern drawl.

I grinned.

She was a poor-looking lady of the stringy type, who probably had never been away from her home town before. I asked her what part of the States she came from. She said Arkansas—which better explained her immediate interest in color. The next two days, as she sat beside me at the teacher's desk, and I went over with her the different types of courses the students had—the conversation for the girls from Señorita Padilla's school, and the business English for the pupils of the academy—she kept looking at me out of the corners of her eyes as if she thought maybe I might bite her.

At the end of the first day, she said: "Ah never come across an

educated Ne-gre before." (Southerners often make that word a
slur between *nigger* and *Negro.*)

I said: "They have a large state college for colored people in
Arkansas, so there must be some educated ones there."

She said: "Ah reckon so, but Ah just never saw one before." And
she continued to gaze at me as her first example of an educated
Negro.

I was a bit loath to leave my students, with whom I had had so
much fun, in charge of a woman from one of our more backward
states, who probably felt about brown Mexicans much as my father
did. But there was no alternative, if they wanted to learn English
at all. Then, too, I thought the young ladies from Señorita Padilla's
academy might as well meet a real *gringo* for once. Feminine gender:
gringa.

WHEN THE NEGRO WAS IN VOGUE

The 1920's were the years of Manhattan's black Renaissance. It began
with *Shuffle Along, Running Wild,* and the Charleston. Perhaps some
people would say even with *The Emperor Jones,* Charles Gilpin,
and the tom-toms at the Provincetown. But certainly it was the
musical revue, *Shuffle Along,* that gave a scintillating send-off to that
Negro vogue in Manhattan, which reached its peak just before the
crash of 1929, the crash that sent Negroes, white folks and all rolling
down the hill toward the Works Progress Administration.

Shuffle Along was a honey of a show. Swift, bright, funny, rollick-
ing, and gay, with a dozen danceable, singable tunes. Besides, look
who were in it: The now famous choir director, Hall Johnson, and
the composer, William Grant Still, were a part of the orchestra.
Eubie Blake and Noble Sissle wrote the music and played and acted
in the show. Miller and Lyles were the comics. Florence Mills sky-
rocketed to fame in the second act. Trixie Smith sang "He May Be
Your Man But He Comes to See Me Sometimes." And Caterina
Jarboro, now a European prima donna, and the internationally
celebrated Josephine Baker were merely in the chorus. Everybody
was in the audience—including me. People came back to see it in-
numerable times. It was always packed.

To see *Shuffle Along* was the main reason I wanted to go to
Columbia. When I saw it, I was thrilled and delighted. From then
on I was in the gallery of the Cort Theatre every time I got a chance.
That year, too, I saw Katharine Cornell in *A Bill of Divorcement,*

Margaret Wycherly in *The Verge,* Maugham's *The Circle* with Mrs. Leslie Carter, and the Theatre Guild production of Kaiser's *From Morn Till Midnight.* But I remember *Shuffle Along* best of all. It gave just the proper push—a pre-Charleston kick—to that Negro vogue of the 20's, that spread to books, African sculpture, music, and dancing.

Put down the 1920's for the rise of Roland Hayes, who packed Carnegie Hall, the rise of Paul Robeson in New York and London, of Florence Mills over two continents, of Rose McClendon in Broadway parts that never measured up to her, the booming voice of Bessie Smith and the low moan of Clara on thousands of records, and the rise of that grand comedienne of song, Ethel Waters, singing: "Charlie's elected now! He's in right for sure!" Put down the 1920's for Louis Armstrong and Gladys Bentley and Josephine Baker.

White people began to come to Harlem in droves. For several years they packed the expensive Cotton Club on Lenox Avenue. But I was never there, because the Cotton Club was a Jim Crow club for gangsters and monied whites. They were not cordial to Negro patronage, unless you were a celebrity like Bojangles. So Harlem Negroes did not like the Cotton Club and never appreciated its Jim Crow policy in the very heart of their dark community. Nor did ordinary Negroes like the growing influx of whites toward Harlem after sundown, flooding the little cabarets and bars where formerly only colored people laughed and sang, and where now the strangers were given the best ringside tables to sit and stare at the Negro customers—like amusing animals in a zoo.

The Negroes said: "We can't go downtown and sit and stare at you in your clubs. You won't even let us in your clubs." But they didn't say it out loud—for Negroes are practically never rude to white people. So thousands of whites came to Harlem night after night, thinking the Negroes loved to have them there, and firmly believing that all Harlemites left their houses at sundown to sing and dance in cabarets, because most of the whites saw nothing but the cabarets, not the houses.

Some of the owners of Harlem clubs, delighted at the flood of white patronage, made the grievous error of barring their own race, after the manner of the famous Cotton Club. But most of these quickly lost business and folded up, because they failed to realize that a large part of the Harlem attraction for downtown New Yorkers lay in simply watching the colored customers amuse themselves. And the smaller clubs, of course, had no big floor shows or a name band like the Cotton Club, where Duke Ellington usually held forth, so, without black patronage, they were not amusing at all.

Some of the small clubs, however, had people like Gladys Bentley, who was something worth discovering in those days, before she got famous, acquired an accompanist, specially written material, and conscious vulgarity. But for two or three amazing years, Miss Bentley sat, and played a big piano all night long, literally all night, without stopping—singing songs like "The St. James Infirmary," from ten in the evening until dawn, with scarcely a break between the notes, sliding from one song to another, with a powerful and continuous underbeat of jungle rhythm. Miss Bentley was an amazing exhibition of musical energy—a large, dark, masculine lady, whose feet pounded the floor while her fingers pounded the keyboard—a perfect piece of African sculpture, animated by her own rhythm.

But when the place where she played became too well known, she began to sing with an accompanist, became a star, moved to a larger place, then downtown, and is now in Hollywood. The old magic of the woman and the piano and the night and the rhythm being one is gone. But everything goes, one way or another. The '20's are gone and lots of fine things in Harlem night life have disappeared like snow in the sun—since it became utterly commercial, planned for the downtown tourist trade, and therefull dull.

The lindy-hoppers at the Savoy even began to practise acrobatic routines, and to do absurd things for the entertainment of the whites, that probably never would have entered their heads to attempt merely for their own effortless amusement. Some of the lindy-hoppers had cards printed with their names on them and became dance professors teaching the tourists. Then Harlem nights became show nights for the Nordics.

Some critics say that that is what happened to certain Negro writers, too—that they ceased to write to amuse themselves and began to write to amuse and entertain white people, and in so doing distorted and over-colored their material, and left out a great many things they thought would offend their American brothers of a lighter complexion. Maybe—since Negroes have writer-racketeers, as has any other race. But I have known almost all of them, and most of the good ones have tried to be honest, write honestly, and express their world as they saw it.

All of us know that the gay and sparkling life of the so-called Negro Renaissance of the '20's was not so gay and sparkling beneath the surface as it looked. Carl Van Vechten, in the character of Byron in *Nigger Heaven,* captured some of the bitterness and frustration of literary Harlem that Wallace Thurman later so effectively poured into his *Infants of the Spring*—the only novel by a Negro about that fantastic period when Harlem was in vogue.

It was a period when, at almost every Harlem uppercrust dance or party, one would be introduced to various distinguished white celebrities there as guests. It was a period when almost any Harlem Negro of any social importance at all would be likely to say casually: "As I was remarking the other day to Heywood—," meaning Heywood Broun. Or: "As I said to George—," referring to George Gershwin. It was a period when local and visiting royalty were not at all uncommon in Harlem. And when the parties of A'Lelia Walker, the Negro heiress, were filled with guests whose names would turn any Nordic social climber green with envy. It was a period when Harold Jackman, a handsome young Harlem school teacher of modest means, calmly announced one day that he was sailing for the Riviera for a fortnight, to attend Princess Murat's yachting party. It was a period when Charleston preachers opened up shouting churches as sideshows for white tourists. It was a period when at least one charming colored chorus girl, amber enough to pass for a Latin American, was living in a pent house, with all her bills paid by a gentleman whose name was banker's magic on Wall Street. It was a period when every season there was at least one hit play on Broadway acted by a Negro cast. And when books by Negro authors were being published with much greater frequency and much more publicity than ever before or since in history. It was a period when white writers wrote about Negroes more successfully (commercially speaking) than Negroes did about themselves. It was the period (God help us! when Ethel Barrymore appeared in blackface in *Scarlet Sister Mary*! It was the period when the Negro was in vogue.

I was there. I had a swell time while it lasted. But I thought it wouldn't last long. (I remember the vogue for things Russian, the season the Chauve-Souris first came to town.) For how could a large and enthusiastic number of people be crazy about Negroes forever? But some Harlemites thought the millennium had come. They thought the race problem had at last been solved through Art plus Gladys Bentley. They were sure the New Negro would lead a new life from then on in green pastures of tolerance created by Countee Cullen, Ethel Waters, Claude McKay, Duke Ellington, Bojangles, and Alain Locke.

I don't know what made any Negroes think that—except that they were mostly intellectuals doing the thinking. The ordinary Negroes hadn't heard of the Negro Renaissance. And if they had, it hadn't raised their wages any. As for all those white folks in the speakeasies and night clubs of Harlem—well, maybe a colored man could find *some* place to have a drink that the tourists hadn't yet discovered.

Then it was that house-rent parties began to flourish—and not always to raise the rent either. But, as often as not to have a get-together of one's own, where you could do the black-bottom with no stranger behind you trying to do it, too. Non-theatrical, non-intellectual Harlem was an unwilling victim of its own vogue. It didn't like to be stared at by white folks. But perhaps the downtowners never knew this—for the cabaret owners, the entertainers, and the speakeasy proprietors treated them fine—as long as they paid.

The Saturday night rent parties that I attended were often more amusing than any night club, in small apartments where God knows who lived—because the guests seldom did—but where the piano would often be augmented by a guitar, or an odd cornet, or somebody with a pair of drums walking in off the street. And where awful bootleg whiskey and good fried fish or steaming chitterling were sold at very low prices. And the dancing and singing and impromptu entertaining went on until dawn came in at the windows.

These parties, often termed whist parties or dances, were usually announced by brightly colored cards stuck in the grille of apartment house elevators. Some of the cards were highly entertaining in themselves:

WE GOT YELLOW GIRLS, WE'VE GOT BLACK AND TAN
WILL YOU HAVE A GOOD TIME? – YEAH MAN!
A SOCIAL WHIST PARTY
—GIVEN BY—
MARY WINSTON
147 WEST 145TH STREET   APT. 5
SATURDAY EVE. MARCH 19TH, 1932
GOOD MUSIC   REFRESHMENTS

H U R R A Y
COME AND SEE WHAT IS IN STORE FOR YOU AT THE
TEA CUP PARTY
GIVEN BY MRS. VANDERBILT SMITH
AT 409 EDGECOMBE AVENUE
NEW YORK CITY
APARTMENT 10-A
ON THURSDAY EVENING, JANUARY 23RD, 1930
AT 8:30 P.M.
ORIENTAL — GYPSY — SOUTHERN MAMMY — STARLIGHT

AND OTHER READERS WILL BE PRESENT

MUSIC AND TALENT — — REFRESHMENTS SERVED

RIBBONS-MAWS AND TROTTERS A SPECIALTY

FALL IN LINE, AND WATCH YOUR STEP, FOR THERE'LL BE

LOTS OF BROWNS WITH PLENTY OF PEP AT

A SOCIAL WHIST PARTY

GIVEN BY

LUCILLE & MINNIE

149 WEST 117TH STREET, N. Y. GR. FLOOR, W,

SATURDAY EVENING, NOV. 2ND 1929

REFRESHMENTS JUST IT   MUSIC WON'T QUIT

IF SWEET MAMMA IS RUNNING WILD, AND YOU ARE LOOKING

FOR A DO-RIGHT CHILD, JUST COME AROUND AND

LINGER AWHILE AT A

SOCIAL WHIST PARTY

GIVEN BY

PINKNEY & EPPS

260 WEST 129TH STREET   APARTMENT 10

SATURDAY EVENING, JUNE 9, 1928

GOOD MUSIC   REFRESHMENTS

RAILROAD MEN'S BALL

AT CANDY'S PLACE

FRIDAY, SATURDAY & SUNDAY,

APRIL 29-30, MAY 1, 1927

BLACK WAX, SAYS CHANGE YOUR MIND AND SAY THEY

DO AND HE WILL GIVE YOU A HEARING, WHILE MEAT

HOUSE SLIM, LAYING IN THE BIN

KILLING ALL GOOD MEN.

L. A. VAUGH, PRESIDENT

OH BOY   OH JOY

THE ELEVEN BROWN SKINS

OF THE

EVENING SHADOW SOCIAL CLUB

ARE GIVING THEIR

SECOND ANNUAL ST. VALENTINE DANCE

SATURDAY EVENING, FEB. 18TH, 1928

AT 129 WEST 136TH STREET, NEW YORK CITY

GOOD MUSIC   REFRESHMENTS SERVED

SUBSCRIPTION   25 CENTS

SOME WEAR PAJAMAS, SOME WEAR PANTS, WHAT DOES IT MATTER

JUST SO YOU CAN DANCE, AT

A SOCIAL WHIST PARTY

GIVEN BY

MR. & MRS. BROWN

AT 258 W. 115TH STREET, APT. 9

SATURDAY EVE., SEPT. 14, 1929

THE MUSIC IS SWEET AND EVERYTHING GOOD TO EAT!

Almost every Saturday night when I was in Harlem I went to a house-rent party. I wrote lots of poems about house-rent parties, and ate thereat many a fried fish and pig's foot—with liquid refreshments on the side. I met ladies' maids and truck drivers, laundry workers and shoe shine boys, seamstresses and porters. I can still hear their laughter in my ears, hear the soft slow music, and feel the floor shaking as the dancers danced.

HARLEM LITERATI

The summer of 1926, I lived in a rooming house on 137th Street, where Wallace Thurman and Harcourt Tynes also lived. Thurman was then managing editor of the *Messenger*, a Negro magazine that had a curious career. It began by being very radical, racial, and socialistic, just after the war. I believe it received a grant from the Garland Fund in its early days. Then it later became a kind of Negro society magazine and a plugger for Negro business, with photographs of prominent colored ladies and their nice homes in it. A. Phillip Randolph, now President of the Brotherhood of Sleeping Car Porters, Chandler Owen, and George S. Schuyler were connected with it. Schuyler's editorials, à la Mencken, were the most interesting things in the magazine, verbal brickbats that said sometimes one thing, sometimes another, but always vigorously. I asked Thurman what kind of magazine the *Messenger* was, and he said it reflected the policy of whoever paid off best at the time.

Anyway, the *Messenger* bought my first short stories. They paid me ten dollars a story. Wallace Thurman write me that they were very bad stories, but better than any others they could find, so he published them.

Thurman had recently come from California to New York. He was a strangely brilliant black boy, who had read everything, and whose critical mind could find something wrong with everything he read. I have no critical mind, so I usually either like a book or don't. But I am not capable of liking a book and then finding a million things wrong with it, too—as Thurman was capable of doing.

Thurman had read so many books because he could read eleven lines at a time. He would get from the library a great pile of volumes that would have taken me a year to read. But he would go through them in less than a week, and be able to discuss each one at great length with anybody. That was why, I suppose, he was later given a job as a reader at Macaulay's—the only Negro reader, so far as I know, to be employed by any of the larger publishing firms.

Later Thurman became a ghost writer for *True Story,* and other publications, writing under all sorts of fantastic names, like Ethel Belle Mandrake or Patrick Casey. He did Irish and Jewish and Catholic "true confessions." He collaborated with William Jordan Rapp on plays and novels. Later he ghosted books. In fact, this quite dark young Negro is said to have written *Men, Women, and Checks.*

Wallace Thurman wanted to be a great writer, but none of his own work ever made him happy. *The Blacker the Berry,* his first book, was an important novel on a subject little dwelt upon in Negro fiction—the plight of the very dark Negro woman, who encounters in some communities a double wall of color prejudice within and without the race. His play, *Harlem,* considerably distorted for box office purposes, was, nevertheless, a compelling study—and the only one in the theater—of the impact of Harlem on a Negro family fresh from the South. And his *Infants of the Spring,* a superb and bitter study of the bohemian fringe of Harlem's literary and artistic life, is a compelling book.

But none of these things pleased Wallace Thurman. He wanted to be a *very* great writer, like Gorki or Thomas Mann, and he felt that he was merely a journalistic writer. His critical mind, comparing his pages to the thousands of other pages he had read, by Proust, Melville, Tolstoy, Galsworthy, Dostoyevski, Henry James, Sainte-Beauve, Taine, Anatole France, found his own pages vastly wanting. So he contented himself by writing a great deal for money, laughing bitterly at his fabulously concocted "true stories," creating two bad motion pictures of the "Adults Only" type for Hollywood, drinking more and more gin, and then threatening to jump out of windows at people's parties and kill himself.

During the summer of 1926, Wallace Thurman, Zora Neale Hurston, Aaron Douglas, John P. Davis, Bruce Nugent, Gwendolyn Bennett, and I decided to publish "a Negro quarterly of the arts" to be called *Fire*—the idea being that it would burn up a lot of the old, dead conventional Negro-white ideas of the past, *épater le bourgeois* into a realization of the existence of the younger Negro writers and artists, and provide us with an outlet for publication not available in the limited pages of the small Negro magazines then existing, the *Crisis, Opportunity,* and the *Messenger*—the first two being house organs of inter-racial organizations, and the latter being God knows what.

Sweltering summer evenings we met to plan *Fire*. Each of the seven of us agreed to give fifty dollars to finance the first issue. Thurman was to edit it, John P. Davis to handle the business end, and Bruce Nugent to take charge of distribution. The rest of us were to serve as an editorial board to collect material, contribute our own work, and act in any useful way that we could. For artists and writers, we got along fine and there were no quarrels. But October came before we were ready to go to press. I had to return to Lincoln, John Davis to Law School at Harvard, Zora Hurston to her studies at Barnard, from whence she went about Harlem with an anthropologist's ruler, measuring heads for Franz Boas.

Only three of the seven had contributed their fifty dollars, but the others faithfully promised to send theirs out of tuition checks, wages, or begging. Thurman went on with the work of preparing the magazine. He got a printer. He planned the layout. It had to be on good paper, he said, worthy of the drawings of Aaron Douglas. It had to have beautiful type, worthy of the first Negro art quarterly. It had to be what we seven young Negroes dreamed our magazine would be—so in the end it cost almost a thousand dollars, and nobody could pay the bills.

I don't know how Thurman persuaded the printer to let us have all the copies to distribute, but he did. I think Alain Locke, among others, signed notes guaranteeing payments. But since Thurman was the only one of the seven of us with a regular job, for the next three or four years his checks were constantly being attached and his income seized to pay for *Fire*. And whenever I sold a poem, mine went there, too—to *Fire*.

None of the older Negro intellectuals would have anything to do with *Fire*. Dr. DuBois in the *Crisis* roasted it. The Negro press called it all sorts of bad names, largely because of a green and purple story by Bruce Nugent, in the Oscar Wilde tradition, which we had included. Rean Graves, the critic for the *Baltimore Afro-American*, began his review by saying: "I have just tossed the first issue of *Fire* into the fire." Commenting upon various of our contributors, he said: "Aaron Douglas who, in spite of himself and the meaningless grotesqueness of his creations, has gained a reputation as an artist, is permitted to spoil three perfectly good pages and a cover with his pen and ink hudge pudge. Countee Cullen has written a beautiful poem in his 'From a Dark Tower,' but tries his best to obscure the thought in superfluous sentences. Langston Hughes displays his usual ability to say nothing in many words."

So *Fire* had plenty of cold water thrown on it by the colored critics. The white critics (except for an excellent editorial in the *Bookman* for November, 1926) scarcely noticed it at all. We had no way of getting it distributed to bookstands or news stands. Bruce Nugent took it around New York on foot and some of the Greenwich Village bookshops put it on display, and sold it for us. But then Bruce, who had no job, would collect the money and, on account of salary, eat it up before he got back to Harlem.

Finally, irony of ironies, several hundred copies of *Fire* were stored in the basement of an apartment where an actual fire occurred and the bulk of the whole issue was burned up. Even after that Thurman had to go on paying the printer.

Now *Fire* is a collector's item, and very difficult to get, being mostly ashes.

That taught me a lesson about little magazines. But since white folks had them, we Negroes thought we could have one, too. But we didn't have the money.

Wallace Thurman laughed a long bitter laugh. He was a strange kind of fellow, who liked to drink gin, but *didn't* like to drink gin; who liked being a Negro, but felt a great handicap; who adored bohemianism, but thought it wrong to be a bohemian. He liked to waste a lot of time, but he always felt guilty wasting time. He loathed crowds, yet he hated to be alone. He almost always felt bad, yet he didn't write poetry.

Once I told him if I could feel as bad as he did *all* the time, I would surely produce wonderful books. But he said you had to know how to *write*, as well as how to feel bad. I said I didn't have to know how to feel bad, because, every so often, the blues just naturally overtook me, like a blind beggar with an old guitar:

> *You don't know,*
> *You don't know my mind—*
> *When you see me laughin',*
> *I'm laughin' to keep from cryin'.*

About the future of Negro literature Thurman was very pessimistic. He thought the Negro vogue had made us all too conscious of ourselves, had flattered and spoiled us, and had provided too many

easy opportunities for some of us to drink gin and more gin, on
which he thought we would always be drunk. With his bitter sense
of humor, he called the Harlem literati, the "niggerati."

Of this "niggerati," Zora Neale Hurston was certainly the most
amusing. Only to reach a wider audience, need she ever write books—
because she is a perfect book of entertainment in herself. In her
youth she was always getting scholarships and things from wealthy
white people, some of whom simply paid her just to sit around and
represent the Negro race for them, she did it in such a racy fashion.
She was full of side-splitting anecdotes, humorous tales, and tragi-
comic stories, remembered out of her life in the South as a daughter
of a traveling minister of God. She could make you laugh one
minute and cry the next. To many of her white friends, no doubt,
she was a perfect "darkie," in the nice meaning they give the term
—that is a naïve, childlike, sweet, humorous, and highly colored
Negro.

But Miss Hurston was clever, too—a student who didn't let college
give her a broad *a* and who had great scorn for all pretensions,
academic or otherwise. That is why she was such a fine folk-lore
collector, able to go among the people and never act as if she had
been to school at all. Almost nobody else could stop the average
Harlemite on Lenox Avenue and measure his head with a strange-
looking, anthropological device and not get bawled out for the at-
tempt, except Zora, who used to stop anyone whose head looked
interesting, and measure it.

When Miss Hurston graduated from Barnard she took an apart-
ment in West 66th Street near the park, in that row of Negro houses
there. She moved in with no furniture at all and no money, but in
a few days friends had given her everything, from decorative silver
birds, perched atop the linen cabinet, down to a footstool. And on
Saturday night, to christen the place, she had a *hand*-chicken dinner,
since she had forgotten to say she needed forks.

She seemed to know almost everybody in New York. She had
been a secretary to Fannie Hurst, and had met dozens of celebrities
whose friendship she retained. Yet she was always having terrific
ups-and-downs about money. She tells this story on herself, about
needing a nickel to go downtown one day and wondering where on
earth she would get it. As she approached the subway, she was
stopped by a blind beggar holding out his cup.

"Please help the blind! Help the blind! A nickel for the blind!"

"I need money worse than you today," said Miss Hurston, taking
five cents out of his cup. "Lend me this! Next time, I'll give it
back." And she went on downtown.

Harlem was like a great magnet for the Negro intellectual, pulling him from everywhere. Or perhaps the magnet was New York—but once in New York, he had to live in Harlem, for rooms were hardly to be found elsewhere unless one could pass for white or Mexican or Eurasian and perhaps live in the Village—which always seemed to me a very arty locale, in spite of the many real artists and writers who lived there. Only a few of the New Negroes lived in the Village, Harlem being their real stamping ground.

The wittiest of these New Negroes of Harlem, whose tongue was flavored with the sharpest and saltiest humor, was Rudolph Fisher, whose stories appeared in the *Atlantic Monthly*. His novel, *Walls of Jericho,* captures but slightly the raciness of his own conversation. He was a young medical doctor and X-ray specialist, who always frightened me a little, because he could think of the most incisively clever things to say—and I could never think of anything to answer. He and Alain Locke together were great for intellectual wise-cracking. The two would fling big and witty words about with such swift and punning innuendo that an ordinary mortal just sat and looked wary for fear of being caught in a net of witticisms beyond his cultural ken. I used to wish I could talk like Rudolph Fisher. Besides being a good writer, he was an excellent singer, and had sung with Paul Robeson during their college days. But I guess Fisher was too brilliant and too talented to stay long on this earth. During the same week, in December, 1934, he and Wallace Thurman both died.

Thurman died of tuberculosis in the charity ward at Bellevue Hospital, having just flown back to New York from Hollywood.

GURDJIEFF IN HARLEM

One of the most talented of the Negro writers, Jean Toomer, went to Paris to become a follower and disciple of Gurdjieff's at Fontainebleau, where Katherine Mansfield died. He returned to Harlem, having achieved awareness, to impart his precepts to the literati. Wallace Thurman and Dorothy Peterson, Aaron Douglas, and Nella Larsen, not to speak of a number of lesser known Harlemites of the literary and social world, became ardent neophytes of the word brought from Fontainebleau by this handsome young olive-skinned bearer of Gurdjieff's message to upper Manhattan.

But the trouble with such a life-pattern in Harlem was that practically everybody had to work all day to make a living, and the cult of Gurdjieff demanded not only study and application, but a large amount of inner observation and silent concentration as well. So while some of Mr. Toomer's best disciples were sitting long hours concentrating, unaware of time, unfortunately they lost their jobs, and could no longer pay the handsome young teacher for his instructions. Others had so little time to concentrate, if they wanted to live and eat, that their advance toward cosmic consciousness was slow and their hope of achieving awareness distant indeed. So Jean Toomer shortly left his Harlem group and went downtown to drop the seeds of Gurdjieff in less dark and poverty-stricken fields.

They liked him downtown because he was better-looking than Krishnamurti, some said. He had an evolved soul, and that soul made him feel that nothing else mattered, not even writing. From downtown New York, Toomer carried Gurdjieff to Chicago's Gold Coast—and the Negroes lost one of the most talented of all their writers—the author of the beautiful book of prose and verse, *Cane.*

The next thing Harlem heard of Jean Toomer was that he had married Margery Latimer, a talented white novelist, and maintained to the newspapers that he was no more colored than white—as certainly his complexion indicated. When the late James Weldon Johnson wrote him for permission to use some of his poems in the *Book of American Negro Poetry,* Mr. Johnson reported that the poet, who, a few years before, was "caroling softly souls of slavery" now refused to permit his poems to appear in an anthology of *Negro* verse —which put all the critics, white and colored, in a great dilemma. How should they class the author of *Cane* in their lists and summaries? With Dubose Heyward and Julia Peterkin? Or with Claude McKay and Countee Cullen? Nobody knew exactly, it being a case of black blood and white blood having met and the individual deciding, after Paris and Gurdjieff, to be merely American.

One can't blame him for that. Certainly nobody in Harlem could afford to pay for Gurdjieff. And very few there have evolved souls.

Now Mr. Toomer is married to a lady of means—his second wife —of New York and Santa Fe, and is never seen on Lenox Avenue any more. Harlem is sorry he stopped writing. He was a fine American writer. But when we get as democratic in America as we pretend we are on days when we wish to shame Hitler, nobody will bother much about anybody else's race anyway. Why should Mr. Toomer live in Harlem if he doesn't care to? Democracy is democracy, isn't it?

PARTIES

In those days of the late 1920's, there were a great many parties, in Harlem and out, to which various members of the New Negro group were invited. These parties, when given by important Harlemites (or Carl Van Vechten) were reported in full in the society pages of the Harlem press, but best in the sparkling Harlemese of Geraldyn Dismond who wrote for the *Interstate Tattler*. On one of Taylor Gordon's fiestas she reports as follows:

> What a crowd! All classes and colors met face to face, ultra aristocrats, Bourgeois, Communists, Park Avenuers galore, bookers, publishers, Broadway celebs, and Harlemites giving each other the once over. The social revolution was on. And yes, Lady Nancy Cunard was there all in black (she would) with 12 of her grand bracelets. . . . And was the entertainment on the up and up! Into swell dance music was injected African drums that played havoc with blood pressure. Jimmy Daniels sang his gigolo hits. Gus Simons, the Harlem crooner, made the River Stay Away From His Door and Taylor himself brought out everything from "Hot Dog" to "Bravo" when he made high C.

A'Lelia Walker was the then great Harlem party giver, although Mrs. Bernia Austin fell but little behind. And at the Seventh Avenue apartment of Jessie Fauset, literary soirées with much poetry and but little to drink were the order of the day. The same was true of Lillian Alexander's, where the older intellectuals gathered.

A'Lelia Walker, however, big-hearted, night-dark, hair-straightening heiress, made no pretense at being intellectual or exclusive. At her "at homes" Negro poets and Negro number bankers mingled with downtown poets and seat-on-the-stock-exchange racketeers. Countee Cullen would be there and Witter Bynner, Muriel Draper and Nora Holt, Andy Razaf and Taylor Gordon. And a good time was had by all.

A'Lelia Walker had an apartment that held perhaps a hundred people. She would usually issue several hundred invitations to each party. Unless you went early there was no possible way of getting in. Her parties were as crowded as the New York subway at the rush hour—entrance, lobby, steps, hallway, and apartment a milling crush of guests, with everybody seeming to enjoy the crowding. Once, some royal personage arrived, a Scandinavian prince, I believe, but his equerry saw no way of getting him through the crowded

entrance hall and into the party, so word was sent in to A'Lelia
Walker that His Highness, the Prince, was waiting without. A'Lelia
sent word back that she saw no way of getting His Highness in,
either, nor could she herself get out through the crowd to greet
him. But she offered to send refreshments downstairs to the Prince's
car.

A'Lelia Walker was a gorgeous dark Amazon, in a silver turban.
She had a town house in New York (also an apartment where she
preferred to live) and a country mansion at Irvington-on-the-Hudson,
with pipe organ programs each morning to awaken her guests gently.
Her mother made a great fortune from the Madame Walker Hair
Straightening Process, which had worked wonders on unruly Negro
hair in the early nineteen hundreds—and which continues to work
wonders today. The daughter used much of that money for fun.
A'Lelia Walker was the joy-goddess of Harlem's 1920's.

She had been very much in love with her first husband, from
whom she was divorced. Once at one of her parties she began to
cry about him. She retired to her boudoir and wept. Some of her
friends went in to comfort her, and found her clutching a memento
of their broken romance.

"The only thing I have left that he gave me," she sobbed, "it's
all I have left of him!"

It was a gold shoehorn.

When A'Lelia Walker died in 1931, she had a grand funeral. It
was by invitation only. But, just as for her parties, a great many
more invitations had been issued than the small but exclusive
Seventh Avenue funeral parlor could provide for. Hours before the
funeral, the street in front of the undertaker's chapel was crowded.
The doors were not opened until the cortège arrived—and the
cortège was late. When it came, there were almost enough family
mourners, attendants, and honorary pallbearers in the procession to
fill the room; as well as the representatives of the various Walker
beauty parlors throughout the country. And there were still hundreds
of friends outside, waving their white, engraved invitations aloft
in the vain hope of entering.

Once the last honorary pallbearers had marched in, there was a
great crush at the doors. Muriel Draper, Rita Romilly, Mrs. Roy
Sheldon, and I were among the fortunate few who achieved an
entrance.

We were startled to find De Lawd standing over A'Lelia's casket.
It was a truly amazing illusion. At that time *The Green Pastures* was
at the height of its fame, and there stood De Lawd in the person of
Rev. E. Clayton Powell, a Harlem minister, who looked exactly

like Richard B. Harrison in the famous role in the play. He had the same white hair and kind face, and was later offered the part of De Lawd in the film version of the drama. Now, he stood there motionless in the dim light behind the silver casket of A'Lelia Walker.

Soft music played and it was very solemn. When we were seated and the chapel became dead silent, De Lawd said: "The Four Bon Bons will now sing."

A night club quartette that had often performed at A'Lelia's parties arose and sang for her. They sang Noel Coward's "I'll See You Again," and they swung it slightly, as she might have liked it. It was a grand funeral and very much like a party. Mrs. Mary Mc-Cleod Bethune spoke in that great deep voice of hers, as only she can speak. She recalled the poor mother of A'Lelia Walker in old clothes, who had labored to bring the gift of beauty to Negro womanhood, and had taught them the care of their skin and their hair; and had built up a great business and a great fortune to the pride and glory of the Negro race—and then had given it all to her daughter, A'Lelia.

Then a poem of mine was read by Edward Perry, "To A'Lelia." And after that the girls from the various Walker beauty shops throughout America brought their flowers and laid them on the bier.

That was really the end of the gay times of the New Negro era in Harlem, the period that had begun to reach its end when the crash came in 1929 and the white people had much less money to spend on themselves, and practically none to spend on Negroes, for the depression brought everybody down a peg or two. And the Negroes had but few pegs to fall.

But in those pre-crash days there were parties and parties. At the novelist, Jessie Fauset's, parties there was always quite a different atmosphere from that at most other Harlem good-time gatherings. At Miss Fauset's, a good time was shared by talking literature and reading poetry aloud and perhaps enjoying some conversation in French. White people were seldom present there unless they were very distinguished white people, because Jessie Fauset did not feel like opening her home to mere sightseers, or faddists momentarily in love with Negro life. At her house one would usually meet editors and students, writers and social workers, and serious people who liked books and the British Museum, and had perhaps been to Florence. (Italy, not Alabama.)

I remember, one night at her home there was a gathering in honor of Salvador de Madariaga, the Spanish diplomat and savant, which somehow became a rather selfconscious gathering, with all Harlem writers called upon to recite their poems and speak their pieces. But afterwards, Charles S. Johnson and I invited Mr. Madariaga to Small's Paradise where we had a "ball' until the dawn came up and forced us from the club.

In those days, 409 Edgecombe, Harlem's tallest and most exclusive apartment house, was quite a party center. The Walter Whites and the Aaron Douglases, among others, lived and entertained here. Walter White was a jovial and cultured host, with a sprightly mind, and an apartment overlooking the Hudson. He had the most beautiful wife in Harlem, and they were always hospitable to hungry literati like me.

At the Aaron Douglases', although he was a painter, more young writers were found than painters. Usually everbody would chip in and go dutch on the refreshments, calling down to the nearest bootlegger for a bottle of whatever it was that was drunk in those days, when labels made no difference at all in the liquid content— Scotch, bourbon, rye, and gin being the same except for coloring matter.

Arna Bontemps, poet and coming novelist, quiet and scholarly, looking like a young edition of Dr. DuBois, was the mysterious member of the Harlem literati, in that we knew he had recently married, but none of us had ever seen his wife. All the writers wondered who she was and what she looked like. He never brought her with him to any of the parties, so she remained the mystery of the New Negro Renaissance. But I went with him once to his apartment to meet her, and found her a shy and charming girl, holding a golden baby on her lap. A year or two later there was another golden baby. And every time I went away to Haiti or Mexico or Europe and came back, there would be a new golden baby, each prettier than the last—so that was why the literati never saw Mrs. Bontemps.

Toward the end of the New Negro era, E. Simms Campbell came to Harlem from St. Louis, and began to try to sell cartoons to the *New Yorker*. My first memory of him is at a party at Gwendolyn Bennett's on Long Island. In the midst of the party, the young lady Mr. Campbell had brought, Constance Willis, whom he later married, began to put on her hat and coat and gloves. The hostess asked her if she going home. She said: "No, only taking Elmer outside to straighten him out." What indiscretion he had committed at the party I never knew, perhaps flirting with some other girl, or taking a drink too many. But when we looked out, there was Constances giving Elmer an all-around talking-to on the sidewalk.

And she must have straightened him out, because he was a very nice young man at parties ever after.

At the James Weldon Johnson parties and gumbo suppers, one met solid people like Clarence and Mrs. Darrow. At the Dr. Alexander's, you met the upper crust Negro intellectuals like Dr. DuBois. At Wallace Thurman's, you met the bohemians of both Harlem and the Village. And in the gin mills and speakeasies and night clubs between 125th and 145th, Eighth Avenue and Lenox, you met everybody from Buddy de Silva to Theodore Dreiser, Ann Pennington to the first Mrs. Eugene O'Neill. In the days when Harlem was in vogue, Amanda Randolph was at the Alhambra, Jimmy Walker was mayor of New York, and Louise sang at the old New World.

DOWNTOWN

Downtown there were many interesting parties in those days, too, to which I was sometimes bidden. I remember one at Florine Stettheimer's, another at V. F. Calverton's, and another at Bob Chandler's, where the walls were hung with paintings and Louise Helstrom served the drinks. Paul Haakon, who was a kid then whom Louise had "discovered" somewhere, danced and everybody Oh'ed and Ah'ed, and said what a beautiful young artist! What an artist! But later when nobody was listening, Paul Haakon said to me: "Some baloney—I'm no artist. I'm in vaudeville!"

I remember also a party at Jake Baker's, somewhere on the lower East Side near the river, where I do not recall any whites being present except Mr. Baker himself. Jake Baker then had one of the largest erotic libraries in New York, ranging from the ancient to the modern, the classic to the vulgar, the *Kama Sutra* to T. R. Smith's anthology of *Poetica Erotica*. But since Harlemites are not very familiar with erotic books, Mr. Baker was never able to get the party started. His gathering took on the atmosphere of the main reading room at the public library with everybody hunched over a book—trying to find out what white folks say about love when they really come to the point.

I remember also a big cocktail party for Ernestine Evans at the Ritz, when she had got a new job with some publishing firm and they were celebrating her addition to the staff. Josephine Herbst was there and we had a long talk near the hors-d'œuvres, and I liked Josephine Herbst very much. Also I recall a dinner party for Claire

Spencer at Colin McPhee's and Jane Belo's in the village, where Claire Spencer told about a thrilling night flight over Manhattan Island in a monoplane and also another party in the Fifties for Rebecca West, who knew a lot of highly amusing gossip about the Queen of Rumania. I remember well, too, my first party after a Broadway opening, the one Horace Liveright gave for Paul Robeson and Fredi Washington, following the premiere of Jim Tully's *Black Boy*. And there was one grand New Year's Eve fête at the Alfred A. Knopf's on Fifth Avenue, where I met Ethel Barrymore and Jascha Heifetz, and everybody was in tails but me, and all I had on was a blue serge suit—which didn't seem to matter to anyone—for Fifth Avenue was not nearly so snooty about clothes as Washington's Negro society.

Downtown at Charlie Studin's parties, at Arthur and Mrs. Spingarn's, Eddie Wasserman's, at Muriel Draper's, or Rita Romilly's, one would often meet almost as many Negro guests as in Harlem. But only Carl Van Vechten's parties were *so* Negro that they were reported as a matter of course in the colored society columns, just as though they occurred in Harlem instead of West 55th Street, where he and Fania Marinoff then lived in a Peter Whiffle apartment, full of silver fishes and colored glass balls and ceiling-high shelves of gaily-bound books.

Not only were there interesting Negroes at Carl Van Vechten's parties, ranging from famous writers to famous tap dancers, but there were always many other celebrities of various colors and kinds, old ones and new ones from Hollywood, Broadway, London, Paris or Harlem. I remember one party when Chief Long Lance of the cinema did an Indian war dance, while Adelaide Hall of *Blackbirds* played the drums, and an international assemblage crowded around to cheer.

At another of Mr. Van Vechten's parties, Bessie Smith sang the blues. And when she finished, Margarita D'Alvarez of the Metropolitan Opera arose and sang an aria. Bessie Smith did not know D'Alvarez, but, liking her voice, she went up to her when she had ceased and cried: "Don't let anybody tell you you can't sing!"

Carl Van Vechten and A'Lelia Walker were great friends, and at each of their parties many of the same people were to be seen, but more writers were present at Carl Van Vechten's. At cocktail time, or in the evening, I first met at his house Somerset Maugham, Hugh Walpole, Fannie Hurst, Witter Bynner, Isa Glenn, Emily Clark, William Seabrook, Arthur Davison Ficke, Louis Untermeyer, and George Sylvester Viereck.

Mr. Viereck cured me of a very bad habit I used to have of thinking I had to say something nice to every writer I met concerning his work. Upon being introduced to Mr. Viereck, I said, "I like your books."

He demanded: "Which one?"

And I couldn't think of a single one.

Of course, at Mr. Van Vechten's parties there were always many others who were not writers: Lawrence Langner and Armina Marshall of the Theatre Guild, Eugene Gossens, Jane Belo, who married Colin McPhee and went to Bali to live, beautiful Rose Rolanda, who married Miguel Covarrubias, Lilyan Tashman, who died, Horace Liveright, Blanche Dunn, Ruben Mamoulian, Marie Doro, Nicholas Muray, Madame Helena Rubinstein, Richmond Barthe, Salvador Dali, Waldo Frank, Dudley Murphy, and often Dorothy Peterson, a charming colored girl who had grown up mostly in Puerto Rico, and who moved with such poise among these colorful celebrities that I thought when I first met her she was a white girl of the grande monde, slightly sun-tanned. But she was a Negro teacher of French and Spanish, who later got a leave of absence from her school work to play Cain's Gal in *The Green Pastures*.

Being interested in the Negro problem in various parts of the world, Dorothy Peterson once asked Dali if he knew anything about Negroes.

"Everything!" Dali answered. "I've met Nancy Cunard!"

Speaking of celebrities, one night as one of Carl Van Vechten's parties was drawing to a close, Rudolph Valentino called, saying that he was on his way. That was the only time I have ever seen the genial Van Vechten hospitality waver. He told Mr. Valentino the party was over. It seems that our host was slightly perturbed at the thought of so celebrated a guest coming into a party that had passed its peak. Besides, he told the rest of us, movie stars usually expect a lot of attention—and it was too late in the evening for such extended solicitude now.

Carl Van Vechten once wrote a book called *Parties*. But it is not nearly so amusing as his own parties. Once he gave a gossip party, where everybody was at liberty to go around the room repeating the worst things they could make up or recall about each other to their friends on opposite sides of the room—who were sure to go right over and tell them all about it.

At another party of his (but this was incidental) the guests were kept in a constant state of frightful expectancy by a lady standing in the hall outside Mr. Van Vechten's door, who announced that she was waiting for her husband to emerge from the opposite apartment, where he was visiting another woman. When I came to the party, I saw her standing grimly there. It was her full intention to kill her husband, she said. And she displayed to Mrs. Van Vechten's maids the pistol in her handbag.

At intervals during the evening, the woman in the hall would receive coffee from the Van Vechten party to help her maintain her vigil. But the suspense was not pleasant. I kept feeling goose pimples on my body and hearing a gun in my mind. Finally someone suggested phoning the apartment across the way to inform the erring husband of the fate awaiting him if he came out. Perhaps this was done. I don't know. But I learned later that the woman waited until dawn and then went home. No husband emerged from the silent door, so her gun was not fired.

Once when Mr. Van Vechten gave a bon voyage party in the Prince of Wales suite aboard the Cunarder on which he was sailing, as the champagne flowed, Nora Holt, the scintillating Negro blonde entertainer de luxe from Nevada, sang a ribald ditty called, "My Daddy Rocks Me With One Steady Roll." As she ceased, a well-known New York matron cried ecstatically, with tears in her eyes: "My dear! Oh, my dear! How beautifully you sing Negro spirituals!"

Carl Van Vechten moved about filling glasses and playing host with the greatest of zest at his parties, while his tiny wife, Fania Marinoff, looking always very pretty and very gay, when the evening grew late would sometimes take Mr. Van Vechten severely to task for his drinking—before bidding the remaining guests good night and retiring to her bed.

Now, Mr. Van Vechten has entirely given up drinking (as well as writing books and smoking cigarettes) in favor of photography. Although his parties are still gaily liquid for those who wish it, he himself is sober as a judge, but not as solemn.

For several pleasant years, he gave an annual birthday party for James Weldon Johnson, young Alfred A. Knopf, Jr., and himself, for their birthdays fall on the same day. At the last of these parties the year before Mr. Johnson died, on the Van Vechten table there were three cakes, one red, one white, and one blue—the colors of our flag. They honored a Gentile, a Negro, and a Jew—friends and fellow-Americans. But the differences of race did not occur to me until days later, when I thought back about the three colors and the three men.

Carl Van Vechten is like that party. He never talks grandiloquently about democracy or Americanism. Nor makes a fetish of those qualities. But he lives them with sincerity—and humor.

Perhaps that is why *his* parties were reported in the Harlem press.

SHOWS

During the *Fire* summer, I earned my living by writing lyrics and sketches for an intimate musical revue for Caroline Dudley (then Mrs. Reagan), sister of Dorothy Dudley, who wrote a fine study of Theodore Dreiser, and who introduced the Italian poet Carnevali to America.

Mrs. Reagan lived in an apartment in an old house in, I believe, West 11th Street, with a courtyard garden in the rear. And the apartment was all aflurry with excitement over the prospect of an intimate Negro revue, to star Paul Robeson, and to include the sparkling Nora Holt. And to present many of the then unexploited Negro folksongs. All the material, music, and sketches were to be by Negro writers. I was helping Mrs. Reagan plan the revue, and later Rudolph Fisher came in on some of the skits. The house was alive with the continual comings and goings of Negro artists having auditions, tap dancers in one room, tramp bands in another, the ear-splitting voice of George Dewey Washington bursting the walls of the parlor, and comedians looking dumb in the courtyard.

In the midst of it all, Dorothy Dudley, who had suffered a broken toe, lay on a chaise longue, looking very pretty and bird-like, taking it all in, making charming comments, and waiting for her husband, Henry Harvey, to come home from his office. Then, if he were still working in the early evening, Mrs. Reagan would send out for a chicken or two, some peas and beans and cucumbers, and put them all in a grilling pan and run them in the oven, where everything cooked at once and automatically came out tasting very good, while everybody went on talking about the revue and writing things down and only looking once or twice in the oven to see what the chicken and cucumbers and peas were doing. And they would be doing very nicely, and would be eaten in the midst of writing, talking, and singing.

I continued to come up to New York from college weekends most of the winter to work on the revue. But meanwhile, Paul Robeson had gone to London to appear in *Showboat*. He made such a tremendous hit there that he refused to come back, although he was under contract to Mrs. Reagan, so Mrs. Reagan went to law. Paul's wife, Essie Robeson, came back to New York, but could not settle the matter, it seems, and was forced to flee over the Harlem roof tops with baby Paul in her arms, like Eliza in *Uncle Tom's Cabin*, in order to escape the clutches of Mrs. Reagan's process servers.

But Essie Robeson got to the boat, escaped, and was off to England again. So then Mrs. Reagan went to London and sued Paul Robeson there. She won her case and got several thousand pounds, so it was said in Harlem, where the people Mrs. Reagan had under contract were paid what was due them on her return.

But the revue never went on. Delay and trouble broke it up. So Mrs. Reagan went to Paris and married a French poet and lived in the south of France and no longer worried about show business.

Mrs. Reagan had bad luck with Negro shows. It was she who took *La Revue Nègre* to Paris, with Maude Russell, Claude Hopkins, settings by Miguel Covarrubias, and the then unknown Josephine Baker. Miss Baker, with her Charleston and her verve, stole the show from the more veteran Negro performers and overnight became the hit of Paris, stepping immediately from the chorus to stardom.

There is a story about Josephine Baker's first month in Paris, which the Parisians find very amusing. They say a wealthy and distinguished old Frenchman was so entranced with Miss Baker that he came every night to see *La Revue Nègre*. He sent daily bouquets of flowers to the dusky youngster from St. Louis, who could fling her limbs about in such amazing directions to the rhythm of Harlem music. He even went so far as to insist that Miss Baker accept the use of one of his town cars and a chauffeur in uniform. All of which Miss Baker accepted—but still paid the wealthy and elderly gentleman no mind. Finally, he asked her, in the best English that he could muster, just why she did not find his attentions to her liking.

Miss Baker naïvely replied: "But, Monsieur, I thought you said you gave me all these things because you loved my art!"

Of course, after that she no longer had the town car nor the chauffeur nor the flowers from the same monsieur. But she did have many bids for her appearances in the various large theaters of Europe. She accepted one of these offers and left the American show to go to Berlin. And because she was under age, Mrs. Reagan could not prevent her going. With Josephine lost, the show was forced to close. And that was the end of *La Revue Nègre*.

In those days, most of Harlem's actors were kept busy either on the Broadway stage, in night clubs, or in London or Paris. Aubrey Lyles, the comedian, rode up and down Seventh Avenue in a long red car with solid ivory trimmings. It was the first car Harlem had seen that could be turned into a sort of Pullman sleeper at will, the back seats sliding out to make a bed.

Another car that excited the colored world was that of Jules Bledsoe, who originated "Old Man River" in *Show Boat*. One day he appeared in the streets of Harlem with an expensive, high-powered motor, driven by a white chauffeur in livery. Mr. Bledsoe, who is dark, explained to the delight of Harlem that he had a white-uniformed chauffeur so that the public could tell which was the chauffeur and which the owner of the car.

Somewhat later, I recall a sincere but unfortunate attempt on Jules Bledsoe's part to bring "Art" to Harlem. He appeared in Eugene O'Neill's *The Emperor Jones* at the old Lincoln Theater on 135th Street, a theater that had, for all its noble name, been devoted largely to ribald but highly entertaining, vaudeville of the "Butterbeans and Susie" type. The audience didn't know what to make of *The Emperor Jones* on a stage where "Shake That Thing" was formerly the rage. And when the Emperor started running naked through the forest, hearing the Little Frightened Fears, naturally they howled with laughter.

"Them ain't no ghosts, fool!" the spectators cried from the orchestra. "Why don't you come on out o' that jungle—back to Harlem where you belong?"

In the manner of Stokowski hearing a cough at the Academy of Music, Jules Bledsoe stopped dead in his tracks, advanced to the footlights, and proceeded to lecture his audience on manners in the theater. But the audience wanted none of *The Emperor Jones*. And their manners had been all right at all the other shows at the Lincoln, where they took part in the performances at will. So when Brutus continued his flight, the audience again howled with laughter. And that was the end of *The Emperor Jones* on 135th Street.

In those days Ethel Waters was the girl who could thrill Harlem. Butterbeans and Susie could lay them in the aisles. Jackie Mably could stop any show. Snakehips was a permanent "solid sender," and Louis Armstrong a killer!

But who wanted *The Emperor Jones* running through the jungles?

Not Harlem!

POETRY

I think it was at a party at 17 Gay Street in the Village, where Dorothy and Jimmy Harris lived, that I first heard people talking about New Mexico and Taos, and about writers and artists heading west to the desert and the Indians. It was about that time, too, that I first met Genevieve Taggard, Robert Wolf, and Ernestine Evans. And heard Eli Siegel read "Hot Afternoons There Have Been in Montana."

I met a lot of very exotic and jittery writers and artists of that period, too. And the more exotic and jittery they were, the more they talked of heading for Taos and the desert and the Indians. So I began to wonder what the Indians would think about their coming and if they would drink as much in Taos as they did in the Village. When I got back to Washington, after one of my prize-money trips to New York, I was walking home from work one night when this poem came to me. I named it "A House in Taos."

RAIN

Thunder of the Rain God:
   And we three
   Smitten by beauty.

Thunder of the Rain God:
   And we three
   Weary, weary.

Thunder of the Rain God:
   And you, she and I
   Waiting for nothingness.

Do you understand the stillness
Of this house in Taos
Under the thunder of the Rain God?

SUN

That there should be a barren garden
About this house in Taos
Is not so strange,
But that there should be three barren hearts
In this one house in Taos—
Who carries ugly things to show the sun?

MOON

Did you ask for the beaten brass of the moon?
We can buy lovely things with money,
You, she and I,
Yet you seek,
As though you could keep,
This unbought loveliness of moon.

WIND

Touch our bodies wind.
Our bodies are separate, individual things.

Touch our bodies, wind,
But blow quickly
Through the red, white, yellow skins
Of our bodies
To the terrible snarl,
Not mine,
Not yours,
Not hers,
But all one snarl of souls
Blow quickly, wind,
Before we run back into the windlessness
With our bodies—
Into the windlessness
Of our house in Taos.

It was a strange poem for me to be writing in a period when I was writing mostly blues and spirituals. I do not know why it came to me in just that way, but I made hardly a change in it after I put it down.

A year or so later from Lincoln University, during my first term there, I submitted the poem to *Palms,* as an entry in Witter Bynner's Intercollegiate Undergraduate Poetry Contest. It was given the First Award of one hundred and fifty dollars and published in *Palms* in 1927. Then amusing things began to happen. I did not know anybody in Taos, nor had I ever been there, but the Greenwich Villagers all seemed to know people there and even houses that the poem fitted, and I received a number of gossipy and amusing letters about it from folks I had never met. In one letter there was even a series of snapshots of what the writer claimed to be the very house of my poem—Mabel Dodge Luhan's house in Taos.

At that time, I had never heard Mrs. Luhan's name, nor did I know she had married an Indian, or that Jean Toomer had been a guest in her home. The red, yellow, and white of my poem came from the Indian corn colors of the desert. Three was a mystic number. The rain, sun, moon, and other nature words I used in contrast with the art-houses being built by the exotics from the Village.

Years later, when I met Mrs. Luhan in Carmel, the first thing she said to me was: "My house is not a bit like that." And she invited me to come and see for myself.

In New York in the summer of 1926, I wrote a poem called "Mulatto" which was published in the *Saturday Review of Literature.* I worked harder on that poem than on any other that I have ever written. Almost every night that summer I would take it out of the table drawer and retype it and work on it, and change it. When I read it one night at a gathering at James Weldon Johnson's, Clarence Darrow said it was more moving than any other poem of mine he had read. It was a poem about white fathers and Negro mothers in the South.

From the time when, as a small child in rompers in Lawrence, I had played with a little, golden-haired boy whose mother was colored and whose father, the old folks whispered, was white, and when, as this boy grew up, he went over into the white world altogether, I had been intrigued with the problem of those so-called "Negroes" of immediate white-and-black blood, whether they were light enough to pass for white or not. One of my earliest poems was:

CROSS

My old man's a white old man
And my old mother's black.
If ever I cursed my white old man
I take my curses back.

If ever I cursed my black old mother
And wished she were in hell,
I'm sorry for that evil wish
And now I wish her well.

My old man died in a fine big house.
My ma died in a shack.
I wonder where I'm gonna die,
Being neither white nor black?

The problem of mixed blood in America is, to be sure, a minor problem, but a very dramatic one—one parent in the pale of the black ghetto and the other able to take advantage of all the opportunities of American democracy. Later I presented one phase of this problem in my play, *Mulatto,* on Broadway. And I have written several short stories about it.

My second book of poems, *Fine Clothes to the Jew,* I felt was a better book than my first, because it was more impersonal, more about other people than myself, and because it made use of the Negro folk-song forms, and included poems about work and the problems of finding work, that are always so pressing with the Negro people.

I called it *Fine Clothes to the Jew,* because the first poem, "Hard Luck," a blues, was about a man who was often so broke he had no recourse but to pawn his clothes—to take them, as the Negroes say, to "the Jew's" or to "Uncle's." Since the whole book was largely about people like that, workers, roustabouts, and singers, and job hunters on Lenox Avenue in New York, or Seventh Street in Washington or South State in Chicago—people up today and down tomorrow, working this week and fired the next, beaten and baffled, but determined not to be wholly beaten, buying furniture on the installment plan, filling the house with roomers to help pay the rent, hoping to get a new suit for Easter—and pawning that suit before the Fourth of July—that was why I called my book *Fine Clothes to the Jew.*

But it was a bad title, because it was confusing and many Jewish people did not like it. I do not know why the Knopfs let me use it, since they were very helpful in their advice about sorting out the bad poems from the good, but they said nothing about the title. I might just as well have called the book *Brass Spittoons,* which is one of the poems I like best:

BRASS SPITTOONS

> *Clean the spittoons, boy!*
> *Detroit,*
> *Chicago,*
> *Atlantic City,*
> *Palm Beach.*
> *Clean the spittoons.*
> *The steam in hotel kitchens,*
> *And the smoke in hotel lobbies,*
> *And the slime in hotel spittoons:*
> *Part of my life.*
> *Hey, boy!*
> *A nickel,*
> *A dime,*
> *A dollar,*
> *Two dollars a day.*
> *Hey, boy!*
> *A nickel,*
> *A dime,*
> *A dollar,*
> *Two dollars*
> *Buys shoes for the baby.*
> *House rent to pay.*
> *Gin on Saturday,*
> *Church on Sunday.*
> *My God!*

Babies and gin and church
and women and Sunday
all mixed up with dimes and
dollars and clean spittoons
and house rent to pay.
> *Hey, boy!*
A bright bowl of brass is beautiful to the Lord.
Bright polished brass like the cymbals
Of King David's dancers,
Like the wine cups of Solomon.
> *Hey, boy!*
A clean spittoon on the altar of the Lord,
A clean bright spittoon all newly polished—
At least I can offer that.
> *Com'mere, boy!*

Fine Clothes to the Jew was well received by the literary magazines and the white press, but the Negro critics did not like it at all. The Pittsburgh *Courier* ran a big headline across the top of the page, *LANGSTON HUGHES' BOOK OF POEMS TRASH.* The headline in the New York *Amsterdam News* was *LANGSTON HUGHES— THE SEWER DWELLER.* The Chicago *Whip* characterized me as "The poet lowrate of Harlem." Others called the book a disgrace to the race, a return to the dialect tradition, and a parading of all our racial defects before the public. An ironic poem like "Red Silk Stockings" they took for literal advice:

Put on yo' red silk stockings,
Black gal.
Go out and let the white boys
Look at yo' legs.

Ain't nothin to do for you, nohow,
Round this town—
You's too pretty.
Put on yo' red silk stockings, gal,
An' tomorrow's chile'll
Be a high yaller.

Go out an' let de white boys
Look at yo' legs.

Benjamin Brawley, our most respectable critic, later wrote: "It would have been just as well, perhaps better, if the book had never been published. No other ever issued reflects more fully the abandon and the vulgarity of its age." In the Negro papers, I believe, only Dewey Jones of the Chicago *Defender* and Alice Dunbar-Nelson of the Washington *Eagle* gave it a sympathetic review.

The Negro critics and many of the intellectuals were very sensitive about their race in books. (And still are.) In anything that white people were likely to read, they wanted to put their best foot forward, their politely polished and cultural foot—and only that foot. There was a reason for it, of course. They had seen their race laughed at and caricatured so often in stories like those by Octavus Roy Cohen, maligned and abused so often in books like Thomas Dixon's, made a servant or a clown always in the movies, and forever defeated on the Broadway stage, that when Negroes wrote books they wanted them to be books in which only good Negroes, clean and cultured and not-funny Negroes, beautiful and nice and upper class were presented. Jessie Fauset's novels they loved, because they were always about the educated Negro—but my poems, or Claude McKay's *Home to Harlem* they did not like, sincere though we might be.

For every Negro intellectual like James Weldon Johnson, there were dozens like Eustace Gay, who wrote in the Philadelphia *Tribune*, of February 5, 1927, concerning my *Fine Clothes to the Jew:* "It does not matter to me whether every poem in the book is true to life. Why should it be paraded before the American public by a Negro author as being typical or representative of the Negro? Bad enough to have white authors holding up our imperfections to public gaze. Our aim ought to be present to the general public, already mis-informed both by well meaning and malicious writers, our higher aims and aspirations, and our better selves."

I sympathized deeply with those critics and those intellectuals, and I saw clearly the need for some of the kinds of books they wanted. But I did not see how they could expect every Negro author to write such books. Certainly, I personally knew very few people anywhere who were wholly beautiful and wholly good. Besides I felt that the masses of our people had as much in their lives to put into books as did those more fortunate ones who had been born with some means and the ability to work up to a master's degree at a Northern college. Anyway, I didn't know the upper class Negroes well enough to write much about them. I knew only the people I had grown up with, and they weren't people whose shoes were always shined, who had been to Harvard, or who had heard of Bach. But they seemed to me good people, too.

So I didn't pay any attention to the critics who railed against the subject matter of my poems, nor did I write them protesting letters, nor in any way attempt to defend my book. Curiously enough, a short ten years later, many of those very poems in *Fine Clothes to the Jew* were being used in Negro schools and colleges.

I Wonder as I Wander

MARY McLEOD BETHUNE

When Zell and I got to Miami in the spring of 1931, we found the car unmovable. In storage through the long summer heat, the tires had gone flat. The rims of the wheels had cut through one of them and damaged the others. To get the car out, buy a secondhand tire and four new inner tubes, took all the money we had. We had to pawn my camera and everything else, except the two Haitian voodoo drums we had lugged from the Cap. These drums we would not part with under any circumstances. The pawnshops did not consider Zell's paintings of any cash value. Neither did the secondhand tire dealer. I had thirty-four dollars in the bank in New York, but I knew no one in Miami through whom I could cash a check. We were broke—and exactly 1,383 miles from New York.

"All I know to do," I said, "is use what little change we have left for a few gallons of gas to get to Daytona. There I'm sure Mrs. Bethune will cash a check for me at her college."

We starved all the way to Daytona, more than half the length of Florida. But once there, Mrs. Bethune received us cordially, sat us down to dinner, and cashed a thirty-dollar check without question.

"Boys," said Mrs. Bethune, "I was intending to go North myself in a few days by train, so I might as well ride with you and save that fare."

Our little Ford coupe had only one seat, a rather small seat at that. Mrs. Bethune was no small woman. Zell was stocky, too. How the three of us, in hot September weather, would fare on a single seat in a small car all the way from Daytona to Manhattan, I could not surmise.

"We'll make it," Mrs. Bethune said.

With America's leading Negro woman as our passenger, we hit the road early the next morning and drove all day toward the Carolinas. What luck for us! All along the highway, Mary McLeod Bethune had friends. So whenever we got hungry on the road, we stopped at the home of some friends of hers in some Southern village. According to a popular saying in Florida, before Mrs. Bethune reached the wayside home of any friend anywhere, the chickens, sensing that she was coming, went flying off frantically seeking a safe hiding place. They knew some necks would surely be wrung in her honor to make a heaping platter of Southern fried chicken. Colored folks all along the Eastern seaboard spread a feast whenever Mary McLeod passed their way. Zell and I ate well on that trip. We didn't have to spend a penny for food or lodging. When nightfall came, the leading Negroes in the nearest town on the highway, with no advance warning other than a knock on the door, would roll out the red carpet for Mrs. Bethune and ourselves.

"A poet! An artist! What an honor! You always were interested in young people, Mary McLeod. Come in, make yourselves at home! Have you eaten yet? Do you want a bath? We'll get the beds ready whenever you-all get sleepy." And so it went, genial Southern hospitality all the way to Washington.

Mrs. Bethune, aside from her fame in educational circles, was a power in lodge and club activities. She was known far and wide at conclaves, conventions and church meetings. She had spoken at every colored school in the South, too. People loved her, so they showed it by offering her their best. That best, tired and hungry Zell and I shared on this journey. We shared Mrs. Bethune's wit and wisdom, too, the wisdom of a jet-black woman who had risen from a bare-footed field hand in a cotton patch to be head of one of the leading junior colleges in America, and a leader of her people. She was a wonderful sport, riding all day without complaint in our cramped, hot little car, jolly and talkative, never grumbling.

We avoided segregation by not having to seek food or sleeping accommodations in public places along the Southern highways. But we did have to get gas and sometimes use the gas-station rest rooms, usually one for MEN, one for LADIES—and a single one marked COLORED somewhere away out in the back for both men and women, if Negro. To the attendant at such stations, Mrs. Bethune would usually say, "Young man, do I have to avail myself of that shanty rest room away around there in the bushes?"

If there were no whites about, the embarrassed attendant might say, "Ma'am, just use the one marked LADIES." But if the station were busy, he would indicate that the COLORED toilet was meant for her. Then Mrs. Bethune would say gently, "Aren't you ashamed, young man?"

The young man would usually turn red and answer, "Yes, ma'am, I really am."

We arrived one day at Cheraw, South Carolina, just before noon.

Mrs. Bethune said, "Let's stop at Coulter Academy and dine with the teachers, Langston, and you read some of your poems for the students."

We pulled up before a large frame building. As soon as the teachers and students saw Mrs. Bethune getting out of the car, word spread and commotion began. Classes greeted her with applause and an assembly for the whole school was ordered. She made a warm-hearted little talk, then introduced me as a poet whom she wanted the South to know better. I read the students a few of my poems, and was gratified at the warm response they received.

"You see," said Mrs. Bethune as we drove away, "you must go all over the South with your poems. People need poetry."

TRAGEDY AT HAMPTON

In New York the depression was in full sway. Had I started looking for work, a job would have been hard to find. Thousands were out of work. But I did not want a job. I wanted to continue to be a poet. Yet sometimes I wondered if I was barking up the wrong tree. I determined to find out by taking poetry, *my* poetry, to my people. After all, I wrote about Negroes, and primarily *for* Negroes. Would they have me? Did they want me?

Mrs. Bethune had said, "They need poetry."

Sitting half hungry in my tiny room in the West 135th Street Y in Harlem, her words encouraged me to do something about it. I got a *Negro Year Book* from the nearest library. In it is a list of educational institutions, so I began to write to the presidents of all the Negro colleges in the South. Almost immediately answers came back from several institutions, offering to book me. My next problem would be how to get to these colleges. I had heard of the Rosenwald Fund to aid Negro education, so I wrote a letter outlining my plan for a tour of the South. The Rosenwald Fund granted me a thousand dollars toward the reading of my poems at educational centers.

I bought a Ford. But I could not drive and I had no license. I found a former classmate of mine at Lincoln University, Radcliffe Lucas, who was then a part-time Red Cap at the Pennsylvania Station. He could drive, and had a good business head, I knew, because he had worked his way through college running a weekend taxi service from Lincoln's campus in the country to South Street in Philadelphia.

"Raddie, how would you like to make a tour of the South with me reading poetry and you driving?" I proposed. "You can be my business manager, and we'll share the profits."

Raddie said, "It beats being a Red Cap in these tipless times. Let's go."

So we set out about five o'clock one October morning, headed South. The back seat of the car was filled with luggage and books of mine to sell on tour. I carried along also a large number of books by other contemporary Negro writers for a cultural exhibit. As we left Harlem, the sun was rising. All was well.

My first engagement Monday was at Dowingtown, a colored boarding school in Pennsylvania. The youngsters, mostly country kids, seemed to like my poetry. They gave be a big hand. We spent the night at Downingtown, but had to get up at dawn the next morning for a ten o'clock assembly at Morgan College in Baltimore —a very early hour for people to be listening to poetry. But they gave me a big hand, too. That afternoon I read my poems to some English classes at Howard University in Washington. Then we drove into Viriginia through the bright red and gold of autumn. At Richmond the students of Union were cordial. And at Virginia State College in Ettrick I saw hanging in a place of honor a large picture of my great-uncle, John Mercer Langston, first president of the college. At Hampton Institute, Booker T. Washington's alma mater, on Friday night, I faced my first large audience, more than a thousand Negro students, a sea of dark faces before me. Spontaneous applause followed many of my poems, and at the end of the program the students gave me an ovation. Thus ended my first week on tour.

Hampton is the most beautiful of Negro campuses, green and lovely, surrounded by inlets from the bay. I was invited to spend the weekend there. It was that weekend that I first met Dorothy Maynor, then a chubby teen-age student choir singer with long black curls. My meeting with her was the beginning of a realization that I was in the South, the troubled Jim Crow South of ever-present danger for Negroes. That weekend two tragic things happened.

Juliette Derricotte, former traveling YWCA executive, beloved of all girl students and then Dean of Women at Fisk University, away from her campus on a speaking trip, had been seriously injured in an automobile wreck on a country road in Georgia. She had been denied treatment at the nearest hospital, a white hospital, and had died before she could be driven to a colored hospital miles away. And that Saturday afternoon a former Hampton athlete, just graduated the spring before and now coaching at Alabama Normal

College for Negroes, had been beaten to death by a Southern mob on the way to see his football team play their first game of the season. Dorothy Maynor had known and admired both these people, as had the entire Hampton student body, so the whole campus mourned—and all were horrified at the manner in which their friends had died, victims of Southern prejudice.

Early on Saturday evening it was Dorothy Maynor who brought me the news of these tragic events. I had never seen Miss Maynor before word came to my rooms in Holly Tree Inn that a student wished to see me in the lobby. There stood Dorothy with a troubled face. When the news of the two deaths, with segregation and mob violence involved, had reached Hampton, a group of students had met after supper and decided to hold a memorial protest meeting in the chapel. Dorothy Maynor had been chosen to come and ask if I would speak. As the leading soloist of the student chorus under Nathaniel Dett, Dorothy Maynor was a popular campus figure, but her voice was not yet known in the great concert halls, and I had never heard her name.

Now she stood before me almost in tears, protesting, "A woman like Juliette Derricotte, such a noble woman! How could any hospital refuse to take her in, injured, bleeding—just because she's colored? And one of our football stars beaten to death by an Alabama mob because he parked his car in a white parking lot by mistake!"

Juliette Derricotte I had known in New York and Paris, and I had found her a charming and cultured woman. That she should die of injuries, neglected on a Georgia road because the medical facilities of the South were segregated, horrified me, too. It just did not make sense—not *decent, humane* sense, at any rate. Of course, I would speak at the student protest meeting. Just let me know what time, I told Miss Maynor.

But no such meeting was held at Hampton. The elderly white and Negro heads of the Institute would not permit the students to hold a protest meeting. They—and I—were told at a student committee gathering, "That is not Hampton's way. We educate, not protest."

So on Sunday I left Hampton, sadder and wiser concerning Southern Negro education. The further I penetrated into the Deep South, the sadder I became in this regard. The old abolitionist spirit out of which, during the Civil War and in Reconstruction times, many Negro colleges had grown, had now turned strangely conservative in regard to contemporary problems. It was the year of the Scottsboro case, 1931, yet on many Negro campuses the nine black teen-agers on trial for their lives in Alabama were not even to be mentioned.

"We educate, not protest."

COLOR AT CHAPEL HILL

In Virginia I ran into an incident of Jim Crowism more amusing than serious. It was a very warm day driving, and Raddie and I became thirsty. We spotted a roadside refreshment hut so I suggested we pull up there and I would jump out and get some cold sodas. Since I knew we could not eat or drink inside—there is legal Jim Crow in Virginia—it was my intention to purchase the cool drinks and bring them out to the car. But when I put my hand on the knob of the screen door it did not open. I pulled on the door again and discovered to my amazement that a white man just inside was holding the door.

He shouted through the screen, "What do you want?"

I said, "I'd like some sodas."

He said, "Get 'em through the hole."

Puzzled, I said, "What hole?"

He answered, "We got a hole cut for you-all people on the side."

He continued determinedly to hold the door, so I went around the side of the little frame building and there, sure enough, with a sign marked COLORED above it, was a square hole in the wall through which Negroes were served. I did not buy, but I had to laugh. The strange, silly pathetic South!

In North Carolina I spent almost the whole month of November giving programs of my poems. And from the playwright, Paul Green, and the sociologist, Guy B. Johnson, I received a cordial invitation to appear at the University of North Carolina. About a week before I was scheduled to arrive at Chapel Hill, I received a note from a student, Anthony Buttita, asking me to be the guest of himself and his roommate, Milton Abernathy. Buttita said that since the white state University would not house a Negro on the campus, being dyed-in-the-wool Southern, he wanted to show me there were students who did not believe in such stupidities. I accepted Buttita's invitation. He and Abernathy ran a little bookshop near the campus and published an unofficial student paper called *Contempo*. In connection with my coming, they had requested a poem or an article of mine to publish in their paper. I promptly sent them a poem and an article, both about the then famous Scottsboro Case. They

printed my two contributions on the front page of *Contempo* which
was distributed all over the campus the day I arrived. I was as
surprised as were most of the Southerners at Chapel Hill, to see
my work in *Contempo*.

My article, a satirical one, was called "Southern Gentlemen, White
Women, and Black Boys." Since the Scottsboro Case concerned nine
Negro youths accused of raping two white prostitutes in an open
coal car on a freight train traveling through Alabama, I inquired
in the piece why chivalrous Southern gentlemen allowed their
women to ride in a coal car in the first place, even if the women
were of doubtful character. By the time I reached the town of Chapel
Hill the daily papers had reproduced my "inflammatory" lines, and
the white citizenry were claiming mortal insult. When they learned
that I was to stop overnight with two white students, Buttita and
Abernathy had been promptly ejected from their lodgings, and had
nowhere to stay themselves.

My poem, "Christ in Alabama," on the front page of Contempo
created even more excitement than did my article. It was an ironic
poem inspired by the thought of how Christ, with no human father,
would be accepted were He born in the South of a Negro mother,
and it ended:

> Most Holy Bastard
> Of the bleeding mouth:
> Nigger Christ
> On the cross of the South!

The theatre of the University at Chapel Hill was packed to the
doors the night I read my poems there, and special police were on
guard to prevent trouble since considerable pressure had been put
upon the University to cancel my lecture. Courageously, the Univer-
sity refused to do so. But a leading politician of the town attempted
to get police protection for the program withdrawn, stating that I
should be run out of town before I had a chance to speak. "It's
bad enough to call Christ a bastard," he cried, "but to call Him a
nigger—that's too much!"

Buttita and Abernathy were delighted at the commotion their
student paper, *Contempo,* had caused. So they greeted me, the center
of it all, with open arms. They ordered luncheon brought in to the
bookshop from a nearby restaurant and invited several liberal white
students to share the food. That went so well that, in defiance of
Southern custom, they decided to take me to a public restaurant for
dinner. Since I could not be their house guest—for they themselves
evicted, had nowhere to lay their heads except on the floor of their

shop—I would at least, they said, be their guest for meals. I had by afternoon been housed with the leading Negro family of the town. But that evening I dined with my two intrepid white hosts at a *white* café on the main street in the company of several other white students. If they were willing to go through with dinner in a public restaurant in the tense atmosphere of that small town, I was willing, too.

After dinner, when I got back to my stopping place to dress for the lecture, my Negro hosts asked me where I had dined. When I told them at a downtown restaurant, the man of the house said, "What a shame you had to eat in the kitchen."

I said, "No, I ate at a table in the dining room."

His mouth flew open in astonishment. "It's the first time such a thing ever happened in Chapel Hill," he said.

The next morning all the newspapers in the state carried dispatches concerning the excitement attendant upon my appearance at Chapel Hill. At succeeding stops in other Carolina towns my audiences were overflowing. Negroes were delighted at my having, so they said, "walked into a lion's den, and come out, like Daniel, unscathed."

PLANTATION HOSPITALITY

On I went, driving down the road, deeper and deeper into Dixie with poetry as a passport. That fall and winter I covered every state in the South. Thousands of students heard me, and I sold many books. Alfred A. Knopf issued a special dollar edition of *The Weary Blues* for me to sell on tour. And, because it was depression times —even a dollar was a lot of money to some people—I prepared a smaller booklet of some of my newer poems to sell for a quarter. Its title poem was "The Negro Mother." Prentiss Taylor, a young artist in Greenwich Village, designed the booklet, endowed it with a dozen handsome black and white drawings, and supervised the printing of it. Since Prentiss Taylor was white, a Southerner from Virginia, and I, colored, I thought maybe such a book, evidence in itself of interracial collaboration and good will, might help democracy a little in the South where it seemed so hard for people to be friends across the color line. Few white people bought our book. But to Negroes I sold three large printings.

Poetry took me into the hearts and homes of colored people all over the South. But it took me into no more white colleges after

Chapel Hill, and into very few white homes. However, I did go to call on a white lady one day on an enormous plantation in South Carolina. The lady was the writer, Julia Peterkin, whom I had met at literary gatherings in New York at the Knopfs' and at Carl Van Vechten's. A charming woman then very much in the literary news, Mrs. Peterkin and I had gotten on well at Manhattan cocktail parties. She had been awarded in 1928 the Pulitzer Prize for her novel of Negro plantation life, *Scarlet Sister Mary.* From this novel a drama had been made in which Ethel Barrymore starred, playing Mary in blackface. Julia Peterkin had written other novels of Negro life, too, *Green Thursday, Black April* and *Bright Skin,* and later a text for a lovely picture book about her Dixie plantation, *Roll, Jordan, Roll.* The materials of Mrs. Peterkin's distinguished literary career were entirely derived from Negro life in the Deep South, so, when we met, we talked about Negroes and about writing. Graciously—in New York—Mrs. Peterkin had invited me to stop and see her plantation if ever I came to South Carolina.

It was a sunny autumn afternoon when Raddie drove me to the village of Fort Mott and we inquired the whereabouts of Lang Syne Plantation. When we found its entrance, we drove some distance on the plantation grounds through fields of cotton before we located the Big House. In front of a wide veranda my car came to a stop and I got out. There on the high porch alone sat a tall, middle-aged white man.

"Good afternoon," I said, as I mounted the steps.

The man stared at me in unfriendly surprise, and did not reply.

"I'm from New York," I said, "where I knew Mrs. Peterkin, who suggested I stop by, if ever I passed this way, and see the plantations she writes about."

"She's not home," he said.

"My name's Langston Hughes," I volunteered, still on the steps. "Would you be so kind as to tell her that I called?"

"She's not home," he growled a second time. And that is all I ever got out of the man on the porch.

"Please give Mrs. Peterkin my message then and tell her I'm sorry to have missed her," I said.

"She's not at home," he insisted.

As we drove away, I looked back to see the man staring at me openmouthed.

But, in contrast to this strange behavior, at Columbia a distinguished collector of Negro folk lore, the venerable physician, Dr. A. C. L. Adams, came to my program, sat on the front row in the audi-

torium and invited me out to his plantation the next day. My Negro
host, Dr. Green, who knew Dr. Adams professionally, offered to drive
me to his country place. When I told some of the colored citizens of
Columbia where I was going, they said, "Oh, old Dr. Adams will
introduce you to a lot of his colored relatives. That plantation is run
by the doctor's relatives on the colored side. And he is a fine old
white man himself."

He was a fine old man, exactly my idea of what a *true* Southern
gentleman should be. Dr. Adams' *Congaree Sketches* and other vig-
nettes I had enjoyed very much, as I had relished his Negro dialogues
and bits of folklore that had frequently appeared in *Harper's*. When
we arrived on his plantation, he greeted us cordially in front of the
Big House and invited us in. My host from Columbia, the colored
doctor, got out of the car as he spoke to Dr. Adams, but did not
come into the house. He remained outside, smoking in the car. There
was nothing inhibiting or self-consciously Southern about Dr. Adams,
in so far as I could tell. He invited me to have a seat in the living
room, sat down himself, conversed most cordially, and made me
fell quite at home. Presently he sent to the fields for the plantation
hands whose dialogues he featured in his stories. They came and
they, too, seemed perfectly at home, joking and telling tales. One
of them brought a guitar and hit a few tunes. We had a very good
time that afternoon, but my Negro host from Columbia puzzled me
by remaining in the yard. A buxom colored woman in a neat head-
rag and spotless apron brought in food and drinks, and served the
white doctor and myself as the taletelling and music went on. I was
having a wonderful time, but did not wish to keep my colored
driver-host waiting too long, so finally I begged away and started
back to town. Dr. Adams and all his Negroes waved to us from
the porch.

On the road to Columbia, I got up the courage to ask Dr. Green
why he had not come into Dr. Adams' plantation house with me.
Dr. Green said, "Well, in the South, there are some things colored
people who live here just can't do. Dr. Adams is a fine man. To
him my coming in would mean nothing. But had I gone through
the front door of that house as a guest, and word of it got around
among the white people of Columbia, it could ruin my hospital.
The white drugstores might refuse to honor my prescriptions, and
no more white businessmen would contribute to our building fund
for the new hospital Negroes hope to erect. That is why I stayed
outside, Mr. Hughes, and did not come in."

WARNING IN MISSISSIPPI

On the Sunday afternoon when I read my poems at Bethune-Cook-man College with Mary McLeod Bethune presiding, I closed with "The Negro Mother" from my new booklet. "Imagine," I said, "a black woman of old in her starched white apron and bright bandanna."

> Children, I come back today
> To tell you a story of the long dark way
> That I had to climb, that I had to know
> In order that our race might live and grow.
> Three hundred years in the deepest South:
> But God put a dream and a sing in my mouth.
> God put a dream like steel in my soul.
> Now, through my children, I'm reaching my goal.
> Now, through my children, young and free,
> I realize the blessings denied to me. . . .
> I nourished the dream that nothing could smother
> Deep in my breast, the Negro Mother. . . .

"My son, my son!" cried Mrs. Bethune, rising with tears in her eyes to embrace me on the platform. In closing, her choir sang, "We Are Climbing Jacob's Ladder," as the largely white audience of winter visitors from the big Daytona Beach hotels filled the baskets with checks and greenbacks.

Mrs. Bethune knew how to get things done. She once told me, "People wonder how I can move into action these poor colored women's clubs in some of our backward towns, get them building their own clubhouses and community centers and setting up libraries, and doing something else besides just meeting and eating. Well, when I am presiding over a district meeting, I simply tell these women what I want done. I say, 'Now, I want Sister So-and-So to make a motion to do this, that or the other thing, whatever it is . . . Now, I want you, Sister, over there to second this motion . . . Now I want everybody here—I said *everybody*—to vote, Aye!— Let's vote . . . Motion carried.' "

In Miami, I gave a program in an undertaker's parlor, since Negroes had no auditorium there. Then from Florida we drove along the Gulf to New Orleans where I was presented at Straight College. After the program a teen-age girl came up to me with a

sheaf of poems, which I glanced at quickly, between shaking hands
and autographing books that Raddie was selling. I took the poems
to be the usual poor output so often thrust into my hands at public
gatherings. Then, almost immediately, I saw that these poems
showed talent, so I spent an hour after the program going over them
with the girl and pointing out to her where I thought they might
be improved. The youngster's name was Margaret Walker. A
dozen years later her first book of poems, *For My People,* received
the Yale University Younger Poets Award. The author sent me an
advance copy inscribed:

> To Langston—in gratitude
> for his encouragement even
> when the poems were no good.
>   Sincerely,
>   Margaret Walker

Southern University on the Mississippi near Baton Rouge, with
its charming old campus beneath the live oaks and hanging moss,
was our next stop. Then into the State of Mississippi, to Jackson,
Piney Woods, Holly Springs and Meridian. At Meridian a kindly
old white gentleman in the audience came up and said gently,
"I just want to warn you that you shouldn't be reading those race-
equality poems in Meridian, and you'd better be careful selling
your books. There are folks in this state who wouldn't like what
you say."

I knew that there were towns in Mississippi where Negro news-
papers from the North were not allowed to be sold openly. Vendors
had to bootleg Negro papers containing democracy-for-all editorials,
and one man I'd met had been run out of town for selling *The
Chicago Defender.* Mississippi was a state where few Negroes then
dared to vote for fear of violence. In that year, 1931, there had been
twelve lynchings in the South. Several of my poems were about
voting and lynching; and I always read some of them on each
program, as well as one or two poems about the Scottsboro Case.
It was my poetry of this type which caused the kindly old white
man to warn me about his fellow Mississippians. But, in contrast,
at Greenville, Mississippi, in the very heart of the levee country,
the leading white poet of the state, Will Alexander Percy, acted as
the chairman of my program at a Negro church. He introduced
me most graciously to the audience. Later he sent me an inscribed
copy of his autobiography, *Lanterns on the Levee,* and over the
years that followed I had several beautiful letters from him. But I
met less than half a dozen such gentlemanly Southerners on my

winter-long tour. Instead, I found a great social and cultural gulf between the races in the South, astonishing to one who, like myself, from the North, had never known such uncompromising prejudices. Of course, a Negro traveler soon got accustomed to—even if never able to accept emotionally—the many visible evidences of legal segregation: the WHITE and COLORED signs everywhere from station waiting rooms to public water fountains, the Jim Crow cars on the trains, the COLORED ENTRANCE placards in the alleys where movie stairways led up to the highest gallery, the restaurants where Negroes could not eat, and so on. But the unpredictable and unexpected things that suddenly happened are the things I never forget.

Once I was late for an evening engagement because, at a river crossing where the bridge was under repair, a ferry was being used. But all the Negro cars on the road had to wait until *all* the white cars in line, no matter how far back, had gotten on the boat. The ferry captain would fill his boat up with white automobiles and leave the Negro cars standing there. By the time the boat crossed the river and came back, more white drivers had gathered. The ferry master would again motion the whites onto the boat ahead of the Negroes. Finally I was allowed to get across the river.

A less irritating but more fantastic incident happened in Savannah. In New York every Sunday, due especially to my interest in the *Book Review* section, I always bought the *Times*. It was not always easy to find a Sunday *Times* in the South. But whenever I stopped in a large city, I tried to find it.

In Savannah I learned that the *Times* might be purchased at a newsstand in one of the railway stations, so I walked down to the station one afternoon to secure a copy. In the colored waiting room there was no newsstand, so I went outside on the sidewalk and around into the white waiting room where I bought the *Sunday Times* without incident. But, coming out of the station, just at the door, a white policeman stopped me.

He yelled, "You can't come in and out this door."

"There's no newsstand in the colored waiting room," I explained.

"I don't care nothing about that!" he barked. "You can't come in this door. This is for white folks."

"Oh," I said, "I am going out now."

"You can't go out this way neither," said the cop as I started through the door.

This puzzled me, as there was no other way out of the station except through the train sheds. "I just came in this way," I said.

"Well, you can't go out this way," barked the cop. "Niggers can't use this door."

"How do I get out then?" I asked.

"Only way I see," said the cop seriously, "is for you to walk the tracks.' '

In order to get out of the Savannah station with the *New York Times* that day, I had to go through the train gates and follow the railroad tracks to the nearest crossing to reach the street. I had never experienced anything so absurd before. The seriousness of that white policeman and the utter stupidity of being *at* a door, but not permitted to go *through* it, made me burst out laughing as I walked along with my paper from Manhattan.

I remembered, when I was in my teens, coming up from a summer in Mexico on my return to school in Cleveland, I had gone into the dining car one evening as the train was heading through Texas. I was seated alone when a white man came in. Without looking, he sat down opposite me. When I glanced across the table, I saw that the man was staring at me with a look of utter amazement. Suddenly the man jumped as though he had been shot and cried, "Why, you're a nigger, ain't you?" Then the man fled from the dining car as though he had sat down in front of a lion by mistake. As many Negroes as there are in Texas, what could there be about just *one* at a table in a public dining car that could so startle a white man? The colored waiters who saw the incident laughed, and so did I.

This was the sort of thing that continually puzzled and amused me in the South. Certainly the much lauded Southern gentility and aristocratic good manners are seldom shown toward Negroes. The man on Julia Peterkin's porch never did rise to greet me, a stranger, as would almost anyone in the North. The Savannah policeman did not say, "Sir, I am sorry, but you are in the wrong place." He simply barked, "You can't come in here!" When I thought about these things seriously, they were not funny. They were boorish and stupid. Some years later when I asked Carson McCullers, the Georgia writer, why white people in the South behaved so badly toward Negroes, Mrs. McCullers said, "Their hind brains don't work."

PERSONAL AUTOGRAPH

My standard fee for a program was one hundred dollars. This seemed like a very large amount of money to me—simply for reading from a book of poems—especially since I was completely without platform experience. But most of the larger Negro colleges were willing to pay that amount; and some of the biggest ones would pay even more.

On the other hand, not all of my sponsors, by any means, could pay a hundred dollars. But Raddie and I worked out a technique of letter writing that nine times out of ten brought an engagement *of some sort.* Using *The Negro Year Book's* listing of schools and colleges as a starting point for selecting the area we intended to cover, we would, in our first letters to prospective sponsors, state that within a given period I expected to be in the vicinity, and that my fee for a program was one hundred dollars, plus board and lodging, although shelter was taken for granted, anyway, since in the South public accommodations for Negro travelers are very poor, or often lacking altogether. As an afterthought, we would add that, of course, some adjustment of the fee might be made if one hundred dollars seemed exorbitant, since our main purpose was the spreading of culture through poetry. Should a reply plead poverty, my second letter would suggest seventy-five dollars in lieu of one hundred. Should this turn out to be too much, Raddie would then write that, since we would be in the vicinity, anyhow, as a *special* concession Langston Hughes would come for fifty dollars.

However, should even fifty dollars prove too large a fee—and in that depression era it was a considerable sum to some communities—I would instruct my tour manager on my behalf to say that, being nearby and having a free evening, I would give a program for expenses, say twenty-five dollars. If the school or church wrote back that they could not afford even that meager sum, we still did not give up. If I was without a speaking date to fill an empty evening in the area, we would reply that we were planning to stop in their town overnight, and so would—contingent, of course, upon being permitted to offer my books for sale —give a *free* program for culture's sake. When all other offers failed, that one almost always worked. The end result was that almost every evening for months was booked solid, and sometimes Sunday afternoons, as well. In this way we kept a full itinerary, driving several hundred miles a week, and I introduced my poems to every major city, town, and campus in the South that year. No matter how small a dot on the map a town was, we did not scorn it, and my audiences ranged all the way from college students to cotton pickers, from kindergarten children to the inmates of old folks homes.

Entertainment was the hardest part of my tour. White authors and lecturers on a similar tour could always take refuge at a hotel after a program. Negro speakers, barred out of hotels, were at the mercy of private hosts in private homes from whom there was no escape. If the house was small and a party was given in my honor, there was no possibility of going to bed until the last guest had gone. Southerners are great ones for hospitality. Warm and amiable and friendly as it was, I was nevertheless almost killed by entertainment, drowned in punch, gorged on food, and worn out with handshaking. I must have eaten at least a thousand chickens that winter. And I lost a great deal of sleep being entertained from town to town so continuously.

My name I must have written a million times that season on printed programs, in books, on scraps of paper, and even on paper napkins at rural receptions. But, my most personal autograph is, I suppose, obliterated by now. I inscribed it unawares in a small town in Mississippi near the Alabama state line. I was reading my poems that evening for a colored church. I was housed with one of the pillars of the church in a tiny home, spotlessly clean and filled, when I arrived, with the fumes of wonderful cooking. Tired and dusty after a day-long drive, I wanted nothing so much as a good hot bath before dinner. My hostess in preparation for my coming had done a little painting, freshing up all the baseboards and things with white paint. At the very last moment, it seemed, in her zeal to have everything spick-and-span, she had even freshly painted the bathtub, outside and *in,* with white enamel. Unfortunately, the enamel had not quite dried when I arrived. But, unaware of this fact, I blithely ran the bath tub full of hot water and sat down therein, soaking myself happily as I lathered my hair. But then minutes later, when I started to get up, I could not tear myself loose. I was stuck to the bottom of the tub! With great deliberateness, slowly and carefully pushing myself upward, I finally managed to rise without leaving any skin behind. But I certainly left imprinted on that bath tub a most personal autograph.

That evening as I sat stiffly in the seat of honor at church, I was covered with enamel where I sat. But I didn't tell my hostess what had happened, not wishing to embarrass her. In the next town I bought a gallon of turpentine and took a bath in it.

MAKING POETRY PAY

By midwinter I had worked out a public routine of reading my poetry that almost never failed to provoke, after each poem, some sort of audible audience response—laughter, applause, a grunt, a groan, a sigh, or an "Amen!" I began my programs quite simply by telling where I was born in Missouri, that I grew up in Kansas in the geographical heart of the country, and was, therefore very American, that I belonged to a family that was always moving; and I told something of my early travels about the Midwest and how, at fourteen, in Lincoln, Illinois, I was elected Class Poet for the eighth-grade graduating exercises, and from then on I kept writing poetry.

After this biographical introduction I would read to my audiences the first of my poems, written in high school, and show how my poetry had changed over the years. To start my reading, I usually selected some verses written when I was about fifteen:

> I had my clothes cleaned
> Just like new.
> I put 'em on but
> I still feels blue.
>
> I bought a new hat,
> Sho is fine,
> But I wish I had back that
> Old gal o' mine.
>
> I got new shoes,
> They don't hurt my feet,
> But I ain't got nobody
> To call me sweet.

Then I would say, "That's a sad poem, isn't it?" Everybody would laugh. Then I would read some of my jazz poems so my listeners could laugh more. I wanted them to laugh a lot early in the program, so that later in the evening they would not laugh when I read poems like "Porter":

> I must say,
> Yes, sir,
> To you all the time.
> Yes, sir!
> Yes, sir!
>
> All my days
> Climbing up a great big mountain
> Of yes, sirs!

> Rich old white man
> Owns the world.
> Gimme yo' shoes to shine.
>
> Yes, sir, boss!
> Yes, sir!

By the time I reached this point in the program my nonliterary listeners would be ready to think in terms of their own problems. Then I read poems about women domestics, workers on the Florida roads, poor black students wanting to shatter the darkness of ignorance and prejudice, and one about the sharecroppers of Mississippi:

> Just a herd of Negroes
> Driven to the field,
> Plowing, planting, hoeing,
> To make the cotton yield.
>
> When the cotton's picked
> And the work is done,
> Boss man takes the money
> And you get none.
>
> Just a herd of Negroes
> Driven to the field.
> Plowing, planting, hoeing,
> To make the cotton yield.

Many of my verses were documentary, journalistic and topical. All across the South that winter I read my poems about the plight of the Scottsboro boys:

> Justice is a blind goddess.
> To this we blacks are wise:
> Her bandage hides two festering sores
> That once perhaps were eyes.

Usually people were deeply attentive. But if at some point in the program my audience became restless—as audiences sometimes will, no matter what a speaker is saying—or if I looked down from the platform and noticed someone about to go to sleep, I would pull out my ace in the hole, a poem called "Cross." This poem, delivered dramatically, I had learned, would make anybody, white or black, sit up and take notice. It is a poem about miscegenation—a very provocative subject in the South. The first line—intended to awaken all sleepers—I would read in a loud voice:

> My old man's a white old man. . . .

And thus would usually arouse any who dozed. Then I would pause before continuing in a more subdued tone:

> My old mother's black.

Then in a low, sad, thoughtful tragic vein:

> But if ever I cursed my white old man
> I take my curses back.
>
> If ever I cursed my black old mother
> And wished she were in hell,
> I'm sorry for that evil wish
> And now I wish her well.
>
> My old man died in a fine big house,
> My ma died in a shack.
> I wonder where I'm gonna die,
> Being neither white nor black.

Here I would let my voice trail off into a lonely silence. Then I would stand quite still for a long time, because I knew I had the complete attention of my listeners again.

Usually after a résumé of the racial situation in our country, with an optimistic listing of past achievements on the part of Negroes, and future possibilities, I would end the evening with:

> I, too, sing America.
>
> I am the darker brother.
> They send me
> To eat in the kitchen
> When company comes,
> But I laugh,
> And eat well,
> And grow strong.
>
> Tomorrow
> I'll sit at the table
> When company comes.
> Nobody'll dare

Say to me,
"Eat in the kitchen,"
Then.

Besides,
They'll see
How beautiful I am
And be ashamed.

I, too, am America.

BOMBS IN BARCELONA

Nicolás Guillén went with me to Spain in the spring of 1937 as
a correspondent for a Cuban paper. Since everybody said food in
that war-torn country was scarce, we took along with us an enor-
mous basket of edibles. But we ate it all on the train. Guillén
was a jovial companion with whom to travel and on the way to
Barcelona he entertained me with Cubanismos and folk songs:

> *Oyelo bien, encargada!*
> *Esta es la voz que retumba—*
> *Esta es la ultima rumba*
> *Que bailamos en tu morada.*

At the border between France and Spain there is a tunnel, a long
stretch of darkness through which the night express from Paris
passes in the early morning. When the train comes out into the
sunlight, on the Spanish side of the mountain, with a shining blue
bay where children swim in the Mediterranean, you see the village
of Port Bou. The town seemed bright and quiet that morning. But
as I left the train, I noticed that almost all of the windows of the
station were shattered. There were machine-gun marks on the
walls of the custom-house and several nearby houses were in ruins,
gutted by bombs. In the winding streets of Port Bou there were
signs, REFUGIO, pointing to holes in the mountains to be used in
case of air raids. And on old walls there were new Loyalist posters.
One read: "It's better to be the tail of a lion than the head of a
rat." This was my first view of war-time Spain, this little town
by the blue sea where travelers changed trains.

In the country they were harvesting the wheat, and as we chugged
southward, men and women were swinging primitive scythes in the

fields. The Barcelona train was very crowded that day and all around me folks kept up a rapid fire of conversation in various accents. Guillén and I were the only Negroes on the train, so I thought, until at one of the stations when we got out to buy fruit, we noticed a dark face leaning from a window of the coach ahead of us. When the train started again, we went forward to investigate. He was a brownskin boy from the Canary Islands in a red shirt and a blue beret. He had escaped from the Canaries by the simple expedient of getting into his fishing boat with the rest of her crew and sailing toward French Morocco. From there he had gotten to France. The Canary Islands were a part of Spain, he said, but the fishermen did not like the men who had usurped power, so many of them sailed their boats away and came to fight with the Loyalists. This young man spoke a strange Spanish dialect that was hard for Guillén to understand, but he told us that many folks in the Canaries are colored, mixed with African and Spanish blood.

What should have been a short trip from the French border to Barcelona, took all day and well into the night. When our blacked-out train pulled into the blacked-out city near midnight, Nicolás Guillén was so tired that he had stopped talking or singing, and wanted nothing so much as a good bed. There were no lights whatsoever on the platform of the Barcelona station, so we followed the crowd moving slowly like shadows into the station where one lone lantern glimmered behind a ticket wicket. I was loaded down as usual with bags, books, records and a typewriter. Guillén had sense enough to travel light with mostly just his songs and himself. He helped me carry things, and clung to what little remained of our hamper of food. We took a bus through pitch-black streets to a hotel on the Ramblas—there was no gas for taxis and only one bus met each train. I was so tired that night that I slept right through an air-raid alert. Hotel instructions were that all guests were to assemble in the lobby when an alert sounded. Since the hotel had no basement, the ground floor was considered safest. But the so-called ground floor of this hotel was really several feet above street level. The lobby had enormous French doors and windows opening on a balcony. It did not look very safe to me. But I learned later that in a bombing no place was really safe, and that the Spaniards had two rather fatalistic theories about protection. One was during an air raid to go to the roof of a building and fall down with it if a bomb struck. The other was go to the ground floor and, in case of a hit, be buried at once under debris.

One could tell that Barcelona was jittery from the terrific bombing it had undergone the day before I arrived. But nothing happened during the first twenty-four hours I was there, so Guillén and I walked about, looking at the destruction and at the antiaircraft guns on most of the busy corners, the flower sellers on the tree-lined Ramblas, and the passing crowds everywhere, with folks clinging to the overcrowded street cars all day long. Sitting in the cafés, whenever the public radios started to blare out the latest war news, everybody would jump. Nerves were certainly on edge. But there were no planes overhead all day.

As Guillén and I sat at a sidewalk table on the Ramblas that afternoon, a dark young man passed, turned, looked back at me and spoke. He recognized me, he said, because he had heard me read my poems at the library in New York. He was a Puerto Rican named Roldan, who had come from Harlem to serve as an interpreter in Spain. At that moment he was on his way to a dance at a little club where the Cubans and other Spanish-speaking peoples from the Caribbean gathered. He invited us to come with him. The club had a beautiful courtyard and a little bar where rum drinks were mixed. The party that afternoon was in honor of the International Brigaders on leave, among them several Spanish-speaking Negroes and a colored Portugese. Catalonian soldiers and their girls mingled gaily with the Negro guests. And Guillén, lionized as Cuba's most famous poet, was in his element, surrounded by girls.

That night back at our hotel we knew it was wartime because, in the luxurious dining room with its tuxedoed waiters, there was only one fixed menu with no choice of food. The dinner was good, but not elaborate. Later we went to an outdoor café for coffee. Until midnight we sat watching the crowds strolling up and down the tiled sidewalks of the Ramblas. The fact that Barcelona was lightless did not keep people home on a warm evening. There was a wan bulb behind the bar inside to help the barman find his bottles, but other than that no visible light save for the stars shining brightly. The buildings were great grey shadows towering in the night, with windows shuttered everywhere and curtains drawn. There must be no visible lights in any windows to guide enemy aviators.

At midnight, the public radios on many corners began to blare the war news and people gathered in large groups to hear it. Then the café closed, and we went to the hotel. I had just barely gotten to my room and begun to undress when the low extended wail of a siren began, letting us know that Fascist planes were coming. They came, we had been told, from Mallorca across the sea at a

terrific speed, dropped their bombs, then circled away into the
night again. Quickly, I put on my shirt, passed Guillén's room,
and together we started downstairs. Suddenly all the lights went out
in the hotel. We heard people rushing down the stairs in the
dark. A few had flashlights with them. Some were visibly frightened.
In the lobby a single candle was burning, casting giantlike shadows
on the walls. In an ever-increasing wail the siren sounded louder
and louder, droning its deathly warning. Suddenly it stopped. By
then the lobby was full of people, men, women and children, speak-
ing in Spanish, English, French.

In the distance we heard a series of quick explosions.

"Bombs?" I asked.

"No, antiaircraft guns," a man explained.

Everyone became very quiet. Then we heard the guns go off again.

"Come here," a man called, leading the way. Several of us went
out on the balcony where, in the dark, we could see the search-
lights playing across the sky. Little round puffs of smoke from the
antiaircraft shells floated against the stars. In the street a few
women hurried along to public bomb-proof cellars.

Then for a long while nothing happened. No bombs fell. After
about an hour, the lights suddenly came on in the hotel as a signal
that the danger had ended. Evidently, the enemy planes had been
driven away without having completed their mission. Everyone
went back upstairs to bed. The night was quiet again. I put out
out my light, opened the window and, never being troubled with
sleeplessness, I was soon sound asleep. The next thing I knew was
that, with part of my clothes in my arms, I was running in the
dark toward the stairs. A terrific explosion somewhere nearby had
literally lifted me out of bed. Apparently I had slept through an
alert, for almost all the other guests in the hotel had already as-
sembled in the lobby, huddled in various stages of dress and undress.
At the foot of the stairs I put my trousers on over my pajamas
and sat down shaking like a leaf, evidently having been frightened
to this dire extent while still asleep, because I had hardly realized
I was afraid until I felt myself shaking. When I put one hand on the
other, both hands were trembling. There were the sounds of what
seemed like a major battle going on in the streets outside—but this
was only the antiaircraft guns firing at the sky, so someone near me
explained. Suddenly I developed the worst stomachache I've ever
had in my life. I managed to find my way to a MEN'S ROOM about
the time a distant explosion sounded, far away, yet near enough
to cause the hotel to shake. When I came back, by the light of the
single candle at the desk, I managed to find Guillén, sitting calmly

like Buddha on a settee under a potted palm. He said, *"Ay, chico, eso es!"* Well, this is it! Which was of little comfort.

Gradually I began to be fully awake and less frightened, so I sat down, too. smoked a cigarette, and got acquainted with some of the other folks in the lobby. After perhaps a half hour, when the crackling of the antiaircraft batteries had died down, an all clear sounded, and the desk clerk said we might return to our beds. He blew out his candle before opening some of the French doors leading onto the balcony overlooking the Ramblas. Some of us went out on the balcony to see what was happening in the streets. An occasional military motor passed without lights, and a few people moved up and down—police and rescue workers, I supposed. As I stood there with the others a sudden crackle of shots rang out in our direction from across the corner square. Glass came down all over us from windows on the upper floors. A machine gun was firing directly at the hotel! We almost fell over each other getting back inside the lobby. Doors and shutters were slammed again. Shortly some soldiers entered from the street and said that someone on an upper floor had turned on a light. (Their orders were to fire at any exposed light in any building.) Sternly they mounted the stairs in search of the offender. Later I learned that some foreigner (not knowing the rules) had turned on a bedside bulb after he had opened his window for air. So the guards simply blasted away at the lighted room. The frightened guest was severely reprimanded. And I had cause to quake all over again. It was quite a while before I went back to sleep that night.

Eventually, however, I got used to air raids in Spain—the Junkers, Heinkels, Savoias and Capronis going over—and the sound and the feel of bombs bursting. But I never got used to the alerts—those baleful, high, eerie, wailing sirens of warning.

SWEET WINE OF VALENCIA

Somewhere along the line, the railroad to Valencia had been bombed, and no one knew just when the train service would be resumed. So Guillén and I, with others in the hotel who wished to go south, managed to hire a car to drive down the coast. Bright and early one morning through the Catalonian countryside we went speeding, through villages as old as the Roman Empire, and along the dancing Mediterranean, blue beneath the morning sky. We passed fields of wheat, groves of olives and oranges, and cities that recently had been bombed from the air or shelled from the sea. Sometimes elderly peasants in the fields lifted a clenched fist in the government salute. On walls half ruined by explosives, slogans were freshly painted hailing the People's Army. And in village squares young men were drilling to go to the front. The beautiful landscape of Spain rolled by as our car went down the road south, the Spain that had for more than a year occupied the front pages of the world, the Spain of the huge Madison Square Garden meetings in New York, the Spain that I had seen placarded in the main streets of cities like Buffalo and Denver and Salt Lake when I had lectured there: AID BESIEGED MADRID! . . . MILK FOR THE BABIES OF SPANISH DEMOCRACY! . . . MEDICAL SUPPLIES TO THE LOYALISTS! . . . The Spain to which had come from all over the world young men—including many Negroes—to fight in the International Brigades. The Spain that had brought up thousands of young Moors from Morocco as shock troops for Franco. Divided Spain, with men of color fighting on both sides. To write about them I had come to Spain.

Among the things I wanted to find out was what effect, if any, the bringing by Franco of dark troops to Spain from North Africa, had had on the people in regard to their racial attitudes. Had color prejudice been created in a land that had not known it before? What had been the treatment of Moorish prisoners by the Loyalists? Were wounded Moors segregated in the prison hospitals? Were there any Moors at all on the government side? How were American Negroes received in the cities of Spain when they came on furlough from the Brigades?

As I wondered about these things, our car began to slow down in the late afternoon for traffic was growing heavier on the road. Now burros, trucks and oxcarts mingled in increasingly long lines. Fords and oxen, peasants on muleback and soldiers in American trucks, the old and the new vied for dusty passage. On either side of us were orange groves as fas as one could see. I thought of *Cuentos Valencianos* and the novel, *Entre Naranjos,* by Blasco-Ibáñez that I had read in Mexico. About sunset I saw in the distance medieval towers, mingling with tall modern structures. We were approaching a city, a big city.

"Valencia," the chauffeur said.

Ancient Mediterranean seaport, now the seat of the Spanish government. From my days as a merchant seaman, I had happy memories of Valencia. That night as I looked out the windows in the Hotel Londres with the crowded Plaza Castelos below, I was glad to find myself again in that pleasant coastal town. Valencia was a rest center for Loyalist troops and numbers of foreign sailors were in and out, too, including some Americans on boats bringing supplies to Spain. The cafés were full morning to night—even long after dark, for Valencia did not take care to black out as completely as Barcelonia, although the city was shelled from the sea and bombed from the air with frequency. But the Valencians just didn't seem to care much. They had good wine and good food—fresh fish, melons and the sweetest of oranges and grapes—much more food than any other city I visited in Spain. And there were parks and bathing beaches, music and dancing, antiaircraft guns making fireworks in the sky every night, and tracer bullets arching like Roman candles in the air as Franco's bombs lighted up the port. The docks were miles from the heart of Valencia, so whenever an alert sounded, the citizens would say, "Oh, they're just going to bomb the port, not us." And they kept right on doing whatever they were doing. Nobody bothered much to seek shelter. People were always being nicked by bits of antiaircraft shrapnel showering down on them as they stood in the street or on rooftops trying to see the enemy planes when they should have been indoors.

I spent a week or so in Valencia before moving on to Madrid and the battle fronts. Word of our coming had already been sent ahead from Paris to the House of Culture in Valencia, so the poet, Miguel Hernandez and several other writers made Guillén and me welcome, and soon found for us a guesthouse where we might stay much cheaper than at a hotel. But the day we arrived the House of Culture was draped in mourning and the body of Gerda Taro, young Hungarian photographer, was lying in state there. Taking pictures at the front during an attack, she had been smashed between a tank and a truck the day before. She was Robert Capa's friend in Spain, and like him took wonderful photographs, everyone said. Valencia honored her as the first foreign newspaperwoman to die in battle during the war.

From Valencia I wrote a long letter to the girl I was in love with then, Elsie Roxborough, in Detroit. Elsie had staged a play of mine, *Emperor of Haiti,* and was ambitious to become a director in the professional theater, radio, or motion pictures. She was a lovely-looking girl, ivory-white of skin with dark eyes and raven hair like a Levantine. Each time that we met in Detroit or Cleveland or Chicago, Elsie would tell me about her dreams, and wonder whether or not it would be better for her to pass for white to achieve them. From what I knew of the American entertainment field and how Negroes were then almost entirely excluded from the directorial or technical aspects of it, I agreed with her that it was difficult for any

colored person to gain entrance except as a performer—as a director
or technician, almost impossible—and for a colored woman I would
think it harder even than for a man. Elsie was often mistaken for
white in public places, so it would be no trouble at all for her to
pass as white. While I was in Spain she wrote me that she had made
up her mind to do so. She intended to cease being colored. The
intervals between her letters to me gradually became greater, until
finally no letter came at all. When I got back to the United States,
Elsie had disappeared into the white world. None of her friends saw
her any more, nor did I. But every Christmas for several years she
sent me a carefully chosen little present—with no return address on
the packet.

That summer in Spain the beach at Valencia was as lively as
Coney Island on the Fourth of July. The sand and surf were crowded
with soldiers on leave and their girls. In the surf I saw one afternoon
an ebony-dark young man, bathing with a party of Spaniards. Think-
ing he was perhaps an American or a Jamaican from one of the In-
ternational Brigades, when he came out of the water I spoke to him
in English, but he replied in Spanish. He was an African from
Guinea on the West Coast, who had some to study in Spain before
the war. He had enlisted in the People's Army, he told me, but
having been a university student, he was assigned to the officers'
school in Valencia to study for a commission.

I asked this young African what he thought about the war. He
said, "I hope the government wins because the new Republic stands
for a liberal colonial policy with a chance for my people in Africa to
become educated. On Franco's side are all the old dukes and counts
and traders who have exploited the colonies so long, never giving us
schools or anything else. Now they are making the Africans fight
against the Spanish people—using the Moors and my own people,
too, to try to crush the Republic. And the same Italians who dropped
bombs on Ethiopia now come over here to help Franco bomb Span-
iards. You can pick up shrapnel in Valencia with Italian markings on
it."

When he learned I was from New York, he wanted to know all
about Harlem, and if I had ever met Joe Louis. He said he would
like to come to America some day.

"To stay?" I asked him.

"No," he said, "just to visit. I like Spain. My wife is Spanish."

"I like Spain, too," I said, "only I miss the bullfights."

"I never saw one," he said, "and now all the famous matadors
have run away to Franco where the money is. They are not as brave
at fighting fascists as they are at facing bulls."

A common saying in Valencia was, "All the best bullfighters and all the best whores have gone over to the enemy—but we'll get along without them." That summer I did not see any bullfighters, but the few remaining prostitutes were making a fortune. Valencia, like all Mediterranean seaports, had had a great many houses of pleasure when I was there on a freighter in the early 'twenties. Now there were not nearly so many, although the city was full of soldiers on leave and sailors with bonus pay to spend, looking for agreeable girls. What houses of ill-fame there were now operated only from four in the afternoon until seven in the evening. But during these three hours of operation, the houses were as crowded as a New York subway train at rush hour, and the women did a rushing business. Unlike American soldiers visiting such houses, the Spaniards did not queue up and take their proper turns. Instead, they pushed, shoved and crowded by the hundreds into the parlors of the houses, charging boisterously but amiably like young bulls after each girl who came into view. As soon as a woman was free, she was mobbed by as many men as could reach her at once. Finally the girl would manage to untangle one eager customer from the mob and disappear, to return in a few minutes for another. When the doors were closed at seven, the girls of the houses remained at work until all those within the gates were accommodated.

Such after-hours courtesies, however, did not exist in Madrid, I learned later in the summer. There the houses of prostitution like every other business, had to close promptly on time; unserved patrons, no matter how long they had been waiting, had to leave. Madrid was a fighting city, not a center of furlough pleasures; so the black-out and curfew were strictly enforced. But in Madrid after dark the ladies of the evening took to the streets. In *For Whom the Bell Tolls,* Ernest Hemingway has a vivid description of nocturnal love-making along the avenues of the besieged capital. But I do not recall that he described one of its most picturesque areas. After dark just off the Puerta del Sol in the heart of Madrid, in the block behind the Telefonica—the city's only skyscraper and a favorite target for Franco's artillery—numerous prostitutes and hundreds of soldiers off duty congregated. On moonlight nights these human shadow shapes, milling about, could see other only dimly in the moonlight. On nights of no moon, in the inky blackness between the tall buildings, no one could see anything. But the darkness up and down the street would be pin-pointed by the tiny flames of dozens and dozens of matches being lighted by the soldiers to peer into the faces of the prostitutes walking in the dark. The blacked-out canyon of the street danced with little flames of hope, burning briefly, then flung to the

ground as some young soldier, lighting a match at the sound of a
seductive voice, found himself peering into a broken-down witch's
face.

"*Caramba!* You're older than my grandmother!" was a not infre-
quent exclamation as the match dropped to the pavement and the
soldier in disgust moved on to the next feminine voice calling in the
dark. But sometimes an artillery shell gave a sudden burst of light,
enough for a soldier to see a woman clearly, and perhaps pick out a
partner for his needs.

Concerning the nice girls of the town, there was a very sad story
going the rounds of Madrid that year. In pre-revolutionary Spain,
good maidens did not go out with young men until they were en-
gaged, and only then accompanied by a chaperon. Such girls re-
mained virgin until married. If it were rumored otherwise, and
chastity were doubted, a girl might never get a good husband. But
when the Franco troops besieged Madrid in overwhelming numbers
early in the days of the Civil War, and when it seemed that the city
could hold out no longer, word spread that if Madrid fell to Franco
his Moorish legions would rape all the women in the city. This
pleasure, without hindrance, Franco had promised them. Rather
than be raped, many of the good girls of Madrid decided to give
themselves to their sweethearts—the gallant young men who ex-
pected to die anyway, within a few days, in defense of the city. So,
under the thunder of Franco guns and the bombs of foreign planes,
one thunderous night shaken by gunfire, a sort of mass submission
of the decent maidens of Madrid to their beloveds took place. But
due to the miracle of "*No pasaron!*"—*They Shall Not Pass!*—the
city did not fall—not that week, nor that month, nor that year.
Madrid held out. Then, even in the eyes of their own lovers, thou-
sands of the nice girls of Madrid, since they were no longer virgins,
were held in contempt.

In Madrid, when I went to visit the famous bull ring, it was
empty save for antiaircraft guns mounted in the arena. Madrid's
famous *majas* with their mantillas were gone, too, and the ladies of
the evening were mostly homely hags. The great actors and actresses
and musicians—except for a very few courageous artists—had all fled
to San Sebastián, Salamanca, or Seville along with the rich indus-
trialists and the Franco generals. But one great artist remained, the
flamenco singer, La Niña de los Peines. She refused to leave the city
she loved. When I learned in Valencia that La Niña was still singing
in Madrid under fire, I decided it was time I got my permit validated
for the front. Madrid was the front.

BREAKFAST IN MADRID

My first Sunday in Madrid, having heard that La Niña de los Peines was singing, I found the theater. The performance was at eleven o'clock in the morning—why that odd hour I never knew—but the place was already crowded when I arrived to discover on a bare stage a group of Gypsy guitarists and dancers clapping hands and tapping heels as I entered. In their midst on a wooden kitchen chair sat a middle-aged woman. The performers were not dressed in traditional Gypsy clothing—as in a professional theater presentation—but wore the ordinary working clothes of poor Madrileños. There was nothing visually colorful or picturesque about them. They might have been people out of the audience sitting on the barren stage with no special lighting and no curtains, and without a spotlight, fooling around with a few guitars. Never having seen La Niña before, I asked if she were there. My seat neighbor said, "Yes. The old one in the middle on the chair, that's her."

La Niña de los Peines, Pastora Pavón. She was clapping her hands with the others, but someone else was singing when I sat down. Shortly, without any introduction or fanfare, she herself sat up very straight in her chair and, after a series of quavering little cries, began to half-speak, half-sing a *solea*—to moan, intone and cry in a Gypsy Spanish I did not understand, a kind of raw heartbreak rising to a crescendo that made half the audience cry aloud with her after the rise and fall of each phrase. The guitars played behind her, but you forgot the guitars and heard only her voice rising hard and harsh, wild, lonely and bitter-sweet from the bare stage of the theater with the unshaded house lights on full. This plain old woman could make the hair rise on your head, could do to your insides what the moan of an air-raid siren did, could rip your soul-case with her voice. I went to hear La Niña many times. I found the strange, high, wild crying of her flamenco in some ways much like the primitive Negro blues of the deep South. The words and music were filled with heartbreak, yet vibrant with resistance to defeat, and hard with the will to savor life in spite of its vicissitudes. The poor of Madrid adored La Niña de los Peines—this old Girl with the Combs—who refused to leave her besieged city, and whose voice became part of the strength of Madrid's stubborn resistance under the long-range guns, a few miles away.

The Franco batteries shelled the city almost daily. I wondered, when I first arrived in Madrid, why I was offered my choice of the large and beautifully furnished front rooms on the top floor of the Alianza de Intelectuales, instead of the much smaller former servant's room at the back of the house. With living quarters very scarce in Madrid, and the clubhouse crowded, I wondered why someone was not already occupying these spacious front rooms with a lovely view of the city. Gratefully I accepted one. Guillén, much wiser, took a servant's room belowstairs. I soon learned that my room, being a high corner room, was the room most exposed to shellings in the whole house. In fact, its windows on one side, directly faced the Fascist guns. At night I could see the flash of enemy fire when shells poured into the city. But once I'd moved in, I stayed. Another American and I were the only tenants on the top floor. The Spanish writers, thinking that all Americans were like Ernest Hemingway, anyhow, believed we loved to live facing guns.

My fellow American was away at the front when I arrived. But when he came back, I found him a well-bred Princetonian named Harry Dunham, a young cameraman for Pathé News, who had been in the thick of several battles and had taken some daring sequences. We became quite good friends and he gave me a picture of himself riding atop an armored car with his camera. Some years later Harry was killed in the American Army in the South Pacific. But neither of us were struck by shells that summer in our exposed bedrooms of the Alianza.

The poet, Rafael Alberti and his wife, Maria Teresa Leon, were in charge of the Alianza de Intelectuales at Marques del Duero 7. They lived reasonably safe from shells in a little apartment on the substreet level of the mansion, an apartment that probably had been occupied by a governess or a tutor. The actual servants' rooms were in a two-story wing of their own, and were very small. When I asked Guillén if he did not wish to share my large light airy chamber on the top floor, Guillén said, no, he would keep his servant's room with its one window. Mine, he said, had too much glass to shatter in case a shell struck the house. Guillén said he would hate to be blown up *and cut up by glass also*. With Dunham away most of the time making newsreels, on that third floor all by myself, it was lonely, especially during shellings.

This Alianza was the writers' and artists' club. Few foreigners lived there—Dunham, Guillén and I being the only ones then. It was a richly furnished house of some fifty rooms, the former home of a rebel marquis whose family fortune was derived from the slave trade in the days of the Spanish Main. The walls of the living room were hung with priceless Goyas, El Grecos, and other famous paintings.

There were rare medieval tapestries, enormous porcelain vases, and much antique furniture, including real Louis XV chairs. The marquis had been a great bullfight fan and possessed chests full of spangled toreador suits. Other trunks were filled with ruffled skirts and beautiful lace mantillas, which smart Spanish women sometimes wore to *corridas* and the Feria at Sevilla. There was an entire room full of old armor and suits of mail, too, such as Don Quixote wore. Sometimes on chilly nights when we had nothing better to do, the men would all dress up in matador jackets and the women in dresses from Seville of old and have, to my jazz records, an impromptu costume ball. But we were careful to put everything back properly in the basement, for some of the things were priceless, and we knew they would probably go to a museum when the war was over.

The military bus that brought Guillén and me to Madrid over a shell-scarred road had arrived at night after a thirteen-hour trip from Valencia. Dinner at the Alianza was over, and we were told that there were no restaurants open after dark in the whole city. Anyway, with a curfew no one was allowed abroad late at night without a military pass. I went to bed very hungry. But I slept right through the breakfast hour the next morning. At the Alianza there were only two meals a day, breakfast at nine in the morning and dinner at eight at night. There was not a scrap of food to be found in the house between meals. There were no railroads running into Madrid, and only one highway for the transportation of food—the military road over which our bus had come. A city of a million people was fed entirely by this one road. No wonder there was almost nothing to eat for sale anywhere, nothing on the shelves of the food shops, and restaurants—what few there were—were strictly rationed, with a food card required of each diner.

But on that morning of intense hunger, I refused to believe it would be my fate to starve my first day in Madrid. Guillén had already gotten up and gone out, as had Alberti. So I ventured into the streets alone and found my way through the morning sunlight to the Grand Via. Fortunately, speaking Spanish fairly well, I was able to ask of almost every passer-by where a restaurant might be. Most people looked at me in complete amazement and said they knew of none in operation at that hour anywhere in town. With supplies so short, Madrid restaurants open only at dinner time. A few food stores were pointed out to me, but they had nothing edible to sell, even if I had had a ration card—which I'd not yet secured.

Soon I reached the Puerta del Sol, the Times Square of Madrid, all of whose shops were sandbagged, with just a hole between sandbags for an entrance. There were many broken windows, some

boarded up and some not. But I was too hungry to pay much atten-
tion to the ravages of war. I felt certain there must be *somewhere* in
that city something to eat. I determined to find it. At last I did. A
man in the Puerta del Sol told me that each day in a bar near the
Telefonica, they opened a keg of beer at noon—and with the beer
there were usually appetizers.

I headed post haste for the bar. It was crowded to the doors, but
I managed to wedge my way inside. The keg of beer had not yet been
opened. Finally noon came, and the crowd of soldiers and civilians
surged toward it. I was in the forefront and managed to get, if not at
the bar, at least near it, as the mugs of beer were put on the counter.
I got one. That was my breakfast juice. But where were the tidbits,
the morsels, the appetizers? Everyone else seemed to be waiting hun-
grily, for most eyes were turned expectantly toward a door that led
to the kitchen. At last that door opened and two waiters emerged,
each bearing a big, round tray piled high with I knew not what, since
the contents of their trays were obscured by clouds of steam that rose
from them. The waiters put the trays down, one at either end of the
bar. I lost no time getting to he nearest one. Everyone reached out
and took a handful of whatever was on the trays. I stretched over a
man's shoulder and plunged my hand into the tray, too. My hand
came up full of warm hard grey little objects which turned out to be
tiny swirling little shells. I discovered I had a handful of snails!

I knew that people in the Latin lands ate snails, but I had never
intended to eat one myself. However, at this point I was so hungry
that I did not hesitate, nor even stop to think. I simply pulled a snail
out of its shell and ate it. In fact, as fast as I could, I pulled snails
from their shells and ate them—then I reached just in time for an-
other handful before the tray was emptied. Steamed snails were my
first meal in Madrid.

HARLEM SWING AND SPANISH SHELLS

One of Franco's ways of getting back at besieged Madrid for holding
out so tenaciously was to broadcast daily, from his powerful radio
towers at Burgos or Seville, the luncheon and dinner menus of the
big hotels there, the fine food that the Falangists were eating, and the
excellent wines they drank. (Rioja and the best of wine areas were in
Fascist hands.) One could almost hear rebel diners smacking their
lips on the radio.

Since food was scarce in Madrid, I did not torture myself listening to Franco's succulent broadcasts. But I found myself thinking a great deal about hamburgers, hot dogs, sugared doughnuts and ice cream—things one can get on almost any American corner—not to speak of more substantial items like steak. In Madrid, when I got there, even with the proper ration cards, there was next to nothing to buy. The city was almost surrounded by Franco's troops, who were trying to starve the people out. I, after missing my first breakfast in the city, never missed another one.

Breakfast at the Alianza consisted of a single roll and "Malta coffee"—burnt grain, pulverized and brewed into a muddy liquid. Sometimes there was milk, but no sugar. Guillén and I had brought from Paris several bottles of saccharin tablets which we shared with the others as a sweetener. After breakfast one had the whole day un-interrupted by meals. I spent much of my time trying to discover bars that served tidbits with drinks. There were several that tried to do so each day, circumstances permitting, so by making the rounds between bombardments, I could manage sometimes to eat a small lunch of knick-knacks before night. One very sedate old wine house on Alcala Zamora was still serving ancient expensive sherry—for very rare old sherry was all it had left in its cellars. Here they would attempt every day at five to serve something to go with the sherry—often only chestnuts or green almonds. But sometimes from the slaughter house, the venerable proprietor would secure the hearts, liver and lights of various animals and boil them, then slice them into little hunks to be speared with a toothpick. Each person might have a small saucer of these innards with his sherry. Almost all the writers at the Alianza were to be found in this dusky wood-panel old bar in the late after-noon talking about literature and trying not to seem unduly dis-turbed if the proprietor was unable to furnish anything that day but rare old sherry.

Dinner at the Alianza was beautifully served every evening and delicious, for the club had an excellent cook, who did her best to make what little she could purchase appetizing. She would create a wonderful soup out of almost nothing but a pot of water, a few herbs and some rancid olive oil. It became a very special soup if someone left a few crumbs or crusts of bread on the breakfast table. She would toast and fry these in olive oil at night and put them into the soup. Beans she could flavor superbly. Once in a blue moon we might have meat, a little cube, or a very thin slice for each person. Sometimes, but rarely, there was fresh fish from Valencia. I shall never forget one night when we had fish; we had also a very special guest. He was a venerable Spanish scholar, soft-spoken and grey-haired, who had arrived in Madrid from Valencia, probably on the same truck that brought the city's ration of fish that day. Our distinguished guest had not been in Madrid before during the Civil War, so he had never experienced such slim food rations, since in Valencia people still ate fairly well. And there, of course, came plenty of fish directly from the sea.

When our ration of fish arrived on the table at the Alianza—a dozen beautifully fried but quite small smelts—and the platter was passed to our distinguished guest first, he simply raked all the fish into his own plate, thinking them a single service. As polite as Spaniards generally are, at this moment two or three persons at the table could not resist a groan of anguish. Someone even blurted out before thinking, "Ay, Señor, you've taken all the fish."

Our hostess, Maria Teresa Leon, who presided over the table, quickly and graciously said, "Oh, but they're yours, sir, prepared just for you." However, the bewildered guest could not help but notice the sad faces at the table, so he said, "But won't you all share mine?"

By now everyone had gotten their company manners back, and politely refused. "Oh, thank you, no, those are for you, dear friend, sweet visitor. *Bon apetit!* Eat well!"

A dozen little fish normally would have been a rather small serving for even one person in Spain—just a starter preceding the meat course. In Valencia one person might even in war time have that many fish for a meal. But in Madrid, where everything had to come into the city by trucks using precious gasoline, and over a shell-raked road, it was another matter. Our embarrassed guest entreated in vain that we share his fish. No, we would not! We stuck to the fiction that they were prepared *just* for him. Fortunately, a bowl of *garbanzos,* big old Spanish cowpeas, arrived on the table, so we each had a helping of those for dinner, plus an onion. I never ate so many raw onions in my life as I did that summer. Onions and grapes were the only things to eat that were at all plentiful in Madrid. Sometimes the grapes were very sour and green, but we ate them voraciously.

Beans and onions and grapes at the Alianza were all elegantly brought to table in priceless old china belonging to the marquis who was with Franco in Burgos. I suppose he has gotten all his beautiful dishes back now after the war, as well as his lovely tapestries and priceless El Grecos on the walls. As head of the Alianza, Rafael Alberti, was most careful of its belongings. And everybody's heart bled when a cup or something was broken, which didn't happen often, but when it did the fault usually lay with the club's collective son, Luis, a war orphan the Alianza had adopted. Luis was a gentle boy of sixteen who tried to be as careful as he could, but it seemed his fate to almost always be tripping over a rung near a Venetian mirror, dropping something, or tearing the page of an old book just by looking at it. The writers and artists in the house nicknamed the boy, El Destroyer. But because he had seen his whole family wiped out in a bombing raid on his village, nobody scolded him. Usually Maria Teresa just asked him to *please* be very careful.

At first I thought perhaps the youngster was just careless, until I saw a series of little mishaps, one after another, overtake him through no fault of his own; the lad was accident prone. One night I witnessed what must have been for an adolescent, the most embarrassing moment of his life. This was the evening when the main salon of the mansion, seldom used, had been opened in honor of the visit to Madrid of two American Congressmen, Henry O'Connell of Montana and James T. Bernard from Minnesota. For these American dignitaries the intellectuals of wartime Madrid held a reception at the Alianza. Everybody put on their best clothes for the occasion. After we had all shaken hands with the visiting Americans, there was to be an hour of music. The large drawing room was crowded with visitors, including General Miaja, the defender of Madrid. All went well until the very moment when the music was to begin. As the Congressmen took their seats, the rest of the assemblage found places, too, including El Destroyer. He sat down unobtrusively on one of the little antique golden Louis XV chairs in an out-of-the-way corner near the tail of the grand piano. This chair, generations old, must have held many people in its time. But of all nights, tonight was the night the chair decided to cease performing its function. Just as the first note was about to be struck on the piano and the dignified soprano faced her quiet listeners, with an unduly loud splintering of its tiny legs, the Louis XV chair suddenly gave way beneath the young Spaniard. It sank to the floor with a loud crash, carrying with it an astonished adolescent.

El Destroyer loved American jazz. But fortunately my records were locked away safe from breakage, with the marquis's symphonies in the recreation house across the courtyard from the mansion itself. This room had a splendid record player with modern amplification and was seldom used except during a very heavy shelling of the city. The shells generally came from the west where Franco's artillery was situated. This recreation house was on the western side of the court, protected by a much taller building adjoining it. Shells would have to penetrate this larger building before striking the recreation rooms. So this house was considered by the residents of the Alianza as the safest place to be during a *bombardeo*. When heavy shells began to whistle too near our mansion, or explode within wall-

trembling distance, Maria Teresa would get the key to the game
room and we would all gather there and listen to music until the
bombardment ceased. Before I came, Harry Dunham told me, they
had listened mostly to Beethoven, Brahms, or Wagnerian overtures.
But when I appeared with a box full of swing music, folks would call
for Benny Goodman, Duke Ellington, Lunceford or Charlie Barnet.
Certainly in intensity and volume my records were much better than
the marquis's symphonies for drowning out the sound of Franco's
shells exploding in the streets outside.

The first heavy night shelling of Madrid after my arrival occurred
at about two o'clock in the morning. Busy on an article for the *Afro-
American,* I had not yet gone to bed, and was rather fascinated to
watch from my window artillery flashes in the distance, then a split
second later to hear a shell whistling overhead. Artillery bombard-
ments never frightened me nearly so much as air raids. There were
no baleful warning sirens, screeching eerily, to make the flesh crawl
as there were before air raids. The big guns simply started to go off—
and that was that. But this night shells soon began to fall near the
Alianza. Suddenly a projectile landed at our very corner with a
terriffic explosion, like a thousand tons of dynamite. I jumped up
from my typewriter and started downstairs.

Usually at the Alianza no one bothered to get out of bed during
a late bombardment. But this bombardment was so intense that
almost everyone gathered for company across the court in the recre-
ation hall. As usual, someone began to play records to drown out the
sound of the explosions. The amplifier was turned up very loud—so
loud in fact, that unless a shell had fallen in the courtyard, we could
hardly have heard it. The automatic record player would repeat a
disc innumerable times if one wished. So that night of the big
bombardment, the Jimmie Lunceford record we kept going con-
tinuously until almost dawn was "Organ Grinder's Swing."

DEATH AND LAUGHTER

The rebel gunners seemed to love to fire on Madrid in the middle
of the night, but sometimes there were bombardments in the day-
time, too. There were no air raids directly on the city while I was
there, but enemy planes were used on nearby troop concentrations
and on the bridges and highways in the surrounding countryside.
The one road leading into Madrid was frequently bombed in an
attempt to disrupt its traffic. But just for fun, it seemed, artillery

batteries showered Madrid almost every day, sometimes taking the Telefonica for a target and dropping shells all around that sky-scraper into the heart of the town. At other times, instead of concentrating on the business section, the big guns would be trained fanwise, spraying destruction over a wide area of the city. Sometimes, it seemed to me that enemy gunners just shot up in the air and let their projectiles fall at random for no miliitary reason except to terrorize people. But the people of Madrid, having lived under fire for a year, had gotten over terror by the time I arrived. Most bombardments they treated like showers of rain, simply crossing to the opposite side of the street from that toward which the guns were firing—as one does when the rain is slanting the wrong way and shelter is drier on the other sidewalk.

My first visit to the famous Hotel Florida was to pay a call on Sherwood Eddy, the sixty-five-year-old Y. M. C. A. executive whom I had known in New York. I had run into him the day before, bustling about Madrid in an old overseas cap from World War I, which he said he had put on to make him feel at home under fire. Together that day, Sherwood Eddy and I toured various floors of the Hotel Florida where Ernest Hemingway lived, and where up to that time some twenty artillery shells had penetrated the walls. The street entrance to the Florida was well protected with sandbags. But since it was impossible to sandbag nine stories, some of the front upper floors now had no complete walls at all. Not many guests accepted front rooms anyway any more, and suites with a view were not in demand —since the view from the rise on which the Florida sat was a full panorama of enemy territory just beyond the Casa de Campo. From shattered windowpanes one did not need binoculars to see the enemy trenches.

The Hotel Alfonso, another important hostelry a few blocks from the Florida, had several large shell holes through its four walls, too. Sometimes a shell came in one side and went right on through the other. One of the corridors on an upper floor of the Alfonso led straight into space—its French doors, balcony and all having been shot away. In an unused bedroom I looked slantingly down three floors into the street through an opening made by a projectile that had struck the roof and plowed its way downward to the sidewalk. On the hotel's marble staircase two persons had been killed by shrapnel a few days before.

The safest hotel seemed to be the Victoria, not so near the firing lines. There, Herbert Matthews of *The New York Times* and many other foreign journalists lived. The Victoria had not been struck by shell fire up to the time I left Madrid. But any of its inhabitants who had been in the city long could tell you of narrow escapes in other parts of town. Some journalists I knew, covering a special dinner for a distinguished foreign delegation, had to flee to the cellar of the restaurant with the guests when the big guns started to fire. Shortly a bus boy came down into the basement with a table leg in his hands. A member of the foreign delegation asked, "What's that?"

"That's the table where you were eating," replied the bus boy.

The citizens of Madrid themselves had thousands of humorous tales with a macabre twist. One concerned a man who went into a barbershop to get his hair cut entirely bald, since there was no soap for shampoos and he wished to avoid lice. As he sat in the chair, a shell fell in the street just outside, a sharp piece of shrapnel flew through the window, and he got his *head* cut off instead of his hair. The barber was unharmed—except that he didn't get paid for the haircut.

Another story concerned a Franco projectile that landed with a hiss and a boom one busy afternoon on a sidewalk of the Puerta del Sol. Fortunately, no one was killed. But when the smoke cleared away, people saw a man lying on the sidewalk stunned and speechless, with one leg of his trousers ripped from belt to ankle. Sympathetic strangers crowded around him. "An ambulance right away! Get the poor fellow to a hospital."

But the man, having regained his senses, jumped to his feet, angrily looked at his torn trousers, and cried, "Hospital, hell! I want a tailor."

There were certain sections of Madrid more dangerous than the actual front-line trenches, so people said, since they were more frequently exposed to direct artillery fire. But in spite of the bombardments in the city traffic usually kept on moving and, while I was there, the streetcar service was seldom disrupted. But during a shelling, motormen seemed to have a tendency to increase their speed. So when shells fell, I would often see trams whizzing faster than ever through the streets. A few cars had been hit and passengers killed, so if any passenger wished to get off and take shelter, the motorman would stop the car for him. But the general feeling was that a person was as safe on a streetcar as in a shelter. The car might be struck, but so might the shelter. The streetcar men of Madrid had sent a whole company of their own to the front. Sometimes those at work relieved the men at the front so that they might come back to town and take a turn on leave at running the cars again.

During that second year of the war, there were said to be almost a hundred thousand children in Madrid. Certainly one saw many youngsters playing in the streets, picking up shrapnel for fun, and playing hide-and-seek in shell holes. But mothers in the more exposed sections of the city usually called their children into the house at the first boom of the cannon. The children, often more expert than the grownups in recognizing the sounds of artillery and from just which direction the shells were coming, were sometimes loath to obey. I heard a small boy yell from the street to his mother in an upper window one day, as he kept on playing, "Aw, those are our guns, ma, shooting the other way. Can't you tell by the sound?"

In the early days of the war Madrid was frequently bombed from the air. But after the first few months, the rebels no longer wasted their aviation on nonmilitary targets. However, by that time whole areas of Madrid had already been destroyed. Now the artillery continued the destruction. By 1937, the beautiful Arguelles section of new villas and modern apartment houses was a shambles. One enormous apartment house, covering a whole block, was known as the House of Flowers, because, in its planning, each window had been designed with a window box for plants, and each balcony had its rows of potted flowers or vines. But when I saw this huge dwelling house, it was empty and desolate, with great shell holes in the walls, its window boxes broken and its balconies smashed. But a few flowers were still blooming in some of the windows, and from a number of balconies little green vines still hung. Although the taller buildings, being excellent targets for artillery, were empty, a number of cottages were still occupied. One day in Arguelles, I was told, a shell fell in the study of a bearded old professor of Greek. His wife and daughter came running to see if anything had happened to him. They found the old gentleman standing in the center of the floor, holding a portion of the shell in his hand and shaking his head quizzically.

"This little thing," he said, "this inanimate object, can't do any more than kill us. It's the philosophy that lies behind this little fragment, wife, that is so dangerous."

The Cuban poet, Alejo Carpentier, who had been living in Arguelles, told me that one morning after an especially heavy shelling, he had passed a house, a considerable portion of whose front wall was lying in the yard. A shell had passed through the roof the night before and carried with it not only a portion of the living room wall but the top corner of the family piano as well. Then the shell buried itself in the garden. Nevertheless, early that morning Carpentier saw the little daughter of the house seated at the damaged piano, very clean and starched, her hair brushed and braided, her face shining. Diligently, she was practicing scales from a music book in front of her. The fact that the top corner of the piano had been shot away in the night and that the living room had no wall did not seem to affect the child's concentration. In answer to the Cuban's good morning and his question as to what had happened, the little girl said, "Oh, a shell came through our house last night. I'm going to help clean up after a while, but I have to practice first. Today's the day my music teacher comes."

Madrid, you wondrous city!

were words the Brigade boys had put to an old Spanish folk song, "Mamita Mia." The Madrileños had previously put wartime Spanish words to it, too, about the way their city was holding out under siege:

> *Madrid, que bien resistes!*
> *Madrid, que bien resistes,*
> *Mamita, mia, los bombardeos!*

The will to live and laugh in this city of over a million people under fire, each person in constant danger, was to me a source of amazement. One could forget the possibility of imminent death, but it was impossible not to be cold as winter came, or always half hungry. At the Alianza sometimes, when transportation had been disrupted and our food shop had no rations for our dinner, there would be nothing at meal time but bread soup with bread. The writers around the table would repeat an old Spanish proverb, "Bread with bread—food for fools." Then we would all laugh and tighten our belts as we got up to keep our stomachs from feeling so empty.

I was an American who could go home anytime I wanted to. But the others were Spaniards who lived in Madrid. How much longer could they resist like this, I wondered. Yet it seemed certain that they would never be starved out—perhaps not even shelled out or bombed out, unless overwhelming military forces were unleashed against them. Hemingway and Matthews, Leland Stowe and all the other American journalists in the city agreed that there were no signs of surrender. Yet there were no heroics, no mass meetings, no bands, no great speeches about it. City without heroics, Madrid, *que bien resistes!*

One night that summer, in the center of the city, in one of the larger motion-picture theaters the audience avidly followed the progress of an American-made film. Suddenly a shell fell in the street outside with a tremendous detonation—but nobody moved from his seat. The film continued. Shortly another shell fell, nearer and louder than before, shaking the whole building. The manager of the theater went into the lobby and looked up and down the Grand Via. He saw a billowing tower of smoke at the corner. Overhead the whine of one shell after another caused him to decide to stop the show so that people might seek refuge. He had the film halted and mounted the stage to announce his decision to the audience, and say that in view of the intensity of the shelling, he thought it best to call off the rest of the picture. Before he had gotten the words out of his mouth, he was greeted with such hissing and booing and stamping of feet and calls for the show to go on— plus cries of "Coward!" hurled in his direction—that he shrugged his shoulders, signaled the operator to continue, and left the stage. The magic of Hollywood resumed its spell. While enemy shells whistled dangerously over the theater to crash in nearby streets, the film went its make-believe way to a thrilling climax—a climax in which gunfire played a prominent part. Artillery fire outside and machine-gun fire on the screen mingled, one hardly distinguishable from the other. The picture was *Terror in Chicago*.

BODY HERE, LEG THERE

Just after the big battle of Brunete near the city, I reached Madrid. This was the battle in which the Loyalist troops experienced the heaviest concentration of aerial bombs yet used up to that time anywhere in the world. For more than twenty-four hours, Spanish, Italian and German aviation bombed the government trenches. The whole earth shook, and its trembling was felt all day and all night in Madrid itself. Brunete was an outpost of the defense of Madrid. To go with one of the first groups of American newspapermen to visit that front after the battle, was my good fortune—journalistically speaking. I had never been on any war front before, so I was lucky to be going with experienced men, for the reporters with whom I traveled were Leland Stowe and Richard Mowrer. We went in Mowrer's car, driving over shell-pocked roads until we came within sight of Quijorna on the Brunete front. At the top of a rise a sentry stopped us.

He said, "You'd better leave the car here. Down there in the hollow the road is within range of fascist guns. They might machine-gun a car. If you walk, they'll only snipe."

"Maybe they won't even bother to do that," said Stowe. "Anyway, we'll walk."

So we left the car and started down the road in the brilliant sunlight. The leaves on the trees along the road had all been shot away, and the branches were splintered and broken. This was the first time I'd ever seen battle-scarred trees. While I was looking up at the trees, it seemed that ever so often I heard a bird cheep. But I could not see any birds. Finally I asked my companions, "Where are the birds I keep hearing?"

"Birds?" Stowe said, "There's no birds. Those are sniper bullets whistling by."

"Firing at *us*?" I exclaimed.

"Certainly," said Stowe. "There's nobody else on this road to fire at."

"I never knew bullets sounded like birds cheeping before."

"Well, now you know," Mowrer grinned. "And there's no use to duck. Anyhow, they're probably just shooting at us for fun."

Perhaps for my comfort, Stowe said, "I can tell by the sound the bullets are over our heads."

Chee-eep! . . . Chee-eep! . . . Chee-eep! I didn't know just where the cheep came from, so soft and swift, but Stowe's words were of little comfort. I could see spurts of dust fly up every so often in the road where an occasional bullet landed too near for a feeling of safety.

I was glad when we had crossed that declivity and went up the next rise and down into the outskirts of the ruined village toward which we were headed. Had there been a hotel, or any shelter standing whole, I probably would not have gone back to Madrid until the snipers cleared out. I had never been a *personal* target before, and I did not relish the thought of being a target again that day.

The little town was a scene of complete desolation. Nobody remained there, but there were still portions of the dead in the streets. Whole bodies had been cleared away, but hands, arms, fingers and legs were still lying around, protruding from piles of rubble, smelling not good in the sun. There were no soldiers about, nobody at all, so one could walk into any of the shell-battered houses and bombed-out buildings and take whatever one wished. In some houses books and furniture had not been harmed. In others, everything was smashed, scorched, or otherwise damaged. The records at the little city hall were scattered all over the place in the rubble of its shattered walls. Maybe it had been a very old building, two or three hundred years old, but now it was in ruins. I picked up an old ledger with a leather back, its faint pages indicating records of marriages more than eighty years ago.

There wasn't much to see in the village except ruination, and the stench of death was not pleasant. After I'd ventured into one quite pretty little villa, only partly destroyed, to find a dead man sprawled just inside the door, his left leg a yard or two away from his body, I was none too eager to explore any more of the deserted town. Stowe and Mowrer wanted to check up on the full extent of aerial destruction, so I let them go ahead. It didn't take more than a quick look on my part to verify that it had been devastating, a kind of preview of what happened later to other larger and more famous European cities in World War II—to which some of the newsmen in Madrid predicted Spain was but a prelude.

Some of the men in the International Brigades had told me they came to Spain to help keep war and fascism from spreading. *"War and fascism"*—a great many people at home in American seemed to think those words were just a left-wing slogan. War and fascism! He was not just a slogan, that dead man sprawled on the floor of his house; not just a slogan the chee-eep, chee-eep, chee-eep of what I thought were birds singing; certainly not a slogan the streets I had to traverse through that smashed village with a leg here, a hand there, to get back to the road exposed to snipers' fire to reach our car to return to Madrid.

"Death does not smell good at all," I thought, a little sick at the stomach as I walked away from that Spanish town where nobody lived any more on account of war and fascism.

GENERAL FRANCO'S MOORS

"Imagine," said the Madrileños, "that rebel Franco bringing Mohammedans to Spain to fight Christians! The Crusaders would turn over in their graves. The Moors are back in Spain."

With Dick Mowrer and Leland Stowe, I visited a prison hospital in Madrid and saw my first Moor. We had gone to interview some captured German aviators and Italian ground troops. The Germans were in one ward and the Italians in another. The Italians were the most talkative. They said they had come to Spain because Mussolini had sent them. They had no choice in the matter, and they seemed to have no idea what the war was about—or if they did have, they were careful not to express themselves. They were amiable young fellows, stocky and rough-looking, probably peasants at home or unskilled workers. The Germans, on the other hand, were much less communicative. They had been sent to fight communism, they said, and yes, they bombed cities full of women and children. An airman had to take orders, *nein?* But one of them said that now he knew what a bombardment felt like, as he lay there in this prison hospital that had been struck by fourteen shells.

It was a hot day and smelly in the hospital wards. Since I didn't understand German or Italian well, and the other reporters were dragging out their interviews a very long time, I decided to walk down the corridor and see if I could find some water. If I missed anything, Stowe or Mowrer would tell me later. The hospital hall was empty. But as I got almost to the end where the hall turned, around the corner came one of the darkest, tallest men I have ever seen in my life. His blackness was accentuated by a white hospital gown flopping about his bare legs, and a white bandage around his head. Not having seen a Negro since I'd been in Madrid, the sudden sight of this very dark face almost startled me out of my wits. There at the corner of the corridor the man and I would have collided, had I not stopped in my tracks as he passed me without a word, silently like a black ghost.

I was a bit ashamed of myself for having been startled at the unexpected sight of a dark face in a hospital I had thought filled only with white prisoners. I thought of how once, when I had been walking with some other fellows along a bayou in Louisiana, a white woman had looked out of her hut and cried. "You colored boys get away from here. I'm scared of you." Now, here I was—a Negro myself—suddenly frightened by another dark face!

When I got back to the German ward and asked the nurse about the man I had seen, she said there were a number of Moors in another part of the hospital. While Mowrer and Stowe continued to talk to the Germans, I went with the nurse to find them. In a big room with three rows of cots, a number of Moors sat on their beds in white wrappings and bandages, while others lay suffering quietly, too badly wounded to be up. It was almost impossible for me to carry on any sort of conversation with them. They spoke little or no Spanish and I had no interpreter with me. But finally I came across a small boy who had been wounded at the Battle of Brunete. He looked to be a lad of ten or eleven, a bright smiling child, who spoke Spanish.

"Where did you come from?" I asked.

He named a town I'd never heard of in Morocco.

"How old are you?"

"Thirteen," he said.

"And how did you happen to be fighting in Spain?"

"I came with my mother," he said.

"Your mother?" I exclaimed, for that was the first time I had heard of Moorish women being brought to Spain. The rebels, I learned later, imported women as well as men—women to accompany the troops, to wash and cook for them behind the lines.

"What happened to your mother?"

The little boy closed his eyes. "She was killed at Brunete," he said.

The Moorish troops were colonial conscripts, or men from the Moroccan villages enticed into the army by offers of what seemed to them very good pay. Franco's personal bodyguard consisted of Moorish soldiers, tall picturesque fellows in flowing robes and winding turbans. Before I left home American papers had carried photographs of turbanned Mohammedan troops marching in the streets of Burgos, Seville and Malaga. And a United Press dispatch from Gibraltar that summer said:

> Arabs have been crossing the Straits of Gibraltar from Spanish Morocco to Algeciras and Malaga at the rate of 300 to 400 a day, according to reliable information reaching here. General Franco intends to mass 50,000 new Arab troops in Spain so that he can maintain the strength of the Nationalist army should the Italian volunteers be withdrawn.

According to Madrid papers these shiploads of Moorish mercenaries from Larache provided a strange union of the Cross and the Crescent against Spanish democracy. The Falangist papers reaching Madrid were most religious, even running in their advertisements slogans such as VIVA CRISTO REY! VIVA FRANCO! as if Christ and the General were of equal importance. On the cover of the book, *Espana en la Cruz*, published in rebel territory, the map of Spain was pictured crucified on an enormous cross by the nails of Marxism, Judaism and Masonry, which the book claimed formed the core of the Loyalist government. Yet the Franco insurrectionists, in spite of their Christian cast, had encamped thousands of pagan Moors at Casa del Campo. And General Queipo de Llano was said to have promised one girl in Madrid to each twenty Moors. But I could not find that the enemy's use of these colored troops had brought about any increased feeling of color consciousness on the part of the people of Spain. I was well received everywhere I went, and the Negroes in the International Brigades reported a similar reception.

Negroes were not strange to Spain, nor did they attract an undue amount of attention. In the cities no one turned around to look twice. Most Spaniards had seen colored faces, and many are quite dark themselves. Distinct traces of Moorish blood from the days of the Mohammedan conquest remain in the Iberian Peninsula. Copper-colored Gypsies like La Niña de los Peines are common. There were, too, quite a number of colored Portugese living in Spain. And in both Valencia and Madrid I saw pure-blooded Negroes from the colonies in Africa, as well as many Cubans who had migrated to Spain.

All the Negroes, of whatever nationality, to whom I talked, agreed that there was not the slightest trace of color prejudice in Spain. In that respect they said it was even better than France because in Paris, charming city that it is, some of the big hotels catering to tourists will not register dark-skinned guests. Negro jazz musicians told me that they enjoyed performing in Spain where audiences are most cordial. I found, shortly after my arrival, that one of the most popular variety stars in Madrid was El Negro Aquilino, a Cuban, who played both jazz and flamenco on the saxaphone. Aquilino was then in his third month at the Teatro Calderon, and appeared on the same bill with the famous Pastora Imperio, the great dancer who remained on the Loyalist side. Aquilino traveled all over government Spain, and was a great favorite with the soldiers for whom he played at the front. When I went backstage to interview him for my paper, I asked him about color in Spain. He said, "Color? *No le hace nada en Espana*—it doesn't matter."

Sometimes, amusingly enough, American Negroes in Brigade uniforms were asked if they were Moors fighting on the Loyalist side. One young Negro, Walter Cobb, had a big scare behind the lines on the Aragon front where he was the only American with a French brigade. Cobb spoke both French and Spanish.

"I have to keep in practice with my languages in this man's country," he said. "If I hadn't known Spanish in the last action, I'd have been taken for a Moor and made a prisoner. Man, I was driving a captured Franco truck that we took at Belchite one night, bringing it back behind our own lines to be repaired, and I hadn't had a chance to paint out the Falangist markings on it. I hadn't gone but a few kilometers in the dark before some Loyalist soldiers on patrol duty, Spanish boys, stopped me at a crossroads and threw their flashlights on the truck. When they saw me, dark as I am, and saw that truck with those Fascist insignias on it, they thought sure I was a Moor that had got lost and come across the lines by accident. They yelled at me to jump down quick with my hands up, and they held their guns cocked at my head until I got off that truck. Man, I started talking Spanish right away, explained I was an International.

So they let me show them my papers and tell them how we captured that truck from the Fascists, and that it belonged to us now. Then, man, they almost hugged me! But suppose I didn't keep in practice with my Spanish? As much like a Moor as I look, I might have been dead, driving a Franco truck! It pays to *habla espanol*."

In Arguelles, I saw two posters in a classroom for the Spanish soldiers of the 14th Battalion training to fight the Moors. One poster said: LIKE THE SPANISH PEASANTS, THE INDUSTRIOUS AND DECENT MOOR DOES NOT TAKE UP A GUN, HE TILLS THE SOIL. And the other poster declared: THE MOORS ON THE SIDE OF THE FALANGISTS DO NOT KNOW THEY ARE FIGHTING AGAINST THE REAL SPANISH REVOLUTION. WORKERS, HELP US! RESPECT THE MOORISH PRISONERS.

The International Brigaders were, of course, aware of the irony of the colonial Moors—victims themselves of oppression in North Africa—fighting against a Republic that had been seeking to work out a liberal policy toward Morocco. To try to express the feelings of some of the Negro fighting men in this regard, I wrote these verses in the form of a letter from an American Negro in the Brigades to a relative in Dixie:

International Brigades, Lincoln Battalion, Somewhere in Spain, 1937

> Dear Brother at home:
> We captured a wounded Moor today.
> He was just as dark as me.
> I said, Boy, what you doin' here,
> Fightin' against the free?
> He answered something in a language
> I couldn't understand.
> But somebody told me he was sayin'
> They grabbed him in his land
> And made him join the Fascist army
> And come across to Spain.
> And he said he had a feelin'
> He'd never get back home again.
> He said he had a feelin'
> This whole thing wasn't right.
> He said he didn't know
> These folks he had to fight.
> And as he lay there dyin'
> In a village we had taken,
> I looked across to Africa
> And I seen foundations shakin'—

For if a free Spain wins this war,
The colonies, too, are free—
Then something wonderful can happen
To them Moors as dark as me.
I said, Fellow, listen,
I guess that's why old England
And I reckon Italy, too,
Is afraid to let Republic Spain
Be good to me and you—
Because they got slaves in Africa
And they don't want 'em free.
Listen, Moorish prisoner—
Here, shake hands with me!
I knelt down there beside him
And I took his hand,
But the wounded Moor was dyin'
So he didn't understand.

ARTISTS UNDER SIEGE

Cuidadito, compa' gallo, cuidadito!
Cuidadito, compa' gallo, cuidadito!

Take care, brother rooster, take care! Guillén used to sing as he
came up the stairs to my Alianza room. But one day in late No-
vember, he came up shivering. "Damn, man," he sputtered in his
Cuban Spanish, "it's getting too cold in Madrid for Papa Gallo to
crow any more. But I hear it's still warm in Valencia."

"When are you cutting out?" I asked.

"As soon as I can crowd into a military bus," said Guillén, his
teeth chattering.

I knew it was time for me to be leaving too, but I hated to quit
that city I had grown to love. Like the Madrileños, even under doom,
I did not want to leave. A year or so earlier, when the citizens of
Madrid could have gone and, in fact, the government had begged as
many of them as possible to evacuate the city, they wouldn't go. Now
that they couldn't go, since there was no transportation, they
wouldn't go anyway. But there was no real reason for me, an
American, to stay there any longer, eating up their meager food,
taking up their fighting time. I had gotten the stories for my paper,
overstayed the time for which the editor had agreed to pay me, and
seen almost all there was to see. Still I wanted to remain. It was

mid-December before I left. Franco was threatening to sever the Madrid-Valencia road—and even more than that, to divide Loyalist Spain into two parts, cutting off the north from the south, by a drive through Teruel to the coast. The Americans in Madrid said it would be wise to leave before the city was entirely surrounded and a starvation blockade in force. I brought no winter clothes to Spain and should have gone home before the cold set in. But the longer I stayed in Madrid, the more I liked it. I might get hungry there, but I never got bored. And certainly there were abnormal deprivations plus the normal and great poverty—but not the dull relief W. P. A. kind of worried existence we had at home in Cleveland—with little hope in sight. Here in Madrid, where people had next to nothing— with the guns pointed at them every day to take that little away— they expected soon to have everything. At the Alianza poets were making poems about it, musicians making songs, artists painting pictures, and Maria Teresa Leon preparing plays.

To get tickets to the crowded Madrid theaters was difficult without standing in line a long time, but fortunately through Maria Teresa I was able to see a number of plays, and could always attend the Teatro Lope de Vega, which she administered, or the Zarzuela where she performed and directed an excellent student company in Spanish and other European plays. Maria Teresa Leon, Alberti's wife, was a buxom blonde with a handsome face and a commanding personality. Her hair was very long, her complexion clean and wholesome, and her Spanish very clear and positive. She dressed well. And in Spain, where men always turn around to look at a woman, she was an eye-catcher.

There is an old Spanish custom taken for granted that a man may whistle or even speak to a pretty girl on the street without offense. But if the girl so much as turns her eyes, then—but only then—she may be insulted by a direct proposition. So long as the woman does not notice the admiration of the unknown male, she is safe from intrusion, but may hear after she has passed a whispered compliment to her pretty legs. Only loose women ever turn around to acknowledge such compliments. But with revolutionary zeal, some of the more ardent Loyalist ladies in Spain set out to put an end to what they felt was "intrusive and uncomradely" in this traditional Spanish way of flirting. Women, they said, were workers and citizens just like men, not mere objects of sex, and so should not be subjected to personal remarks from unknown admirers on the public streets. In Paris, London, New York, and other truly cultured centers where she had been, Maria Teresa said, such behavior on the part of men toward women was unknown. The new Spain should not tolerate it either.

One day, walking alone down the Paseo de Recoletos in Madrid, Maria Teresa was the subject of a passing soldier's ardent compliments, "Wow! What a blonde! Gee, *chica,* you're pretty!" Most women, secretly pleased, would have walked straight on, eyes ahead without the flicker of a lash. But Maria Teresa decided to teach the young soldier a lesson. She turned her head to tell him that that was no way for any comrade in Loyalist Spain to behave toward another —since he did not even know her name. But before she got the words out of her mouth, the young soldier took for granted that, having turned her head, she was a streetwalker, so he playfully slapped her on her shapely behind. Maria Teresa screamed indignantly. The corner policeman recognized the popular actress and immediately laid hands on the young soldier for daring to strike her, and she permitted the bewildered youth to be hauled off to police court.

That night at dinner, when Maria Teresa told the assembled diners about it, the few women there, of course, voiced indignation concerning the amourous soldier's uncouth behavior. But the men all looked embarrassed, and even Maria's husband did not support her position very strongly. Spanish males were all for preserving the right to whistle at a pretty face or figure in passing, and to give vent to a few fleeting sidewalk compliments.

But at the Alianza de Intelectuales, whose president was the Catholic writer, José Bergamin, and Alberti the executive secretary, women were on a par with men. There were few amorous doings there anyway. Everybody was too busy working: making posters for the war effort or the liquidation of illiteracy campaign, or editing and publishing books. I was busy translating, with the aid of Rafael Alberti and Manuel Altolaguirre, the "Gypsy Ballads" of Federico Garcia Lorca, and his play, *Bodas de Sangre.* Alberti, Altolaguirre, and Arturo Barea had known Lorca well and still grieved for his execution at the hands of the Fascists. With workshops at the Alianza, Miguel Prieto had established a satirical puppet theater, La Tarumba, touring the trenches right up to the front lines. But most male members of the Alianza were soldiers and so able to work at art only when in Madrid on leave. The leading man at Maria Teresa's theater came in from the trenches at University City to play his roles, then went back to the front after his performance.

Maria Teresa's student group presenting Lorca's *Marianna Pineda* often took their play to the battle fronts to perform in the open for the soldiers, many of the men standing throughout the whole show.

Maria Teresa told me of a peasant soldier watching the play who suddenly exclaimed, "All my life I have done nothing but dig in the earth. Now here I am like a lord watching a play." After a performance the actors and the director made it a point to mingle with the soldiers and discuss the play with them.

"What we want to do—our theater groups," Maria Teaesa Leon told me, "is make the peasants and workers, even while they are soldiers, realize that they too can learn to make up plays, direct plays, and act in them. The soldiers can talk with our actors if they want to, and they can become actors themselves."

Alberti added, "What the members of the Alianza want to do is make art life, and life art, with no gulf between the artists and the people. After all, as Lorca said, 'The poem, the song, the picture is only water drawn from the well of the people, and it should be given back to them in a cup of beauty so that they may drink—and in drinking, understand themselves.' Now our art is at the service of the Republic to help win the war, since we do not want the books we write to be burned in public squares by Fascists, or blown into bits on library shelves by bombs, or censored until all their meaning is drained away. That is why we artists help to hold Madrid against Franco."

HOW TO EAT A CAT

Miguel Hernandez, a young poet in peasants' shoes, came from Valencia to visit us at the Alianza for a week. He had been a shepherd boy. The Cuban writer, Pablo de la Torriente-Brau, had passed by the house earlier that year on his way to the trenches where he was killed. Miguel Hernandez, who had fought with him in the same regiment, told us about it. Louis Aragon from Paris and Egon Ervin Kish from Central Europe had visited the Alianza, too, and the painter, Alfredo Siquieros from Mexico. But since the Alianza was more a work place than a center of entertainment, not too many foreign writers dropped by during their visits to the beleaguered city, for there was no food and little drink to offer a guest. If a guest came, and pesetas were available, the guest might be taken in the late afternoon to the old bar that had the good sherry. There, when other knick-knacks were lacking, a big bowl of walnuts or almonds might be placed on the table along with several little hammers. Sometimes at the cocktail hour, the cracking of nuts at tables was louder than the gunfire at the front. There being less and less food in Madrid as fall became winter, one did not leave a single kernel of a single nut uneaten.

Late at night I could hear the emaciated lions roaring in the Madrid Zoo just beyond the Retiro near the Alianza. I always wondered what they fed these animals. Some said they fed them the skinny horses that dropped dead of starvation. At the nearly abandoned American Embassy there was a famous dog, a great Dane, that some foreigner had left behind in the embassy's care. The dog could eat more meat than a whole family of people. The Spanish caretakers at the embassy slighted themselves to feed this dog the little that they were able to give him during the war. The dog was still surviving when I left the city, looking at visitors with big sad eyes.

The Gypsy dancers were still dancing in the music halls and El Niño Perez playing his guitar. Albacin, son of Madrid's prettiest Gypsy flower seller, was appearing in *La Copla Andaluza*. *Don Juan Tenorio* was playing at the Español. And at the Calderon Pastora Imperio, the famous Argentinita, had just come back from two hundred performances for the soldiers in the trenches. In the early fall a delegation of Mexican writers and painters brought to Madrid a stunning exhibition of art and posters. Every evening during the Mexican exhibition there were literary programs in which Spanish poets like Rafael Alberti and Leon Felipe took part, as well as the visiting Mexican writers, Jorge Mansisidor, Maria Luisa Vera, Juan de la Cabada, and the young poet, Octavia Paz. Silvestre Revueltas conducted the Madrid Symphony Orchestra in a program of his works. I found the jovial Revueltas a likable man, very simple in manner, and almost as stout as Diego Rivera. Revueltas set my "Song for a Dark Girl" to music, and it was later published in New York with both the English and Spanish text.

Revueltas, like most Mexicans I've known, had a keen sense of humor. He enjoyed the ironic anecdotes and wry jokes about the bombardments, the war, Franco, Mola and Queipo de Llano that continually went the rounds of Madrid. One joke concerned the pregnant wife of an African savage who asked her husband what they should name their son, Lion, Hyena or Leopard. The husband answered, "None of those, wife, they're not savage enough. We'll call him Mussolini." Another tale was that when Franco went to make a speech to a division of his troops at Cordova, as he stood up before them, he asked, "Does anybody here know Spanish?" And a little story that the Madrileños thought very funny concerned a soldier who, after weeks of eating nothing but rice in the trenches, came home on leave and his mother prepared a surprise dish for him for dinner. When she put it on the table, it was a pot of rice! In an almost lunchless city a common question was, "What did you have for lunch?" The answer might be, "Boiled mule's tongue." Whereupon, the questioner, not to be outdone, would say, "Why, we had fried pony."

The bombardments that fall seemed heavier than ever in the city and the hard metallic bang of exploding shells clearer and sharper in the cold autumn air. Loyalist Intelligence Agents said the rebels were now trying out new model Krupp cannons, firing on Madrid from the Garabitas Hills a few miles beyond the city limits. The government was answering back from Carabanchel with the same old guns they had been depending upon for months. In the Plaza de Castelar just down the street from the Alianza, a shell had broken the nose off one of the lions hitched to the chariot of the Goddess of the Fountain of Cibeles. Now that the fountain had been belatedly covered with sandbags, the wits of Madrid called her, "Beauty Under Covers."

With a Spanish soldier friend who came into town often on leave, I went to visit his parents in the Cuarto Caminos section of Madrid, a poor neighborhood East of University City. There every house had been damaged by shrapnel or flying shells. But the neighborhood was still thickly populated, with children scampering in the streets, women washing clothes in courtyards, and old men sitting in the chilly sunlight to absorb what warmth was left before the freezing weather came. My friend, Vincente, gave me packs of "draft killers," the hard little black cigarettes supplied the troops, which he lighted from one end of a fuselike rope-lighter he wound about his waist. He said its long smoldering tip was used to touch off dynamite charges at the front. I in turn gave Vincente saccharin tablets to sweeten the family coffee. He introduced me to the little bodegas, wineshops, in Antocha, a roughneck section of Madrid near the railroad yards where every night seemed like Saturday, in spite of the frequent crack of rifle fire, the staccato run of machine guns, and the boom of trench mortars and hand grenades on the Madrid front. When the enemy artillery opened up on the town and you knew again you weren't just *near* action, but *in* it, the folks in Antocha simply closed the wineshop doors to keep flying shell fragments from bursting a wine keg—and the good times kept on. What people, those Madrileños!

The sixteen-story Telefonica had closed down operations on its upper floors since they were riddled with shell holes, and no elevators were running, but the lower five floors were still in use. The telephone girls still sat at their switchboards, and you could put through a call to Paris if you wished. The Madrid Post Office near the Alianza had hardly any windows left, but the mail went out on schedule by plane to Valencia. Across the plaza from the post office, the flower stand that had been at the curb for years still did business, in spite of the fact that the Ministry of War, at which the Fascists regularly aimed a shell or two, was only a few hundred yards away.

Ralph Heinzen, the United Press man in Madrid called the siege of the city one of the most notable of modern times, and one "that will go down in history with the sieges of Troy, Sagunto, Paris and Verdun." During the months that I was there, it was estimated that more than three thousand shells fell in Madrid, almost a thousand people were killed, some three thousand wounded, and twenty-seven hundred buildings rendered uninhabitable, many totally demolished. By the end of the war there were to be six thousand civilian dead and some twenty thousand Madrileños wounded. The Associated Press correspondent whom I knew, Charles P. Nutter, wrote, *"They Shall Not Pass (no pasaron)* still remains the blood-stained motto of war-battered Madrid, cold, hungry, forlorn, the capital of Spain."

War and hunger were daily companions there. With the coming of autumn and the scarcity of fresh vegetables from the country, even onions became less plentiful. Potato peelings and sausage skins were boiled in Madrid to make soup. At the Alianza even horse meat became a luxury, its coarse-grained flesh prepared to look as much like pot roast as possible by our skillful cook. She was adept at making gravies to cover up the peculiar looks of things. With lentils in one of the beautiful antique bowls belonging to the marquis, horse meat in gravy made a right nice dinner.

In extremely poor sections like Antocha and Cuarto Caminos, it was said that people sometimes ate their cats. I asked my friend, Vincente, about this, He shrugged. *"Quien sabe?* Might be," he said. "But I wouldn't eat a cat by itself, would you? The best way to eat a cat is stewed with a rabbit—then you don't know when you have a mouthful of what. Each time you take a bite, you can imagine it's rabbit."

SALUD MADRID

On my last night in Madrid I did not go to bed at all. I had intended to go to bed, but I neglected to pack any of my belongings before I went out into the streets—and once out, I did not get back home until after three in the morning. The bus for Valencia left at five from a point a long way from the Alianza. On my return I had to pack hurriedly and start walking, for, with all the things I had to carry, I knew it would take me a long time to get to the bus stand. There was no transportation available save my own feet, no taxis, not even a push cart.

Herbert Matthews, Ernest Hemingway, and some of the other newspapermen were giving a little farewell party for me at the Hotel Victoria that night about ten. Earlier in the evening Bunny Rucker had come in town from the Auto Camp to say goodbye and invited me out for a drink. We went to a café off the Puerto del Sol and when it closed, it being not quite time to go to the Victoria, I started to walk with Bunny to the point where his truck was parked. He was due back at camp by ten. One of the heaviest shellings I'd encountered in Madrid began while we were groping our way through a pitch-dark side street on the way to the truck. It was the hour for the theaters and cafés to close that the enemy often chose to shell Madrid in order to terrorize the throngs headed home from what little public pleasures were available in that city after dark. In the chill December air, the clarity of the preliminary BOOM! and whiz and SPANG! of shells passing, then striking the stone of a building or the concrete pavement, made each hit seem very near. No doubt, some were very near. Bunny and I took refuge in a wineshop that we found still open. Tables and counter were crowded with Spaniards who greeted us with friendly *Saluds!*

"Internationals, welcome!" they said. Almost all the men in the place insisted on buying us wine, glass after glass.

SPANG! . . . BANG! . . . SPANG! . . . The shells continued to fall, mostly toward the center of the city, it seemed, but often so near that their vibrations were distinctly felt inside the little bodega.

Some of the men at a long table began to sing, folk songs and flamenco, and everybody turned to listen while they drank. One husky, hairy Spaniard with a range from bass to high falsetto, threw back his head and cried some verses that were almost as frightful in their intensity as the crash of the shells. Flamenco and explosives on my last night in Madrid became an unforgettable combination! Wine and two candles burning in the crowded little wine house, and Bunny saying, "I guess I won't get back to camp by ten o'clock tonight." BANG! . . . One of the men began to sing:

> *Madrid, que bien resistes,*
> *Madrid, que bien resistes,*
> *Mamita mia, los bombardeos!*

This everyone knew, and when the contemporary wartime stanzas were exhausted, they sang together the old folk verses about the four mule drivers. Then they asked us to sing something in our language. I, who could never carry a tune, was unable to oblige. But Bunny sang "Go down, Moses, and tell old Pharaoh to let my people go." The men stamped and shouted for more, so he sang another spiritual, and another. Then the Spaniards sang some more, and the singing and drinking kept up all the time the shells were falling. Each time that there was a lull in the firing and I thought we could leave, by the time another farewell round was set up, the Franco batteries had turned loose on the city again. It was past eleven o'clock before Bunny and I, both far from sober, left the bar. We shook hands on a pitch-black corner in a canyon of enormous darkened buildings; then I found my way to the Victoria. Six or eight journalists were waiting for me there with wine and bottles of Scotch on the table. Later a few others who had been delayed by the shelling arrived, and we sat talking and drinking until after two o'clock. Hemingway and some others headed for the Florida or the Alfonso, so we shook hands on a dark corner, and I went down the Grand Via in the opposite direction toward the Alianza.

The lightless streets of Madrid were quite deserted, except for military patrols. The sandbagged shops and offices were solid walls of darkness, their roof tops dim silhouettes against an inky sky. An occasional sentry at a crossing watched me as I went by, but only one stopped me as I passed the Banco de Espana and asked to see my permit to be aboard after the curfew.

He said, *"Pase, comarada. Salud!"*

"Salud," I said. *"Salud, Madrid!"* I knew this was the last time I would walk through the main streets of this city. *"Salud, Madrid!"*

A shell earlier in the evening must have grazed the corner of a building just across the street for there was scattered rubble and the fallen stone of what looked like a broken cornice all over the sidewalk as I went up the Paseo past the War Ministry toward the street where I lived. Guillén, who was catching the bus, too, was in bed sleeping soundly, his single bag already packed and sitting ready just inside his door. I did not wake him but went on to my room to gather my various belongings into some portable form. Because I had so little time, I stuffed my suitcases carelessly and quickly as full as I could get them. Then I stood in the middle of the floor puzzled as to what I should do with all the other things I had to carry—books by the dozens which various writers had given me, warmly inscribed; gifts and souvenirs, including a handsome pair of bullfight banderillas that a famous torero had placed in the neck of a bull at a great corrida and which a friend presented to me when he learned that I was an *aficionado;* a bottle of wine in a wicker holder another friend had brought me to drink on the way to Valencia; a box of pieces of shrapnel I had picked up in the streets after shellings, and a ledger from the rubble of the city hall at Quijorna; a lace mantilla one of the women of the Alianza was sending to my mother; and my typewriter and manuscripts! The situation looked hopeless, for I had no transportation to get me to the bus a mile away, and no porters to help me lug so much. Besides, I was drunk.

The wine of the bodega, and the Scotch of the Victoria's party had finally gone to my head. I observed my belongings through an alcoholic fog. Drunk or sober, it was hard to figure out at that late hour what to discard. I couldn't bear to part with the banderillas, so I tied them together with a string. Of the books and ledger and manuscripts, I made a single heavy package. I stuffed my overcoat pockets full of shrapnel and other souvenirs. And I decided to hang the wine bottle around my neck. With two bags, the enormous package, my typewriter, the banderillas, and the bottle, I had no recourse but to hope that the amiable Guillén would not object to being a pack mule. Fortunately, he didn't, so about four o'clock, both of us, loaded down, started on foot toward the distant bus. I was so tired, so sleepy, and so unsteady on my legs, and the things I had in my hands, under my arms, and in my pockets were so heavy that I had to stop every few hundred yards and put everything down to rest. Guillén declared we were going to miss the bus if I didn't hurry. To get another permit for another bus on another date from the military authorities might take weeks. I replied that I didn't care—to go ahead if he wanted to—just drop my stuff on the ground and leave me.

"*Caramba, chico,*" Guillén cried, "Madrid might be cut off from the rest of the world soon—you might never get out."

"*Nichevo,*" I said. "*Que le hace?* Damn if I care! I can't walk any faster with this stuff—and I'm *not* going to leave my typewriter here, and these books the writers have given me, nor my banderillas, and my few clothes I've got. So go ahead."

But Guillén stuck with me, and we finally reached the bus, standing in the dark almost ready to depart and already crowded. When the motor began to sputter and bark and backfire, and the bus took off with a jerk and lurched through the dusky streets before dawn and past the bull ring at the edge of town, from the wine and the whisky, the weariness and the flamenco and the shells and the goodbyes of the night before to the men and women with whom I'd shared for so long the dangers of Madrid—plus the sadness of leaving a city that I loved—I began to feel sick at my stomach and in my soul. I rode the long way to Vanencia all day until well after dark feeling very sick.

Filled with refugees from the ruined villages and towns near the fronts, Valencia was more crowded than ever. But the weather was mild and sunny, and there was still much more to eat than in Madrid. Some of the hotels even had hot water for a hot bath. But the nights were enlivened with sirens and air raids, searchlights cutting across the sky, bombs falling, and occasional shellings from the sea, and the air was full of desperate rumors. It was said that the government was preparing to move to Barcelona. Months ago it had moved from Madrid to Valencia. Now in the eventuality that Loyalist Spain were cut in two, it intended to move to Barcelona. Said the maid at my hotel, "The big shots can always go, señor. Governments can always move, *but the people have to stay.*"

For a week or so it looked as if I might have to stay in Valencia, too. There was no transportation available to the north. The trains to Catalonia were booked up for weeks ahead and crowded to the gunwales. Ticket queues were unending at the station, and there were no more tickets available for Barcelona for a month. People of means were streaming northward toward the French border— just in case. Cars could no longer be rented, since all transport now belonged to the military. Even Constancia de la Mora, the charming aristocrat in charge of the Government Press Bureau, to whom members of the foreign press appealed for everything, could be of no immediate help to me.

"So many people all of a sudden seem to want to go to Paris," said Constancia. (Everyone called her by her first name.) "Maybe after the rush is over, I can get you a seat on a train, perhaps by Christmas."

I had thought I might spend Christmas at home in Cleveland with my folks, but that hope grew dimmer as the days passed. Finally, an idea occurred to me. Almost every day I passed the downtown office of Cook's Travel Service. But no one ever seemed to be going in or out of the travel bureau, and it did not appear to be doing any business. There were no tourists coming to Valencia, and the posters in Cook's unwashed windows were all old and dusty. But the door was open. I knew that the night train for Barcelona carried one de luxe *wagon-lit* coach. I had, of course, asked at the station about a berth on this coach long ago, and was told that usually all its space was taken by the government for diplomats or military men. The stationmaster said that there was a long civilian waiting list for any free space in this car for weeks ahead.

Guillén wanted to get to Barcelona, too, where he intended to remain a few weeks doing some pieces on the Catalonians for his paper. So I said one day, "Guillén, I think I'll try Cook's." But Guillén laughed at the idea of a mere tourist bureau being able to get us tickets, when the Government Press Bureau itself could not.

"Cook's is open," I said. "They must be open for *some* reason, so no harm to try."

My one previous experience with Cook's Travel Service had been an unpleasant one. The first time I had gone to Havana from New York, I had sought to purchase a steamship ticket and make hotel reservations at the Fifth Avenue office of Cook's in New York, first phoning for information, and being assured that space was available both on the boats and in the hotels. But when I went to the office, an astonished clerk, seeing that I was colored, hurried off to confer with others, and came back to tell me in a somewhat embarrassed manner that Cook's was not equipped to give Negroes service in the Caribbean areas.

"But Cubans are all mixed with Negroes," I said. "Havana is full of colored people."

The clerk reddened and stammered, and said he was sorry. But I did not get my ticket to Cuba from Cook's nor from any American steamship agency or line. I sailed from New York on a British cruise boat and sought out my own hotel after I got to Havana.

In Valencia, however, I did not expect to find any such color difficulties. And there were none. I simply walked into Cook's bureau one morning and asked if there were two places available on the Barcelona *wagon-lit* any night that week.

The English clerk asked, "When would you like to go?"

I said, "Tomorrow."

He said, "Yes, I can give you a compartment for two."

It was that simple. I had heard from many travelers that the British-controlled Cook's was wonderfully dependable all around the world, and I had never heard of anyone having difficulties with them except Negroes in the color-conscious United States. When I found that Cook's in Valencia had tickets to Barcelona—when no one could get them for love or money—and the clerk made no fuss about it, but quite nonchalantly stamped them, I thought, "What a firm!"

Guillén was amazed when I got back to the hotel with the tickets, although a bit astonished at the price for such de luxe accommodations. We traveled the following night to Barcelona in style in a private room with plenty of space, while in other coaches people were packed in like sardines.

When I bought the morning papers at a stand on the Rambla de las Flores, I noticed the Barcelona Symphony Orchestra—the Orquesta Simfonica Catalana—would be performing that evening George Gershwin's "Rhapsody in Blue." I went to the concert and heard it beautifully played with Maria Campmany at the piano. The other numbers were "Scheherezade," "La Revoltosa," and the "Overture to Tannhauser." And, for once, no air-raid warnings sounded during the concert. The following afternoon I went to a music hall to see some Basque dancers. At the top of the printed programs there was a notice signed by Spain's two great labor unions to this effect:

JUST A MOMENT, COMRADE

The United Syndicate of Public Spectacles begs you to have the greatest respect for all the comrades you are going to see on the stage. They are workers just as you are. DON'T DISTURB the show and spoil its performance. Take art as it should be taken.

The Joint Committee

of

CNT—UGT

The CNT, the National Confederation of Labor, was an anarchist union, and the UGT, the General Union of Workers, was Socialist-Communist controlled. They had formerly been bitter rivals, and even now in the midst of war, they did not always see eye to eye. Certainly, a visitor did not have to be in Loyalist Spain long to see that it was not a Communist land, as many outside Spain claimed it to be. If there were Russians fighting in Spain, I never saw them. I saw German Nazis and Italian Fascists in Madrid's Prison Hospital, but of the thousands of Russians some papers said were aiding the Loyalists, I saw not a one. The only Russian whom I came across in Spain, other than reporters like Kolsov, was a nurse in one of the hospitals. In the cabinet of the Republican coalition government, when I was there, if I remember correctly, only one post was occupied by a Communist, that of the Ministry of Agriculture. In Madrid, Valencia and Barcelona, it was easy to tell from the press and the daily conversations of the people that political opinions varied widely. In fact, it seemed to me a major weakness of Loyalist Spain that even in regard to the conduct of the war, action and opinion varied so greatly between the Socialist, Communist, Anarchist, and Republican parties as to cause not infrequent confusion in military plans. The Communists, although an important party, by no means controlled the government, the military forces, the press, the arts, or anything else so far as I could see. At Maria Teresa's theater in Madrid, for example, the actors and stagehands belonged to the UGT, and the members of the orchestra to the CNT. At one performance which I attended, the lights in the orchestra pit were turned on full during a scene on the stage that required darkness. When I asked Maria Teresa why that was, she said, "Because the CNT musicians union will not co-operate with the actors who belong to the UGT." Even to an outsider like myself, not only in the theater was such disunity evident, but in much else in government Spain. Alvarez del Vayo, Socialist Minister of Foreign Affairs, once asked, "Why is it Spain's people are so great, but her leaders so small?"

On one thing, however, all parties seemed united. That was to lift the cultural level of the peasants and workers, teach them to read and write, have good manners, appreciate their national arts, and take care of public property—including the churches. Some had wanted to destroy the churches—particularly the Anarchists, who took advantage in the early days of the Civil War to try to settle by violence their long feud with Catholicism. But in the trench schools I had visited there were teachers of all parties working with the illiterates. And in the public parks of Madrid—where the anti-aircraft batteries were stationed under the trees—there were also signs that read:

CITIZENS, how we respect plants and animals is an index of culture. Trees, plants and flowers have life, just as do men and women. Look upon them as we do ourselves. A sincere regard for nature will lead you to respect all its works.

On a visit to a kindergarten in Barcelona, I found the children being told not to mark with their crayons on the walls of the buildings. Walls that the enemy did not mind marring with ten-ton bombs were being protected from children with chalk.

After a few days in Barcelona, I left Guillén there, and went on alone across the border to Tour de Carol, a charming French village in the Pyrenees. There I took the night express to Paris, bags, banderillas, books, typewriter, shrapnel and all still intact. But I no longer had any phonograph records to lug. Those I left with my friends in Madrid to play during the bombardments.

Out of earshot of shells and bombs for the first time in six months, at Tour de Carol that day high in the snow-covered mountains I sat down in the station buffet and ordered an enormous meal. Just across the border on the Spanish side, there had been nothing at all to eat. Now, less than a mile away, there was everything: fat cheeses, smoked turkey, hanging hams overhead, tarts, cakes and all sorts of pastries, long loaves of crackly French bread protuding from a wicker basket on the floor, a dozen brands of cigarettes and packets of chocolates on the newsstand counter. What a difference a border makes: on one side of an invisible line, food; on the other side, none. On one side, peace. On the other side, war. On one side, quiet in the sunlight. On the other side the dangerous chee-eep, chee-eep, chee-eep that was not birds, the BANG! of shells, the whine of sirens, and the bursting of bombs over crowded cities.

I stood alone on the platform of the little station at Tour de Carol that bright December day and looked down the valley into Spain and wondered about borders and nationalities and war. I wondered what would happen to the Spanish people walking the bloody tightrope of their civil struggle. In the last few years I had been all around the embattled world and I had seen people walking tightropes everywhere—the tightrope of color in Alabama, the tightrope of transition in the Soviet Union, the tightrope of repression in Japan, the tightrope of the fear of war in France—and of war itself in China and in Spain—and myself everywhere on my tightrope of words.

Anybody is liable to fall off a tightrope in any land, I thought, and God help you if you fall the wrong way.

PAGEANT

The Glory of Negro History

A Pageant

It *is* glorious—this history of ours! It is a *great* story—that of the Negro in America! It begins *way* before America was America, or the U. S. A. the U. S. A. It covers a wide span, our story. Let me tell it to you:

(Sound effect: boom of sea waves)
(Sound effect: whistle of wind)

Hear the wind in the sails of the ships of Columbus? They say one of his pilots, Pedro Alonso Niño, was a Negro. That was in 1492. Certainly by the early 1500's, *black* explorers were coming to the New World. One of them was Estavan—or Estavanico, his nickname—which means in Spanish "Kid Steve."

"Tierra! Ahi esta tierra!" From the deck of a Spanish galleon he cried, "Land! There is land!" when he first sighted the coast of what is now Florida. On that coast his ship was wrecked and Estavan, with four Spaniards, were the only men left alive. Perhaps because he was colored, Estavan got along well with the Indians. He learned their various languages, and soon became a famous guide and translator for other explorers who could not communicate with the Indians. All the way across the southern part of what is now the United States, and as far as Mexico City, for eight years Estavan wandered. From Mexico in 1539 he set out with Friar Marcos de Niza on an expedition toward the North to find the fabled Seven Cities of Cibola, which were said to be built of gold. Estavan was the only Negro in the group. The Spaniards held out until they got as far as what is now Texas. Then the heat and the dust overcame them. They asked Estavan if he would go ahead with the Indian guides and send word back to them as to what he found.

Estavan did not find the Cities of Gold, but he did find rich

Indian pueblos with houses of sunbaked brick, whose doorways were decorated with turquois. And he discovered the rich and beautiful country of gold, copper, cotton, and flowers that is now Arizona. So you see, the first Negroes did not come to America as slaves. They came as explorers. History says that. When Balboa discovered the Pacific, thirty colored men were in his party.

1619 was the year when the roots of slavery began in Virginia. Then ships filled with captured black men and women began to sail across the Western Ocean to our shores. In chains, crowded in the dark holes of the slave ships, they sang their mournful songs:

(Sound effect: African chant)

Sometimes whole groups of Africans, taken on deck at night for air, would leap into the sea—committing mass suicide rather than go into slavery. As soon as they were landed and sold, some would run away into the forest and join the Indians. No man wanted to be a slave. But thousands of Africans were brought by force to America to plant cotton, rice, corn, and wheat, to build the roads and clear the forests, to do almost all the hard work that went into the early building of America.

Most slave masters were heartless and cruel, but there were some who were kind. Such a master was the tailor, John Wheatley. One day he went down to the dockside in Boston to buy, from a newly arrived slave ship, a little servant girl for his wife. The child he bought was from Senegal, maybe seven or eight years old, very dark and cute and shy—and frightened, too, for she could not understand people when they asked her what her name was. So her master and mistress called her Phillis. Later, she took their last name, Wheatley. Before she was twenty, that name, Phillis Wheatley, began to be famous all over the New England colonies—for she became a poet. General George Washington wrote Phillis a letter commending her talent. Because of her genius, Phillis was given her freedom. But, in a land of slavery, when Phillis Wheatley wrote one of her famous poems about the freedom of the American colonies after the Revolutionary War, she must have been looking forward to the future freedom of her own people, too. This is a part of her poem, "Liberty and Peace, 1784":

> Lo freedom comes! The prescient muse foretold
> All eyes the accomplished prophecy behold:
> Her port described, "She moves divinely fair,
> Olive and laurel bind her golden hair." . . .
> To every realm shall peace her charms display
> And heavenly freedom spread her golden ray.

The first man to fall for American freedom was a Negro, Crispus Attucks. When a group of Bostonians, who did not like being ruled by the King, protested, and the Red Coats fired, Crispus Attucks was shot dead. Today in Boston Common there is a monument to Crispus Attucks, the Negro who died for American freedom.

OH, FREEDOM

Oh, freedom!
Oh, freedom!
Oh, freedom over me!

In 1783, America became a free nation—the U. S. A. That is, all were free except the Negro, still a slave. But not willing—no man likes to be a slave. In 1800, a young Negro, Gabriel, organized a revolt in Virginia that involved thousands of black men and women. But on the day when the uprising was to have started, a great storm and a flood wrecked their plans. The leaders were discovered, and Gabriel and some thirty-five others were put to death by the slave owners. They died silently.

OH, FREEDOM *(Hum)*

In 1831 another great slave rebellion broke out in Virginia, led by Nat Turner. In this one some sixty slave owners were killed. More than a hundred Negroes lost their lives before this uprising was suppressed. Seventeen slaves were put to trial and hanged. But Nat Turner had no regrets. Just before he was led to the scaffold to die, he said, "I was intended for some great purpose." In his mind, that purpose was freedom. More and more restless did those in bondage become, more and more did they revolt. In increasing numbers, too. they were escaping to the North.

One who had been a slave, but went away to freedom, was a woman named Isabella. In New York City she had a vision, so she changed her name to Sojourner Truth, and she began to make speeches all over the North against slavery:

"Now about my name, the Lord gave me Sojourner, because I was to travel up and down the land showin' the people their sins and bein' a sign unto them. Afterwards I told the Lord I wanted another name, 'cause everybody else had two names. And the Lord gave me Truth, because I was to declare the truth to the people. I've had five children, and I've seen 'em most all sold off into slavery. Where they be, I don't know—and my children don't know where I be. But I look at the stars, and they look at the stars, and somehow I feels better. Now I walks the world lookin' for truth. I think of the *great* things of God, not the little things. I's a sojourner lookin' for truth!"

Truth to her was freedom—not just for herself, *but for all.* That's what it meant to Harriet Tubman, too, in the dark, in the deep woods, singing:

STEAL AWAY

> Steal away,
> Steal away,
> Steal away to Jesus.
> Steal away,
> Steal away home.
> I ain't got long to stay here . . . . .

But that "steal away" did not mean, as the slave masters thought, stealing away to Jesus. Harriet Tubman used that song as a great secret call—to steal away to freedom, to steal away through the swamp, and follow the North Star to freedom! After she had made her own escape alone from a Maryland plantation, Harriet Tubman went back into slave territory many times to rescue relatives and friends, and guide them to the North:

STEAL AWAY

> My Lord, he calls me.
> He calls me by the thunder.
> The trumpet sounds within-a my soul.
> I ain't got long to stay here.
> Steal away . . . . .

"Home! Home is where freedom is! Home ain't nowhere, children, but where freedom is. The house can be ever so nice with a soft bed, and fine food, and fire in the fireplace—but it ain't home, if it ain't where freedom is. Houseboy! I hear you cryin' in the Big House where you eat the Missus' cake. Huh! Freedom ain't there! Coachman! I hear you cryin' on the carriage seat where you drive them fine bays. Freedom ain't there! Rosie, I hear you cryin' as the master slips a coin in your hand when the mistress ain't lookin'— because you's pretty. Money ain't freedom! I live where the fire is out, where the bed is hard, and the bread is scarce, and maybe you work, and maybe you eat—and maybe you don't—the North.

But freedom is there! Do you want to go? I know you do—freedom is where *I's* gwine! Come with me—through swamp, through mire, past patter-rollers with their bloodhounds and dogs, past danger, past even death. Freedom is there! Come with me!"

SWING LOW, SWEET CHARIOT

Swing low, sweet chariot,
Comin' for to carry me home.
Swing low, sweet chariot
Comin' for to carry me home . . . .

Do you think she was singing about the chariot of death? Not Harriet Tubman! Called at one time the most dangerous woman in America, with a price of $40,000 on her head, put up by the slave owners for her capture, going back and forth in the South to rescue slaves, a great conductor of the Underground Railroad to freedom, a nurse for the Union soldiers in the Civil War, a spy for the Union Armies, Harriet Tubman was singing about the chariot of freedom. But not all slaves had a Harriet Tubman to help them escape from slavery. Thousands ran away alone. This is a song about a slave named Riley who escaped "like a turkey through the corn," and about a bloodhound named Rattler who could not pick up his scent:

OL' RILEY

Riley walked de water.
Here, Rattler, here!
Ol' Riley walked de water.
Here, Rattler, here!
Riley's gone like a turkey through de corn.
Here, Rattler, here!
Ol' Riley's gone like a turkey through de corn.
Here, Rattler, here!
Ol' Rattler come when I blow my horn.
Here, Rattler, here!
Ol' Rattler come when I blow my horn.
Here, Rattler, here!
Toot! Toot-toot!
Here, Rattler, here!
Toot! Toot-toot!
Here, Rattler, here . . .

No use calling Rattler, master. Old Riley's gone, long gone, North! What was slavery like—that men rebelled against it, women risked their lives to escape, that upset the whole South, and eventually brought war to the nation?

"Once when I were trying to clean the house like Old Miss tell me, I finds a biscuit. I's so hungry I et it, 'cause we never see such a thing as a biscuit. We just have corn bread and syrup, but when I et that biscuit and she comes in and say, "Where is that biscuit?" I say, "Miss, I et it 'cause I's so hungry." Then she grab that broom and start to beating me over the head with it and calling me low-down, and I guess I just clean lost my head, 'cause I knowed better than to fight her, if I knowed anything't all, but I started to fight her, and the driver, he comes in and he grabs me and starts beating me with that cat-o'nine-tails, and he beats me till I fall to the floor nearly dead. He cut my back all to pieces."

"When a slave died, they buried him duh same day. They'd cart 'em down to duh graveyard on duh place and didn't even bury them deep 'nough so dat duh buzzards wouldn't come circling 'round lookin' for dere bodies. In them days they wasn't no time for mournin'."

"My papa was strong. He never had a licking in his life. But one day the master says, "Si, you got to have a whopping," and my papa says, "I never had a whoopin' and you can't whop me." And the master says, "But I can kill you," and he shot my papa down. My mama took him in the cabin, and put him on a pallet—and he died."

Frederick Douglass, in his autobiography, describes a beating which a Maryland slave-breaker gave him when he was a boy, in order to tame him for his master, who wanted his spirit broken:

"He rushed at me, tore off the few clothes I had on and proceeded to wear out on my back the heavy goads he had cut from a gum tree. Under his blows my blood flowed freely. Wales were left on my back as large as my little finger. During the first six months I was there I was whipped, either with sticks, or cow-skins, every week."

So no wonder Frederick Douglass said to himself:

"I'll run away. I have only one life to lose. It cannot be, I shall live and die a slave."

OH, FREEDOM

Oh, freedom!
Oh, freedom!
Oh, freedom over me!
And before I'll be a slave
I'll be buried in my grave
And go home to my Lord and be free . . . . .

Douglass was twenty-one when he ran away. He got a job in New England, began to make anti-slavery speeches, and eventually

> Glory, glory, halleluiah!
> Glory, glory, halleluiah!
> His soul goes marching on!

Thousands believed that Brown was right and slavery was wrong, that Frederick Douglass was right and slavery wrong, Harriet Tubman was right to steal slaves away from their masters—and the masters were wrong. Then Abraham Lincoln became President, Julia Ward Howe wrote a song, and armies of men began to march for freedom:

(Sound effect: Bugle call)

Frederick Douglass called for Negro volunteers in aid of Lincoln. "Go! Go quickly—and help fill up the first *colored* regiment from the North. Remember Denmark Vesey of Charleston; remember Nat Turner; remember John Brown."

Frederick Douglass sent his own two sons to war against the slave masters. Harriet Tubman became a nurse in the Union Armies, and later a spy behind the rebel lines. Colonel Robert Gould Shaw led the Negro troops at the assault of Fort Wagner. And the cannon boomed:

(Sound effect: Cannon)

But when the camps were quiet in the lull between battles, through the darkness of night:

BATTLE HYMN OF THE REPUBLIC

> Mine eyes have seen the glory of the coming of the Lord.
> He is trampling out the vintage where the grapes of wrath are stored.
> He has loosed the fateful lightning of his terrible swift sword.
> His truth is marchin' on.
> Glory, glory, halleluiah . . .

And from the Negro slave cabins, sometimes even before freedom came, the song came:

BATTLE HYMN OF THE REPUBLIC *(Harmonica)*

And in the ranks of the Union Armies, from tents pitched on a ridge in the starlit night:

BATTLE HYMN OF THE REPUBLIC

> John Brown's body lies a-moulderin' in the grave.
> John Brown's body lies a-moulderin' in the grave.
> John Brown's body lies a-moulderin' in the grave,

became one of the Great American abolitionists, founding a pape
called "The North Star," writing and speaking for freedom. Stron
societies of white abolitionists, including people of every faith, gre
up in the Northern cities. Many escaped slaves worked with th
white abolitionists. Some limited their activities to speaking an
writing and fund raising in the North, while others, like Harrie
Tubman, risked their lives to go into the South to help slaves escap

GO DOWN, MOSES

Go down, Moses,
Way down in Egypt's Land,
Tell ol' Pharaoh
Let my people go!

And there came a kind of Moses intending to lead the slaves t
freedom. His name was John Brown, old and tall, white, with a
flowing white beard, a Bible in one hand and a gun in the other
John Brown believed that God had called him to help free the
Negro people. In a speech on the Fourth of July, 1852, Frederick
Douglass said:

"It is not light that is needed, but fire. It is not the gentle shower,
but thunder. We need the storm, the whirlwind, and the earth-
quake."

John Brown brought the thunder and the earthquake. A group
of white men and Negroes together, 23 in number, one Octobe
night in 1859, marched on the government arsenal at Harper'
Ferry, Virginia, intending to seize the arms and give them to th
slaves. Some were killed and the rest were taken prisoners. Joh
Brown's uprising was a failure in so far as freeing the slaves th
went. But it shook the empire of slavery to its foundations.
startled the world. It aroused the conscience of the nation. It g
courage to the bondsmen and struck terror into their masters. J
Brown was hanged. But it was only a matter of time before the wl
of the Union Armies began to march for freedom. John Br
died on the scaffold, but his soul went marching on in song
story:

JOHN BROWN'S BODY

John Brown died that the slaves might be free.
John Brown died that the slaves might be free.
John Brown died that the slaves might be free,
But his soul goes marching on.
Glory, glory, halleluiah!

And truth goes marchin' on.
Glory, glory, halleluiah . . . .
And the truth is marchin' on.

And then, after many men had died on the battlefields, the President of the United States, Abraham Lincoln, put his name to a paper that said:

"On the first day of January, in the year of our Lord one thousand eight hundred and sixty-three, all persons held as slaves within any State, or designated part of a State, the people whereof shall then be in rebellion against the United States, shall be then, thenceforward, and forever free . . ."

BATTLE HYMN OF THE REPUBLIC

Glory, glory, halleluiah!
Glory, glory, halleluiah!
Glory, glory, halleluiah!
And the truth is marchin' on!

PART II. THE GLORY

When lilacs last in the dooryard bloom'd.
And the great star early droop'd in the western sky in the night,
I mourn'd, and yet shall mourn, with ever-returning spring.
Ever-returning spring, trinity sure to me you bring
Lilac blooming perennial, and drooping star in the west,
And thought of him I love.
O powerful western fallen star!
O shades of night! O moody, tearful night!
O great star disappear'd . . . . .

So wrote Walt Whitman on the death of Abraham Lincoln, killed in Washington, a martyr to our freedom.

The Civil War was over, Lincoln was dead. Emancipation had begun, and the period historians call the Reconstruction. For a little while freedom was wonderful. There were Negro Representatives from the South in Congress. Negroes held city and state offices. Then the reaction set in. The vote was taken away from the freedmen in many states. The Ku Klux Klan began to ride. Jim Crow cars made their appearance on the railroads. Negro churches and schools were burned. White teachers were driven away from the South. Freed with nothing, the former slaves were poor and often hungry. The night was dark. But hope was there, and ambition, and the desire for learning. even though the road was hard:

TROUBLE IN MIND

Trouble in mind! I'm blue,
But I won't be always.
The sun's gonna shine
In my backdoor someday,

I'm all alone at midnight
And the lights are burnin' low.
Never had so much trouble
In my life before.

One I love's done quit me
And it sure do grieve my mind.
Sometimes I feel like livin',
Sometimes I feel like dyin'.

I'm gonna lay my head
On some lonesome railroad line
And let the 2:19 train
Satisfy my mind.

Trouble in mind! I'm blue,
But I won't be always.
The sun's gonna shine
In my backdoor someday.

The Blues! But the sun is going to shine in my back door some-day. . . . . Shortly before the Civil War began a boy was born in slavery. He stood with bare feet before the Big House to hear the Emancipation Proclamation read, and he saw the tears run down his mother's face at the news of freedom. Then, still a child, he went to work in the salt pits of West Virginia. He wanted to learn to read and write. So did his mother. But there was no teacher for Negroes anywhere around so, all by themselves, they pored over an old blue-backed speller at night by the firelight. Finally the colored people of the town raised enough money to send away and get themselves a teacher. Then the boy went to school, working in the early mornings before school in the salt mines, and again after school until dark came. On his first day in class, the teacher asked all the children their names—and each child *but him* had two names. He was ashamed to have only one name, Booker. So when his turn came, out of the clear blue sky, he added Washington—"Booker

Washington," he said. Later he added an initial, T,—he gave himself a full name: Booker T. Washington.

When he was about fifteen Booker walked almost all the way to Hampton on the coast to study, arriving there with no money. But the kind white teachers accepted him, and he became their most famous student. After graduation, he himself founded a school, Tuskeegee. And he became one of the great American Negroes, an educator and a diplomat—a kind of link between the freedmen and the powers that be—a counselor to Presidents, and the "official" leader of his race. At the Cotton States Exposition in Atlanta in 1895, addressing the largest crowd to whom a Negro had ever spoken in the United States, he made a famous speech that went in part like this:

"One-third of the population of the South is of the Negro race. No enterprise seeking the material, civil, or moral welfare of this section can disregard this element of our population and reach the highest success. . . . . . Once a ship lost at sea for many days suddenly sighted a friendly vessel. From the mast of the unfortunate vessel was seen a signal, "Water, water! We die of thirst!" The answer from the friendly vessel came back, "Cast down your bucket where you are." A second time the signal, "Water, water! Send us water!" ran up the distressed vessel and was answered, "Cast down your bucket where you are." The captain of the distressed vessel, at last heeding the injunction, cast down his bucket—and it came up full of fresh sparkling water from the Amazon River.

"To those of my race who underestimate the importance of cultivating friendly relations with the Southern white man, who is their next-door neighbor, I would say, "Cast down your bucket where you are." Cast it down in making friends in every manly way of the people of all races by whom we are surrounded. Cast it down in agriculture, mechanics, in commerce, in domestic service, and in the professions. No race can prosper till it learns there is as much dignity in tilling a field as in writing a poem. . . . . To those of the white race, I would repeat what I say to my own race, 'Cast down your bucket where you are.' Cast it down among the eight millions of Negroes whose habits you know, whose fidelity you have tested. Cast down your bucket among these people who have tilled your fields, cleared your forests, and brought forth treasures from the bowels of the earth. Cast down your bucket among my people, help and encourage them to the education of head, hand, and heart. There is no defense or security for any of us except in the highest intelligence and development of all. This will bring to our beloved South a new heaven and a new earth."

Tuskeegee became a model industrial school. Educators came from all over the world to study its methods of teaching people how to "let down their buckets" where they are, getting the most out of the soil and surroundings they live in. To Tuskeegee Booker T. Washington brought a young agricultural chemist, George Washington Carver, who was to become just as famous as the founder of the school. Carver developed hundreds of new products from the peanut, the sweet potato, and the soil of Alabama itself— from paints to cooking oils, plastics to rubber compounds, peanut butter to linoleum. His discoveries enriched the whole South, indeed the whole world, not just the Negro people.

While Washington and Carver were working at Tuskeegee, other Negroes all over the country were doing important things, too. Great Negro newspapers were being founded, colored insurance companies were coming into being, books were being written, and among other things, Jazz was on its way to being born:

DALLAS RAG (*Instrumental*)

Meanwhile in Dayton, Ohio, a colored elevator boy was writing poetry. His father and mother had been slaves. And it was young Paul Laurence Dunbar, as a child in school, who helped his mother learn to read and write. Dunbar grew up to publish many books, to lecture in England and to write Broadway shows. One of Dunbar's poems, famous at the turn of the century, is about a father coming home from a long day's work, playfully picking up his baby son, and saying:

LITTLE BROWN BABY

Little brown baby wif spa'klin' eyes,
    Come to you' pappy an' set on his knee.
What you been doin', suh—makin' san' pies?
    Look at dat bib—you's ez du'ty ez me.
Look at dat mouf—dat's merlasses, I bet;
    Come hyeah, Maria, an' wipe off his han's.
Bees gwine to ketch you an' eat you up yit,
    Bein' so sticky an' sweet—goodness lan's!

Little brown baby wif spa'klin eyes,
    Who's pappy's darlin' an' who's pappy's chile?
Who is it all de day nevah once tries
    Fu' to be cross, er once loses dat smile?
Whah did you git dem teef? My, you's a scamp!
    Whah did dat dimple come f'om in yo' chin?

Pappy do' know yo—I b'lieves you's a tramp;
　Mammy, dis hyeah's some ol' straggler got in!

Let's th'ow him outen de do' in de san',
　We do' want stragglers a-layin' 'roun' hyeah;
Let's gin him 'way to de big buggah-man;
　I know he's hidin' erroun' hyeah right neah.
Buggah-man, buggah-man, come in de do',
　Hyeah's a bad boy you kin have fu' to eat.
Mammy an' pappy do' want him no mo',
　Swaller him down f'om his haid to his feet!

Dah, now, I t'ought dat you'd hub me up close.
　Go back, ol' buggah, you sha'n't have dis boy.
He ain't no tramp, ner no straggler, of co'se;
　He's pappy's pa'dner an' playmate an' joy.
Come to you' pallet now—go to yo' res';
　Wisht you could allus know ease an' cleah skies;
Wisht you could stay jes' a chile on my breas'—
　Little brown baby wif spa'klin' eyes!

Down in New Orleans a little brown boy in the band at the Waif's Home began to play on a battered old cornet the music that he had always heard. This lad played so beautifully that the people stopped on the streets to stand at the curb whenever his band passed. Later this boy from New Orleans became one of the great kings of jazz—Louis Armstrong:

I'M NOT ROUGH (Instrumental)

That's Louis! And he's playing a blues—the blues that were to have such a great influence on American music. In 1914, W. C. Handy wrote "The St. Louis Blues," now sung around the world. And in 1924 George Gershwin first performed his "Rhapsody in Blue" that has become an American classic. Its themes are derived from the Negro blues.

The blues are sad songs, but with an undercurrent of hope and determination in them. Thus it was with Negro life for a long time, with pools of prejudice and segregation at the doorstep, but with hope and determination always there. In 1905 a group of courageous colored men met at Niagara Falls to initiate a movement to do something about the many problems which colored people—and democracy—faced. Out of their conference eventually grew the National Association for the Advancement of Colored People—the

N. A. A. C. P., began to try to bring into being full democracy for all the people in our land.

In 1915, Dr. Carter G. Woodson, to whom this recording is dedicated, established the Association for the Study of Negro Life and History. Later he founded Negro History Week. This Association soon began to publish "The Journal of Negro History" and the "Negro History Bulletin," also Dr. Woodson's book, *The Negro in Our History*. They brought out many other valuable records of our past and present.

Following the First World War there were 70 lynchings within a year. In 1919, there were 25 bloody race riots in the United States. In some towns returning Negro soldiers were beaten and forced to discard their uniforms. Mobs burned Negro homes. Segregation grew. In the violent Chicago race riot, millions of dollars worth of property was destroyed and many people killed. Then it was that the poet, Claude McKay, wrote his famous sonnet:

IF WE MUST DIE

If we must die, let it not be like hogs
Hunted and penned in an inglorious spot,
While round us bark the mad and hungry dogs,
Making their mock at our accursed lot.
If we must die, O let us nobly die,
So that our precious blood may not be shed
In vain; then even the monsters we defy
Shall be constrained to honor us though dead!
O kinsmen! We must meet the common foe!
Though far outnumbered let us show us brave,
And for their thousand blows deal one deathblow!
What though before us lies the open grave?
Like men we'll face the murderous, cowardly pack,
Pressed to the wall, dying, but fighting back!

But for civilized men, violence should be no solution for their problems, so the N. A. A. C. P. kept working for equal enforcement of the laws of our Constitution, particularly for the colored citizen who did not have legal equality or full protection by the police. But little by little, we have seen these objectives come more and more into being in recent years, largely through the affirmation of the Supreme Court's upholding the great provisions of our Constitution. In those states were Negro tax money was spent for beautiful state universities to which Negroes could not go, the lawyers for the N. A. A. C. P. convinced the Supreme Court that this should not be, and the Court declared it wrong. Again, through the N. A. A. C. P. restrictive covenants denying colored people the right to buy homes anywhere were broken down. Segregation in interstate travel has been declared against the national interest. And, most recently, the right of all children to a full and equal education without discrimination has been upheld. The Urban League has had great effect in opening up to Negro workers employment in plants, and factories, and offices, and shops where formerly no colored people worked. The large National Association of Colored Women's Clubs, under the guidance for many years of Mary McLeod Bethune, has been a force for good in race relations, too. During the Second World War, Mrs. Bethune became an advisor to the President, and an internationally known speaker for the rights of all peoples.

Meanwhile, books by Negro writers began to be published in increasing numbers, and to be translated abroad. Our music, from jazz to the symphonies of William Grant Still, has been heard around the world. And Joe Louis became the heavyweight champion of the world. Jackie Robinson became a member of the Dodgers, and our music is still traveling. Here is Ella Fitzgerald:

ORGAN GRINDER'S SWING

All the children tag along
Just to listen to his song.
Monkey dancing on a string
To the Organ Grinder's Swing.
Hy-ho! . . . Hy-ho!
Hy-ho! . . . Hy-ho!
I swing it!
So do you!

In the United Nations, the highest ranking American official on the permanent staff is Dr. Ralph Bunche, a Negro, second only to the Secretary-General. Born in Detroit, educated in California and at Harvard University, Ralph Bunche is an expert on the affairs of minority groups and smaller nations. He was the recipient of the Nobel Peace Prize in 1950. Looking at the years ahead of us, Dr. Bunche says:

"I have great faith that the kind of world we all long for can and will be achieved. It is the kind of world the United Nations is working incessantly to bring about; a world at peace; a world in which people practice tolerance and live together in peace with one another as good neighbors; a world in which there is full respect for human rights and fundamental freedoms for all without distinction as to race, sex, language, or religion; a world in which all men shall walk together as equals and with dignity."

Ralph Bunche is speaking for all mankind. But, in speaking for mankind, he is speaking for the Negro in America, too. We have wanted those *very* things since the beginnings of our history in the United States. Our efforts to achieve them—and our very great achievements—make up the story of—indeed the glory of—Negro history in America. All the way from the Negro pilot who was with Columbus to Ralph Bunche at the United Nations—from Estavan and the explorers with Balboa to Henson who went to the North Pole with Perry—from the Colonial poet, Phillis Wheatley to Margaret Walker and dozens of other excellent colored writers— from Crispus Attucks, the first man to fall for American independence to Doire Miller, a hero of World War II, from the anonymous Negro singers on the slave ships to Marian Anderson, from the players of African drums to Duke Ellington and the hundreds of famous makers of music today—from Harriet Tubman to Mary McLeod Bethune—who speaks to us now in her own voice:

"We have known what it is to suffer; we are prepared to understand suffering. We have known what it is to be underprivileged; we are prepared by history to redeem others from want. For years I have felt that despite the difficulties and obstacles in the way, our great American nation was moving toward integration and solidarity. I have always believed that some day we would find greater peace and harmony among the many elements which make up the American people. There is now before us an unparalleled opportunity. This is our day! Doors will open everywhere. The floodtide of a new life is coming in."

BATTLE HYMN OF THE REPUBLIC

Glory, glory, halleluiah!
Glory, glory, halleluiah!
Glory, glory, halleluiah!
His truth is marching on!

ARTICLES AND
SPEECHES

LANGSTON HUGHES' SPEECH AT NATIONAL ASSEMBLY OF AUTHORS AND DRAMATISTS SYMPOSIUM: "THE WRITER'S POSITION IN AMERICA," ALVIN THEATRE, NEW YORK CITY, MAY 7, 1957

Bruce Caton spoke today of the writer's chance to be heard. My chance to be heard, as a Negro writer, is not so great as your chance if you are white. I once approached the Play Service of the Dramatists Guild as to the handling of some of my plays. *No,* was the answer, they would not know where to place plays about Negro life. I once sent one of my best known short stories, before it came out in book form, to one of our oldest and foremost American magazines. The story was about racial violence in the South. It came back to me with a very brief little note saying the editor did not believe his readers wished to read about such things. Another story of mine which did not concern race problems at all came back to me from one of our best known editors of anthologies of fiction with a letter praising the story but saying that he, the editor, could not tell if the characters were white or colored. Would I make them definitely Negro? Just a plain story about human beings from me was not up his alley, it seems. So before the word *man* I simply inserted *black,* and before the girl's name, the words *brown skin*—and the story was accepted. Only a mild form of racial bias. But now let us come to something more serious.

Censorship, the Black List: We Negro writers, just by being black, have been on the blacklist all our lives. Do you know that there are libraries in our country that will not stock a book by a Negro writer, not even as a gift? There are towns where Negro newspapers and magazines cannot be sold—except surreptitiously. There are American magazines that have *never* published anything by Negroes. There are film studios that have never hired a Negro writer. Censorship for us begins at the color lines.

As to the tangential ways in which many white writers may make a living: I've already mentioned Hollywood. Not once in a blue moon does Hollywood send for a Negro writer, no matter how famous he may be. When you go into your publishers' offices, how many colored editors, readers, or even secretaries do you see? In the

483

book review pages of our Sunday supplements and our magazines, how often do you see a Negro reviewer's name? And if you do, nine times out of ten the Negro reviewer will be given a book by another Negro to review—seldom if ever, THE SEA AROUND US or AUNTIE MAMIE—or COMPULSION—and yet a reviewer of the calibre of Arna Bontemps or Anne Petry or J. Saunders Redding could review anybody's books, white or colored, interestingly. Take Lecturing: There are thousands and thousands of women's clubs and other organizations booking lecturers that have never had, and will not have, a Negro speaker—though he has written a best seller.

We have in America today about a dozen top flight, frequently published and really good Negro writers. Do you not think it strange that of that dozen, at least half of them live abroad, far away from their people, their problems, and the sources of their material: Richard Wright—"Native Son" in Paris; Chester Himes—"The Primitives" in Paris; James Baldwin—"Giovanni's Room" in Paris; William Denby—"Beetle Creek" in Rome; Ralph Ellison—"Invisible Man" in Rome; Frank Yerby—of the dozen best sellers, in South France; and Willard Motley—"Knock On Any Door" in Mexico. Why: Because the stones thrown at Autherine Lucy at the University of Alabama are thrown at them, too. Because the shadow of Montgomery and the bombs under Rev. King's house, shadow them and shatter them, too. Because the body of little Emmett Till drowned in a Mississippi river and no one brought to justice, haunts them, too. One of the writers I've mentioned, when last I saw him before he went abroad, said to me, "I don't want my children to grow up in the shadow of Jim Crow."

And so let us end with children. And let us end with poetry—since somehow the planned poetry panel for which I was to have been a part, did not materialize. So, therefore, there has been no poetry in our National Assembly. Forgive me, then, if I read a poem. It's about a child—a little colored child. I imagine her as being maybe six or seven years old. She grew up in the Deep South where our color lines are still legal. Then her family moved to a Northern or Western industrial city—one of those continual migrations of Negroes looking for a better town. There in this Northern city—maybe a place like Newark, New Jersey, or Omaha, Nebraska, or Oakland, California, the little girl goes one day to a carnival, and she sees the merry-go-round going around, and she wants to ride. But being a little colored child, and remembering the South, she doesn't know if she can ride or not. And if she can ride, where? So this is what she says:

Where is the Jim Crow section
On this merry-go-round,
Mister, cause I want to ride?
Down South where I come from
White and colored
Can't sit side by side.
Down South on the train
There's a Jim Crow car.
On the bus we're put in the back—
But there ain't no back
To a merry-go-round:
Where's the horse
For a kid's that's black?

MEMORIES OF CHRISTMAS

My first memories of Christmas center in Kansas, which is the very
center of our U.S.A. Christmas trees, candles, cotton snow, and pot-
bellied stoves are all mixed up in these early memories. The stove
is there because my first Christmas trees always stood in the corner
behind the pot-bellied stove. On account of the cotton snow, we
had to be careful of the stove, and of the candles on the tree. If the
stove got red-hot, or the candles fell down, the cotton snow might
catch on fire. The idea of snow catching on fire intrigues me to this
very day. Early in life I had a love of excitement, and I always
rather hoped the snow would catch on fire, but it never did.

For poor children, Santa Claus seldom lives up to expectation. I
never remember finding on Christmas morning *all* of the things
I had asked Santa Claus to bring. But always I would find at least
one of the hoped-for gifts, and the surprise and happiness of that
one would make up for those lacking. The big presents would always
be under the tree. But hope for the missing B-B gun or the long
desired cowboy suit would not be downed until the very toe of
each hanging stocking was also searched. But out of the stockings
would usually come mostly oranges, nuts, and hard candies. Cer-
tainly, not even Santa Claus could get an air rifle in a stocking!

Christmas without presents must be a strange Christmas indeed
for an American child. But as I grew older, I learned that there
are children (even in this richest of all countries) whose parents
and whose Santa Claus sometimes cannot afford presents. I was
twenty-one before I knew a Christmas without presents. That year

I was working in the merchant marine, and in early December we sailed out of New York harbor for Rotterdam. The boat had a new crew. Of the forty seamen aboard, none of us had ever met or worked together before. Christmas Eve we were at anchor in a strange Dutch port whose dock fronts and gabled houses were covered with the same white snow I had known in Kansas. Rotterdam's canal lights gleamed with a frosty glow as a half dozen of us took a motor launch across the harbor to the main part of the city where we found a cozy bar. There we greeted the Christmas dawn in a warm glow of Holland gin. Back aboard ship the next day, we had chicken for Christmas dinner, but no tree, and none of the crew exchanged presents.

That was my only Christmas without giving or receiving something. Even in the Soviet Union, where I spent a Yuletide away down in the heart of Uzbekistan in Central Asia, there were presents. Some thirty or forty miles from Tashkent there was at that time a colony of American Negro cotton chemists and growers teaching the Asiatics how to raise cotton Alabama style. Among them was the late Colonel Young's son, and some others who had been teachers at Hampton and other of our Southern colleges. With their wives, they invited Bernard Powers, a Negro road engineer working in Tashkent, and myself, to spend the holidays with them.

When I left Moscow for Central Asia in November, the citizens of the Soviet capital said they envied me going to the warm part of the Soviet Union for the winter. I pictured myself as basking in a kind of Florida sunshine while Moscow suffered their customary twenty below zero temperature. Well, to a Moscovite the climate of Tashkent may be warm—but to me it was just as cold as Topeka or Kansas City or Chicago. In Uzbekistan the snow was half way up to my knees by December and, although the mercury never hit zero, it did get mighty near there. But to a Russian *that was warm!*

The day before Christmas, Powers and I hailed a passing sled, horse-drawn—that took the place of taxis in snow-covered Tashkent —and off we went to the railroad station. There was a line of country-bound travelers a block long outside waiting to purchase tickets. When we finally got on the train it was crowded to the doors and beyond. Polite as Soviet citizens are to foreigners, often making way for them to have seats in a crowded coach, these coaches were too crowded for anyone to even move to let us inside. Powers and I had to stand on the open platform between the coaches in the bitter cold.

As the train pulled out, it started to snow again. Before we had gone ten miles, all the human beings who were crowded together on these old-time open platforms between the cars were covered from head to toe with the driving snow, until we looked like snow-men ourselves. After a half hour of this, the snow with which we were coated began to turn to ice, fanned as it was by prairie winds and the speed of the moving train. First my face, then my hands, then my feet froze—and the cold finally penetrated to the very marrow of my bones. After a while, it did not matter any more. That sweet don't-care-ness that I have always heard comes with freezing to death, came over me. At last the train came to a station in the stormy wilderness. Some of the people in the coaches got off. But by then it did not matter whether I got inside the train or not. I was frozen stiff—and Powers and I both were so covered with snow that we could have passed for white in Mississippi.

Finally we reached the farm where the Negro agricultural experts lived. There was warmth and good-will, good food and presents— and a Christmas tree. But it took Powers and I all night to thaw out and finally really realize that Christmas had come. For Christmas dinner we had fried rabbit and wonderful hot biscuits that one of the colored wives made. There was pie, too! And it was just like being back home in Kansas although we were in the ancient land of Tamerland and Ghengis Khan and the Thousand And One Nights.

Other memorable Christmases for me in foreign lands have been the Yuletides of Mexico and of France. Paris has its charming features all the year round, but Christmas there—if you live with and know French people—has a heart-warming delight all its own.

In Mexico the holidays possess picturesque joys I have seen no-where else. For nine days before Chritsmas there is a series of neigh-borhood parties each night from house to house known as *"las posadas."* At the *"posadas"* each guest takes a candle and a procession is formed that goes from room to room and door to door around the patio of the house singing:

> *Humildes peregrinos.*
> *Maria, Jésus, José. . . .*

as Mary, with child, and her husband, Joseph, walked centuries ago seeking shelter in Bethlehem so that the Child might be born. But no door opens, so the procession moves on. The old story of man's lack of interest in his brother is acted out each night.

But each night it all ends in happiness and feasting, dancing and a party—and after nine such nights comes Christmas! Perhaps it simply means—this symbolic *"posada"*—that after the hard days, the long months (maybe even the bitter years), there comes somehow to everyone the clean white snow, the sparkling tree, the gifts, and the new birth of friendship and life that is Christmas, holiday of the new-born Child.

MY MOST HUMILIATING JIM CROW
EXPERIENCE

It happened in Cleveland years ago when I was in High School, and the Great Migration of Negroes from the South during World War I was at its height. Jim Crow, new to Cleveland in most public places, was beginning to raise its ugly head.

Our High School French class had gone to see a matinee performance of the late great Sara Bernhardt, with her wooden leg, in Cleopatra's death scene, where the asp stings her in the bosom. The magic of Sara's famous golden voice still rings in my ears.

But of that afternoon, there is an even more vivid memory. Following the performance, with one of my white classmates, a Polish-American boy, I went across the street from the theatre into one of Cleveland's large cafeterias. Its self-service and low prices appealed to our school-boy pocket-books. Its long cases and counters and steam-tables loaded with appetizing food whetted our appetites. We took our trays and got in line. My white school-mate was just in front of me.

We passed around in front of the colorful green salads, the sweet, good looking desserts, the white and pink and chocolate frosted cakes, the long steam table with its soups and vegetables and meats. Each of us selected our foods, and stopped with our trays before the cashier's desk. She rang up my friend's bill, he paid her, and passed on to seek a table.

But when the white woman looked at me and then down at my tray, I thought she would never stop striking the keys on the cash register. It rang and rang and rang. The amount it registered on the black and white tabs behind its glass strip became larger and larger. Finally the cashier pulled out a check and flung it on my tray. It was *Eight Dollars and Sixty-Five Cents!*

My friend's check had been only about forty-five or fifty cents. I had selected about the same amount of food. I looked in amazement at the cashier.

"Why is mine so much?" I asked.

"That is just what you will pay if you eat in here," said the cashier.

"But I don't have that much food," I said.

"That is what you will pay to eat it," said the cashier, her face growing more and more belligerent, her skin turning red and her eyes narrowing. I could see the hatred in her face.

"But it doesn't cost that much," I said.

"Pay your check—or else put your tray down and leave it," she shouted. "You are holding up the line. That's what it costs if you want to eat!"

I put my tray down and left it there in front of her. I had not run into anything like that before in Cleveland, but I know it was because I was colored. I went up to the table where my white classmate was eating and said, "Come on, let's get out of here. They won't let me eat in this place."

He was astonished, and it took a long time to explain it to him, because he did not know that such things went on in this democratic land that his parents had travelled way across the sea to find. But neither one of us made any protest. We were only fifteen or sixteen, and we did not know what to say. He and I both were embarrassed.

Some years later a large group of Communists picketed that same restaurant and others like it in Cleveland. Negro and white workers together went in and insisted on service for all. In that way they broke down the color line and ended that kind of un-American Jim Crow in the downtown cafeterias in Cleveland. I do not believe such an incident would happen to a High School boy there today. At least, I hope not. Such things are harder to take when one is young.

TEN THOUSAND BEDS

Often I hear a person say, "I can't sleep in strange bed." Such a person I regard with wonder and amazement, slightly tinged with envy. Wonder and amazement that such a small change as a strange bed would keep a person from sleeping, and envy that there are people who stay put so well that any bed other than their own upsets them. At a most conservative estimate, I figure I have slept in at least ten thousand strange beds.

As a child I was often boarded out, sent to stay with relatives, foster-relatives, or friends of the family. And my family itself was always moving, so quite early in life I got used to a variety of beds from the deep feather beds of the country to the studio couches of the town, from camp cots to my uncle's barber chair in Kansas

City elongated to accommodate me. If strange beds had been given to upsetting me, I would have lost many a good night's sleep in my life. And there is nothing I like better than to sleep.

This year of our Lord, 1948, for example, I have slept in beds from Montreal, Canada, to New Orleans, Louisiana, from St. Petersburg, Florida, to Spokane, Washington, from Elizabeth City, North Carolina, to Los Angeles, California. Nowhere did I pass a sleepless night. Since January I have slept on trains in lower berths, upper berths, roomettes, and bedrooms, and on planes with the seat reclining flying over mountains and deserts. In anything moving, from cars to trains, boats to planes, I can sleep like a log. I can also sleep in movies, lectures, and theatres, not to speak of concerts, although I do not consider it polite to do so, and I try my best to stay awake.

Sometimes I hear a person say, "I always take a book to bed with me to read myself to sleep." How I envy such a person. I often wish that I could read for an hour or so at night in bed, but I usually go to sleep before I get to the bottom of a page. And it is a nusiance to have to wake up and close the book and put out the light.

I know many people who say they cannot drink coffee at night because it keeps them awake. Often I have wished that coffee would have such an effect on me. I have drunk several cups at times quite late at night, but sleep came down just the same. And once in bed, I did not even dream. I have never had the need to count sheep. I have tried sometimes to see if I could count a hundred, but I never remember getting beyond thirty-six. I lost all interest in the sheep, being asleep.

Once, having undergone an experience that should have upset my nerves, a physician friend prescribed for me some sleeping pills. That night I said to myself, "If I wake up I will take a pill." So I placed the bottle beside the bed. But I did not wake up until noon the next day, so I never took the sleeping pills. I think I am the kind of fellow who needs pills to wake up rather than to go to sleep. The first night I was in Madrid during the Spanish Civil War, I slept through a Franco bombardment and did not even turn over.

Once in a hotel in the Middle West I was awakened by a loud altercation in the next room. A lady's boy friend was accusing her of infidelity with her dog. And one time in Samarkand, in Central Asia, in the early dawn some camels got to fighting and screaming among themselves just outside the window. Their unholy screeching aroused me before the master of the caravan subdued them. But as a rule I am not easily aroused. And I do not come to my senses immediately upon awakening. I have always admired those persons who can jump out of bed as bright as a dollar as soon as they open their eyes in the morning.

Some writers tell me they do their best writing by arising early and working three or four hours before breakfast. At five A.M. their minds are as clear as a bell. For them I have the greatest admiration. Also for persons like Edison, who can sleep only four or five hours a night, arising refreshed and full of creative powers, I have respect and admiration. Unfortunately, nature endowed me with quite a different constitution. Ten hours sleep suits me much better than five. And twelve hours really restores my soul. I consider it unfortunate that I am not able to get along very well with less than eight hours sleep. On the other hand, I suppose I am fortunate in being able to sleep in any bed, any time, any place anywhere. Ten thousand beds and not a sleepless night although I did wake up once when those folks quarrelled next door, and again when the camels fought outside my window before the caravan set out.

HOW TO BE A BAD WRITER
(In Ten Easy Lessons)

1. Use all the clichés possible, such as "He had a gleam in his eye," or "Her teeth were white as pearls."

2. If you are a Negro, try very hard to write with an eye dead on the white market—use modern stereotypes of older stereotypes—big burly Negroes, criminals, low-lifers, and prostitutes.

3. Put in a lot of profanity and as many pages as possible of near-pornography and you will be so modern you pre-date Pompei in your lonely crusade toward the best seller lists. By all means be misunderstood, unappreciated, and ahead of your time in print and out, then you can be felt-sorry-for by your own self, if not the public.

4. Never characterize characters. Just name them and then let them go for themselves. Let all of them talk the same way. If the reader hasn't imagination enough to make something out of cardboard cut-outs, shame on him!

5. Write about China, Greece, Tibet, or the Argentine pampas—anyplace you've never seen and know nothing about. Never write about anything you know, you home town, or your home folks, or yourself.

6. Have nothing to say, but use a great many words, particularly high-sounding words, to say it.

7. If a playwright, put into your script a lot of hand-waving and spirituals, preferably the ones everybody has heard a thousand times from Marion Anderson to the Golden Gates.

8. If a poet, rhyme June with moon as often and in as many ways as possible. Also use *thee's* and *thou's* and *'tis* and *o'er*, and invert your sentences all the time. Never say, "The sun rose, bright and shining." But, rather, "Bright and shining rose the sun."

9. Pay no attention really to spelling or grammar or the neatness of the manuscript. And in writing letters, never sign your name so anyone can read it. A rapid scrawl will better indicate how important and how busy you are.

10. Drink as much liquor as possible and always write under the influence of alcohol. When you can't afford alcohol yourself, or even if you can, drink on your friends, fans, and the general public.

If you are white, there are many more things I can advise in order to be a bad writer, but since this piece is for colored writers, there are some things I know a Negro just will not do, not even for writing's sake, so there is no use mentioning them.

JAZZ AS COMMUNICATION

You can start anywhere—Jazz as Communication—since it's a circle, and you yourself are the dot in the middle. You, me. For example, I'll start with the Blues. I'm not a Southerner. I never worked on a levee. I hardly ever saw a cotton field except from the highway. But women behave the same on Park Avenue as they do on a levee: when you've got hold of one part of them the other part escapes you. That's the Blues!

Life is as hard on Broadway as it is in Blues-originating-land. The Brill Building Blues is just as hungry as the Mississippi Levee Blues. One communicates to the other, brother! Somebody is going to rise up and tell me that nothing that comes out of Tin Pan Alley is jazz. I disagree. Commercial, yes. But so was Storeyville, so was Basin Street. What do you think Tony Jackson and Jelly Roll Morton and King Oliver and Louis Armstrong were playing for? Peanuts? No, money, even in Dixieland. They were communicating for money. For fun, too—because they had fun. But the money helped the fun along.

Now; To skip a half century, somebody is going to rise up and tell me Rock and Roll isn't jazz. First, two or three years ago, there were all these songs about too young to know—*but.* . . . The songs are right. You're never too young to know how bad it is to love and not have love come back to you. That's as basic as the Blues. And that's what Rock and Roll is—teenage *Heartbreak Hotel*—the old songs reduced to the lowest common denominator. The music goes way back to Blind Lemon and Leadbelly—Georgia Tom merging into the Gospel Songs—Ma Rainey, and the most primitive of the Blues. It borrows their gut-bucket heartache. It goes back to the jubilees and stepped-up Spirituals—Sister Tharpe—and borrows their I'm-gonna-be-happy-anyhow-in-spite-of-this-world kind of hope. It goes back further and borrows the steady beat of the drums of Congo Square—that going-on beat—and the Marching Bands' loud and blatant *yes!!* Rock and roll puts them all together and makes a music so basic it's like the meat cleaver the butcher uses—before the cook uses the knife—before you use the sterling silver at the table on the meat that by then has been rolled up into a commercial filet mignon.

A few more years and Rock and Roll will no doubt be washed back half forgotten into the sea of jazz. Jazz is a great big sea. It washes up all kinds of fish and shells and spume and waves with a steady old beat, or off-beat. And Louis must be getting old if he thinks J. J. and Kai—and even Elvis—didn't come out of the same sea he came out of, too. Some water has chlorine in it and some doesn't. There're all kinds of water. There's salt water and Saratoga water and Vichy water, Quinine water and Pluto water—and Newport rain. And it's all water. Throw it all in the sea, and the sea'll keep on rolling along toward shore and crashing and booming back into itself again. The sun pulls the moon. The moon pulls the sea. They also pull jazz and me. Beyond Kai to Count to Lonnie to Texas Red, beyond June to Sarah to Billy to Bessie to Ma Rainey. And the Most is the It—the all of it.

Jazz seeps into words—spelled out words. Nelson Algren is influenced by jazz. Ralph Ellison is, too. Sartre, too. Jacques Prevert. Most of the best writers today are. Look at the end of the *Ballad of the Sad Cafe*. Me as the public, *my* dot in the middle—it was fifty years ago, the first time I heard the Blues on Independence Avenue in Kansas City. Then State Street in Chicago. Then Harlem in the twenties with J. P. and J. C. Johnson and Fats and Willie the Lion and Nappy playing piano—with the Blues running all up and down the keyboard through the ragtime and the jazz. House rent party cards. I wrote *The Weary Blues*:

      Drowning a drowsy syncopated tune . . . . . . etc. . . . . .

Shuffle Along was running then—the Sissle and Blake tunes. A little later *Runnin' Wild* and the Charleston and Fletcher and Duke and Cab. Jimmie Lunceford, Chick Webb, and Ella. Tiny Parham in Chicago. And at the end of the Depression times, what I heard at Minton's. A young music—coming out of young people. Billy—the male and female of them—both the Eckstein and the Holiday—and Dizzy and Tad and the Monk. Some of it came out in poems of mine in *Montage of a Dream Deferred* later. Jazz again putting itself into words:

POEMS FROM "MONTAGE"

But I wasn't the only one putting jazz into words. Better poets of the heart of jazz beat me to it. W. C. Handy a long time before. Benton Overstreet. Mule Bradford. Then Buddy DeSilva on the pop level. Ira Gershwin. By and by Dorothy Baker in the novel—to name only the most obvious—the ones with labels. I mean the ones you can spell out easy with a-b-c's—the word mongers—outside the music. But always the ones of the music were the best—Charlie Christian, for example, Bix, Louis, Joe Sullivan, Count.

Now, to wind it all up, with you in the middle—jazz is only what you yourself get out of it. Louis's famous quote—or misquote probably—"Lady, if you have to ask what it is, you'll never know." Well, I wouldn't be so positive. The lady just might know—without being able to let loose the cry—to follow through—to light up before the fuse blows out. To me jazz is a montage of a dream deferred. A great big dream—yet to come—and always *yet*—to become ultimately and finally true. Maybe in the next seminar—for Saturday—Nat Hentoff and Billy Strayhorn and Tony Scott and the others on that panel will tell us about it—when they take up "The Future of Jazz." The Bird was looking for that future like mad. The Newborns, Chico, Dave, Gulda, Milt, Charlie Mingan. That future is what you call pregnant. Potential papas and mamas of tomorrow's jazz are all known. But THE papa and THE mama—maybe both—are anonymous. But the child will communicate. Jazz is a heartbeat—its heartbeat is yours. You will tell me about its perspectives when you get ready.

SWEET CHARIOTS OF THIS WORLD

Swing low, sweet chariot,
Coming for to carry me home!

So sang the lowly of a century ago. But even way back yonder there were those who did not wait for that final chariot to ride sweetly. Then as now, if you had what it took to make the wheels go around, you could ride about in grand style. Even in ante-bellum days in the South, wealthy free Negroes were transported in elegance as great, if sometimes not greater, than wealthy whites. Long before the Civil War there were in New Orleans free Creoles of color and quadroon belles who rode down Canal Street in a coach-and-four—the equivalent then of a special built Cadillac today. Handsome surreys and handsome bays were the property of well-to-do colored folks as well as well-to-do whites.

Before the days of motor cars, in areas where there were bayous, rivers, or canals, water travel was not uncommon. Boats and barges were a convenient mode of private transportation. In the early 1800's a free Negro woman in Florida persuaded her mate, a wealthy white planter, to have built for her a palatial barge propelled by six black slaves at the oars. It had a silken canopy and was painted in gorgeous colors. Reclining among the cushions like a new-world Cleopatra, this beautiful ebony woman would ride regally up and down the Sewanee River in the cool of the evening to the envy and astonishment of all the whites along its banks. When their envy finally became too great for comfort, she persuaded her mate to book passage for her, the children, and himself to Santo Domingo where they settled down and where their descendants are among the leading families of that island today.

Just after the Civil War several of the Reconstruction congressmen of color drove from their Washington mansions to the Capitol in the handsomest rigs money could buy behind the finest horses available. Congressman John M. Langston possessed a sleek black rubber-tired carriage, drawn by two snow-white horses with a coachman at the reins. He lived in LeDroit Park near Howard University, whose Law School he founded. To get home he had to pass through a well-to-do white neighborhood whose inhabitants did not relish seeing a Negro ride in such style. Some of them put up a wooden barrier across the street to keep him from passing. Mr. Langston did not believe in barriers, so one day on the way home from the Halls of Congress he stopped at a hardware shop on Pennsylvania Avenue and bought himself an axe. When his carriage reached the wooden barrier he got out, took his axe and chopped it down while the coachman held his gloves. From then on. without hindrance, he rode behind his snow-white horses through the streets of Washington, the ebony spokes of his highly lacquered carriage wheels gleaming—such wheels being the nearest thing in those days to the contemporary elegance of white-walled tires.

When motor cars were first made, no sooner were they acquired by white folks than they were acquired by Negroes. Just who the first Negro in America to own an automobile was, I do not know. But old New Yorkers tell me Avery and Hart, a famous dancing team of the early 1900's, and Oscar Hammerstein, colored man-about-town, were among the first to be seen speeding up Broadway in long open cars, all occupants dressed in linen dusters to keep the rush of air from blowing their garments into disarray. One of the first Negro-owned cars on record to attract wide attention belonged to Jack Johnson, the heavyweight champion of the world. Jack, at one point in his career, was not satisfied to own an ordinary automobile, so legend says. He bought an armored car.

In the Golden Era of the 20's when the so-called "Negro Renaissance" of the theatre and the arts was in full bloom, money was free and the Harlem nightclubs packed with downtown whites, some very elegant chariots sped through Central Park from Lenox Avenue to Broadway and back. One of them belonged to Aubrey Lyles of Miller and Lyles, the comedy stars of "Shuffle Along." The Lyles car was as long as a Pullman. Its back seat opened up into a bed when its owner took to the road. And its decorations and accessories were all of pure white ivory. It was the kind of car that attracted a crowd whenever and wherever it was parked. It was frequently sighted near the famous tree of hope in front of the old Lafayette Theatre on Seventh Avenue, with the Rhythm Club nearby where Bojangles and other greats of the theatrical and sporting world went for recreation. Always there would be a curious admiring group of people about Lyles' chariot. Lyles himself was a very little fellow and he looked lost in so large and fine a car. But the car itself was most imposing. Lesser vehicles gave way before it when it took out, its horn sounding off. Historians call that era in American life the "Roaring Twenties." The horn on Lyles' car formed a part of its roar.

A few years later the great Negro actor and baritone, Jules Bledsoe, who originated the role of Joe in "Show Boat" and first sang "Ole Man River," appeared on the streets of Harlem in a long black Rolls Royce, sleek and striking in its funereal simplicity, and obviously very expensive. But even more startling to the Harlemites of those days than the car, was the fact that Mr. Bledsoe had a white chauffeur in full uniform. Jules Bledsoe was very dark. With his great sense of humor, he explained to his friends that he had a *white* chauffeur so folks could better tell who was the chauffeur and who the owner of the car, otherwise there might be a mistake. But the envious and small-minded had another explanation that they whispered about. They said the chauffeur went with the car of necessity, supplied by the firm, because the Rolls Royce people would not let anybody else drive it until the car was at least half paid for. Such a rumor, however, did not prevent Jules Bledsoe from emerging from his Broadway dressing room after a performance to settle his dark self among the soft cushions of the rear seat, and call through a speaking tube to his white chauffeur, "Home, James."

When "Rhapsody in Black" was playing with its wonderful cast including Ethel Waters, Valaida Snow, and the Berry Brothers, Miss Snow purchased a mauve-colored Mercedes Bentz of a striking orchid tone. She had her designer make for her an orchid suit trimmed in silver fox. Miss Snow had a pet monkey so for the monkey, too, a suit was made and a little cap to match. Her chauffeur also had a specially designed uniform to set off the car. When the show went on the road, Valaida Snow toured in her mauve-orchid chariot, causing the natives of such places as Terre Haute, Indiana, to stand agape with wonder as, chauffeur at the wheel and monkey on shoulder, she would draw up to the door of the local colored rooming house in her gorgeous foreign-made car. As the softly purring motor went still and the chauffeur jumped out to open the door, the beautiful brownskin Miss Snow would rise and walk with dignity into the dingy third-rate kind of a hotel which was the only sort of lodging place where Negro performers touring the Middle West could stop in those days. Her chariot was a dream, but many other factors in the lives of touring artists of color were less glamorous. A monkey could stay at a white hotel, but not a colored star.

That was before the second World War for democracy. Things are a bit better now. When Lena Horne steps out of her new foreign-made car and into the lobby of almost any hotel in the larger cities of the North, she will be received with courtesy. The curious outside will ask: "Whose car is that?" "What make is it?" "From what country did it come?"

In the early 1950's, the mode among celebrities of color seems to have turned more than ever to cars of foreign make. Domestic Packards and fish-tail Cadillacs no longer incite much comment, being far too numerous for notice in Harlem, Hollywood, and Chicago's South Side. For this reason, no doubt, Mr. Billy Eckstein, I hear, has recently purchased a silver-toned Jaguar of French make. Several English and a few Italian cars, too, are to be seen about Harlem these days. But Sugar Ray turned the tables by taking with him to Europe a canary-yellow *U.S.A.* Cadillac that became the talk of Paris. This cheerful chariot helped to gild the lily of this young fighter's reputation as one of the two greatest things

America has produced since the War—these things being Sugar Ray and the Marshall Plan.

It's a far cry from the elegant horse-drawn carriages of antebellum days or the canopied barges of the Swannee River to the colorful cars of today and the sleek white yachts of some successful Negroes—for Negroes have yachts, too, sailing nonchalantly up the Harlem River. In whatever style others ride, we ride. There are even those of us who have private planes. Several well-to-do Southern professional men of color possess them, taking to the air for a pleasure flight or a trip to Harlem at will. But I have not yet had the thrill of riding in any of these private planes, so I cannot tell you about them. I only know that now *our* bright chariots have wings, too, and some of us, anytime we wish, without waiting for heavenly chariots to swing low, may cleave the air. As soon as rockets to the moon are made, no doubt we will possess a few, probably faster, longer, and brighter than most others. When estates on the moon become more fashionable than mansions in St. Albans, West Chesterfield, or Blueberry Hill, there will most certainly be Negroes (probably movie stars or public relations executives) who will step into their rocket planes and call to a uniformed pilot, "Home, James!" Elegantly taking off—out of this world.

THE FUN OF BEING BLACK

It is a shame to say it, but apparently mankind thrives on conflict. A nation is never so alert and alive as when it is a nation at war. Literature, science, and art may thrive on peace, but the ordinary human being seems to have a hell of a good time out of conflicts, whether they be wars, political battles, arguments, athletic contests, debates or just plain old free-for-alls.

Some of the world's most stirring songs are songs of conflict. One that belongs to France but is loved by the whole world is "La Marseillaise" which begins somewhat to this effect, "Let's go, sons of our country! The bloody flag of tyranny is raised against us." And then proceeds to unfurl some of the most stirring martial words in musical literature.

One of America's greatest songs is, "The Battle Hymn of the Republic" which starts:

> Mine eyes have seen the glory
> Of the coming of the Lord. . . .

> He has loosed the fateful lightning
> Of His terrible swift sword. . . .

In other words, He is ready to fight.

One of our most venerable Christian hymns goes:

> Onward, Christian soldiers,
> Marching as to war. . . .

So I do not know why some folks (me included) are always lamenting the particular fact that we have a race conflict in America—because a great many people get a great deal of fun out of our contemporary white-Negro battles, not to speak of the jobs that are held as a result. Look at the number of Civil Rights lawyers who make a living and a reputation suing white folks, or fighting Jim Crow vote cases or teacher's salary inequalities right on up to the Supreme Court—and what a kick they get out of defeating some of our reactionary white folks. Look at the joy with which the NAACP attacks a segregation problem, or the delight with which the Urban League goes after factory owners who won't hire Negroes.

And did you ever hear Mary McLeod Bethune make a speech about Negro rights? Do you recall with what pride and joy she lifted her ample bosom to the enemy? And those of us who remember Roscoe Conkling Simmons, can never forget the vim, vigor, vitality —and pleasure—with which he lashed into the problems of the Negro race and, incidentally, tied them all up in the hold of that ship which is the Republican Party to which all else to him is the sea.

Crusaders—off the public platform—are some of the happiest-looking people you could ever hope to meet, possibly because they are so sure of the ultimate triumph of their causes. Negroes in Georgia have told me that the late Eugene Talmadge was really a most amiable man if you met him at home—but he was a hellion in favor of white supremacy in public. That venerable old lady of Communism, Mother Bloor was in person as sweet and full of sunshine as she could be—yet she battled the capitalists tooth and nail for seventy years. Individuals, like nations, seem to thrive on struggle. Look at Joe Louis, still as fat and sassy as he can be after all of his battles!

This racial struggle of ours in America has so many intricate and amusing angles that nobody taking an active part in it can ever be bored. It's very variety from North to South—from Boston where New England Negroes side with New England whites in opposing black southern migration, to Mobile on the Gulf where a Negro dare not oppose anybody—keeps the contest exciting. In the far West a Negro can sometimes eat in a Mexican restaurant but he cannot eat in a Chinese restaurant—so it is fun figuring out just where you can eat. In some towns a colored man can sit in the balcony of a theatre, but in others he has to sit in the last three rows on the left downstairs because the balcony is for whites who smoke. So, trying to see a movie in the United States can be for a Negro as intriguing as working a crossword puzzle.

Those of us engaged in this racial struggle in America are like knights on horseback—the Negroes on a white horse and the white folks on a black. Sometimes the race is terrific. But the feel of the wind in your hair as you ride toward democracy is really something! And the air smells so good!

MY AMERICA

This is my land America. Naturally, I love it—it is home—and I am vitally concerned about its mores, its democracy, and its well-being. I try now to look at it with clear, unprejudiced eyes. My ancestry goes back at least four generations on American soil—and, through Indian blood, many centuries more. My background and training is purely American—the schools of Kansas, Ohio, and the East. I am old stock as opposed to recent immigrant blood.

Yet many Americans who cannot speak English—so recent is their arrival on our shores—may travel about the country at will securing food, hotel, and rail accommodations wherever they wish to purchase them. I may not. These Americans, once naturalized, may vote in Mississippi or Texas, if they live there. I may not. They may work at whatever job their skills command. But I may not. They may purchase tickets for concerts, theaters, lectures wherever they are sold throughout the United States. I may not. They may repeat the Oath of Allegiance with its ringing phrase of "liberty and justice for all," with a deep faith in its truth—as compared to the limitations and oppressions they have experienced in the Old World. I repeat the oath, too, but I know that the phrase about "liberty and justice" does not fully apply to me. I am an American—but I am a colored American.

I know that all these things I mention are not *all* true for *all* localities *all* over America. Jim Crowism varies in degree from North to South, from the mixed schools and free franchise of Michigan to the tumbledown colored schools and open terror at the polls of Georgia and Mississippi. All over America, however, against the Negro there has been an economic color line of such severity that since the Civil War we have been kept most effectively, as a racial group, in the lowest economic brackets. Statistics are not needed to prove this. Simply look around you on the Main Street of any American town or city. There are no colored clerks in any of the stores—although colored people spend their money there. There are practically never any colored street-car conductors or bus drivers—although these public carriers run over streets for which we pay taxes. There are no colored girls at the switchboards of the telephone company—but millions of Negroes have phones and pay their bills. Even in Harlem, nine times out of ten, the man who comes to collect your rent is white. Not even that job is given a colored man by the great corporations owning New York real estate. From Boston to San Diego, the Negro suffers from job discrimination.

Yet America is a land where, in spite of its defects, I can write this article. Here the voice of democracy is still heard—Roosevelt, Wallace, Willkie, Agar, Pearl Buck, Paul Robeson. America is a land where the poll tax still holds in the South but opposition to the poll tax grows daily. America is a land where lynchers are not yet caught—but Bundists are put in jail, and majority opinion condemns the Klan. America is a land where the best of all democracies has been achieved for some people—but in Georgia, Roland Hayes, world-famous singer, is beaten for being colored and nobody is jailed—nor can Mr. Hayes vote in the State where he was born. Yet America is a country where Roland Hayes *can* come from a log cabin to wealth and fame—in spite of the segment that still wishes to maltreat him physically and spiritually, famous though he is.

This segment, however, is not all of America. If it were, millions of Negroes would have no heart for this war in which we are now engaged. If it were, we could see no difference between our ideals and Hitler's, in so far as our own dark lives are concerned. But we know, on the other hand, that America is a land in transition. And we know it is within our power to help in its further change toward a finer and better democracy than any citizen has know before. The American Negro believes in democracy. We want to make it real, complete, workable, not only for ourselves—the fifteen million dark ones—but for all Americans all over the land.

L. H. February, 1943.

ALSO BY LANGSTON HUGHES

POETRY   The Weary Blues, 1926; The Dream Keeper, 1932; Shakespeare in Harlem, 1942; Fields of Wonder, 1947; One-Way Ticket, 1949; Montage of a Dream Deferred, 1951; Cuba Libre (by Nicolas Guillen, translated from the Spanish by Langston Hughes and Benjamin Carruthers), 1948; Selected Poems of Gabriele Mistral (translated from the Spanish by Langston Hughes), 1957; The Poetry of the Negro (edited by Langston Hughes and Arna Bontemps), 1949.

HUMOR   Simple Speaks His Mind, 1950; Simple Takes a Wife, 1952; Simple Stakes a Claim, 1957.

AUTOBIOGRAPHIES   The Big Sea (1st volume), 1940; I Wonder As I Wander (2nd volume), 1956.

NOVELS   Not Without Laughter, 1930; Masters of the Dew (by Jacques Roumain, translated from the French by Langston Hughes and Mercer Cook), 1947.

BIOGRAPHIES   Famous American Negroes, 1954; Famous Negro Music Makers, 1955; Famous American Negro Heroes, 1958.

JUVENILES   Popo and Fifina (with Arna Bontemps), 1932; First Book of Negroes, 1952; First Book of Rhythms, 1954; First Book of Jazz, 1955; First Book of the West Indies, 1956.

SHORT STORIES   The Ways of White Folks, 1934; Laughing To Keep From Crying, 1952.

PHOTO ESSAY   The Sweet Flypaper of Life, 1955.

HISTORY   Pictorial History of the Negro in America (with Milton Meltzer), 1956.

PLAYS, MUSICALS AND OPERAS   Mulatto, 3 Act Tragedy, 1935; Little Ham, 3 Act Comedy, 1936; Soul Gone Home, 1 Act Tragi-Comedy, 1937; Joy To My Soul, 3 Act Comedy, 1937; Emperor of Haiti, 3 Act Tragedy, 1938; Don't You Want To Be Free? 1 Act Historical Panorama, 1937; Front Porch, 3 Act Comedy Drama, 1939; When the Jack Hollers, 3 Act Folk Comedy (with Arna Bontemps), 1936; The Sun Do Move, 2 Act Music Drama, 1942; Simply Heavenly, 2 Act Comedy with Music, 1957; Tambourines to Glory, 2 Act Music Drama, Unproduced; Street Scene, 2 Act Musical Drama, Book by Elmer Rice, Music by Kurt Weill, Lyrics by Langston Hughes, 1947; Just Around the Corner, 2 Act Musical, Book by Abby Mann and Bernard Drew, Music by Joe Sherman, Lyrics by Langston Hughes, 1951; Troubled Island, Opera, Music by William Grant Still, 1949; The Barrier, Opera, Music by Jan Meyerowitz, 1950; Esther, Opera, Music by Jan Meyerowitz, 1957; Port Town, 1 Act Opera, Music by Jan Meyerowitz, Work in progress; Five Wise, Five Foolish, Opera, Music by Jan Meyerowitz, Work in progress; Wide, Wide River, 1 Act Opera, Music by Granville English, Work in progress.